John R. M. Gledhill

**How to Translate
Thomas Mann's Works**

To John

From John

John R. M. Gledhill

How to Translate
Thomas Mann's Works

A Critical Appraisal of Helen Lowe-Porter's Translations of Death in Venice, Tonio Kröger and Tristan

VDM Verlag Dr. Müller

Bibliografische Information der Deutschen Nationalbibliothek:
Die Deutsche Nationalbibliothek verzeichnet diese Publikation in der Deutschen
Nationalbibliografie; detaillierte bibliografische Daten sind im Internet über
http://dnb.d-nb.de abrufbar.

Copyright © 2007 VDM Verlag Dr. Müller e. K. und Lizenzgeber
Alle Rechte vorbehalten. Saarbrücken 2007
Kontakt: VDM Verlag Dr. Müller e.K., Dudweiler Landstr. 125 a,
D-66123 Saarbrücken, Telefon 0681/9100-698, Telefax 0180 5060 3388 4322,
Email: info@vdm-verlag.de
Coverbild: www.purestockx.com
Covererstellung: Nina Michaltzik

Herstellung:
Schaltungsdienst Lange o.H.G., Zehrensdorfer Str. 11, D-12277 Berlin
Books on Demand GmbH, Gutenbergring 53, D-22848 Norderstedt

Zugelassen: Erfurt, Universität Erfurt
              Diss., 2003

ISBN: 978-3-8364-1399-2

To Madeleine

Acknowledgements

I am very much indebted to the University of Erfurt for giving me the opportunity to write and present this dissertation. Even though the official process began in 1999, thanks are due initially to Professor Dr. Ulrich Boas (Erfurt) who was the first to suggest that I should write a doctoral thesis in 1994 when he was Head of the Institute of American and British Studies at the Pedagogical University of Erfurt/Mühlhausen. Professor Dr. Fritz-Wilhelm Neumann (Erfurt) kindly offered his services as supervisor despite his heavy workload. His support has not only been very encouraging but was also tinged with a very English sense of humour. In addition, he provided his doctoral students with a very stimulating colloquium supervised by Professor Dr. K. Tetzeli von Rosador (Münster).

Professor Dr. Karlfried Knapp (Erfurt) unhesitatingly undertook the onerous task of marking the thesis as second examiner as well as participating in the oral examination. Professor Dr. Eberhard Klein (Erfurt) was also an oral examiner who gave his unstinting help and support throughout the preparatory period. Professor Dr. Karl Heinemeyer (Erfurt) was always very open and helpful in his capacity as Chairman of the Examinations Committee.

I have benefited from the support and help from dedicated lecturers and research workers in Erfurt's English Department. Dr. Dagmar Haumann (Erfurt) and Professor Sabine Schülting (Berlin) provided invaluable support not only with their painstaking proofreading but also with their useful criticisms and help with initial computer problems.

Even though I am used to speaking German in many demanding situations, the prospect of a public doctoral defence in German did seem to be daunting. In this context, my Erfurt colleagues Ursula Renziehausen-Espelage M.A. (Latin Lector), Dr. Andreas Marshollek and PD Dr. Helmut Schwarztrauber helped both with the stylistic aspects for the final presentation in German and with the practical problems faced by a technophobe giving a power presentation. Indeed, the team spirit and animated discussions I enjoyed during the final preparation stage was one of the most positive aspects of the whole undertaking.

As I wrote my dissertation whilst working full-time as a lector and part-time as a translator, a special debt of gratitude is due to my wife Madeleine to whom the dissertation is dedicated and who never complained when holiday time had to be sacrificed, but, on the contrary, who always willingly helped with the proofreading, typing and the presentation of the ideas contained in the thesis. Thanks are also due to my son Andrew Gledhill (B.A. German First Class Honours) who not only contributed to the discussion of ideas but also provided his own original poetry for purposes of illustration. He has found the approach in this thesis to be of practical value in his work as a translator. I very much hope he continues the family tradition of translation and will one day give his own contribution to the debate.

Finally, I would like to express my appreciation to my teaching colleagues at Erfurt, Dr. Angelika Bonczyk and Christina Seyfarth, who in their capacity as co-ordinators took my academic work into consideration when planning the time-table.

TABLE OF CONTENTS

Chapter I: Introduction

Although this dissertation is mainly concerned with translation theory, the controversy, or rather, scandal concerning Helen Lowe-Porter's English translations of the following three works by Thomas Mann: *Tonio Kröger, Tristan* and *Der Tod in Venedig* will be discussed. These translations will be compared with David Luke's versions of the same stories.

As a result of the comparison of the two versions, new aspects pertaining to the theory of translation will be developed and a new approach will emerge which, for the sake of convenience, will be called *the strategic approach*. This is not a radically new departure from contemporary theories, but is more a case of a more flexible and less dogmatic application of some present-day theories to the practical problems of translation. The theoretical basis for this approach reflects Wittgenstein's (1963) notion of *language games*. The translator needs first to identify the nature of the 'game', and then use the translation strategy most appropriate for the particular language game. It will be seen that this strategy puts an end to the sterile debate between *les belles infidèles* as opposed to close translators by offering a radically new definition of fidelity based partly on a semiotic approach (as defined in Chapter V (e)) and partly on the insights of post-Derridean translation theorists. A humorous source text should have similarly humorous translation. A dense philosophical text may be even clearer in translation if the translator has faithfully reproduced the structure of the argumentation from the original. A dense literary text, on the other hand, deserves an equally or, at least similarly, rich translation as the original. It will be seen from the comparison of the two translators in question that their approach fails drastically at the high literary level.

It could be argued that there is sufficient material for two dissertations: one giving a detailed comparison of the two translations and another developing a new approach to literary translation. However, a fundamental aspect of the methodology of this dissertation is that theory should be closely based on practice and an acceptable comparison of two translations should in turn involve theory. It is usual practice in contemporary translation studies to keep close links between practice and theory as attested, for example, by Koller (1992: 13) and by Bassnett (1980):

> The need for systematic study of translation arises directly from the problems encountered during the actual translation process and it is essential for those working in the field to bring their practical experience to theoretical discussion, as it is for increased theoretical

1

perceptiveness to be put to use in the translation of texts. To divorce the theory from practice, to set the scholar against the practitioner as has happened in other disciplines, would be tragic indeed. (Bassnett 1980: 7)

Thus, this study involves a constant interaction between theory and practice, which is made possible by having a rich source of concrete examples in the three texts for the purposes of illustration and comparison.

One of the reasons for the choice of Thomas Mann as a translated writer is that most of the difficulties of literary translation can be found in his work, and, indeed, in the three stories chosen for detailed analysis. Difficult areas include the following elements: dense, rich musical prose; covert poetry; philosophical disquisition; dialect and word-play. Although elements of all these are found in all three stories, the poetic and philosophical aspects of translation are analysed mainly in conjunction with *Der Tod in Venedig*, dialect in *Tonio Kröger* and irony, humour and word-play in *Tristan*. The long chapter of philosophical dialogue (or more accurately monologue) in *Tonio Kröger* (i.e. Chapter IV) is covered mainly in Appendix I under the heading "A Selection of Errors" whereas the more subtle aspects of philosophical translation are discussed by analysing in detail a passage taken from *Der Tod in Venedig* in Chapter VII.

The Lowe-Porter translation has been selected mainly because her translations of Thomas Mann's literary works are by far the most widely read in the world[1]. The whole of her oeuvre is published in Penguin paperback and is available in virtually every bookshop in the English-speaking world which sells standard literary classics. Indeed, several critics have asserted that some of Thomas Mann's books are probably more widely read in English than in German. Lowe-Porter is also one of the few translators in the English-speaking world who has had articles, a book and a dissertation written about her work and methods. She is also one of the few, if not the only, American twentieth-century translator, in whose name a university prize in quality translation used to be awarded annually. At the same time, her oeuvre has probably been the most controversial in the twentieth century for literary translation from German into English. Roughly speaking, opinion about her in both the literary world and the world of translation studies is equally divided. In 1995, there was a heated debate about the quality of her translations in the *Times Literary Supplement*.

---

[1] Over 100,000 copies of Dr Faustus were sold to the USA Book of the Month Club alone. (See Buck 1996: 918-919.)

2

This will be discussed in detail in Chapter II, part (f). The main purpose of the dissertation is by no means to join in what is often a passionate and vitriolic attack on her work as a translator although the conclusion cannot be avoided that Lowe-Porter's translations are very often a long way below what is generally regarded as a minimal standard for professional translators. Indeed, it can be seen in the Error Appendix that many of her mistakes are typical for students who have a poor grasp of a foreign language. Part (a) of Chapter II, however, will show that she was an extremely conscientious worker and was respected and admired by many highly qualified academics and literary people including Thomas Mann himself despite his initial misgivings. If any attack is intended, it is more on the publishing world which, as pointed out by one of her major critics, David Luke himself, has continued to print the same versions despite numerous mistakes (including printing errors) and despite several critics pointing out some of the grosser mistakes. The seventy-five-page Error Appendix classifying 187 basic mistakes pertaining mainly to *Tristan* and *Tonio Kröger* gives an indication of the scale and density of the distortions which exist in Lowe-Porter's fundamentally flawed translation. A brief scan selecting typical errors will establish that David Luke was correct when he stated that what is in question here are basic errors or "schoolboy howlers" revealing a deep misunderstanding of German grammar and vocabulary, sometimes at the most elementary level. Even more scandalously, many errors reveal a similar lack in her mother tongue. Chapter III establishes that these errors are by no means harmless as has been argued by her numerous defenders, but that they can lead to a misreading of some of the basic themes in Mann's works. To a certain extent, the debate itself is a scandal in the world of translation criticism because her work is often of such poor quality that it is very difficult to understand how she can have so many defenders. Chapter II gives biographical detail to help to explain how such poor quality translations can still be the main version in print and how a translation prize for quality in translation can be offered in her name.

The strategy that is defined in this study as the *academic approach* will be seen to apply to both Lowe-Porter and Luke. This approach is discussed in detail in Chapter II, but it can be roughly defined as the conventional approach which tries to balance fidelity to the source text whilst at the same aiming at being readable and fluent in the target language. In other words, it is what many people usually understand by the word *translation*, indeed, so much so that it will be seen that there are many linguists who would assert that any thing else is not translation, but another activity[2]. It will, however, be shown throughout the dissertation that this narrow approach has very limited use for high literary translation. Luke's translation methods run parallel to those of Lowe-Porter and some parts are almost identical (even to the point of his copying Lowe-Porter's errors!), but it will also be seen that Luke essentially succeeds in his task of producing a reliable translation of Thomas Mann's work with regard to the content or surface meaning whereas Lowe-Porter's version often fails drastically even at this basic level.

It will also be shown that even if the *academic strategy* succeeds in its own terms, the resulting translation is often dull and always fails totally at the high literary level. Two alternative strategies with sample translations are offered in this dissertation. These 'suggested' versions, which I have produced for this dissertation, are theoretically based on Peter Newmark's (1981) classification of "semantic" and "communicative" translation, but they are by no means intended to be ideal translations of Thomas Mann, because they are presented as examples of how a different approach can work better by the very use of a particular strategy. It will also be seen that the *academic strategy* is doomed from the start for high literary translation even though this is still the strategy used by most translators. This is not to imply that the *academic strategy* does not have its uses, but the emphasis in this context has to be made on 'high' literary translation. The translation of what the theoreticians Leech and Short (1981) classify as *transparent* literature might well succeed with the *academic approach* at the level of adequacy even though here it will be seen that other strategies are preferable. To make further use of Leech and Short's

---

[2] The term *academic approach* has been coined for the purposes of this dissertation to emphasise the fact that this approach is *one* strategy in the context of the polyvalency implied by the *strategic approach*. In defining the whole process of translation as such, Lowe-Porter (1977: 72) inadvertently defines what is meant by the *academic approach*, when she refers to translation as "a sleight-of-hand", a balancing "trick" between the Charybdis of fidelity and the Scylla of felicity: "And herein [felicity] lies the Scylla of translators: the Charybdis would be the faithful rendering of the sense. The translator steers as warily as may be; but however conscientious, he is likely to be blamed for steering on to one or the other. [...]. I have often thought that translation is a trick, and a good translator, like a sleight-of-hand artist who must concentrate the reader's attention on something so that the latter will not notice something else which might spoil the effect." (Thirlwall 1966: 59) Similarly, she refers to this dichotomy by quoting the well-known phrase to describe 'free' translation as *les belles infidèles*, but in the hope that that 'true' translation will manage to achieve both felicity and accuracy: "*Les traductions sont comme les femmes: lorsqu'elles sont belles, elles ne sont pas fidèles, et lorsqu' elles sont fidèles elles ne sont pas belles.* From a more familiar source we are instructed that 'to have honesty coupled to beauty is to have honey a sauce to sugar.' And on the highest authority of all we know that the price of a virtuous woman, with no mention of other charms, is above rubies. All things considered, what remains to hope is only that the English version of *Doctor Faustus* here presented may at least not conjure up the picture of a *femme ni belle ni fidèle*." (Thirlwall 1966: 103)

terminology, *opaque* texts are in need of a different strategy. Linguistic theory on literary translation tends implicitly to support the *academic strategy* by stressing the search for equivalents. The practised translator, however, knows that readily available equivalents often simply do not exist, which does not necessarily entail a policy of despair, but, on the contrary, the attempt to solve this problem is one of the cardinal features of the *strategic approach* in which alternative strategies are suggested. However, broader definitions of equivalence such as 'functional' or 'dynamic' equivalence or the semiotic approach of Levý (1969) will be seen as essential to any discussion on the *strategic approach* to translation theory.

It is a fundamental aspect of *strategic approach* to translation that there are many forms of translation, all of which have their validity depending the translator's aims and circumstances. These range from close translation to re-creations and include intermediary stages such as adaptations, poetical rewriting and loose translation (i.e. based on the work of a particular author). Many would contend that the extreme free adaptations or re-creations are not really translations, but translation at the theoretical level within this dissertation is seen as an umbrella term for the many different kinds of translation strategies as summarised by Wilss (1977). There is no one single ideal strategy, but each strategy can be appropriate for translating a particular kind of text or for a particular purpose in the target language. Using Wittgenstein's theory of language games, it is important for the translator to identify the kind of language game that is being played in the source text and to establish the language game aimed at in the target text as SL and TL games are not always identical. This point will be made very clear in the ensuing chapters in which poetic, philosophical, humorous and dialectal texts can be seen as different kinds of language games. The very proliferation of words, particularly in German, which can be subsumed under the general heading of translation, implies a great variety of approaches. The following definitions with equivalents and brief explanations taken from Wilss (1977) are given in English in note form for many specifically German concepts:

Übertragung: - 'transfer' (not necessarily in the Derridean sense of διαφερειν. See Chapter V on post-Derridean translation for a discussion of this concept.)

Umsetzung - 'transposition' - even transliteration in some contexts; also *convert* in a mathematical sense - a very relevant concept in commercial translation for highly specialised data such as an accountant's break-down sheet.

Abbildung - 'simulation' - used more in non-linguistic contexts, but can be a translation metaphor for presenting information or 're-presenting'.

Nachbildung - 'replication' - (limited to very specific contexts e. g. the reproduction of a translated document in its original form).

Nachdichtung - 'free rendition' - a very important concept in translation theory which is only roughly translated by 'free rendition' because of the negative connotations sometimes associated with this approach such as a 'loose' translation - rather than a 're-creation' based on another work as is the case in German.

Umdichtung - 'recasting' - this term can be used metaphorically such as when a poem may be recast into another metre or rhythm whilst retaining the spirit and diction of the original.

Neuschöpfung - re-creation' - this is a very useful concept in translation theory - the semantic stress may be on the first syllable *re-* or on *creation*, but, whatever, an interactive dynamic is set up by this strategy.

At the same time as this dissertation was in the process of being written, Krasweski (1998) was developing his receptor-based theory of literary translation strategies in which he identifies four basic translation strategies: *informational* (analogous to a copyist painter), *corrective* (analogous to an art restorer) *critical* (analogous to a literary critic or art historian) and *proselyting* (analogous to a theatre director). Krasweski bases his arguments on close textual analysis of translations into and from Polish, Czech, Greek, French, German and English and offers his own tentative solutions not in a spirit of *reine Besserwisserei* (to quote Koller 1992: 14), but as concrete points of comparison and criticism within translational discourse. Indepedently, I have used a similar approach with my own translations of several passages in Thomas Mann. The very fact that sometimes two or more versions are offered is a reflection of the strategic approach. My only criticism of Krasweski's book is that it could create the impression that there are only four possible strategies as quoted above using the author's own analogies. That is the reason why I refer this strategic theory to Wittgenstein's language games because the possible number of games and hence, strategic translation approaches, is limited only to the possible number of human discourse types and is thus effectively unlimited. It would take another thesis to develop fully the strategic approach, but here it will be argued only that this direction is very fruitful when criticising or creating literary translations.

The alternative translations I have produced are offered in the spirit of dialogue and debate. A very good exercise in advanced translation classes is, of course, to compare various versions. Appendices II and III contain seven versions of the same two passages taken from *Der Tod in Venedig*: five published versions by Lowe-Porter (1978), Luke (1988), Burke, (1971), Koelb (1994) and Chase (1999) in that order as well as the unpublished 'semantic' and 'communicative' versions which have been written for the purpose of this comparison only.

The nature of translation criticism unfortunately involves pointing out mistakes and a dogmatic, schoolmasterly tone may ensue. However, if each statement is qualified by too many reservations, the dissertation would become unwieldy and unreadable. For this reason, many of the criticisms are given in note form in Appendix I. Although the majority of errors are clear-cut (spelling mistakes, gross grammatical errors and typical "schoolboy howlers" (Luke: 1988)), a few 'corrections' may be open to dispute, and there are also a few grey areas. Nevertheless, there has been little controversy about the mistakes themselves, but there has been widely differing views as to their frequency. It is for this reason that the rather negative task of carrying out a thorough quantitative error analysis was undertaken. Even though 187, on average serious, errors have been identified in two stories alone, the analysis does not claim to be exhaustive. It does, however, disprove the thesis upheld by Lowe-Porter's supporters that the errors are few and far between. This aspect will be discussed in Chapter III in conjunction with Appendix I. Luke's reliable translation following the same principles as in Lowe-Porter's versions usually acts as a useful yardstick of comparison.

Chapter II summarises the biography of Lowe-Porter and her translation methods. This involves a brief account of her thirty-year literary relationship with Thomas Mann and this chapter discusses the reception of her work in both the literary and academic worlds. Chapter II also attempts to show how such deeply flawed translations came to be accepted as the "official d version" (Berlin: 1992b: 4) and how such a vitriolic controversy about her work has, in the meantime, arisen. This controversy is still going on, but it is to be hoped that detailed analyses will put an end to what has so far been yet another "scandal"[3] in the world of literary translation.

Chapter III discusses the reliability of Lowe-Porter's translation in the light of both her detractors and her defenders. This chapter involves a detailed analysis of the errors which lead to a fundamental misreading of the main themes in *Der Tod in Venedig* at the most elementary level of surface meaning. There is also a detailed discussion of some of the more drastic mistakes discovered by Luke. This chapter is intended to be read in conjunction with Appendix I where the 187 errors are classified according to their various types.

Chapter IV begins with the general problem of translating stylistic features and then goes on to discuss the difficulties involved in translating Thomas Mann's elaborate and deliberately planned sentence structure. Two critical discussions of the Lowe-Porter translations with particular reference to Mann's stylistic features are incorporated into this chapter. The problem of 'style' is tackled at a highly intensive micro level by comparing a detailed and comprehensive *explication du texte* on one sixteen-line sentence in *Der Tod in Venedig* with Lowe-Porter's and Luke's translations. Structural, poetic, rhythmic and even musical features are subjected to a micro-analysis alongside the more usual discussion of nuance and connotation. I have offered both a semantic and a communicative version of the same passage as a basis of comparison together with three other published versions.

Chapter V involves a theoretical discussion on the (im)possibility of translating poetry or poetic features in literary prose and a refutation of the scientific approaches which are very much based on the concept of *equivalence* as the key notion in translation theory. This chapter includes a formal refutation of Holmes' mathematical approach to the theory of poetry translation by using the methods of mathematical logic. The cognitive linguist or scientific approach is seen as a strategy which has little to offer with regard to the translation of poetry. In this chapter, other radically different approaches to the translation of poetry are explored including Levý's semiotic analysis (1969) of Wilson Knight's translation of a Christian Morgenstern 'non-sense poem' (1990). Also in this chapter, there is a study of two examples of successful literary translation at the highest level within the framework of post-Derridean translation theory: the poet Hölderlin's translation of a passage taken

---

[3] Venuti's (1998) book is entitled *Scandals in Translation.*

from Sophocles' *Antigone* and the writer James Joyce's own translation of *Finnegans Wake* into Italian. The purpose of this chapter is to refute the 'untranslatability' school by showing that literary translation can succeed at the highest level. These two translators are seen as model practitioners for the *strategic approach*, which reveals how translation is possible at the highest level and that this kind of translation is of the same order as literary creation.

Chapter VI shows that Thomas Mann's work contains elaborate metrical and rhythmical features akin to formal classical verse even though these features may be covertly embedded in the text. The Luke and Lowe-Porter versions this time are compared with one French and three Italian versions which reflect the poetic aspects more successfully than their English counterparts. Again, an alternative approach will be offered as another aspect of the *strategic approach*.

Chapter VII discusses the problem of translating 'philosophical' texts in general and literary philosophical works in particular, as well as touching upon the difficulty of dialect translation. It is shown that within the *strategic approach*, fidelity to the structure of argumentation is of key importance. This point is illustrated by using techniques taken from formal logic, which are then applied to a specific philosophical text from *Der Tod in Venedig*. As in some of the previous chapters, there is a detailed analysis of Lowe-Porter's and Luke's versions together with my own two suggested versions. Three more versions of the same philosophical passage are given in Appendix III for further comparison. In a similar vein, this chapter tries to throw some light on the (un)translatability of dialect in literary works by aiming at a more precise definition of dialect and offering possible strategies. Finally in this chapter, the translations of the unnamed Hamburg's businessman's speech in *Tonio Kröger* are compared and alternative strategies are suggested as part of the *strategic theory*.

Chapter VII discusses the difficulties involved in translating paranomasia, humour and gentle irony in general, but with particular reference to Lewis Carroll's *Alice's Adventures in Wonderland* and to Unger's (1996) discussion of Gotter's *Der argwöhnische Ehemann* (1785), a translation of Benjamin Hoadly's (1776) comedy *The Suspicious Husband* (first published 1747). These examples prove that successful translation is also possible in an area which is usually regarded as untranslatable by cognitive linguists. Certain passages in *Tristan* are also discussed in detail within the framework of the *strategic theory*. Again, alternative examples and strategies are offered.

Chapter IX summarises the conclusions to be drawn not only with regard to the two translators, but also with regard to translation theory, translation criticism and the teaching and practice of translation. The characteristics of the *strategic theory* of translation which has emerged from this study will also be summarised.

Chapter II: The Background to the Lowe-Porter Translations

(a) Introduction

Helen Tracey Lowe-Porter was probably the most prominent literary translator in the English-speaking world working from German to English in the twentieth century. Opinions range from giving Lowe-Porter the status as a model translator to those who question her competence at the minimal level. The controversy is still continuing today amongst some of the most distinguished theoreticians and practitioners. One reason why this particular translator was chosen for detailed study is to examine which criteria are in operation to result in such a diverse and vitriolic disagreement amongst translation critics. Another is to end this controversy which has become a "scandal" in translation criticism. The assessment of the quality of her translations is intended not only to contribute the debate about this particular translator but also to place the debate within the context of translation theory in general and to add to translation criticism theory in particular.

(b) A Brief Outline of the Life of Helen Lowe-Porter

Helen Tracey Porter was born in 1877 in Towanda in north-eastern Pennsylvania and graduated from Wells, a women's college in Aurora, New York. In 1964, one year after her death on 27 April 1963, the college set up an annual award for 'superior translation' in honour of Helen Lowe-Porter, thus enabling her to become one of the very few translators in the English-speaking world ever to receive such public acclaim. (Interestingly, the award now longer exists.) She had her first translations published in the *Poet Lore* edited in Boston by her aunt, Charlotte Endymion Porter. This connection facilitated her entry into the world of translation and literature by giving her a platform to publish translations from a variety of sources. Her main translation activity was based on her thirty-year literary relationship with Thomas Mann whose name she became associated with for the rest of her life. Thirlwall (1966) describes this relationship in hyperbolic terms typical of many accolades to this translator which help towards understanding how Lowe-Porter attained such a high status:

> But her thirty-year relationship with Thomas Mann, with whom her name became as closely united as Carlyle's was with Goethe, Constance Garnett's with Dostoievski, or Scott Moncrieff's with Proust, was the backbone of her life's work. Without her translations, the

name of Thomas Mann might well have been as little known to the English-speaking world as that of his brother Heinrich. (Thirlwall 1966: vi)

In 1921, the American publisher Alfred A. Knopf (1892-1984) gained exclusive rights to publish all the English translations of Thomas Mann's works under the proviso that at least one work should be published every year. Helen Lowe-Porter was commissioned as the translator of Thomas Mann, a status she retained till the end of her life.

(c) Lowe-Porter's Own Comments on Translation

Lowe-Porter wrote relatively little on her methods and theory of translation. Her most quoted statement appeared in her "Translator's Note", to *Buddenbrooks* (1954) which was first published in 1924:

> Yet it was necessary to set oneself the bold task of transferring the spirit first and the letter so as might be; and above all, to make certain that the work of art, coming as it does to the ear, in German, like music out of the past, should, in English, at least *not* come out like a translation - which is, God bless us, a thing of naught. (Lowe-Porter 1954: Frontpiece)

Her rather odd formulation, "the letter so as might be", presumably is intended to mean that an *ad hoc*, pragmatic approach is recommended with regard to meaning. Her theory of translation reflects the well-known Ciceronian dichotomy between spirit and letter[4] and St Jerome's famous dictum *non verbum e verbo sed sensum exprimere de sensu*, (i.e. not a word-for-word translation, but a translation that should express the sense as derived from the general meaning). In line with what has already been defined as the *academic approach* in Chapter I, Lowe-Porter claimed that the art of translation consisted in the balancing act of writing natural English and yet conveying the sense of the original. The 'sense and letter' dichotomy remained to be her main theoretical concern throughout her professional life. This letter-spirit dichotomy has dominated European translation theory for the past two millennia as stated by Snell-Hornby (1988):

> By far the most influential concept in the history of translation is that age-old dichotomy of word and sense, which traditional translation theory never managed to overcome, and which still besets translation studies today. (Snell-Hornby 1988: 9)

---

[4] Albrecht (1998: 53-55) argues convincingly that Cicero was not the champion of free translation as has been traditionally understood throughout the centuries. The formulation "nec converti ut interpres sed ut orator" is, according to Albrecht, to be referred only to Cicero's use of Greek sources for his speeches whereas other comments show that his ideas reflected the close-translation approach of his time.

This delicate balancing of the letter-spirit dichotomy adopted by both Lowe-Porter and Luke is one which is familiar to any student of foreign languages. This approach has until now had no name. Indeed, many people think that this is the only approach to translation. This strategy has already been referred as the *academic approach* in the introduction. The essence of this approach is this very balancing act between fluency and fidelity to which Lowe-Porter refers. I have called this the *academic approach* as it is the approach that traditionally any British university teacher of translation (as language practice rather than a teacher of translation theory) uses when required to produce the 'key' to a test translation such as a newspaper article. It involves a delicate balancing act between trying to reflect every detail, every nuance of the original text connotation whilst at the same time producing a version that reads like an original text in the target language. This approach is unproblematic in texts where the aim is to convey information i.e. where the denotative aspects predominate. However, in a text where features such as form, rhythm, wordplay, ambiguity and assonance are of equal, if not greater importance, then the *academic approach* is woefully inadequate. The latter features apply very much to Thomas Mann's texts.

Lowe-Porter's view of the inadequacy of translation to do justice to a poetic text does not reflect the inadequacy of translation as such in all its possible forms but the inadequacy of the *academic approach*. Only in this context can her extremely self-deprecating comments be seen as consistent when she dismisses literary translation as a "perverse pleasure":

> I cannot defend literary translation against the charge that it is a perverse pleasure, and that the translator would be better employed as a philologist or a language teacher. Everybody who ever writes verse or tries to turn a poem into another language than the original, knows that the result, in the measure that it is good as literature, is not the same poem. Try to translate Rilke, for instance! This must be so. (Thirlwall 1966: 197)

In summary, it can be seen that Lowe-Porter's theory of translation reflected the academic and literary prejudices of the time. There is no evidence, however, that she was ever involved in the theoretical debates of her contemporaries such as Pound, Benjamin, Nabokov or I. A. Richards. Like Thomas Mann, she believed that literature is fundamentally untranslatable; hence, many of her self-deprecating comments on the translator's task[5].

---

[5] Another example of her self-deprecating comments is to be found in her preface to her translation of *The Magic Mountain* when she refers to her work as "lame": "The translator wishes to thank, in this

(d) Lowe-Porter's Literary Relationship with Thomas Mann

Their thirty-year literary relationship started off on a rather formal footing, but later became more cordial. The low point was reached when Thomas Mann expressed preference for another translator for the English version of *Der Zauberberg*. In later years, however, their relationship grew increasingly cordial so that in the end she was almost regarded as a close friend of the family.

Thomas Mann's attitude to Lowe-Porter's ability as a translator seemed, as might be expected, to be ambiguous. His contribution to the debate concerning the quality of Lowe-Porter's translations only helps to fuel the controversy. On the one hand, many statements from his correspondence with her and from letters to others concerning her suitability as his translator would appear to give a generally favourable picture whereas some of his other remarks show that he had serious doubts with regard to her competence.

His letter referring to her first assignment for him the translation of *Buddenbrooks* had a very positive tone. He seemed, in fact, to be delighted with the result in his letter to her on 11th April, 1924:

> Sehr geehrte Frau,
>
> [...] ich darf Sie beglückwünschen zu Ihrer Leistung, *die ich ungewöhnlich feinfühlig und gelungen finde.* Wie gewandt und schlagend sind z. B. die gelegentlich vorkommenden Verse übertragen! Und die Schwierigkeit, die Sie im Vorwort erwähnen, und die die Unübersetzbarkeit des Dialekts betrifft, haben Sie auf eine Weise zu überwinden gewußt, *daß bei mir kein Entbehrungsgefühl aufkam.* (Berlin 1992a: 290. My emphasis.)

This is high praise, indeed. The last phrase, "daß bei mir kein Entbehrungsgefühl aufkam," would imply total satisfaction with the translation.

Similarly, Thomas Mann's first visit to the Lowe-Porters' seems to have been a success when almost a month later, Thomas and Katja Mann met Lowe-Porter in Oxford. He referred to the visit as "the real culmination of our journey" in his letter of 20th May, 1924:

> Dear Mistress Lowe!

---

place, a number of scholars, authorities in the various fields entered by *The Magic Mountain*, without whose help the version in all humility here offered to English readers, *lame as it is,* must have been more lacking still." (Thirlwall 1966: 15. My italics.)

> [...] Thanks to you and Dr Lowe's solicitude and guidance we are greatly tempted to consider
> our stay in Oxford as the real culmination of our journey. [...] (Thirlwall 1966: 7)

Lowe-Porter, on the other hand, seemed to be overawed by Thomas Mann and was only too aware of her deficiencies and inadequacies as a translator. In her essay "On Translating Thomas Mann", she wrote of their first meeting in very modest terms:

> I felt shy, ignorant, and insecure. Such qualifications as I had for the role of translator to
> Thomas Mann retreated from my own consciousness and made me painfully aware of *my*
> *faulty speaking German*[6] and the poor impression I must be making. (Thirlwall 1966: 81. My
> emphasis.)

Thomas Mann obviously took an interest in the translations of his work as is evidenced by the former letter, but his register of idiomatic English was understandably very weak as is shown by the unfortunate reference to *Mistress Lowe* for 'Mrs. Lowe.'[7] Even at this early stage, however, there is still some ambiguity in Mann's attitude to Lowe-Porter as his translator as is shown in his letter to Knopf almost a year later on 20th April, 1925 concerning the most suitable translator for *Der Zauberberg*. Lowe-Porter had a rival in the form of a certain Dr. Herman George Scheffauer who had already translated *Bashan and I* and *Disorder and Early Sorrow*. He had been Mann's co-editor for the series *Romane der Welt* and was also Mann's preferred translator as is clear from his letter to Knopf of 20th April, 1925[8].

---

[6] Presumably, this phrase is supposed to mean *faulty spoken German*. It will be clear in the course of the dissertation that she often uses similar either infelicitous or ungrammatical formulations in her translations.

[7] Hayes cites an amusing example of Thomas Mann's level of English. It may seem rather cruel, but it is necessary to bear this fact in mind for the occasions when Mann makes a pronouncement about English style: "But it must be mentioned that Mann's qualifications to make such a pronouncement were somewhat dubious; his English often shows an unmistakably German coloration. For example, in a frantic hand-written postscript to one letter, otherwise entirely in German, he writes: 'I forgot how far I sent you the Joseph-Manuscript, until which page, please, tell me!'" (Hayes 1974: 59)

[8] As Mann's misgivings are clearly stated in this letter, it is worth quoting in full: "Sehr geehrter Herr Knopf, ich habe von Mrs. Lowe die Nachricht, daß Sie sie beauftragt haben, mit der Übersetzung des 'Zauberberg' sogleich zu beginnen, und indem Herr Herman George Scheffauer mir den Inhalt Ihres letzten Schreibens an ihn übermittelt, gibt er mir eine Bestätigung dieser Nachricht. Obgleich ich Ihnen schon einmal, so eindringlich ich konnte, in dieser Sache geschrieben habe, möchte ich Ihnen doch noch einmal sagen, daß, so sehr die Tatsache der bevorstehenden Übersetzung mich erfreut, mich doch eine offenbar nicht ungerechtfertigte und von vielen vertrauenswürdigen Seiten gestützte Besorgnis quält, *ob Sie mit Ihrer Übersetzerwahl das Richtige getroffen haben*, ich meine das Richtige im Interesse des Buches und im Ihrem eignen künstlerischem und geschäftlichen Interesse daran. Mrs. Lowe war gewiß die Persönlichkeit, die ein Buch wie 'Buddenbrooks', d. h. ein geistig-sprachlich sich wesentlich in bürgerlicher und relativ schlichter Sphäre bewegendes Buch, in Ihre Sprache zu übertragen, obgleich meine Zweifel eben darauf beruhen, daß mir von verschiedenen Personen, denen ich vertrauen muß, versichert worden ist, *daß das Buch in dieser Übersetzung schwer gelitten habe.*" (Berlin 1992a: 293-294. My emphasis.)

On writing to Lowe-Porter on 25th April, 1925 concerning the translation of *Zauberberg*, he tried tactfully to reject her in favour of Scheffauer on the (ludicrous) grounds that such a task would be too demanding for a woman:

> I question whether the personality of a translator perfectly fit as it was for transmitting the essence of 'Buddenbrooks', would be able to manifest its special talents equally successfully for 'Der Zauberberg'. This new book is essentially different from the former one [...] the new book with its deeply intellectual and symbolic character makes quite other demands on the translator - *demands which I deem would sometimes be more readily met by a male rather than a female temperament.* (Thirlwall 1966: 9. My emphasis.)

It is not surprising that, after receiving this letter, Lowe-Porter was very angry. She scribbled a rough draft reply on the back of the letter which is still preserved and quoted in full by Berlin[9]. It is also not surprising after this that she decided to resign as Mann's translator "with mingled feelings of pride, defeat, and relief."

Berlin's view that Thomas Mann might have preferred a male translator because of the embarrassment which could have been caused by homo-erotic elements in the work seems unlikely since there seemed to be no such scruples regarding *Der Tod in Venedig*. On the other hand, it might simply have been an excuse to prepare her for the shock in case he finally chose Dr. Scheffauer as his main translator. That Scheffauer was his preferred choice is supported by his very positive and unambiguous assessment of his character and abilities and is, moreover, confirmed by his entry in his diary in October, 1928, after the latter's death (which Thomas Mann had taken to be suicide when Scheffauer mysteriously died by either falling or jumping out of a high window):

> Ich hatte den Mann [Scheffauer] persönlich gern, ich war ihm dankbar, weil er mehrere meiner Arbeiten *mit außerordentlicher Kunst und Liebe* ins Englische übersetzt hatte, zudem galt er als ausgezeichneter Kenner der angelsächsischen Literaturen. (Thomas Mann 19 60-761. My emphasis.)

Dr. Scheffauer's sudden death finally clinched the matter and Lowe-Porter, possibly as Mann's second choice, continued her services as Mann's main translator into English. Certainly his letter to Knopf less than six months later dated 7th October,

---

[9] With regard to Thomas Mann's idea that the translation of *Der Zauberberg* required a "männliche Konstitution", she wrote down her immediate reactions: "I need not say to you, for you know it, I suppose, that just that "männliche Konstitution" which is the fibre of the book, and just those speculations on *Zeitrechnung*-relativity, and just those searching parallels between flesh and spirit, are what I should enjoy worming my way into." (1992a: 302)

1925, displays no sign of his earlier misgivings with regard to Lowe-Porter. Instead, the tone is very optimistic and encouraging:

> Sehr geehrter Herr Knopf
>
> es freut mich sehr, zu hören, daß die Übersetzung des 'Zauberberges' gut vorschreitet, und ich sehe dem Erscheinen des Werkes in englischer Sprache mit Spannung entgegen. Wenn Mrs Lowe-Porter irgendwelche Auskünfte wünscht, stehe ich natürlich gern zur Verfügung. (Berlin 1992a: 305)

The fact that at least the *Zauberberg* translation was progressing well may also explain his more conciliatory tone in his letters to Lowe-Porter.

The American sales of *The Magic Mountain* were very successful and Thomas Mann's rather resigned acceptance turned to delight, but he did not entirely 'leave translation to the experts', because he still continued to take an interest in the English translations of his work as is evidenced by his letter of 22nd May, 1927:

> [...] yesterday I received several copies of *The Magic Mountain* and the emotions which I felt on receiving the book in its English version urged me above all to express to you my sincere appreciation of the great and the stirring effort which you have made to give this difficult unwieldy work its form and character for the English reading public. Insofar as I have been able to apply myself to reading it to date - and within the limits of my knowledge of the language - it seems to me that your efforts and your faithfulness to the original have been crowned with signal success. (Thirlwall 1966: 14-15)

During the period of 1945-1948 when Lowe-Porter was translating *Dr Faustus*, Thomas Mann was very happy with her work and progress. In his letter of 4th August, 1945, for example, he wrote:

> It is an impossible task, of which I am fully aware. You ought to hate me for having been born and being such a nuisance! (Thirlwall 1966: 103-104)

It was also during this time that relations between them became far less formal and far more cordial, as Thirlwall rightly notes in their forms of address to each other:

> During the three years of writing and translation, their relationship warmed from a 'Liebe Frau Lowe' to 'Liebe Freundin', and then to 'Dear Helen', while he became 'Dear Tommy' to her. (Thirlwall 1966: 106)

The last translation Lowe-Porter was to do for Thomas Mann was *Der Erwählte* (*The Holy Sinner*) by which time there seemed to be no more doubts on Mann's behalf with regard to Lowe-Porter's suitability as his translator. In his letter of 25 October, 1951, addressed to her, he wrote:

In New York [...] Knopf gave me a copy of *The Holy Sinner*, and I have since occupied myself a great deal with your translation. I have good reason to write to you and to express to you my gratitude for your achievement and your patience and, as far as I can see, the highly successful elimination of all difficulties which also in this case, and perhaps particularly in this case, presented themselves. Better judges than myself have acknowledged your success, as I saw from many reviews. (Thirlwall 1966: 131)

After this time, Lowe-Porter wanted to devote more time to her own writing. Her health deteriorated and she suffered from such severe depression that she no longer wanted to continue the Mann oeuvre, which Thomas Mann regretted very much, confirming the fact that, in the end, she was his preferred translator[10]. In his letter of 18th December, 1953, he unambiguously expressed his regret that she was no longer his translator:

It remains an uncanny idea for me that you will no longer be my English interpreter. It seems very dubious to me that an equivalent substitute has been found or will be found. But your health and your work take precedence. (Thirlwall 1966: 142)

(e) Thomas Mann's Own Comments on Translation

In this letter of 9th August, 1926, Thomas Mann made one of his very rare statements on translation methodology, leaving no doubt that he was of the 'semantic' or source-text oriented school of translation, though still within the confines of *academic* translation, as evidenced by his formulation: "als es die fremde Sprache nur irgend gestattet":

Ich bin grundsätzlich für eine so wörtliche und genaue Wiedergabe, als es die fremde Sprache nur irgend gestattet. (Berlin 1992a: 306)

It is well worth quoting this second paragraph of the letter in full as this brief description of his expectations from literary translation represents the first dialogue between Thomas Mann and Lowe-Porter regarding translation methodology:

Prinzipiell möchte ich sagen, daß mir eine allzu freie Übertragung der Peeperkorn'schen Abgerissenheiten nicht sympathisch wäre. Ich bin grundsätzlich für eine so wörtliche und genaue Wiedergabe, *als es die fremde Sprache nur irgend gestattet*, und so meine ich auch, daß man die Redensarten und Sprachbrocken Peeperkorns tunlichst *mit den entsprechenden englischen Worten und Redensarten wiedergeben soll*, ohne irgendwelche Übertragung und Umarbeitung. Es *müssen* sich ja für deutsche Ausdrücke wie 'Perfekt', 'Absolut', 'Erledigt' und dergleichen mehr Wendungen finden lassen, die im Englischen in ähnlichem Sinn gebräuchlich sind. (Berlin 1992a: 306. My emphasis.)

---

[10] Lowe-Porter had declined to translate the *Felix Krull* fragment on health grounds and because she wanted to do her own literary work even though she had already made a start on the *Krull* project.

The second italicised phrase in the quotation, "mit den entsprechenden englischen Worten und Redensarten wiedergeben", confirms his assumption that translation essentially consists in searching for suitable equivalents in the target language. He also reflected the assumptions of the more naive theoreticians of the equivalence approach in his optimistic assumption that equivalent words and phrases "must" exist. On the other hand, Thomas Mann also realised that at times, the complexity of his prose was so extreme that it would be impossible to find English equivalents so that he ultimately belonged to the 'untranslatability' of literature school. His ideas on translation strategy reflected the assumptions typical for his time. They can be summarised as below:

1. Where possible, the exact word (*le mot juste*) with the same connotations.

2. If 1 fails, then an equivalent word or phrase with a corresponding effect in the target language.

3. If 1 and 2 fail, then there is no solution, thus a failed translation confirming the ultimate untranslatability of great literature.

This idea of ultimate untranslatability applied particularly to the translation of poetry and poetic prose. Thus, Thomas Mann despaired of ever having a good translation of his works as expressed in his letter to his Hungarian translator, Jenö Gömöri, dated November 15, 1951, as translated in Thirlwall (1966):

> *It is generally known that lyric poetry cannot really be translated.* That this is also the case with more refined prose is known only to a few - most likely only the sensitive translators themselves, many of whom have complained to me about it. Such prose (prosa) is usually perverted, its rhythm is destroyed, the subtle shades of meaning are lost, its inner intention, its mental attitude and intellectual atmosphere diverted up to a point of complete misunderstanding. This reminds me of the time when my American translator and friend, Helen Lowe-Porter, said to me while she was at work on the translation of *Lotte in Weimar*, deploringly, 'I am committing murder!' (Thirlwall 1966: 51. My emphasis.)

(f) The Reception of Lowe-Porter's Translations in the Literary and Academic Worlds[11]

---

[11] For the purposes of this study, the phrase 'literary world' refers to those statements published in literary journals aiming at a wide readership and with a wide range of subjects such as is the case with *Times Literary Supplement* whereas the phrase 'academic world' refers to reactions published in scholarly journals often connected to a university.

There has been a great variety of reactions to her work in both the literary and academic worlds. Some of the reactions are documented in Hayes (1974), who rightly notes that:

> In the welter of Thomas Mann criticism in English, there is surprisingly little notice taken of the fact that his words are filtered through the mind of a translator. (Hayes 1974: 67)

Despite the relative paucity of references to the translations themselves, Hayes then gives a very brief survey of the reactions to Lowe-Porter's translations of Thomas Mann. They display a wide variety of opinions ranging from "heavy and drear", (West 1969: 127), "not very well translated" (Connolly 1936: 3) to "elegant" (Adelberg 1936: 3), "superb" (Follett 1936: 5) and "ironic and pyrotechnical" (Ziolkowski 1961: 5). In the light of so many conflicting lapidary opinions of reviewers, Hayes' rather dismissive assertion seems to be more than justified:

> The truth probably is that too few reviewers have sufficient command of any other language to enable them to comment intelligently on the quality of a translation. (Hayes 1974: 69)

The first known mention of Lowe-Porter in Britain was in Cyril Connolly's article in the *New Statesman and Nation* in 1936. As he was such an eminent literary man, it is worth quoting the reference in full because it also shows the Olympian dismissive contempt even distinguished English critics could display with regard to the whole areas of both German literature and literary translation:

> It is <u>obvious</u> that the later stories in *Stories of Three Decades* are the best. *Mario the Magician* (sic), *Disorder and Early Sorrow*, are little masterpieces. *Death in Venice* is a borderline case. For one thing alone among these stories, it is not very well translated. (Connolly 1936: 3. My underlining.)

Koch-Emmery (1953) was the first academic to take translation seriously in the field of German studies so that his article has something of a 'pioneering' tone:

> Mrs H. T. Lowe-Porter, the indefatigable translator of Thomas Mann has tackled an almost impossible task. Yet she succeeded in introducing Thomas Mann's works to the English-speaking world. We find her translations in every bookshop and in every library; the number of those who read Thomas Mann in translation must be as large as those who read the original. (Koch-Emmery 1953: 275)

Although Koch-Emmery was well aware of the complexity of Thomas Mann's style and of the inadequacies of the Lowe-Porter versions, he avoids any direct, harsh criticism of Lowe-Porter's work. As is typical of the 'untranslatability' school predominant in academe at that time, he refers to her "almost impossible task". His faint praise of her work refers more to the quantity of her work than to its quality:

> Nobody can help admiring Mrs. Lowe-Porter's enterprise and perseverance. Thomas Mann's
> works have now grown to quite a *formidable* collection of *large* volumes, and, with very few
> exceptions, she has translated them *all*. (1953: 275. My emphasis.)

His analysis of stylistic features will be discussed in Chapter IV.

Lowe-Porter's translations of Thomas Mann remained protected by copyright until 1970 when David Luke's translation *Thomas Mann: Tonio Kröger and Other Stories* was published by Bantam Press. His over-forty-page-long introduction to his own translations not only offers some interesting insights into Luke's methods and theories as a translator but also provides a detailed, critical analysis of Lowe-Porter's translations. His appraisal is very negative:

> Like all her translations of Mann, as is increasingly recognised, it [*Death in Venice*] is of very
> poor quality. (Luke 1988: xlv. My insertion.)

Luke's intriguing phrase, "as is increasingly recognised", is not supported by any reference to the published literature on Lowe-Porter. He supports his arguments by citing "omissions and flagrant mistranslations" which will be discussed in detail in the next chapter. At this point, it is perhaps relevant to quote Luke's assignment of culpability in this context:

> No one is exempt from liability to such oversights and errors, and in many cases we may no
> doubt blame the incompetence of Mrs. Lowe-Porter's copy editors. But the fact remains that
> these omissions and the other flagrant mistranslations have continued, unrectified and largely
> unnoticed, through all the reprintings of Mann's work for about the last sixty years. (Luke
> 1988: xlix-l)

On the other hand, Hayes (1974) whose comparison of the Burke and Lowe-Porter translations, takes note of Luke's criticisms, but basically defends the Lowe-Porter version of *Death in Venice* simply on the grounds of its commercial success and survival. This will be discussed in further detail in the next chapter. Hayes' final verdict on the Lowe-Porter translation is positive even though he concedes that there are many deficiencies:

> Still, nearly all of Mann's works are known in this country through her translations, and her
> accomplishments were of a quality that continued to be saleable enough to assure her status as
> the authorised translator from the 1920's to the early 1950's. This is a deceptive point.
> Marketability is a businessman's yardstick; it is not an assurance that a translation is reliable.
> Yet, still today, it remains the primary consideration about whether or not to publish the
> translation of a work of art like *Der Tod in Venedig*. (1974: 266)

21

Mandel (1982) also has a positive assessment of Lowe-Porter's ability as a translator whilst admitting there are many "flaws" in her oeuvre:

> Despite such flaws, Lowe-Porter's translation of Mann's works throughout three decades still remains monumental. It does mean though that scholars and critics will need to review the entire range of translations for infelicities that affect the meaning and sense of the original texts and suggest revisions and provide annotations. (1982: 39)

It is a pity that up to the present time, Mandel's recommendation, like that of Luke, has still not been heeded.

The Lowe-Porter translations came to be regarded as the 'standard' translation and were later published in paperback by Penguin Books in 1955. Berlin (1992a) regards the Lowe-Porter translations as the one which is most generally used in the universities and high schools of the USA:

> The Lowe-Porter translation is usually designated as the 'official' English-language version of Mann's work [...] (Berlin 1992b: 4)

The situation with regard to the Lowe-Porter translations, even as late as 1992, is described in the same paragraph in terms of a *monopoly*:

> [...] for many years the Lowe-Porter's translation's of Mann's works have monopolised the market (Berlin 1992: 4).

Despite the numerous errors and mistranslations listed in Luke's criticisms, the text has still not been subjected to close critical or editorial scrutiny and was essentially the same text as her original translation of 1928 published by Martin Secker & Warburg. Her translation oeuvre remained relatively 'invisible' in the wider literary world until it became the subject of a heated correspondence in the *TLS* in 1995. This was initiated by Timothy Buck's article in the *TLS* of October 13th, 1995. It was entitled: "Neither the Letter nor the Spirit" with the subtitle: "Why Most English Translations of Thomas Mann are So Inadequate". The article was mainly concerned with Lowe-Porter's translations but also to a certain extent with Wood's translation of *Buddenbrooks*. Buck referred extensively to Luke's introduction to his own translation. Although the general thrust of Buck's argument that Lowe-Porter's work was "seriously flawed" does not add any fundamentally new insights to Luke's analysis, its importance lies in bringing the whole issue of literary translation and, in particular the translations of Mann, to a much wider public. Buck's criticisms are even more scathing than those of Luke. He questions her competence at the most basic level:

> But as detailed comparisons - by means of random sampling - between the originals and their translation reveal, she clearly did not always understand the meaning of the German she was translating, and moreover, felt entitled to take unnecessary liberties that are tantamount to a distortion of what the author wrote.

Buck then cites several examples to substantiate his argument. As these concern *Buddenbrooks*, it is sufficient to note that he quotes seven gross mistranslations in his next paragraph[12]. He then made an even more virulent attack on her work:

> Countless other such examples could be quoted, not only from *Buddenbrooks* but also from the other works. Lowe-Porter's linguistic incompetence remained astonishingly constant throughout the quarter-century during which she translated Mann's 'oeuvre', no improvement is detectable in all that time.

It is not surprising that Buck's comments provoked a strong response. Lawrence Venuti came to her defence in his letter in the *TLS* dated 24th November, 1995. The tone of his letter is even more polemical than that of Buck:

> Timothy Buck's screed on the English translators of Thomas Mann raises to new heights of thoughtlessness the typical academic condescension toward translation.

Venuti's attack is mainly directed at the academic establishment and its dismissal of translation as "hack-work, unworthy of research or serious critical attention," as already quoted, but he does make some relevant points in her defence. His argument can be summarised as follows: since her translations so far seemed to have worked as texts in themselves, it is both pedantic and churlish to start pointing out errors fifty years later. He claims that her translations took a 'belletristic' approach which for her meant a 'Victorian poeticism' and that they can be defended on the grounds of 'readability':

---

[12] As with Luke, Buck has found errors that can only be described as "schoolboy howlers": "A trawl through selected chapters of *Buddenbrooks* yielded a number of extraordinary mistranslations: *breitbeinig* (with his legs apart) rendered as 'with big bones'; *kurzweilig* (entertaining) 'brief'; *er war stark gewachsen in letzter Zeit* (he had grown a great deal of late) 'he had grown strong and sturdy'; *mit Tatkraft und Umsicht* (with vigour and discretion) 'with tact and discretion'; *Ich habe eine Bratwurst* (I have got a bratwurst) 'the joint is in the oven'; *sein weitläufiges Grundstück* (his extensive property) 'his spacious ground floor'; *wenn ihm etwas zustieße* (if anything were to happen to him) 'if any thing hit him'; *ihre Tränen waren versiegt* (her tears had dried up) 'her tears were conquered'."(Buck 1995: TLS)

Both [This judgement also refers to J. E. Woods translation. J.G.] slighted precision for readability and literary effect in English. And in this they were undoubtedly successful, judging from the 1951 *TLS* article that praised Lowe-Porter.

The obvious weakness in Venuti's argument is the 'ad verecundiam' fallacy in his merely referring to another critic for authoritative support. This position is further weakened when the critic referred to in her defence is the *TLS* critic already quoted who damned Lowe-Porter with the faint praise that she was "competent and devoted." Venuti does, however, have some valid points to make in that translations are to be seen as whole texts rather than a set of academic exercises containing an abundance of errors. His defence is essentially polysystemic by being based on the fact that they have succeeded in the English-speaking world and thus through conflicting semiotic cultural systems so that it is untoward for academics to point out lexical and grammatical errors more than a half century later. Venuti defends her translations by referring indirectly to a target-language oriented approach with his use of the phrase "according to domestic values":

> Buck's attack on Lowe-Porter's 'imprecision - in which the translator reinterprets the author's words' - naively assumes that translation can be a simple communication of the foreign text, uncomplicated by the translator's reinterpretation of it according to domestic values. Hence, when he complains that Lowe-Porter's *Death in Venice* gives a 'false perception' of the interaction between Aschenbach and Tadzio, his examples indicate not so much deliberate distortion as a recasting of the erotic dynamic between the characters, perhaps for an American audience in the 1930s.

The intensity of the debate continued to increase with Luke's reply to Venuti in the *TLS* of 8th December, 1995. The attacks become almost personally abusive as can be seen from the opening remarks with his use of words such as "leaping", "wilfully" and, at a later stage, "pretends":

> Lawrence Venuti in *leaping* to the defence of Helen Lowe-Porter and John E. Woods as translators of Thomas Mann, *wilfully* misses the main point of Timothy Buck's recent criticism of Mann. Perhaps I may try to make his point again more clearly, or *more rudely*. (My emphasis.)

Luke argues that the gravity of Lowe-Porter's mistranslations excludes the defence of their being a case of reinterpretation, but should be regarded as simply gross errors proving that the translation as a whole is below standard. Luke makes this point very forcefully:

I described the defects of the Lowe-Porter versions and gave a list of examples, pointing out, there too, that this is not a question of 'interpretation', or even primarily of style, but of *unwitting factual misrepresentations of the meaning, due to obvious incomprehension of the German vocabulary*. (My emphasis.)

The vitriolic tone then almost reaches the point of fury:

Venuti does not understand that what we are each trying to confront is the type of mistranslation that used to be called *schoolboy howlers*. Well, let us promote them to undergraduate howlers; they are the daily bread of any teacher of German at a British university. (My emphasis.)

Luke quotes some examples of mistranslations which will be discussed in detail in the next chapter. Luke's conclusion is, however, very pertinent to the main argument and purpose of the thesis and so deserves to be quoted in full:

Readers with a scholarly knowledge of German will not normally read Mann's work in translation, and the ordinary reader with little or no German will not notice the mistakes anyway. This no-win situation is what incompetent translators and materialistic publishers rely on in order to get away with translations. The rare pedant who points out the facts is a crank and a nuisance, rocking the boat, crying stinking fish. But it is more than high time that this boat was rocked. *The continued circulation of debased versions of one of the great German writers of this century is a continuing scandal.* (My emphasis.)

The final comment in this debate should go to Buck Timothy Buck who summarises the 'scandal' of Lowe-Porter's translations:

In the series of grossly distorted and artistically diminished versions on which most Anglophones' perception of Mann's work is based, the loss, not only of accuracy but also of quality, is inestimable and – widely unrecognised. The botching of the English translation of Mann arose as the result of a powerful publisher's fiat bringing about the mismatch of an author of world stature with an ambitious, startingly underqualified translator who did not know her limitations. (Buck 1996: *MLA* 919)

(f) Conclusion

It can be seen from this chapter alone that there has been a great variety of critical responses to the Lowe-Porter translations ranging from the highest adulation to the most extreme vitriolic attacks as quoted above, and yet including all the various intermediate shades of grey. There also seems to be a transatlantic divide in that her staunchest defenders are all Americans and virtually all the attackers are British. This could, however, also be due to the divide between the literary and the academic worlds as indicated by Venuti in his letter quoted above. These factors emphasise the urgent need of a dispassionate detailed criticism for one of the most important translation oeuvres of this century. One of the main purposes of this thesis is not merely to contribute to this debate but to develop a critical theory of appraisal for literary translations which will emerge from the study of these particular versions. The first and most urgent point to be tackled is to decide whether the "howlers" referred to by Luke are, in fact, errors or merely "recastings" as referred to by Venuti. This matter will be discussed in the next chapter.

Chapter III: Gross Errors or "Recastings"

(a) General discussion

This chapter aims at throwing light onto the two entrenched positions with regard to the quality of Lowe-Porter's translations encountered in the previous chapter - or, in other words, it needs to be ascertained whether Luke and Buck are, in fact, justified in denouncing Lowe-Porter's mistranslations as "palpable factual mistakes" and "unwitting errors of comprehension" (Luke 1988: xlvi) or whether her apologists such as Venuti or critical defenders of her work such as Mandel (1982) and Hayes, are justified in exonerating them as "recastings", "reinterpretation" (Venuti 1998) and "paraphrasing" (Hayes 1974: 265).

All the critics referred to admit that Lowe-Porter's translations do, in fact, contain errors, but it will be seen in this chapter that the opinions concerning both the frequency and gravity of these errors are extremely diverse. It will also be seen that Luke's and Buck's descriptions of the errors are self-evident to any one with a reasonable knowledge of the two languages. Certainly, in the literature, no one has challenged Luke's and Buck's examples illustrating the specific points made in all their articles. For this reason, it is not necessary to become involved in the debate as to defining what is meant by an error. In any case, Joyce (1997) rightly remarks:

> There are almost as many theoretical differentiations of errors as there are theorists [...]
> (Joyce, 1997: 146)

Buck further substantiated his views on Lowe-Porter's inadequacy for the task of translating Thomas Mann by undertaking an error analysis based on selected sections from various works by Mann and comparing them with the Lowe-Porter translations. His conclusions support the contention that the errors involved here are of the most drastic variety:

> But her credibility as a translator collapses completely when the awful reality of the scale and nature of the errors that mar her work is confronted. It almost beggars belief that the translation of the life's work of one of Europe's leading writers this century should have been entrusted to someone who had such a limited understanding of, and feeling for, German, a deficiency compounded by her at times unnatural handling of English. (Buck 1996: 918)

Even though most of the errors are a case of "undergraduate howlers"[13] as Luke rightly refers to them, Venuti takes an extremely lenient view of their gravity in his letter to the *TLS* of the 24th November, 1995:

> As a result, not only calculated choices, *but errors can work marvellously for the domestic reader*. And what seems fluent at one moment can't be expected to seem so at another. Buck's attack on Lowe-Porter's 'imprecision' - in other words - naively assumes that translation can be a simple communication of the foreign text, uncomplicated by the translator's reinterpretation of it according to domestic values. (My emphasis.)

This opinion was expressed at the height of the *TLS* controversy discussed in Section (f) of the previous chapter, but even after both Luke and Buck had illustrated their arguments with numerous examples of gross errors, Venuti (1998) still remained adamant in his defence of Lowe-Porter's work in his book on translation theory published three years later:

> Yes, translation errors should be corrected, *but errors do not diminish a translation's readability, its power to communicate and to give pleasure.* (Venuti 1998: 32. My emphasis.)

It will be seen that this is an extraordinary statement with regard to Lowe-Porter's errors to which this judgement is referring.

Appendix I shows that there are at least fifty grammatical and seventy-four (grave) stylistic errors in *Tristan* and *Tonio Kröger* alone. These errors vary from relatively trivial to gross, but their cumulative effect detracts seriously from the quality of the work and its readability.

It has been seen in Section (e) of Chapter I that Venuti (1998) refers to these errors as "other possible readings", but even a cursory glance at the error analysis will establish that what is in question here is what Luke correctly described as "schoolboy" or "undergraduate" howlers. Venuti's contention that there is some kind of academic conspiracy against her work is not convincing:

> When texts from the academic canon of foreign literatures are translated by non-specialists, foreign-language academics close ranks and assume a don't tread-on-my-patch attitude. They correct errors and imprecisions in conformity with scholarly standards and interpretations, excluding other possible readings of the foreign text and other possible audiences: for example, belletristic translations that may slight accuracy for literary effect so as to reach a general readership with different values. (Venuti 1998: 33)

Even though there may be an element of truth in Venuti's point in general as a defence of domesticating or target-culture oriented translations, it does not apply to

---

[13] See the previous chapter referring to Luke's reply to Venuti in the *TLS* of 8th December, 1995.

Lowe-Porter whose errors are so frequent and so gross that if there is a 'scandal in translation', it is that, firstly, these errors have been allowed to remain uncorrected to the present day and, even worse, not only that her translations are used as texts in higher education but also that her translations are still being defended in both academia and the literary world. It is even more incredible that Lowe-Porter has supporters who still defend her work after having subjected her translations to academic analysis.

An early example of a Lowe-Porter 'supporter' is Hayes who, in his dissertation on the quality of Lowe-Porter's translation (Hayes 1974), takes a lenient view of the mistakes:

> However, the other examples cited by Luke do not, in my opinion, reveal an inadequate knowledge of German. Rather, they show what happened when Lowe-Porter undressed Mann's thought and put an English garb on it. (Hayes 1974: 265)

It is, however, a pity that Hayes did not research into either the gravity or the frequency of Lowe-Porter's mistakes in his otherwise conscientious study of her translations. Even though the Hayes' study refers to Luke's introduction in which some of Lowe-Porter's gravest errors are listed, Hayes decides against undertaking an error analysis without offering any clear reason for this decision:

> *As little attention as possible* will be paid to errors which are *clearly due to lexical misunderstanding*. I will attempt to show how the two translations differ otherwise with respect to one another and to the original. (Hayes 1974: 26. My emphasis.)

This seems to be a very unfortunate decision in view of the fact that his next heading immediately following the above quotation is a paragraph discussing the criterion of *reliability* for which he gives the following definition:

> Thus I am using the term 'reliability' here to mean 'producing the word-sense and ideas, and suggesting the literary features to an optimum extent'. (Hayes 1974: 26)[14]

If the "word-sense" is completely distorted as Luke strongly contends, then there is a serious loss of reliability according to Hayes' own definition. The decision to give "as little attention as possible" to the errors seems even more incomprehensible in view of

---

[14] Hayes' emphasis on the importance of reliability is worth quoting in full to refute Venuti's underplaying of this aspect: "Over the years little serious attention has been paid to the quality of translations. But in consideration of the increased interest in comparative literary study and the present demand for foreign literature in translation, we must concern ourselves, if not with their aesthetic values, at least with the reliability of translations of works of literature." (Hayes 1974: 11. Hayes' emphasis.)

the fact that Hayes' supposition that the errors are not frequent is based on very unscientific anecdotal evidence:

> Ever since my first acquaintance with *Tod in Venedig,* I have heard repeatedly from many different sides that 'the' [i.e. Lowe-Porter's, J. G.] translation was rather poor because it lacked this or that quality, or because there were so many mistakes in it. The latter charge has often been confined to pointing out *half a dozen or so lexical errors among the 25,000 words of text* and condemning the entire translation on that basis. (Hayes 1974: 26. My emphasis.)

The fact that a few critics may have pointed out "half a dozen or so lexical errors" does not exclude the possibility of there being more mistakes than were noticed by the critics concerned. Hayes subjects the translations under investigation to several quantity analyses, but his very unscientific approach with regard to the errors seems to be deliberate blindness on his part as also appears to be the case with Venuti (1998). The seventy-six-page-long Error Appendix (Appendix I) attests both to the frequency and gravity of the errors which appear in the two novellas *Tonio Kröger* and *Tristan*.

(b) The Quantity and Gravity of the Errors in the Context of Appendix I

The Error Appendix (Appendix I) which highlights 179 errors in *Tristan* and *Tonio Kröger* alone (excluding the eight errors already listed by Luke) is by no means exhaustive. Some of the listed errors may be disputable, but by far the majority are quite clear. The number of errors, defects and omissions are enormous for a mere 106 pages of a paperback edition. The errors in *Der Tod in Venedig* are not, however, included in the Appendix (other than the ones discovered by Luke) as these are studied qualitatively and in depth in the detailed analysis of later chapters and their inclusion would cause the Appendix to become too cumbersome.

Appendix I is a particularly important part of the thesis because for the first time a systematic line-by-line error analysis has been undertaken with regard to the quality of Lowe-Porter's work and the frequency of her mistakes. Any analysis is bound to have a subjective element, but most, if not all, the Appendix I errors listed are clear and uncontroversial – errors in orthography, grammar, usage and lexis - all being the typical errors any teacher of foreign languages deals with on a daily basis. The errors have been checked by colleagues from both the world of professional translation and from academe some of whom are referred to in the acknowledgements in this dissertation. The reaction of every colleague has been one of great surprise that the translator for such an important author can make so many grievously elementary errors. It is, in many ways, a sad task to list the errors of a highly respected translator, but it is necessary to do so in order to end once and for all the debate about the reliability of her translations.

(c) Detailed Analysis of the Errors Identified by Luke

The first example quoted by Luke (1988) refers to Spinell's conversation with Frau Klöterjahn in Chapter VI of *Tristan* in which the aesthete expresses his delight with the Empire-style furnishings of the sanatorium. Part of the humour of this remark is based on Spinell's highly pretentious assertion that there are times when he could not possibly live without the Empire style. The quotation below shows that Lowe-Porter gives the opposite meaning to the effect that the aesthete cannot stand the Empire style:

> *Mann:* Es gibt Zeiten, in denen ich das Empire einfach nicht *entbehren* kann, in denen es mir, um einen bescheidenen Grad des Wohlbefindens zu erreichen, unbedingt nötig ist. (Mann 1977: 171-172)
>
> *Lowe-Porter:* There are times when I cannot *endure* Empire and then times when I simply must have it in order to attain any sense of well-being. (Lowe-Porter 1978: 95)
>
> *Luke:* Now, there are times when I simply cannot *do without* 'Empire', times when it is absolutely necessary to me if I am to achieve even a modest degree of well-being. (Luke 1988: 163)

It is quite clear that Lowe-Porter totally misunderstood the meaning of the verb *entbehren* and probably chose to translate it as "endure" because of its superficial resemblance to the false friends, *entbehren* and 'bear'. This would indeed, be regarded as an example of what Luke condemns as "undergraduate howlers". On the other hand, Lowe-Porter cleverly maintains the general import of the whole sentence to avoid an obvious contradiction by implying that Spinell is very moody so that there are times when he cannot stand "Empire" and other times when he cannot live without it. However, this mistranslation still distorts Mann's intended authorial intention because Spinell is also portrayed by Thomas Mann as a committed aesthete with exquisite tastes rather than a mere moody weakling[15]. Thus, Lowe-Porter's

---

[15] Dittmann (1971) maintains that the portrait of Spinell is based mainly on the writer Arthur Holitscher, partly on the Viennese literary figure Peter Altenberg and partly on the author himself. Dittmann shows that Spinell is not just a moody weakling, but a certain literary type or aesthete: [...] "wichtiger als biographisch fixierbare Einzelheiten ist die Künstlerproblematik der Zeit und der in Spinell getroffene Typ des ästhetisierenden Literaten aus den Jahren um 1900 - für die Darstellung des Problems und dieses Typs leiht sich Thomas Mann Details von den verschiedensten Vertretern des eigenen Berufs." (Dittmann 1971: 53)

downgrading of Spinell's aesthetic commitment involves a minor distortion of his character. Luke's translation, though accurate, lacks humour and force. As an aesthete of exaggerated tastes is involved here, a translation such "There are times when I would simply lie down and die, were I to be deprived of *Empire* surroundings," would not be too 'free' as the satirical perspective on Spinell is brought to the fore. From this first example, it can be seen that Lowe-Porter did indeed commit a "howler", but also that the mistake, in this case, may not be quite so damaging as implied by the ferocious attacks of Buck and Luke.

Similarly, the second example Luke quotes from *Tristan* would also seem to be a "howler" as Lowe-Porter again gives the opposite meaning to a key word. This time the mistranslation has profoundly misleading consequences for any interpretation of the whole passage. The relevant passages occur in Chapter X and refer to Spinell's opening of his letter to Klöterjahn. The aesthete describes how Klöterjahn put an abrupt end to an idyllic scene (*Eden topos*) when Gabriele Eckhof (later to become Klöterjahn's wife) used to sit in a garden with her friends and family. The scene is deliberately described in the most overblown poetic terms:

> Sieben Jungfrauen saßen im Kreis um den Brunnen; in das Haar der Siebenten aber, der Ersten, der Einen, schien die sinkende Sonne heimlich ein schimmerndes Abzeichen der Oberhoheit zu weben. Ihre Augen waren wie ängstliche Träume, und dennoch lächelten ihre klaren Lippen. (Mann 1977: 124-125)

Spinell then maintains that the highly poetic scene came to be destroyed by the gross and prosaic intrusion of Klöterjahn (*Sündenfall topos*). Spinell expresses his outrage in his letter:

> Dies Bild war ein Ende, mein Herr; mußten Sie kommen und es zerstören, um ihm eine Fortsetzung der Gemeinheit und des häßlichen Lebens zu geben? (Mann 1977: 125)

For this reason, Spinell refers to the whole 'story' of Gabriele Eckhof's 'descent' from an idyllic childhood and adolescence down to a prosaic, bourgeois marriage to a philistine in the form of Klöterjahn as "eine ganz kurze, unsäglich empörende Geschichte". At this point, it would be relevant to give the whole quotation together with the two translations:

> **Mann:** [...] ich erzähle lediglich eine Geschichte, eine ganz kurze, unsäglich *empörende* Geschichte [...] (Mann 1977: 124)
>
> **Lowe-Porter:** I will merely tell a story, a brief, unspeakably *touching* story. (Lowe-Porter 1978: 119)

Luke: I merely wish to tell you about something as it was and now is. It is a quite short and unspeakably *outrageous* story. (Luke 1988 123)

It is clear from the above quotation that Lowe-Porter had given the opposite meaning to the adjective *empörend*. As this basic mistranslation refers to Spinell's assessment to Gabriele's whole life story, the error is this time less excusable. This is all the more the case in view of the fact that Spinell was supposed to be a very fastidious writer who took great trouble to find *le mot juste*. (Even the collocation *unspeakably moving* is in itself infelicitous as the qualifier *unspeakably* is usually very negative so that a choice such as *inexpressibly touching* or even *ineffably touching* would demonstrate at least a consistent use of language.) It can be seen from these two examples alone that Luke's judgement of her errors as "flagrant mistranslations" is not without foundation.

This judgement would also apply to the mistakes quoted by Luke in *Tonio Kröger* even though some of these errors may be of less consequence than the one quoted above. Luke's next two examples, though perhaps trivial in themselves, would seem to support Buck's and Luke's contention that Lowe-Porter "had an inadequate knowledge of German" as they represent errors at the most elementary level of simple word recognition and would thus refute Hayes' bald statement that these errors "do not reveal an inadequate knowledge of German" (1974: 7). In Chapter IV of *Tonio Kröger*, there is a description of Lisaveta's easel and canvas in which the latter is covered with a network of lines. Lowe-Porter translates the noun *Liniennetz* as "linen mesh" rather than *network of lines* as can be seen to be correct in the Luke version below:

Mann: Und er betrachtete abwechselnd die farbigen Skizzen, die zu beiden Seiten der Staffelei auf Stühlen lehnten, und die große, mit einem *quadratischen Liniennetz* überzogene Leinwand. (Mann 1977: 221. My emphasis.)

Lowe-Porter: [...] and he looked at the colour-sketches leaning against chairs at both sides of the easel and from them to the large canvas covered with a square *linen mesh.* (Lowe-Porter 1978: 149. My emphasis.)

Luke: And he looked by turns at the color sketches propped against the chair backs on either side of the easel, and at the great canvas marked off *in squares.* (Luke 1988: 153. My emphasis.)

It is obvious, as pointed out by Luke, that Lowe-Porter had confused the noun *Linien* with *Leinen*. Although the mistake is trivial and of little consequence, it is clear that this is a case of confusion rather than an alternative interpretation.

33

The same applies to her translation the adjective *ungewürzt* in Chapter IV of *Tonio Kröger* as *without roots* rather than *savourless* or *without spice*. This is again a basic lexical error, i.e. the confusion of *Würze* with *Wurzel*:

> **Mann:** Sie werden pathetisch, Sie werden sentimental, etwas Schwerfälliges, Täppisch-Ernstes, Unbeherrschtes, Unironisches, *Ungewürztes*, Langweiliges, Banales entsteht unter Ihren Händen. (Mann 1977: 223. My emphasis.)
>
> **Lowe-Porter:** You get pathetic, you wax sentimental; something dull and doddering; *without roots or outlines*, with no sense of humour. (Lowe-Porter 1978: 152. My emphasis.)
>
> **Luke:** You will become solemn, you will become sentimental, you will produce something clumsy, ponderous, pompous, ungainly, unironical, *insipid*, dreary and commonplace. (Luke 1988: 155. My emphasis.)

This passage is one of the more difficult ones in the story so that this mistake could lead to enormous confusions for the reader struggling with the main argument about art. 'Rootless art' may well be the brilliant product of a cynical genius whereas its contrary 'art with roots' is by no means positive in this context, as this could be precisely the sincere, deeply felt, yet banal bourgeois art rooted in emotion and honest feelings, in other words, the very kind of art which the protagonist is condemning. So what is condemned in the original is implicitly praised in the Lowe-Porter translation, thus virtually nullifying the whole of Thomas Mann's argumentation at a stroke. Other aspects of this sentence are also a cause for concern even though they may not be directly subsumed under the heading of gross errors.[16]

---

[16] In this extract, for example, it can also be noted that Lowe-Porter directly translates *pathetisch* as "pathetic". This would also seem to be a mistranslation in view of the fact that *emotional* is not only the more usual translation, but it would also fit much better in the context because *pathetisch* in German is rarely used in the sense of being ridiculous or absurd. The full effect of the 'bourgeois' trying to be an artist could, however, be described as 'pathetic' *as a result* of being emotional so that the full effect of this error is more misleading than grave. Luke's translation of this adjective as 'solemn' may be more appropriate although, within this context, the solemnity is meant in an ironical sense of 'oversolemn' or 'pompous', but *sentimental* or *emotional* would seem to fit better because the point being made is that dullness and banality are a *result* of art based purely on sincere emotions. In this extract, Lowe-Porter also omits some of Thomas Mann's key terms for banal art in his list of definitions: *Schwerfälliges, Täppisch-Ernstes, Unbeherrschtes, Unironisches, Ungewürztes, Langweiliges, Banales* is reduced to "dull and doddering; without roots or outlines, with no sense of humour". (The unique compound *Täppisch-Ernstes* is, for example, ignored completely and no distinction is made between the two differentiated notions *Langweiliges* and *Banales*). The adjective *doddering* is also totally inappropriate translation for *Unbeherrschtes* as *doddering* has connotations with age and decrepitude in the context of persons whereas the actual reference is to banal but well-meaning artistic productions. In this case, Luke's list: "something clumsy, ponderous, pompous, ungainly, unironical, insipid, dreary and commonplace," would seem to be much more accurate although it is strange that both translators avoid the obvious translation of *Banales* as *banal*. This time the cognate word would seem to be appropriate in order to contrast with 'sophisticated' art described in the same paragraph as: "*und künstlerisch sind bloß die Gereiztheiten und kalten Ekstasen unseres verdorbenen, unseres artistischen Nervensystems.*" (ibid.)

Another example of a similarly misleading error cited by Luke can be found in Lowe-Porter's translation of the adjective *heiligend* as *healing* to describe Russian literature:

> **Mann:** Wie also: Die reinigende, *heiligende* Wirkung der Literatur [...] der Literat als vollkommener Mensch, als Heiliger. (Mann 1977: 227)
>
> **Lowe-Porter:** [...] of the purifying and *healing* influence of letters [...] the poet as saint. (Lowe-Porter 1978: 156)
>
> **Luke:** [...] of the purifying, *sanctifying* effect of literature [...] the writer as saint. (Luke 1988: 159)

This mistranslation may seem, at first sight, more innocuous than the other examples quoted above, but this error causes confusion in one of the main themes. Lowe-Porter's misreading would wrongly assign Russian literature to the 'healthy' bourgeois world rather than to the alternative category of the artist as saint, thus representing a false picture of Lisaveta's interpretation of literature, and in particular, of Russian literature[17].

Luke accuses Lowe-Porter of "misconstruction of syntax" with regard to the next example quoted below:

> **Mann:** Nein, Lisawetta, ich folge ihm nicht, und zwar einzig, weil ich hie und da imstande bin, *mich vor dem Frühling meines Künstlertums ein wenig zu schämen*. (Mann 1977: 224)
>
> **Lowe-Porter:** No, Lisabeta, I am not going to; and the only reason is that I am now and again in a position to *feel a little ashamed of the springtime of my art*. (Lowe-Porter 1978: 153)
>
> **Luke:** No, Lisaveta, I shall not follow him; and the only reason I shall not is that I am occasionally capable, *when confronted with spring, of feeling slightly ashamed of being an artist*. (Luke 1988: 156)

Owing to the strange word order in the italicised construction *mich vor dem Frühling meines Künstlertums ein wenig zu schämen*, the formulation would seem to be ambiguous and perhaps deliberately so as a play on the themes of 'springtime' and 'art'. A less ambiguous formulation in German would be: *mich meines Künstlertums vor dem Frühling ein wenig zu schämen*. At the very least, Lowe-Porter's interpretation could be regarded as a genuine translation blunder so that Luke has, in

---

[17] Thomas Mann expresses his view of Russian literature as "holy" (saintly) in the *Betrachtungen eines Unpolitischen:*

> Ist nicht der Russe der menschliche Mensch? Ist seine Literatur nicht die menschlichste von allen, - heilig vor Menschlichkeit? Rußland war immer in tiefster Seele immer demokratisch, ja christlich-kommunistisch, d. h. brüderlich gesonnen. [...] Ein Däne. Hermann Bang, war es, der die russische Literatur zuerst 'die heilige' genannt hat, - was ich nicht wußte, als ich sie im *Tonio Kröger* ebenfalls so nannte. (Mann 1974: 437-438)

this case, been rather harsh in listing this example under the category of 'gross errors' even though his interpretation would seem to be the correct one.

However, there are many other examples which would justify Luke's attribution of some of Lowe-Porter's syntactical errors to an inadequate knowledge of German, as in the following example:

> *Mann:* Fast jedem Künstlernaturell ist ein üppiger und verräterischer Hang eingeboren, *Schönheit schaffende Ungerechtigkeit* anzuerkennen. (Mann 1977: 358)
>
> *Lowe-Porter:* For in almost every artist nature is inborn a wanton and treacherous proneness to side with the *beauty that breaks hearts*. (Lowe-Porter 1978: 31-32)
>
> *Luke:* Inborn in every artistic nature is a luxuriant, treacherous bias in favour of the *injustice that creates beauty*. (Luke 1988: 217)

This syntactical error of failing to distinguish between a subject and object in a preceding noun-qualifying phrase reveals a fundamental lack of knowledge of elementary German syntax. Unfortunately, her work contains many such mistakes. Besides the fifty examples of syntactical errors in Appendix I, there are also frequent similar errors [18] in *Der Tod in Venedig*. In such cases, Luke's translation is far more accurate as there is no reason to doubt that he has an excellent knowledge of German. The notion of the very injustice of life creating a kind of beauty and art is lost in the Lowe-Porter version only to be replaced by the irrelevant cliché, *beauty that breaks*

---

[18] One such example can again be found in the first chapter of *Der Tod in Venedig*, in which Mann describes Aschenbach's feelings about his work:

> *Thomas Mann:* [...] und es schien ihm, als ermangle sein Werk jener Merkmale feurig spielender Laune, die, ein Erzeugnis der Freude, *mehr als irgendein innerer Gehalt, ein gewichtigerer Vorzug, die Freude der genießenden Welt bildeten.* (Mann 1977: 342. My emphasis.)

Lowe-Porter's translation barely makes sense for syntactical reasons:

> *Lowe-Porter*: To him it seemed his work had ceased to be marked by that fiery play of fancy which is the product of joy, and *more, and more potently, than any intrinsic content, forms in turn the joy of the receiving world*. (Lowe-Porter 1978: 11. My emphasis.)

However, Luke's version which takes minor liberties with the rather convoluted German syntax, makes at least some sense to the English reader and generally conveys the import of the original:

> *Luke*: It seemed to him that his work lacked that element of sparkling and joyful improvisation, that quality which *surpasses any intellectual substance in its power to delight the receptive world*. (Luke 1988: 199. My emphasis.)

In Lowe-Porter's version, the subject of the verb *forms* is not clear as the relative pronoun would need to be repeated if the subject is the phrase *play of fancy*. Grammatically, the noun *work* would have to be the subject which would, however, have the effect of depriving the sentence of any sense. The sense is further weakened by the obscure comma in the phrase *and more, and more potently*. This phrase might make sense with some phatic inclusion such as *and what is more, it is all the more powerfully the case that...* in which case the whole sentence would have to be reformulated. Similarly, the collocation *intrinsic content* is obscure. What is meant, in this context, by *intrinsic* content as opposed to *extrinsic* content? The notion of *forming the joy of the receiving world* is also unclear as the noun *joy* tends to be a natural spontaneous sustained emotion rather than a process which can be formed.

hearts. This reduction also considerably diminishes the high literary and philosophical tone of the original even though it could be argued that her 'free' translation reflects the 'art for art's sake' aestheticism which may well have been a familiar concept for the target readership at that time. Hayes' contention in the light of examples such as these would seem to be unsustainable:

> However, as it will be seen in the course of the discussion to follow, I contend that Lowe-Porter's misinterpretations do not result from lexical problems, but from her approach to translating. The difficulty is ultimately literary, not linguistic, despite some demonstrable errors in her work, the charge that she did not know German cannot be allowed: (Hayes 1974: 70-71)

Another example of a case where the syntax had been completely misunderstood at even the most elementary level is quoted by Luke towards the end of her translation of *Death in Venice* when Aschenbach dreams that he is a witness to a Dionysian feast:

> **Mann:** Aber alles durchdrang und beherrschte der tiefe, lockende Flötenton. Lockte er nicht auf ihn, den widerstrebenden Erlebenden, *schamlos beharrlich* zum Fest und Unmaß des äußersten Opfers? (Mann 1977: 393. My emphasis.)
>
> **Lowe-Porter:** But the deep, beguiling notes of the flute wove in and out and over all. Beguiling too was it to him who struggled in the grip of these sights and sounds, *shamelessly awaiting* the coming feast and the uttermost surrender. (Lowe-Porter 1978: 76. My emphasis.)
>
> **Luke:** But the deep enticing flute music mingled irresistibly with everything. Was it not also enticing to him, the dreamer who experienced all this while struggling not to, enticing him *with shameless insistence* to the feast and frenzy of the uttermost surrender. (Luke 1988: 256. My emphasis.)

Lowe-Porter fails to recognise *beharrlich* as an adverb qualifying the verb *lockte* and instead, takes it to be an adjectival predicate referring to Aschenbach. Luke's grammatically correct version makes this point very clear. Lowe-Porter's phrase referring to Aschenbach as *shamelessly awaiting the feast* misses the point that the temptation is portrayed as irresistible and this particular case also falsely attributes the 'shameless' guilt to Aschenbach. It is, of course, a difficult assessment to determine the extent of Aschenbach's responsibility for his own descent, but Lowe-Porter's mistranslation in this case would tip the scales to the wrong balance by placing too much moral responsibility on Aschenbach, thus missing the philosophical import which is expressed throughout both *Tonio Kröger* and *Der Tod in Venedig* that art is a curse which inevitably and of its own nature leads the artist to death and destruction. Together with Lowe-Porter's treatment of the *Würde* theme to be discussed at a later stage in this Section, this interpretation is another item reducing what is a philosophical tragedy to a conventional morality play. In the source text, the phrase *schamlos beharrlich* places some of the guilt on to the irresistibility of the music, thus confirming the key thesis in the *Phaidros* dialogues that the artist's descent into decadence and death is inevitable:

> Der Gegenstand war ihm geläufig, war ihm Erlebnis; sein Gelüst, ihn im Licht seines Wortes erglänzen zu lassen, auf einmal *unwiderstehlich*. (Mann 1977: 375. My emphasis.)

In contrast, however, some of her 'mistranslations' understate the 'immorality' of Aschenbach by playing down the homoerotic elements in the novella. Venuti (1998) argues that this is simply a case of reinterpretation:

> Lowe-Porter's version of Mann's novella *Death in Venice*, criticised for giving a 'false perception' of the 'interaction' between the ageing writer Aschenbach and the enchanting youth Tadzio, could just as well be described as <u>recasting</u> their homoerotic dynamic to suit the greater moral strictness of an American audience during the 1930s. (1998: 33. My underlining)

An example of what Venuti refers to as "recasting their homoerotic dynamic" deserves to be quoted in full with regard to her domestication of the proper noun and monoseme *der Eros* with the vague, polysemic phrase *of the god*:

> **Mann**: Ein Leben der Selbstüberwindung und des Trotzdem, ein herbes, standhaftes und enthaltsames Leben, das er zum Sinnbild für einen zarten und zeitgemäßen Heroismus gestaltet hatte - wohl durfte er es männlich, durfte es tapfer nennen, und es wollte ihm scheinen, als sei *der Eros*, der sich seiner bemeistert, einem solchen Leben auf irgendeine Weise besonders gemäß und geneigt. (Mann 1977: 53. My emphasis.)

> **Lowe-Porter**: It had been a life of self-conquest, a life against odds, dour, steadfast, abstinent, he had made it symbolic of the kind of overstrained heroism the time admired, and he was entitled to call it manly, even courageous. He wondered if such a life might not be somehow especially pleasing in the ey*es of the god* who had him in his power. (Lowe-Porter 1978: 64. My emphasis.)

> **Luke**: A life of self-conquest and defiant resolve, an astringent, steadfast and frugal life which he had turned into the symbol of that heroism for delicate constitutions, that heroism so much in keeping with the times - surely he might call this manly, might call it courageous? And it seemed to him that *the kind of love* which had taken possession of him did, in a certain way, suit and benefit such a life. (Luke 1988: 246. My emphasis.)

Although Luke probably rightly points out that the 'tame' translation of the proper noun *der Eros* as the common noun *the god* could be for reasons of prudery, his own version *the kind of love* seems almost equally vague. The theme of *Eros* is an important element in the litany of Greek deities. The sequential logic of Aschenbach's decline is reflected by the appropriate deity which dominates each corresponding stage of the decline. At first, *Apollo* symbolising form, order, beauty and perfection dominates when Aschenbach admires the formal perfection of Tadzio. At this stage, innocence, beauty and freshness are the dominant associations:

> Dieser Anblick gab mythische Vorstellungen ein, er war wie Dichterkunde von anfänglichen Zeiten, vom Ursprung der Form und von der Geburt der Götter. (Mann 1977: 41)

Later, *Eros* holds Aschenbach in his ban during the stage quoted above when the artist's over-disciplined life begins to be overtaken by obsession. At this stage which overlaps with the 'Apollonian' phase, *Eros* appears in his more innocent form as *Amor* together with all the relatively frivolous rococo associations:

> Amor fürwahr tat es den Mathematikern gleich, die unfähigen Kindern greifbare Bilder der reinen Formen vorzeigen: So auch bediente der Gott sich, um uns das Geistige sichtbar zu machen, gern der Gestalt und Farbe der menschlichen Jugend, die er zum Werkzeug der Erinnerung mit allem Abglanz der Schönheit schmückte und bei deren Anblick wir dann wohl in - Schmerz und Hoffnung entbrannten. (Mann 1977: 53)

Eros then takes over Aschenbach's mind so that the passion becomes an all-consuming obsession as has already been argued in this chapter.

Finally the destructive god *Dionysus* ("der fremde Gott") dominates leading to the inevitable and tragic downfall and death of Aschenbach

> Aber mit ihnen, in ihnen war der Träumende [i.e. Aschenbach, J. G.] nun und *dem fremden Gott* gehörig. Ja, sie waren er selbst, als sie reißend und mordend sich auf die Tiere hinwarfen und dampfende Fetzen verschlangen, als auf zerwühltem Moosgrund grenzenlose Vermischung begann, dem Gotte zum Opfer. Und seine Seele kostete Unzucht und Raserei des Unterganges. (Mann 1977: 394. My emphasis.)

Thus both translators miss an important link within the concatenation of deities.

As with the mistakes quoted from *Tonio Kröger* and *Tristan*, some of the thirteen mistranslations in *Death in Venice* listed by Luke do not adversely affect the main themes, but they do act as an irritant. For example, on page thirteen, she translates the noun *Wertzeichen* as *tributes* rather than as the correct version *postage stamps*, thus distorting once again the basic sense and meaning of this admittedly archaic lexeme:

Mann: Der Vierziger hatte, ermattet von den Strapazen und Wechselfällen der eigentlichen Arbeit, alltäglich eine Post zu bewältigen, die *Wertzeichen* aus allen Herren Ländern trug (Mann 1977: 343)

Lowe-Porter: At forty, worn down by the strains of his actual task, he had to deal with a daily post heavy with *tributes* from his own and foreign countries (Lowe-Porter 1978: 13)

Luke: By the age of forty he was obliged, weary though he might be by the toils and vicissitudes of his real work, to deal with a daily correspondence that bore *postage stamps* from every part of the globe. (Luke 1988: 200-201)

Again the example may be trivial as the plural nouns *tributes* would fit in the context of Aschenbach's eminence as a man of letters and no doubt the etymology of *Wertzeichen* with its ambiguous associations of *Wert* and *Zeichen* (i.e. 'symbols of value') which can have either a purely financial or a moral connotation could well have been a factor for Mann's choice of this word rather than the more familiar *Briefmarken*. Luke is correct in listing this as an error, but it is hardly a gross error. This point is also made by Hayes:

And in this context, her incorrect rendering, "tributes" turns out to be relatively harmless in relation to the work as a whole. (Hayes 1974: 265)

However, Hayes' bias in favour of Lowe-Porter is shown by the fact that this "relatively harmless" rendering is the only error cited by Luke that Hayes discusses in some detail. Indeed, based on the analysis of this one 'harmless' error, Hayes goes on to assert in the next paragraph:

However, the other examples cited by Luke do not, in my opinion, reveal an inadequate knowledge of German. (Hayes 1974: 265)

Lowe-Porter, however, frequently makes lexical or translation errors, forty-seven of which are dealt with in Section B of part (ii) in Appendix I under the heading "lexical errors". All the other gross errors listed by Luke and numerous obvious errors in the text of Lowe-Porter's *Death in Venice* are ignored in Hayes' otherwise thorough study.

In the same chapter of *Der Tod in Venedig*, for example, there is confusion in Lowe-Porter's translation between *Tram* and *train*. (Luke correctly translates *die Tram* as "the tram". Similarly, on page ten of Lowe-Porter's translation, *Fuhrwerk* is wrongly translated by Lowe-Porter as *wagon* whereas Luke's choice of the noun *vehicle* is correct.) There are many other similar irritating examples[19].

---

[19] On page thirteen, Lowe-Porter translates in a totally idiosyncratic way:

Another example of an a minor, but irritating error identified by Luke can be found in her translation of *quer* as "diagonal" on two different occasions. The first is a description of the hotel on his arrival in Venice:

> **Thomas Mann:** [...] und folgte dem Karren durch die Allee, die weißblühende Allee, welche Tavernen, Basare, Pensionen zu beiden Seiten, *quer* über die Insel zum Strande läuft. (Mann 1977: 356. My emphasis.)
>
> **Lowe-Porter:** [...] and followed the hand-car through the avenue, that white-blossoming avenue with taverns, booths and pensions on either *side it*[20] which runs across *diagonally* to the beach. (Lowe-Porter 1978: 29. My emphasis.)
>
> **Luke:** [...] and followed the trolley along the avenue, that white-blossoming avenue, bordered on either side by taverns and bazaars and guesthouses, which runs *straight across* the island to the beach. (Luke 1988: 214-215. My emphasis.)

Similarly, a few pages further on in the same chapter, she translates the phrase *querstehende Hütten* as *diagonal rows of cabins* rather than, as in Luke, *bathing huts at right angles to the main row.*

> **Thomas Mann:** [...] und schaute sich nach den *querstehenden* Hütten um. (Mann 1977: 362. My emphasis.)
>
> **Lowe-Porter:** He looked towards the *diagonal* rows of cabins. (Lowe-Porter 1978: 36. My emphasis.)
>
> **Luke:** [...] he looked round at the *projecting* row of huts (Luke 1988: 221. My emphasis.)

As Luke stated in his preface (1988: xlviii), this error could have been avoided by simply looking at a map.

> **Mann:** [...] sein Talent (war) geschaffen, den *Glauben* des breiten Publikums und *die bewundernde, fordernde Teilnahme* der Wählerischen zugleich zu gewinnen. (Mann 1977: 343. My emphasis.)
>
> **Lowe-Porter:** [...] his genius was calculated to win at once the *adhesion* of the general public and the admiration, both *sympathetic* and *stimulating*, of the connoisseur. (Lowe-Porter 1978: 13. My emphasis.)
>
> Luke's version is again more accurate:
>
> **Luke:** His talent had a native capacity, both to inspire *confidence* in the general public and to win *admiration and encouragement* from the discriminating connoisseur. (Luke 1988: 201. My emphasis.)

In Lowe-Porter's version, the noun *adhesion* is far too physical and combines badly with the adverbial phrase *at once* because the noun *adhesion* refers more to a process than a sudden event. The metaphor is also not made clear. In addition, there is no real justification in adding the adjectives *sympathetic and stimulating* to the text. The adjective *sympathetic* in the phrase *sympathetic admiration* would seem to be a confusion with the 'false friends' *sympathisch* and *sympathetic* because, in English, the collocation *sympathetic admiration* makes little sense.

[20] This should, of course, be 'side *of* it'. It is remarkable that this printing error still exists in all the printed versions and is another reminder that some of the responsibility for the mistakes must be taken by the publishers and (or the lack of) proof readers. See Appendix I Section 2. B (i) for other similar examples.

Far more serious than the elementary errors just quoted is Lowe-Porter's mistranslation of key-words which are connected to the basic motifs running through the novella. The theme of 'dignity' (*Würde*) is one of these central motifs as the novella traces the rapid tragic (also tragi-comic) descent of a highly renowned artist and moralist from his lofty self-disciplined life of *Würde* into passion, obsession, inner depravity, disease and death. The first example taken from Chapter II of *Tod in Venedig* presents *Würde* as the central aim of Aschenbach's life:

> **Mann:** Aber er hatte die *Würde* gewonnen, nach welcher, wie er behauptete, jedem großem Talente ein natürlicher Drang und Stachel eingeboren ist, ja, man kann sagen, daß seine ganze Entwicklung, ein bewußter und trotziger, alle Hemmungen des Zweifels und der Ironie zurücklassender Aufstieg *zur Würde* gewesen war. (Mann 1977: 17. My emphasis.)

> **Lowe-Porter:** But he had attained to *honour*, and *honour*, he used to say, is the natural goal towards which every considerable talent presses with whip and spur. Yes, one might put it that his whole career had been one conscious and *overweening* ascent to *honour*, which left in the rear all the misgivings or self-derogation which might have hampered him. (Lowe-Porter 1978. 16. My emphasis.)

> **Luke:** But he had achieved *dignity*, that goal toward which, as he declared, every great talent is innately driven and spurred; indeed it can be said that the conscious and defiant purpose of his entire development had been, leaving all the inhibitions of skepticism and irony behind him, an ascent to *dignity*. (Luke 1988: 203. My emphasis.)

Lowe-Porter's interpretation implies that Aschenbach is guilty of hubris by her mistranslation of the adjective *trotzig* as *overweening* so that the phrase *overweening ascent to honour* is reminiscent of the notion of *overweening pride*, and thus of hubris. The aspect of *trotzig* understood as heroic defiance of obstacles such as disease and weakness, "Ein Leben der Selbstüberwindung und des Trotzdem" (Mann 1977: 346), is grossly distorted into "overweening" arrogance in the Lowe-Porter version. The fact that this interpretation could seem to be plausible makes it all the more insidious by adding yet another factor to her reduction of the tragedy to a morality play.

Another example of Lowe-Porter's ignoring of the theme of dignity is quoted below:

> **Mann:** [...] und gewiß ist, daß die schwermütig gewissenhafteste Gründlichkeit des Jünglings Seichtheit bedeutet im Vergleich mit dem tiefen Entschlusse des Meister gewordenen Mannes, das Wissen zu leugnen, es abzulehnen, erhobenen Hauptes darüber hinwegzugehen, sofern es

den Willen, die Tat, das Gefühl und selbst die Leidenschaft im geringsten zu lähmen, zu entmutigen, *zu entwürdigen* geeignet ist. (Mann 1977: 346. My emphasis.)

> ***Lowe-Porter:*** And certain it is that the youth's constancy of purpose, no matter how painfully conscientious, was shallow beside the mature resolution of the master of his craft, who made a right-about-face, turned his back on the realm of knowledge, and passed it by with averted face, lest it lame his will or power of action, paralyse his feelings or his passions, deprive any of these of their conviction or *utility*. (Lowe-Porter 1978: 17. My emphasis.)

> ***Luke:*** [...] and it is very sure that even the most gloomily conscientious and radical sophistication of youth is shallow by comparison with Aschenbach's profound decision as a mature master to repudiate knowledge as such, to reject it, to step over it with head held high - in the recognition that knowledge can paralyse the will, paralyse and discourage action and emotion and even passion, and *rob all these of their dignity.* (Luke 1988: 204. My emphasis.)

Lowe-Porter's reading of *zu entwürdigen* as to *deprive* [these] *of their utility* cannot be justified in this context. What is meant by a 'useful' or 'useless' passion and emotion is very unclear and even less clear is the notion of *depriving* a 'useful' passion of its utility[21]. The *Würde* theme continues to be either ignored or misinterpreted by Lowe-Porter when she mistranslates *die Würde des Geistes* as "recognises his own worth":

> ***Mann:*** [...] wenn ein großes Talent dem libertinischen Puppenstande entwächst, *die Würde des Geistes* ausdrucksvoll wahrzunehmen sich gewöhnt und die Hofsitten einer Einsamkeit annimmt [...] (Mann 1977: 347. My emphasis.)

> ***Lowe-Porter:*** [...] when a man of transcendent gifts outgrows his carefree apprentice stage, *recognises his own worth* and forces the world to recognise it too and pay *it* homage though he puts on a courtly bearing [...] (Lowe-Porter 1978: 18. My emphasis.)

> ***Luke:*** [...] when a great talent grows out of its libertinistic chrysalis-stage, becomes an expressive representative of the *dignity of mind*, takes on the courtly bearing of that solitude, [...] (Luke 1988: 205. My emphasis.)

Lowe-Porter's version may superficially seem to be in the spirit of this extract, but the phrase *dignity of intellect* is not the same thing as her mis-translated phrase "the writer's own worth" nor is there any justification for her adding the phrase "forcing the world to recognise it and paying homage to it", i.e. 'to his own worth'. Her free interpretation continues to support the misreading of the work as a morality play. As with her insertion of the phrase "overweening ascent", the idea of this artist

---

[21] Even 'utilitarian' ethics would not help to clear up this difficulty as presumably 'a useful passion' would simply increase the happiness of the greatest number, but even within the principles of the Benthamite *hedonistic calculus*, the notion of will, passions and emotions possessing *inherent* 'utility' would contradict the very spirit of this consequentialist ethic.

'compelling' others *to pay homage* to 'his own worth' would imply that the writer not only has narcissistic tendencies in his self-worship but also that his vanity is so extreme that it has a despotic element in "forcing" the world to pay homage to the artist. Again, by re-introducing her concocted 'hubris' theme, Lowe-Porter continues the process of reducing a philosophical tragedy into a trivial morality play, in which pride is 'justly' punished.

(d) Detailed Analysis of the Omissions Identified by Luke

Besides the "flagrant mistranslations", Luke accuses Lowe-Porter of serious omissions:

> In addition, Mrs. Lowe-Porter was in the habit (and this applies to her translations generally) of unnecessarily and *often* damagingly excising words, phrases and even whole sentences. (Luke 1988: xlix)

Luke then goes on to give two examples of her omissions which contribute to Lowe-Porter's distortion of a major theme. Luke claims that the first example is of lesser importance than the second, which will, however, be shown to be debatable.

The first example takes place in Chapter III in *Der Tod in Venedig* when Aschenbach is hurrying to catch his train to leave Venice. Aschenbach has decided to do the sensible thing and leave Venice on account of the *sirocco* wind which is carrying the cholera epidemic. He has at the same time discovered Tadzio with the result that Aschenbach feels reluctant to leave the city. He tries to persuade himself that it is just Venice that he is leaving. There is, however, a dim awareness that a great though possibly fatal adventure might take place if he stays.[22] The passage in question takes place at the station where he learns that his luggage has gone astray, which gives him an excuse to stay. The conflict, whether to stay in Venice or not, is between his reason and his hidden passions. The whole passage can be argued to be a turning point because, after this incident, Aschenbach's fate is sealed. He is, at the same time, so deeply satisfied with his 'wrong' decision that his mood bursts out into a mild form of delirious hysteria:

> Eine abenteuerliche Freude, eine unglaubliche Heiterkeit erschütterte von innen fast krampfhaft seine Brust. (Mann 1977: 368)

---

[22] "Wunderlich unglaubhaftes, beschämendes, komisch-traumartiges Abenteuer", [. . .]. (Mann 1977: 369).

The whole paragraph needs to be quoted in full together with Lowe-Porter's translation. It will be seen that her version tones down the passage by placing the main emphasis on the external circumstance of the protagonist simply having the irritation of finding that his luggage has been redirected. (It could be argued that the 'lost case' incident, though theoretically trivial in itself, fulfils the structural demand for novellas by acting as an example of an *unerhörtes Ereignis*). In this context, Lowe-Porter's omission of the sentence, "Er will es und will es nicht", is a very serious matter because it shows that Aschenbach was divided about his return home and that the foolhardy decision to stay was at least indirectly willed by him. At the same time, it shows that, at one level, he wanted to do the correct thing. Pure chance or fate has intervened on his side so that the formula, *art→ eros→ decadence→ disease→ death*, takes its inevitable and tragic course. On the other hand, it also reminds the reader that if he really wanted to leave Venice, he merely needed to make alternative travel arrangements. The Lowe-Porter omission of the full sentence gives the impression that circumstances alone decided the outcome despite her indirect reference to the artist being torn between two possibilities. If this is coupled with her 'morality play' interpretation, chance has been allocated the role of nemesis leading to the 'just' downfall and punishment of Aschenbach. As has already been shown, there is no justification for this interpretation from the original passage:

> *Mann:* Unterdessen nähert sich das Dampfboot dem Bahnhof, und Schmerz und Rastlosigkeit steigen bis zu Verwirrung. Die Abreise dünkt den Gequälten unmöglich, die Umkehr nicht minder. So ganz zerrissen betritt er die Station. Es ist sehr spät, er hat keinen Augenblick zu verlieren, wenn er den Zug erreichen will. *Er will es und will es nicht.* Aber die Zeit drängt, sie geißelt ihn vorwärts; er eilt, sich sein Billet zu verschaffen. (Mann 1977: 368. My emphasis.)

In addition to the omitted sentence indicated above, phrases either toning down the original or distorting the sense are indicated in italics in the Lowe-Porter version:

> *Lowe-Porter:* Meanwhile the steamer neared the station landing. *His anguish of irresolution* amounted *almost* to panic. *Torn* between two alternatives, he entered the station. To leave seemed impossible to the sufferer, to remain not less so. It was very late, he had not a moment to lose, Time pressed, it scourged him onward. He hastened to buy his ticket [...]. (Lowe-Porter 1978: 44. My emphasis.)

> *Luke:* In the meantime the vaporetto was approaching the station, and Aschenbach's distress and helplessness increased to the point of distraction. In his torment he felt it to be impossible to leave and no less impossible to turn back. He entered the station torn by this acute inner conflict. It was very late, he had not a moment to lose if he was to catch his train. *He both*

wanted to catch it and wanted to miss it. But time was pressing, lashing him on; he hurried to get his ticket. (Luke 1988: 228. My emphasis.)

The total effect of the Lowe-Porter translation of this paragraph is to lose the momentous urgency of the original. Reed (1994) notes that the importance of this moment is emphasised by Thomas Mann's dramatic use of the present tense and the anonymous reference to the English translation would certainly refer to the Lowe-Porter version, but, in this case, would also apply to Luke's tense usage:

> The botched departure is a classic piece of narrative even in this virtuoso text. There are sad images and rhythms for the 'voyage of sorrow' (made more immediate in the original by the shift to the present tense, *which the English translations do not render*), and then the sprightly rhythms of the return to the Lido, with 'the rapid little boat, spray before its bows, tacking to and fro between gondolas and vaporetti,' the very embodiment of joyful release. Aschenbach is as happy as a 'truant schoolboy.' The literal German sense - an 'escaped' schoolboy - sets off an even more ironic sequence. (Reed 1994: 48. My emphasis.)

In Lowe-Porter's version, the moment of decision leading to the protagonist's ultimate downfall, is trivialised to a mere irritating incident, namely Aschenbach's loss of his baggage and portrays him as simply indecisive ("torn between two alternatives") without any hint of the *Wille* theme in Schopenhauer's use of this concept: i.e. the conflict between the blind *Wille* (in this case, *Eros*) and human reason in the form of the sensible decision to return home and avoid the cholera plague. Thus, not only basic themes and motifs are botched by the Lowe-Porter omission but also any possibility of understanding the structure of the novella is blurred by her toning down of a passage which could be regarded as the *Wendepunkt*.

Luke justifiably expresses outrage at Lowe-Porter's second omission of a full sentence almost at the very end of the story:

> The more crucial and almost incredible case comes at the very end of the story, in the passage describing Aschenbach's final vision and death. (Luke 1988: xlix)

Its context can be placed by quoting the previous sentence referring to Aschenbach's last moments of consciousness:

> *Mann:* Ihm war aber, als ob der bleiche und liebliche Psychagog dort draußen ihm lächle, ihm winke; als ob er, die Hand aus der Hüfte lösend, hinausdehnte, voranschwebe ins Verheißungsvoll-Ungeheure. *Und wie so oft, machte er sich auf, ihm zu folgen.* (Mann 1977: 398. My emphasis.)

Incredibly, Lowe-Porter's version simply omits the last sentence in the penultimate paragraph of the novella (i.e. the italicised sentence in the above quotation), which describes Aschenbach's final action before his death. It shows that the 'author' is still under Tadzio's spell.

> *Lowe-Porter:* It seemed to him the pale and lovely Summoner out there smiled at him and beckoned; as though with the hand he lifted from his hip, he pointed outward as he hovered on before into an immensity of richest expectation. [Omission] (Lowe-Porter 1978: 83)

> *Luke:* But it was as if the pale and lovely soul-summoner out there were smiling to him, beckoning to him: as if he loosed his hand from his hip and pointed outward, hovering ahead and onward, into an immensity rich with unutterable expectation. *And as so often, he set out to follow him.* (Luke 1988: 263. My emphasis.)

Whether this omission is "more crucial" than the former as discussed is debatable, but it is certainly a totally incomprehensible translation act, to which Hayman (1995) in his biography of Thomas Mann also takes exception:

> It was impossible for most English readers to understand the end of *Death in Venice* until a new translation by David Luke appeared in the United States during 1987 and in Britain during 1990. (Hayman 1995: 266)

Although Luke does not indicate what is lost by this omission nor why this omission should be regarded as "very much more" serious than the other omission quoted above, Hayman does give some intimation of its gravity:

> But it's *unforgivable* to jettison the sentence that gives the final glimpse into Aschenbach's consciousness and rounds the story off by adding a layer of inevitability to his death. In Venice, casting aside his habitual self-discipline, he has often trailed Tadzio through the narrow streets; finally he's under the comfortable illusion of succumbing to the same temptation - with the encouragement of a signal. (Hayman 1995: 266. My emphasis.)

In Lowe-Porter's version, the omission gives Aschenbach's death an uncalled-for religious quality leaving a certain ambiguity that there could be an element of the repentant sinner reconciled with death - a dignity unwarranted by the text. The source text implies the opposite of Lowe-Porter's interpretation because the phrase *Wie so oft* refers to Aschenbach's constant, barely concealed obsessive pursuit of Tadzio so that his last act was the last 'sinful' attempt to get up and follow the boy as usual. This is in ironic contrast with the romantic religiosity of the previous sentence, thus adding another layer of irony to the whole situation. Hayman's interpretation is supported by Dittmann (1993) so that the wonderfully vague metaphysical phrase *ins*

Verheißungsvoll-Ungeheure has a hidden ironically sordid subtext because, alongside the highly romantic surface mystical implication, it can and, in this context probably does, refer to illicit sexual adventure. This line of argumentation is derived from Reed and Vaget:

> Daß diese Geste (ins Verheißungsvoll-Ungeheure) als erotisches Signal zu verstehen sei, wird von Reed und Vaget durch den Verweis auf eine teilweise gleichlautende Formulierung in Thomas Manns *Felix Krull* begründet. Die Stelle erscheint in dem frühesten, kurz vor dem *Tod in Venedig* geschriebenen Teil des Romans. Es ist dort von Prostituierten die Rede, die ihre Kunden 'ins Verheißungsvoll-Ungeheure' locken, als erwarte sie 'dort ein ungeheures nie gekostetes und grenzenloses Vergnügen'. (Dittmann 1993: 71).

At the same time, Tadzio plays the role of the *Psychagog* or the *Summoner* seductively beckoning his victim to a blissful sensual death with the result that Aschenbach almost eagerly tries to get up to follow him. In the end, the tragic hero accepts both his nature and the inevitability of his fate. This sentence also underlines the fact that Aschenbach was in a sense true to Tadzio to the point of death as if he had come to terms with his own 'degradation'. These aspects, whether accurately described or not, are totally absent in the Lowe-Porter version so that the reader cannot even enter into dialogue with this theme.

(e) A Brief Selection of Some Other Serious Mistranslations in *Der Tod in Venedig*

At the beginning of *Der Tod in Venedig*, Aschenbach is disoriented by his sudden encounter with a man in the graveyard, a figure reminiscent of the 'Grim Reaper' whose horrific aspect is enhanced by the fact that he is standing in a higher position which increases the impression of his threatening 'superiority'.

> **Mann:** So - und vielleicht trug *sein erhöhter und erhöhender Standort* zu diesem Eindruck bei - hatte seine Haltung etwas herrisch Überschauendes, Kühnes oder selbst Wildes [...] (Mann 1977: 339. My emphasis.)

> **Lowe-Porter:** Perhaps *his heightened and heightening position* helped out the impression Aschenbach received. At any rate, standing there as though at survey, the man had a bold and domineering, even a ruthless air. (Lowe-Porter 1978: 9. My emphasis.)

> **Luke:** [...] and perhaps *the raised point of vantage on which he stood* contributed to this impression - an air of imperious survey, something bold or even wild about his posture. (Luke 1988: 196. My emphasis.)

The phrase *his heightened and heightening position* is virtually meaningless whereas Luke's translation *the raised point of vantage on which he stood* conveys the physical location with perfect clarity. Even Luke misses the important connotation of the adjectival participle *erhöhender* which gives the impression that this mysterious figure is increasing in stature as if it were a supernatural phenomenon.[23]

The next error occurs in the scene when Aschenbach disembarks from a *vaporetto* on his arrival in Venice. At first sight, the mistake may seem to be relatively innocuous, but it reveals a profound ignorance of how English syntax works. This example would seem to be merely infelicitous whereas, in fact, it is shown to be totally ungrammatical[24]:

> *Mann:* [...] sein Koffer hinderte ihn, der eben mit Mühsal die leiterartige Treppe *hinuntergezerrt und geschleppt* wird. (Mann 1977: 352. My emphasis.)

> *Lowe-Porter:* Then came another delay while his trunk was *worried* down the ladder-like stairs. (Lowe-Porter 1978: 25. My emphasis.)

> *Luke:* (He was) held up by his trunk which at that moment was being *laboriously dragged and maneuvered* down the ladder-like stairway. (Luke 1988: 211. My emphasis.)

Whilst Luke's version conveys the sense with perfect clarity, Lowe-Porter's italicised error verges on absurdity, i.e. with the notion of 'a worried trunk'. This was probably a misapplication of the less common transitive verb *to worry* which often applies to animals as in the sentence, *The dog worried the cat.*

The next sentence in the same passage also contains some examples of unidiomatic English usage:

> *Mann:* So sieht er sich minutenlang außerstande den Zudringlichkeiten des *schauderhaften* Alten zu entkommen, [...]. (Mann 1977: 352. My emphasis.)

---

[23] Both translators miss the mythical or even supernatural poetic aspects of the original conveyed by the abstract nominalised adjectives. The magnificently ambiguous formalisation *etwas herrisch Überschauendes* has associations of both 'schaudern' and 'schauern'. However, these are more stylistic aspects which will be dealt with thoroughly in later chapters.

[24] The metaphor may be within the bounds of possibility, but certainly not as the non-existent phrasal verb *to worry down*. If the meaning is purely adverbial, then another qualifier is necessary such as in the sentence, *The dog worried the cat all the way down the stairs*. In the passive form with an omitted agent, even this clear cut case does not work owing to the ambiguity of the construction. Thus, the sentence, *The cat was worried all the way down the stairs* would normally mean that the cat was anxious during its descent down the stairs whereas the progressive form excludes this ambiguity *The cat was being worried all the way down the stairs*, but Lowe-Porter uses the former construction when the latter was the only correct one with the resultant absurdity of the suitcase being anxious during its descent. There are many such examples, six of which are classified under the heading *Confusion of Transitive and Intransitive verbs* in Appendix I (Section 2 (iv)).

> *Lowe-Porter:* Thus he was forced to endure the importunities of the ghastly *young-old* man, (Lowe-Porter 1978: 25. My emphasis.)

> *Luke:* [...] and thus, for a full minute or two, he could not avoid the importunate attentions of the dreadful *old* man, (Luke 1988: 211)

Lowe-Porter's infelicitous and baldly self-contradictory formulation *the young-old man* could almost imply the contrary of the original. A "young-old" man would normally refer to an old man with youthful vigour and appearance rather than, as is quite clearly intended, an old man desperately trying, but failing tragically to look young. The use of the hyphen in this formulation only adds to the absurd effect.

The next few examples all occur on page thirty-three of the Lowe-Porter translation and refer to the incident when Aschenbach first encounters the Polish family:

> *Mann:* Allein das alles hatte sich so ausdrücklich, mit einem solchen Akzent von Zucht, Verpflichtung und Selbstachtung dargestellt, daß Aschenbach *sich sonderbar ergriffen fühlte.* (Mann 1977: 352. My emphasis.)

> *Lowe-Porter:* Yet they had done this all so expressly, with such self-respecting discipline, and sense of duty that Aschenbach *was impressed.* (Lowe-Porter 1978: 33)

> *Luke:* But this had all been carried out with such explicitness, with such a strongly accented air of discipline, obligation and self-respect that Aschenbach *felt strangely moved.* (Luke 1988: 219)

Lowe-Porter's version expresses mere approval, thus missing the theme of *Anstand* which is also closely linked to the *Würde* motif. The sight of the family with their strict discipline has a great emotional effect on Aschenbach as it recalled the strict, ordered lives of his forefathers and also acted as a kind of conscience in contrast to the extravagance of the artistic existence. This theme is much more explicit in *Tonio Kröger*, but even here it serves to explain why Aschenbach felt "sonderbar ergriffen".

At the beginning of Chapter V in *Der Tod in Venedig*, Lowe-Porter mistranslates the adjective *unheimlich* as "singular", so that she misses the atmosphere of evil. Adjectives such as *eerie, disturbing* or even better, *sinister* might be a more appropriate translation:

> *Mann:* In der vierten Woche seines Aufenthaltes auf dem Lido machte Gustav von Aschenbach einige die Außenwelt betreffende *unheimliche Wahrnehmungen.* (Mann 1977: 379. My emphasis.)

Lowe-Porter: In the fourth week of his stay *on* (!) the Lido Gustave made certain *singular observations* touching the world about him. (Lowe-Porter 1978: 59. My italics and exclamation mark)

Luke: During the fourth week of his stay at the Lido Gustav von Aschenbach began to notice certain *uncanny developments* in the outside world. (Luke 1988: 241. My emphasis.)

Although Lowe-Porter's slavish following of the German in mistranslating the preposition *auf* as *on* is merely an irritant, any reader tracing the theme of the gradual emergence of evil would have missed the subtly sinister implications, which add to the major themes of disease, evil and art.

Many other examples could be adduced where Lowe-Porter's translations tone down the source text such as in page 67 when she translates the "frecher" musician described as *halb Zuhälter, halb Komödiant* as "half *bully*, half comedian." Her reluctance to use a more accurate word such as *pimp* is all part of her strategy of underplaying the sexual references in the text.

(f) Conclusion

It is to be hoped that this chapter together with Appendix I will now contribute to ending the debate concerning the reliability of the Lowe-Porter translations at least as far as the three stories are concerned. It is quite clear that her translations are not only very unreliable but that they also tone down and distort the central themes running through the stories. Luke's translations, though still less easily available, can be regarded as at least a reliable workmanlike achievement. Lowe-Porter not only frequently confuses elementary lexical items but also fails to understand more complex syntactical structures. Some of the mistranslations show that she also failed to understand the basic themes which permeate Thomas Mann's oeuvre. Even worse than this, a few of the examples in this chapter as well as the forty-nine grammatical errors and seventy-five lapses in English usage in Appendix I show that her command of English was very poor for a literary translator. The real point is not whether a certain Helen Lowe-Porter was a good translator or not, but that half the literary and academic establishment have, to quote Luke, "leaped" to the defence of very seriously flawed translations and still defend them to this day.

It will be shown in the next few chapters that she seemed to have little inkling of the sophisticated language games Thomas Mann plays whether he is writing in a poetic, philosophical or humorous vein. That her mistakes as demonstrated in this chapter together with Appendix I are often below the level of minimal competence comprises the essence of the Lowe-Porter scandal.

Chapter IV: Problem of Translating a Literary Style with Reference to General Stylistic Features in *Der Tod in Venedig*

(a) The Problem of Transposing a Literary Style

Comparatively little has been written in the field of translation theory about the problem of translating a literary style. Snell-Hornby's (1988) summary of the literature still generally applies to the present situation:

> Style is nominally an important factor in translation, but there are few detailed or satisfactory discussions of its role within translation theory. In their definitions of translation, both Nida and Wilss put style on a par with meaning or content. In Reiß (1971), Wilss (1977) and Koller (1979), references to aspects of style in translation are frequent, and Stolze (1994) devotes a complete section (1982: 300ff.) to the question of style. In all cases, however, the discussion is linked to specific items or examples, and no coherent theoretical approach is attempted. In the recent theories of Vermeer and Holz-Mänttäri the problem of style recedes perceptibly into the background: in Holz-Mänttäri (1984) it is barely mentioned, and in Reiß and Vermeer (1984) the topic is limited to brief references to the general need for a "Stiltheorie" in translation (1984: 22, 219). Up to now this has remained a desideratum. (Snell-Hornby 1988: 119-120)

Snell-Hornby is one of the few theorists to deal directly with the problem of style and she illustrates her arguments with examples of translated texts, which are then subjected to detailed analysis. The same approach will be taken with Luke's and Lowe-Porter's translations. Snell-Hornby's approach seems to be eminently practical:

> With the development of text-linguistics and the gradual emergence of translation studies as an independent discipline in its own right, there has been an increasing awareness of the text, not as a chain of separate sentences, these themselves being a string of grammatical and lexical items, but as complex multi-dimensional structure consisting of more than a mere sum of its parts - a gestalt whereby an analysis of its parts cannot provide an understanding of the whole. Thus textual analysis, which is an essential preliminary to translation, should proceed from the "top down," from the macro to the micro level, from text to sign. (Snell-Hornby 1988: 69)

The other Sections of this chapter will be concerned with textual analysis, which will reveal something of the complexity of Thomas Mann's style as well as the difficulty in 'reproducing' his stylistic effects.

In her study of the concept of style, Snell-Hornby cites Leech's and Short's term *transparent* to describe an easily digestible style (Leech and Short 1981: 19) and a difficult complex literary style is designated as *opaque* (Leech and Short 1981: 29). For the purpose of this study, the term *opaque* can be further defined in terms of *richness* and *density*. The perspective of *richness* refers to the quantity and variety of stylistic features as whereas *density* concentrates both on the interaction of the various features and their frequency per number of words in the text.

In addition to Snell-Hornby, Hatim and Mason (1998) are also amongst the few recent theoreticians who tackle the problem of style directly. They start with the traditional distinction between form and content with the severely practical question:

> Should content be faithfully rendered at all costs, and form only if the translation of content allows? (Hatim and Mason 1998: 8)

It is true that most translators and, particularly the translators discussed in this study, give primacy to content over form or, in other words, to semantics over semiotics. Style is often treated as if it were a dispensable luxury.

The imitation or reproduction of a certain style, however, does have grave dangers if the translator is not fully aware of differing cultural factors. For example, Hatim and Mason quote Nida (1964), who as a Bible translator, is only too conscious of the pitfalls of misapplied cross-cultural transference:

> What is entirely appropriate in Spanish, for example, might turn out to be quite unacceptable 'purple prose' in English, and the English prose we admire as dignified and effective often seems in Spanish to be colourless, insipid and flat. Many Spanish literary artists take delight in the flowery elegance of their language, while most English writers prefer bold realism, precision, and movement. (Nida 1964: 169)

To a certain extent, Nida's 'dilemma' can be resolved by a judicious application of Newmark's distinction between "semantic" and "communicative" translation, or to use the terms "domesticating" and "foreignising" translation as applied by Venuti (1995). A communicative translation would either find a 'functional equivalent' in the target language (for example, parallel wordplay in a humorous text) or, at least produce a stylistically readable TL text. A "foreignising" text, on the other hand, can afford to make more demands on the reader who wishes to experience something of the 'feel' or even 'awkwardness' of the original. Hatim and Mason rightly see the problem of translating style as semiotics:

> The translator, as language user in a setting which is generally not that of the ST [source text] producer, has to be able to judge the **semiotic** value which is conveyed when particular stylistic options are selected. (Hatim and Mason 1998: 10)

An example of semiotic analysis is given in Section (e) of Chapter V with regard to the translation of poetry, where the concept of second-order semiotics is defined and illustrated. Before semiotics, there must, however, be analysis as has already been argued. In the case of Thomas Mann, the scrutiny of stylistic aspects is an enormous undertaking. This is an area which will be seen to provide a fruitful interface between literary analysis and translation. It will also be seen that Thomas Mann's style is both extraordinarily *dense* and *rich*.

It is interesting to see how two other writers on Thomas Mann translations deal with the problem of translating Mann's style. Hellman's (1992) study comparing the French translation of *Der Zauberberg* with the original generally avoids any direct confrontation with the problem of style which is subsumed under different headings such as "Sondersprachen", "Wortbildung", "Abtönung" and "Rhetorische Figuren". It is disappointing, however, that Hellmann (1992) restricts his comments to referring to a few translation deficiencies without offering alternative solutions or embarking on a theoretical discussion of how to deal with these difficulties. Although Hayes (1974) does devote a page to 'style' in his comparison of the Lowe-Porter and Burke translations of *Der Tod in Venedig*, he comes to the rather unhelpful conclusion that style is indefinable:

> Style. The definitions of literary style are as numerous as the definers. (Hayes 1974: 37)

Hayes does, however, tackle many of Thomas Mann's stylistic features, even if indirectly, under headings such as "diction" and "rhetorical figures". There is, however, no general description of Mann's style and he confines his comments to a few examples of Lowe-Porter's mistranslations.

Style is used in this context as an umbrella term for stylistic features including connotation, structure, rhythm and general sonic effects together with their interaction with each other to produce a certain general tone or register. The first step is to analyse the style of a writer such as Mann which includes the study of the works of scholars who have undertaken this task. Just as the technical translator needs to be, or rapidly to become, an expert in the field he or she is translating, so the literary translator needs to work in close harmony with scholarly analyses of the particular writer who is being translated, which unfortunately would not seem to be the case with the Lowe-Porter translation. So much has been written on the stylistic aspects of Thomas Mann's works that it would be virtually impossible even to summarise the research taking place on a world-wide basis. For the purposes of a study of Thomas Mann in translation, it will be sufficient to focus on those aspects which are of interest to the translator. In the case of Thomas Mann, it is fortunate that there are two excellent articles which have concentrated on these key stylistic aspects: Koch-Emmery (1953) and Seidlin (1963). The former article analyses Mann's style in conjunction with the Lowe-Porter translation whereas the latter not only refers explicitly to translation problems but also highlights those very aspects which would seem to be untranslatable.

(b) Koch-Emmery's (1953) Stylistic Analysis of Lowe-Porter's Translations of Thomas Mann

Koch-Emmery outlines the difficulties in the syntactic structure of Thomas Mann's sentences:

> But this is only the beginning of a translator's difficulties. Thomas Mann has inherited from no less a predecessor than Goethe a German style which, in its ponderous, sonorous beauty, is a miracle of logical precision, of flexible phraseology and accumulative vigour. Every single paragraph in Thomas Mann's writings represents a solid structure, it is built to an architect's plan; some of them may be compared to castles, others to cathedrals, others to picture galleries or wayside inns, but they are all solidly constructed. (Koch-Emmery 1953: 275)

The truth of these rather florid assertions will be confirmed even more in the detailed analysis in Sections (b)-(d), which show just how tightly constructed Mann's sentences really are, sometimes demanding the same complexity as poetic form. Thomas Mann was a quite deliberate and self-conscious stylist as statements such as the following example clearly demonstrates:

> Mein Streben ist, das Schwere leicht zu machen; mein Ideal: Klarheit; und wenn ich lange Sätze schreibe, wozu die deutsche Sprache nun einmal neigt, lasse ich es mir, ich glaube, nicht ohne Erfolg, angelegen zu sein, der Periode vollkommene Durchsichtigkeit und Sprechbarkeit zu wahren. Einmal, zu Beginn der Josephgeschichten, habe ich mir den Spaß gemacht, einen Satz zu schreiben, der sich über anderthalb Seiten erstreckt. Die Übersetzer haben ihn *natürlich* in viele kurze zerlegt. Aber wer deutsch versteht, lese sich den Josephsatz nur vor und sehe, ob man dabei ein einziges Mal den Faden verliert. (Mann 1965: 199-200. My emphasis.)

This complexity of Mann's style is confirmed by Koch-Emmery's detailed description:

> The unique secret of German syntax is that you can encase your sentences into each other, interlink and dovetail them in a hundred different ways. This skilful art has been exploited by

56

Thomas Mann with a dazzling, almost uncanny mastery. The result is a word texture so closely knit, so delicately shaped, so subtly suggestive of every shade of thought and emotion, that any less enterprising translator would have despaired of ever rendering it down into comprehensible English. (Koch-Emmery 1953: 275)

It can be seen from the above quotations that both Thomas Mann and Koch-Emmery rule out the possibility of a foreignising translation that could reflect the same complexity of Mann's sentences. Koch-Emmery argues that no matter how competent a translator might be, the stylistic features of Thomas Mann's prose are inevitably lost in translation. To illustrate his argument, his analysis proceeds by contrasting a German sentence with Lowe-Porter's English translation:

In the following I shall place original and translation side by side, not merely to criticise but to arrive at some general criteria of translation from the German. The translator, just because he or she feels that purely literary translation is out of the question, concentrates on detail, *on word-translations but is inclined to overlook the main principle that underlies the sentence structure in the original.* (Koch-Emmery 1953: 276. My emphasis.)

Koch-Emmery's rather unusual coined noun *word-translations* presumably refers to semantic considerations in the form of 'equivalent' words and phrases, or, in other words, the precedence of content over form. The methodology of both Lowe-Porter and Luke is quite clearly word-by-word, phrase-by-phrase and sentence-by-sentence translation with the main stress on semantic accuracy rather than on rendering stylistic or formal features. In addition, Lowe-Porter has a tendency to simplify and break down Thomas Mann's complex syntax into shorter sentences as a deliberate strategy. Her justification for this approach was based on her belief that the stylistic differences were merely the differences between German and English rather than having anything to do with Thomas Mann's particular stylistic genius. It is, of course, also true that German syntax can hold many more subordinate clauses than can English syntax, but there is no reference to Thomas Mann's own specific 'play' with the syntactic features of German. To justify this approach, she wrote:

The German constructs more relative and subordinate clauses, with longer sentences, a different order. So the sentences, in order not to produce clumsy English, must be broken up - with result that nobody is quite satisfied [...]. Sometimes the actual order not only of the words but of the thoughts, the logical sequence, differs in the two languages. (Thirlwall 1966: 199-200)

Koch-Emmery's stylistic criticism is particularly interesting as he does not concentrate only on the connotative aspects, but instead, highlights the structural and syntactic stylistic features of whole sentences. Koch-Emmery claims that the typical structure of a Thomas Mann sentence has a triadic form, consisting of the following elements: *A* an introductory clause (protasis), *B* the principle statement and *C* explanation or elaboration (apodosis). Koch-Emmery uses terminology taken from sacred art, which reflects the 'awe' writers within the literary canon inspired and the veneration academics and literary critics often expressed at that time:

> I also like to refer to it [the structure] as the triptych because it bears a striking resemblance to the three panels of an altar-piece. (Koch-Emmery 1953: 277. My insertion.)

Koch-Emmery copiously illustrates his thesis with nine examples from various works of Thomas Mann. As this material is used to emphasise this same basic point, three examples taken from *Der Tod in Venedig* should suffice to illustrate his analysis:

Example I

> A. Weder auf der gepflasterten Ungererstraße, deren Schienengleise sich einsam gleißend gegen Schwabing erstreckten, noch auf der Föhringer Chaussee war ein Fuhrwerk zu sehen; *(protasis)*
>
> B. hinter den Zäunen der Steinmetzereien, wo zu Kauf stehende Kreuze, Gedächtnistafeln und Monumente ein zweites, unbehaustes Gräberfeld bilden, regte sich nichts, *(principal statement)*
>
> C. und das byzantische Bauwerk der Aussegnungshalle gegenüber lag schweigend im Abglanz des scheidenden Tages. *(apodosis)*

Lowe-Porter's translation is set out in a similar way for the sake of clarity although the structural divisions do not strictly apply to her translation, which, in fact, breaks down the tight unity of the original into three separate sentences:

> A. Not a wagon in sight, either on the paved Ungererstrasse, with its gleaming tramlines stretching off towards Schwabing, nor on the Föhring highway.
>
> B. Nothing stirred behind the hedge in the stone-mason's yard, where crosses, monuments, and commemorative tablets made a supernumerary and untenanted graveyard opposite the real one.
>
> C. The mortuary chapel, a structure in Byzantine style, stood facing it, silent in the gleam of the ebbing day. (Lowe-Porter 1978: 7)

Koch-Emmery expresses his disappointment because of the way Lowe-Porter destroys the (triadic) structure, the rhythm and the tension:

> A large number of Thomas Mann's periods seem to begin with a main clause, which, however, does not contain the principle statement, but only leads up to it. Again the translator feels compelled to cut the period into three independent sentences *and* to reverse the rhythm. (Koch-Emmery 1953: 280)

Lowe-Porter's three sentences have the opposite stylistic effect to the original. They also have a much faster pace and rhythm even though they are supposed to be creating an atmosphere of emptiness and desolation, anticipating the theme of death. The phrase "Not a wagon in sight" in contrast to the source text, "war ein Fuhrwerk zu sehen" has a brisk, cheerful rhythm. Similarly the clause, "Nothing stirred" almost has the effect of an event, even though in this case the lack of movement should be felt as absence. The last sentence does indeed have a poetic effect, but one of dignity, calm and beauty, but not of fading away with a hint of slow, departing death as in the source text. The whole passage, however, fails as a reproduction of Thomas Mann's style, as is validly argued by Koch-Emmery, because the tension and tightness of the structure held together by the syntactic tightness of Mann's prose are totally lost in the translation. In the source text, in part A, there is an almost unbearable tension caused by the long separation from the negative particles in the *weder . . . . noch* construction, which results in giving a 'ghostly' existence to the vehicle in the clause *war ein Fuhrwerk zu sehen* as if reflected in a non-existent negative universe.

In part B in the source text, the 'negative' discourse is continued, creating an increased sense of emptiness, lack of movement and atmosphere of death in the parallel main clause, *regte sich nichts*. In part C, the deathly associations of the stillness are made explicit (*apodosis*) with the reference to the "Aussegnungshalle".

Brilliance, beauty and art are subsidiary themes expressed in the following phrases: *einsam gleißend, das byzantinische Bauwerk* and *im Abglanz,* thus subtly intertwining the themes of art and death. The final effect in part C is one of fading away amidst the dazzling beauty of monumental art with the rhythm reflecting the sense perfectly. The 'hardness' of the potential masculine rhyme in *Abglanz* is set against the gentle rhythm of the parting day with the slow, feminine half-rhyme of *scheidenden* echoing *schweigend* in the same phrase, thus subtly hinting at the themes of slow parting, stillness and death:

[...] lag *schweigend* im Abglanz des *scheidenden* Tages. (My emphasis.)

The final phrase *scheidenden Tages* can scan as a typical hexameter ending (a dactyl followed by a trochee) or, in this case, rather an imperfect spondee (*Tages*) in the genitive ending *es* with the fricative, fading away slowly into the silence of death, and thus bearing the weight of a stressed syllable.

The same kind of criticism Koch-Emmery makes concerning Lowe-Porter's translation could equally apply to Luke's version, even though his translation is semantically more accurate:

> **Luke:** Not one vehicle passed along the Föhringer Chaussee or the paved Ungererstrasse, with its gleaming tramlines stretching off towards Schwabing, nor on the Föhring highway.
>
> Nothing stirred behind the fencing of the stone-masons' yards, where crosses and memorial tablets and monuments, ready for sale, composed a second and untenanted burial ground;
>
> across the street, the mortuary chapel with its Byzantine styling stood silent in the glow of the westering day. (Luke 1988: 195-196)

Luke correctly translates *Fuhrwerk* as "vehicle" and both translators do achieve some poetic effect with the final main clause. In this case, Lowe-Porter's translation "silent in the gleam of the ebbing day" would seem preferable to Luke's "silent in the glow of the westering day" because the idea of *ebbing* as in the sentence *He felt his life ebbing away* is more suggestive of the feeling of slow death than Luke's use of the obscure verb *westering*.

In the next example, Koch-Emmery makes no comment, but the implication is clear that rhythms and tightness of construction are missed in the translation. It concerns the sudden and frightening appearance of the figure in the graveyard who is reminiscent of the 'Grim Reaper':

Example II

A. Mäßig hochgewachsen, mager, bartlos und auffallend stumpfnäsig, *(protasis)*

B. gehörte der Mann zum rothaarigen Typus *(principle statement)*

C. und besaß dessen milchige und sommersprossige Haut. (Mann 1977: 339) *(apodosis)*

Lowe-Porter: He was of medium height, thin, beardless and strikingly snub-nosed; he belonged to the red-haired type and possessed its milky, freckled skin. (Lowe-Porter 1978: 8)

In Section A of the source text, the physical effect of the sinister figure is dramatically portrayed with the accumulation of adjectives contrasting with the humorous and ironic tone of the prosaic, rational explanatory sections, B and C: The 'Grim Reaper' has suddenly become a very ordinary human being. Without subjecting the Lowe-Porter translation to detailed, structured analysis, it is quite evident that the bathos is lost in the translation, which merely offers a neutral, factual description, thus losing all the sinister nuances and ironic effect of the source text. Again, the same loss of rhythmic and structural effect applies to the Luke version which has a cheerful, almost 'chirpy' rhythm. It is, in fact, remarkably close to the Lowe-Porter version:

> *Luke:* The man was moderately tall, thin, beardless and remarkably snub-nosed;
> he belonged to the red-haired type and had its milky, freckled complexion. (Luke 1988: 195)

The third example taken from the same paragraph in *Der Tod in Venedig* displays similar stylistic losses:

Example III

> A. Erhobenen Hauptes, so daß an seinem hager dem losen Sporthemd entwachsenden Halse der Adamsapfel stark und nackt hervortrat, (**protasis**)
>
> B. blickte er mit farblosen, rotbewimperten Augen, zwischen denen sonderbar genug zu seiner kurz aufgeworfenen Nase passend, zwei senkrechte energische Furchen standen, (**principle statement**)
>
> C. scharf spähend ins Weite. (Mann 1977: 339) (**apodosis**)

> *Lowe-Porter:* His chin was up, so that the Adam's apple looked very bald in the lean neck rising from the loose shirt: and he stood there, sharply peering into space out of colourless, redlashed eyes, while two pronounced perpendicular furrows showed on his forehead in curious contrast to his little turned-up nose. (Lowe-Porter 1978: 8-9.)

The majestic dignity of 'Death' expressed in the opening, archaically poetic phrase "Erhobenen Hauptes" has a ludicrous prosaic effect in the English version, "His chin was up", with its inevitable association with collocations such as *Chin up, old boy*! Part A of the original sentence expresses something of both the dignity and horror of death by increasing the tension with the tight and taut structure of part B so that Part C ends in a release of tension with the lordly figure of *Death* looking into the distance whilst, at the same time, the adverb *scharf* reminds us of *Death*'s cruel scythe. The feminine ending of the phrase "ins Weite" heightens the feeling of openness, hinting at infinite space. Many other stylistic points could be made, but Koch-Emmery gives a rather vague, but enthusiastic summary of the stylistic, syntactical features of this sentence:

> The skeleton of the sentence: *Erhobenen Hauptes blickte er scharf spähend ins Weite* is broken up by two long parentheses which give apparently two fortuitous but very characteristic traits; they make the reader feel that he himself watches the scene, that he himself is an onlooker, who has a very clear visual impression. In the translation the description comes after the main clause, it is no part of the first 'striking impression', but tagged on at the end. (Koch-Emmery 1953: 283)

Again, there is a similar stylistic loss in Luke's version:

His head was held high, so that the Adam's apple stood out stark and bare on his lean neck where it rose from the open shirt; and there were two pronounced vertical furrows, rather strangely ill-matched to his turned-up nose, between the colorless red-lashed eyes with which he peered sharply into the distance. (Luke 1988: 195-196)

Luke's version is free of the grosser infelicities to be found in Lowe-Porter's translation referred to above, but again, Thomas Mann's subtle stylistic features are also lost.

In summary, Koch-Emmery's basic argument throughout his article is that the translator or any translator "obsessed with the idea of finding an exact English equivalent for every German word" (Koch-Emmery 1953: 276) invariably misses the subtlety inherent in the structure of Thomas Mann's sentences, thereby losing their essential stylistic features. He argues that the translator (i.e. Lowe-Porter) breaks down one finely structured sentence of the source text into two or three sentences for the sake of simplicity to produce clear, idiomatic prose in the target language with the result that the meaning is conveyed, but stylistic effect is lost. This is a good example that illustrates how the academic approach is inadequate for doing justice to the stylistic features in Thomas Mann's highly poetic prose. Although Koch-Emmery does not explicitly state that the stylistic effect is more important than the semantic content, this is the clear import of the argument. However, Koch-Emmery resorts to the 'untranslatability' argument with regard to great literature, despairing with regard to the possibility of an equivalent stylistic effect being produced.

I would find it very hard to improve on Mrs. Lowe-Porter's translations, yet I am convinced that a careful analysis of the major discrepancies between her version and the German text will help, not only to show up Thomas Mann's *inimitable* artistry, but also to pave the way for a more faithful, a more congenial art of translation, which in the long run, will profit world literature as a whole. (Koch-Emmery 1953: 283-284. My emphasis.)

(c) Mandel's (1982) Stylistic Analysis of Lowe-Porter's Translations of Thomas Mann

Mandel (1982), like Koch-Emmery and Hayes, seems to have been impressed by the sheer quantity and commercial success of the Lowe-Porter oeuvre:

Her near-monopoly of translating Mann's books resulted in more triumphs than failures; no one has claimed perfection for her work but few denied her considerable achievements and integrity. (Mandel 1982: 33)

Mandel does not, however, give as thorough an analysis of Mann's stylistic features as does Koch-Emmery nor does he refer to the latter's article. On the other hand, Mandel does recognise that any fair and thorough treatment of Lowe-Porter's work would require "a book-length study" (Mandel 1982: 36):

Like Thirlwall's book (1966) Mandel's article is essentially an encomium to Lowe-Porter's oeuvre, but Mandel gives a brief analysis of some stylistic features in the opening paragraph of *Der kleine Herr Friedeman*. He compares the source text with three translations into English: those of Scheffauer, Lowe-Porter and Luke in their chronological order:

> *Thomas Mann:* Er war nicht schön, der kleine Johannes; und wie er so mit seiner hohen und spitzen Brust, seinem weit ausladenden Rücken und seinen viel zu langen, mageren Armen auf dem Schemel hockte und mit einem behenden Eifer seine Nüsse knackte, bot er einen seltsamen Anblick.
>
> *Scheffauer:* He was not a beautiful child, little Johannes: and as he sat there on his stool with his pointed pigeon-breast, his hunched-up back, and his all too long, skinny arms, and cracked nuts with a great zest, he offered a most remarkable spectacle.
>
> *Lowe-Porter:* He was not beautiful, little Johannes, as he crouched on his stool industriously *cracking his nuts*. In fact, he was a strange sight, with his pigeon breast, humped back, and disproportionately long arms. (My emphasis.)
>
> *Luke:* Little Johannes was no beauty, with his pigeon chest, his steeply humped back and his disproportionately skinny arms, and as he squatted there on his stool, *nimbly cracking his nuts*, he was certainly a strange sight. (Mandel 1982: 37. My emphasis.)

Like Koch-Emmery, Mandel notes that Lowe-Porter tends to break sentences down in the interests of readability but at the expense of subtle stylistic features whereas, in this case, the other two translators retain something of the structure and tension of the original:

> The long sentence quoted and the translations demonstrate quickly the many options open to translators. Mann's sentence of 46 words is carefully architectured with a leisurely flowing parallelistic series of descriptive phrases. Scheffauer's 45-word sentence is quite faithful to the original. Lowe-Porter compacts matters into 33 words and too easily digestible sentences. As a general principle, she said 'I have felt it sensible to break up the sentences and even to transpose them.' By doing so in this case, she resorts to an unauthorised connective, 'in fact'. Staying with a one-sentence translation, however, Scheffauer and Luke are able to preserve Mann's neatly-wrought frame or envelope which begins and ends with a statement about Johannes. (Mandel 1982: 37-38)

Mandel also spotted the grossly infelicitous translation of using the possessive in the phrase *cracking his nuts* together with Luke's tendency to follow the Lowe-Porter text too closely, even to the point of copying her mistakes:

> In an unguarded moment, Lowe-Porter produces an idiomatically awkward, if not funny, phrase about a boy 'cracking his nuts,' *which is blandly repeated by Luke.* All three translators would have been better advised to use the word 'walnuts,' which was Mann's point of reference in an earlier sentence. Other personal preferences or slips by the translators are discernible and debits and merits crop up impartially. (Mandel 1982: 38. My emphasis.)

Mandel also gives a very brief analysis of a sentence taken from the graveyard encounter already discussed in Section (b) of this chapter. He notes Lowe-Porter's poor rendering of the phrase *Fremdländischen und Weitherkommenden* in the sentence which follows on immediately from the one already quoted:

> **Thomas Mann:** Offenbar war er durchaus nicht bajuwarischen Schlages: wie denn wenigstens der breit und gerade gerandete Basthut, der ihm den Kopf bedeckte, seinem Aussehen ein Gepräge des Fremdländischen und Weitherkommenden verlieh.
>
> **Lowe-Porter:** He was obviously not Bavarian; and the broad, straight-brimmed straw hat he had on even made him look distinctly exotic. (Lowe-Porter 1978: 8-9)

Mandel rightly notes that Lowe-Porter's phrase which "even made him look distinctly *exotic*" does not evoke an alien, strange and frightening personage:

> Readers may remember that Aschenbach in *Der Tod in Venedig* sees someone whose straw hat gave him the appearance of a 'Fremdländischen und Weitherkommenden': Lowe-Porter in *Death in Venice* translates with compression, so that the straw hat 'even made him look distinctly exotic.' Kenneth Burke takes no short cuts and reproduces Mann's double description of the figure who has 'the stamp of a foreigner, of someone who had come from a long distance.' Lowe-Porter's word 'exotic', one may argue has interpretative aptness, but that is not what Mann wished to emphasise. (Mandel 1982: 38)

It would be difficult to argue that her choice of the adjective *exotic* could have any "interpretative aptness" with its contrary positive implications of colour, life and energy. Incredibly, Luke once again slavishly follows Lowe-Porter's translation with his choice of the adjective *exotic*:

> He was quite evidently not of Bavarian origin: at all events, he wore a straw hat with a broad straight rim which gave him an *exotic* air, as of some one who had come from distant parts. (Luke 1988: 195-196. My emphasis.)

In this context, a translation such as the adjective *alien* would be a rough equivalent and even though Luke's phrase "as of some one who had come from distant parts" is adequate for the surface meaning, a bolder translation such as *There was something alien about him as of a stranger who had emerged from some far-flung part of the planet* would emphasise the elements of foreignness and eeriness about the 'Death' figure. The combination of *alien* and *planet* would further underline the 'inhuman' connotations. Mandel also does not refer to the stylistic conceit in the phrase "der breit und gerade gerandete Basthut" which also ends like a classical hexameter with two clear-cut dactyls followed by a spondee. Mandel's conclusion is similar to that of Koch-Emmery in that he argues that, despite her stylistic deficiencies, Lowe-Porter's oeuvre represents a colossal literary achievement. He does concede that her translations are of inferior literary quality:

> By comparison, Lowe-Porter translations often have a harsher edge than those of most other translators mentioned in this essay and do not, for instance, come up to the level of literary finesse gained by Lindley. There is something to her self-characterisation as a sociological rather than a 'literary bird.' It helps to explain her preference for brevity when Mann's phrases seem redundant or literary flourishes, the radical surgery she performed in the 'Johannes' sentence is typical. That approach can have the effect of undercutting Mann's deliberate artistry, symbolic iteration, thematic allusions, and variable repetition. (Mandel 1982: 38)

As has already been seen in this Section, Mandel's analysis of stylistic features displayed in Lowe-Porter's work, however, lacks precise reference and tends to be rather vague with his notions such as "linguistic approximations", "dialect substitutions" and "historical styles different from Mann's", as in the quotation below:

> [...] for in her translating she has invented *her own linguistic approximations*, has made *dialect substitutions*, and has drawn on *historical styles* different from Mann's; at times, she aimed to '*translate etymologically* - the idea - in other words,' and to fit new words into the original contexts. (Mandel 1982: 39. My emphasis.)

Again, it is not quite clear, what he means by "etymological translation" other than non-literal translation or perhaps "word-translation" as used by Koch-Emmery in this chapter. Mandel's phrase, "fitting new words into original contexts" is likewise unclear.

Mandel quotes Lowe-Porter's observation that the reproduction of style is analogous to portraiture rather than photography:

> Lowe-Porter once said that the effect of reproducing the style of the original in general results in a portrait, not a photograph. If translation is portraiture, Lowe-Porter has indeed used a personal palette. (Mandel 1982: 39)

The metaphor of a portrait may be rather too complimentary in her case as good portraiture implies artistic licence to provide an enhanced effect with the result that a portrait can often tell us more than a photograph whereas her translation often completely misses or ignores stylistic features as has been indicated in this chapter, resulting in mere distortion of the original.

Mandel's final conclusion concerning Lowe-Porter's translation oeuvre is very generous again referring to the quantity rather than the quality of her work:

> And yet, each new translation of Thomas Mann's fiction will be measured against Lowe-Porter's prodigious labours and well defined aims (1982: 39).

(d) Seidlin's Detailed Stylistic Analysis of One Sentence in Thomas Mann's *Der Tod in Venedig*

After the examination of general stylistic features in the previous Sections, it is now appropriate to undertake a micro analysis of one paragraph chosen for analysis taken from the opening of the second chapter of *Der Tod in Venedig* (Mann 1977: 149). There are two main reasons for choosing this particular sentence. Firstly, the sentence does not seem to be too complex or obviously poetic, as is the case with many passages in Thomas Mann such as the opening passage of Chapter IV of *Der Tod in Venedig*, which will be discussed in Chapter VI Section (c). Nevertheless, the sentence under close scrutiny will show how incredibly subtle and complex great literary writing can be. The second reason for choosing this sentence is that Seidlin's analysis (1963) is an exemplary, if somewhat effusive study at the micro level, which reveals the complexity involved in defining the concept 'style'.

Seidlin's essay refers to the following sixteen-line opening sentence of this paragraph, which is set out as in Seidlin's analysis together with the rest of the paragraph:

> 1 Der Autor der klaren und mächtigen Prosa-Epopöe vom Leben
> 2 Friedrichs von Preußen; der geduldige Künstler, der in langem
> 3 Fleiß den figurenreichen, so vielerlei Menschenschicksal
> 4 im Schatten einer Idee versammelnden Romanteppich, *Maja*
> 5 mit Namen, wob; der Schöpfer jener starken Erzählung, die
> 6 'Ein Elender' überschrieben ist und einer ganzen dankbaren
> 7 Jugend die Möglichkeit sittlicher Entschlossenheit jenseits
> 8 der tiefsten Erkenntnis zeigte; der Verfasser endlich (und
> 9 damit sind die Werke seiner Reifezeit kurz bezeichnet) der
> 10 leidenschaftlichen Abhandlung über 'Geist und Kunst', deren
> 11 ordnende Kraft und antithetische Beredsamkeit ernste Beur-
> 12 teiler vermochte, sie unmittelbar neben Schillers Raisonne-
> 13 ment über naïve und sentimentalische Dichtung zu stellen:
> 14 Gustav Aschenbach also war zu L., einer Kreisstadt der

15 Provinz Schlesien, als Sohn eines höheren Justizbeamten

16 geboren. (Seidlin 1963: 149)

Seine Vorfahren waren Offiziere, Richter, Verwaltungsfunktionäre gewesen, Männer, die im Dienst des Königs, des Staates, ihr straffes, anständig karges Leben geführt hatten. Innere Geistigkeit hatte sich einmal, in der Person eines Predigers, unter ihnen verkörpert; rascheres, sinnlicheres Blut war der Familie in der vorigen Generation durch die Mutter des Dichters, Tochter eines böhmischen Kapellmeisters, zugekommen. Von ihr stammten die Merkmale fremder Rasse in seinem Äußern. Die Vermählung dienstlich nüchterner Gewissenhaftigkeit mit dunkleren, feurigeren Impulsen ließ einen Künstler und diesen besonderen Künstler erstehen. (Mann 1977: 14)

As with Koch-Emmery, Seidlin's analysis is particularly interesting because it also stresses the syntactic features of Mann's style, a grey area in translation theory as has already been shown in Section (a) of this chapter. Although the whole passage is presented in full in Appendix II, it is relevant at this point to quote the Lowe-Porter translation:

> Gustave Aschenbach was born at L-, a country town in the province of Silesia. He was the son of an upper official in the judicature, and his forbears had all been officers, judges, departmental functionaries - men who lived their strict, decent sparing lives in the service of King and State. Only once before had a livelier mentality - in the quality of a clergyman - turned up among them; but, swifter, more perceptive blood had in the generation before the poet's flowed into the stock from the mother's side, she being the daughter of a Bohemian musical conductor. It was from her he had the foreign traits that betrayed themselves in his appearance. The union of dry, conscientious officialdom and ardent, obscure impulse, produced an artist - and this particular artist: author of the lucid and vigorous prose epic on the life of Frederick the Great; careful, timeless weaver of the richly patterned tapestry entitled *Maia,* a novel that gathers up the threads of many human destinies in the warp of a single idea; creator of that powerful narrative *The Abject,* which taught a whole grateful generation that a man can still be capable of moral resolution even after he has plumbed the depths of knowledge; and lastly - to complete the tale of works of his mature period - the writer of that impassioned discourse on the theme of Mind and Art whose ordered force and antithetic eloquence lead serious critics to rank it with Schiller's *Simple and Sentimental Poetry. (*1978: 17)

The first and most obvious syntactic aspect of Lowe-Porter's translation is that she breaks up the one sixteen-line sentence into three separate sentences. The second point to be made is that this is one of the rare occasions that Lowe-Porter alters the sentence order. The main clause of the original is changed into a complete sentence and is placed at the beginning of the extract as opposed to being at the end. Other sentences within the same paragraph are incorporated within the structure of what was one original sentence. The third feature which is, perhaps, a consequence of the first two alterations, is the great simplification of the original syntax together with an addition of finite verbs and explanatory phrases. These alterations were, no doubt, introduced for reasons of readability and clarity, and indeed, the Lowe-Porter version is easy to assimilate. These changes may seem innocuous. They could even be excused in the case of a free, communicative translation, but as has been shown in the previous chapter, the alterations lose the rhythm, tension and stylistic effect of the original. To illustrate this, it is relevant to quote Seidlin, who refers to a translation which can easily be identified as the Lowe-Porter version:

> Wer die Symbolik dieses Satzbaus nicht versteht, wer das gewaltige Gefüge etwa umstellen, mit dem Geburtsdatum beginnen und mit der Aufzählung der Werke fortfahren wollte (*wie es leider die amerikanische Übersetzerin von* Tod in Venedig *tat*), hat kein Gefühl für die Einmaligkeit und Unantastbarkeit eines großen Stils. (Seidlin 1963: 150. My emphasis.)

The reference to Lowe-Porter as having "kein Gefühl für die Einmaligkeit und Unantastbarkeit eines großen Stils" may seem rather harsh, but it, in fact, only confirms Koch-Emmery's criticisms, even though the latter may have expressed them less forcefully. Lowe-Porter was aware of Seidlin's criticism and even referred to it obliquely:

> I recall receiving a scolding from *a German refugee scholar*[25] for transposing the order of two paragraphs, because it seemed to me the transition would thus be less uneasy for an English reader. (Thirlwall 1966: 200. My emphasis.)

Like Koch-Emmery who also finds architectural imagery to be an appropriate analogy to convey the structural features of Thomas Mann's sentences, Seidlin justifiably refers to the structure of this particular sentence as *Architektur* and forcefully rejects any hint of chance in the construction of this elaborate sentence:

> Das ist Architektur, Architektur eines Satzes, der nicht hingeschrieben, sondern hingebaut ist, nicht in zufälliger Fügung, sondern in planmäßiger Gefugtheit. (Seidlin 1963: 148)

Continuing his architectural analogy, Seidlin divides the sentence into a key-stone (*Schlußstein*) which appears at the end (lines 14-16) and five blocks which are dependent on the key-stone. (This analysis resembles that of Koch-Emmery referred to in with the idea of *the principle statement* with dependent clauses (*protasis*) and (*apodosis*)). In Seidlin's description of this sentence, he maintains that there is a deep

---

[25] The dismissive tone of this remark is further emphasised by the outrageous reference to the refugee status of Oskar Seidlin at that time. There is no doubt that Lowe-Porter could be helpful to refugees; Thomas Mann himself had been a 'German refugee writer'. Her tone implies that the criticism was based on trivial grounds, i.e. simply getting the sentence order wrong rather than, as is clear from the ensuing analysis, being a case of a profound deafness to the musical and literary qualities of Mann's style.

thematic purpose in this structure to the effect that the artist who produces great works of art pays for the price of this achievement by suffering a corresponding impoverishment as a human being. Seidlin gives a line-by-line structural analysis, but the basic structural point is conveyed by the cumulative effect of the five 'blocks' which build up (the great works of art) only to be contrasted with a deliberately bathetic anti-climax: the man himself, Aschenbach, a dwarf of a human being (i.e. the centre of the bathos); a man overshadowed by and exhausted by his immense achievements, which gradually pile up to become a colossal edifice almost crushing the puny individual who appears in the last section of the sentence. It is for such reasons that Seidlin describes the style as "genial":

> Der Schlußstein, auf den der ganze Satz hinausläuft, ist kurz: zwei Zeilen nur - und dem gegenüber steht eine Stauung von dreizehn Zeilen. Die Balance, so könnte man sagen, ist schlecht. Aber sie wird sofort für uns Sinn und tiefe Berechtigung bekommen, wenn wir in Erwägung ziehen, *was* hier balanciert wird. Dreizehn Zeilen sind ausgefüllt mit der Aufzählung und Charakterisierung von Gustav Aschenbachs Werken, dann folgen zwei Zeilen über den Menschen Gustav Aschenbach. *Und diese Verteilung scheint mir eine der genialen stilistischen Symbolgebungen, die wir in der modernen deutschen Literatur finden.* (Seidlin 1963: 149. My emphasis.)

A great stylist uses structure for a purpose and Thomas Mann's sentences are nearly all deliberately and elaborately structured. The sentence under examination is a wonderful example of this effect as Seidlin well illustrates:

> So wie er da steht, erzählt uns dieser Satz durch seinen Bau allein die Lebensgeschichte und das Lebensleid Gustav Aschenbachs: erst das Werk, dann noch einmal das Werk, dann noch einmal das Werk, dann noch einmal das Werk - und dann erst, ganz im Hintergrunde, die Person dessen, der es schuf: das ist die heroische Leistung, die pathetische Größe des Dichters Gustav Aschenbach. (Seidlin 1963: 150)

It is no wonder that after this introductory analysis Seidlin was incensed by the Lowe-Porter translation which simply ignores this brilliant structure by placing the key-stone of the sentence at the beginning of the paragraph, thus nullifying at one stroke the whole purpose of the intended effect by giving more importance to Aschenbach than to his works.

The Lowe-Porter version also fails to reproduce the clear progression displayed in Aschenbach's development from the *Autor* of a historical novel to *Künstler,* then to *Schöpfer* and finally to a *Verfasser* of philosophical and spiritual works. According to Seidlin (1963: 150), Aschenbach's career had four distinct phases: the first as an historical novelist is the lowest because the content and volume predominate over form (*Autor*); the second level is the artist and craftsman who weaves a great carpet of themes in an all-embracing novel with the main achievement being the production of form (*Künstler*); the third phase could be described as the ethical phase in which Aschenbach tried to diagnose the spiritual problems of his time in an original fashion (*Schöpfer*), followed by the final and philosophical phase (*Verfasser*) when he synthesises his works in philosophical treatises which have the depth of the ethical phase combined with the brilliance of his artistic phase so that his final works are not referred to as a grim Germanic *Abhandlung* but a lighter more sparkling French *raisonnement* consisting of dialectical discussion worthy of Schiller himself. Seidlin summarises these stages:

> Es sind die Elemente des schöpferischen Werkes, die hier umschrieben werden, es ist gleichzeitig die Bezeichnung von Aschenbbachs literarischer Entwicklung, die in vier Stufen verläuft: Stoff - Gestaltung - Ethos - Philosophie. Eine Pyramide nannten wir es; es ist der allmähliche Aufstieg von der reinen Materie zum reinen Geist, ein Prozeß progressiver Spiritualisierung. (Seidlin 1963: 153)

After analysing the thematic structure of this sentence, Seidlin then shows how Mann's fastidious choice of vocabulary reflects the subtle modulations of the main ideas together with their nuances. The analysis is enthusiastic and in the midst of full flow, Seidlin offers a very neat and apt definition of style within this context:

> Die völlige Übereinstimmung von Sinn und Ausdruck, jenes völlige Zusammenfallen von Sprachgebung und Bedeuten (*und das ist ja Stil)* macht die unvergleichliche Größe und den einmaligen Zauber des Thomas Mannschen Werkes aus. (Seidlin 1963: 153. My emphasis.)

Each apparent stylistic idiosyncrasy in Thomas Mann's work usually has a clear purpose. At the artist/craftsman stage in lines 2-4, where Aschenbach wove his carpet (*Romanteppich*) consisting of many individual fates and destinies into a philosophically unified whole, Thomas Mann uses the expression *vielerlei Menschenschicksal*. This, at first sight, would seem to be ungrammatical (a plural qualifier with a singular noun), but its purpose is to express unity in diversity:

> der geduldige Künstler, der in langem Fleiß den figurenreichen, so vielerlei Menschenschicksal im Schatten einer Idee versammelnden Romanteppich, *Maja* mit Namen, wob. (3-5)

These kinds of 'idiosyncrasies' contribute to the notion of a 'great literary style'. Seidlin may be criticised for being rather over-enthusiastic when he places this stylistic device on the same level of the theoretically impossible, mathematical process of squaring the circle:

> Die Mathematik behauptet, es sei unmöglich, die Quadratur des Kreises zu finden. Nun, Thomas Mann hat hier das Unmögliche getan. Er hat die Gleichzeitigkeit von Singularität und Pluralität durch eine grammatikalische Wendung geschaffen. (Seidlin 1963: 154)

Nevertheless, his enthusiasm is well-placed. It is only at this most detailed micro level of literary criticism that the subtlety of Thomas Mann style really becomes evident. The literary translator working within the framework of naive semantic equivalence[26] needs not only to read the secondary literature highlighting stylistic features, but also needs to constantly subject the source text to a thorough and sensitive analysis.

Unfortunately, with the Lowe-Porter translation, there seems to be no evidence whatever of understanding the stylistic features of Thomas Mann's prose whereas Luke's translation shows that, at least, there is some superficial consideration of this area, but nothing like the depth displayed in Seidlin's study. This will become clear in the detailed analysis of the translations themselves.

Every phrase, every collocation in Thomas Mann's choice of language is significant. In the same clause, Seidlin goes on to show how the ominous phrase *im Schatten einer Idee* has Dionysian associations which can be further linked with the *Shiva* aspect of the Maya theme. The syntactic features of this clause are, however, even more subtle:

> [...] den figurenreichen, so vielerlei Menschenschicksal im Schatten einer Idee versammelnden Romanteppich.

The tightness of this participial phrase is very difficult to reflect in English, but its very taut density "gestraffte Dichtheit" reflects the artistry of the "carpet weaver":

> Wie leicht wäre es gewesen - und unserem Sprachgefühl sogar entsprechender - das mit Objekten angeschwellte Präsenzpartizip in einen Relativsatz aufzulösen. Aber es durfte nicht geschehen, weil dadurch die syntaktische Einheit der Gruppe gelöst worden wäre. Wie mit einer harten, festen Klammer sind hier Vielheiten zur Einheit gepreßt: gestraffte Dichtigkeit ist das Ziel, so wie es das Ziel des Teppichwebers ist. Und gehen wir zu weit, wenn wir auch noch in der Verbform des Satzes dieses Streben nach gedrängter Dichtheit erkennen wollen? (Seidlin 1963: 155)

---

[26] This does not exclude 'functional equivalence' as defined by Osers: "But let us look more closely at the principle of functional equivalence and see to what extent it may be seen as a translation norm. It states that a translation should have the same impact, or effect, on the TL reader as the original had on the reader of the SL original. I would claim that, in this rather general form, the principal of functional equivalence is nowadays accepted by every reputable literary translator." (Osers 1995: 57-58) See also Nida's discussion of 'dynamic equivalence' in (Nida 2000: 129) and part (c) of Chapter VI.
  The complexity of Thomas Mann's style, however, would need a radical redefinition of this term to the effect that a new level theory would be reached at which point it is questionable whether it is a useful term or not. The present discussion is an attempt to come to terms with the complexity of literary style without being distracted by too many definitions.

Even the syntactic choice of the strong form of *weben* in the same clause is significant according to Seidlin: *wob* in its powerful, strong or masculine form has a mono-syllabic simplicity which acts as a simple and powerful unifying force bringing the strands of the carpet together in contrast to the 'weak' form *webte* where this effect would be lost:

> Es scheint uns mehr als ein belangloser Zufall, daß Thomas Mann die starke Verbform *wob* der schwachen *webte*, die ebenso korrekt und vielleicht sogar geläufiger wäre, vorzieht. Ist doch *wob*, das einsilbige, volltönende Verb, viel gesammelter und versammelnder als das zweisilbige, tonmäßig abfallende *webte* (nicht umsonst nennen wir die eine Form stark, die andere schwach), ist es doch weitaus geeigneter, die Einheit zu suggerieren, die als Leitgedanke über dem hier diskutierten Satzteil steht. (Seidlin 1963: 155)

Seidlin then goes on to list other important words in the sentences with their associations, connotations and sonic qualities. His detailed analysis is very condensed and always enthusiastic and interesting, but for the sake of brevity, these important stylistic aspects in the Thomas Mann sentence can be listed in note form to highlight their main associations:

1. *Epopöe* (line 1): two aspects:

a) Phonological:

> Sicher hat das Klangliche eine Rolle gespielt: das Wort 'Epos' (mit dem Akzent auf der überkurzen ersten Silbe, die nur aus einem Vokal besteht) suggeriert wenig von 'klarer Mächtigkeit,' die uns als das Charakteristische der geschichtlichen Chronik vermittelt werden soll. Dafür erscheint die Langform *Epopöe* schon viel geeigneter. Und noch einen anderen klanglichen Wert gibt das Wort *Epopöe*. Mit dem schweren Akzent auf dem Vokal der letzten Silbe, dem das labial-explosive p vorausgeht und den kein Konsonant abschließt (der im Gegenteil durch das End-e in Länge gezogen wird), mit all diesen Lautqualitäten tönt das Wort wie ein Trompetenstoß. Was im Worte 'Epos' wie eine Schamade erklingen würde, das klingt im Worte *Epopöe* wie eine martialische Fanfare. (Seidlin 1963: 157)

Seidlin may again be criticised for exaggeration as in his use of the phrase *wie eine martialische Fanfare* to express the effect of an open vowel, but his basic argument is not only valid but also highly perceptive.

b) Semantic: such an obscure literary genre has more than a hint of affectation and extreme artistic fastidiousness in keeping with Aschenbach's character both as a man and as an artist.

2. The unusual reference, *Friedrich von Preußen* (line 2) (as opposed to *Friedrich der Große* or *Friedrich II*) provides a link with Silesia together with its associations of Prussian discipline and frugality. There is also the sonic effect of the harsh hissing *s*

sound in Preußen emphasised by the preceding vowel, which according to Seidlin is lost in the relatively sonorous phrase *Friedrich der Große*.

3. *Raisonnement* (line 12): French clarity, logic, precision, wit and elegance.

The syntactic, structural and semantic features represent only a few aspects of the style. Seidlin maintains that the rhythmic or musical aspects are even more important:

> Wir haben bisher von den architektonischen und den symbolischen Elementen des großen Satzes gesprochen. Wir würden das Wichtigste übergehen, wollten wir seine musikalische Meisterschaft unerhört lassen. (Seidlin 1963: 158)

He shows that the sentence starts off with a slow, gentle legato rhythm, which increases speed in the individual clauses to reach a cumulative effect in the penultimate section where the return to legato in the final clause confirms the bathetic effect already displayed by the structural features of the sentence. This basic rhythm is further defined by musical movements: *andante, allegretto, allegro, allegro con brio* and *andante maestuoso*. The clause units can be basically divided into dactyls and iambs. The iambs generally slow down the pace whereas dactyls have the reverse effect with the result that the overall proportion of iambs to dactyls represents the pace of a section. Seidlin calculates the proportion of dactyls to iambs in each section of the sentence and expresses this as a percentage for each clause. For the sake of brevity, it will suffice to summarise Seidlin's results in bar graph form with each bar of the graph representing one of the five clauses:

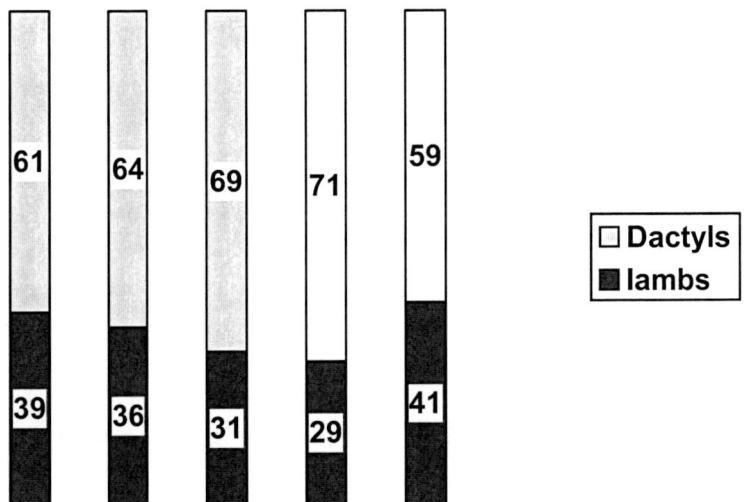

The rhythmic structure reflects the thematic elements: a slow ponderous start reflecting the seriousness and heaviness of his early work, but as the list progresses the pace increases as the great works accumulate until the breathless crescendo in the fourth clause where they reach their final climax in the profound synthesising philosophical work, and suddenly in the fifth and final clause, as Seidlin so well illustrates, the pace reverts to its former rhythm providing us with the appropriate anti-climax: the man himself, Aschenbach, a dwarf in comparison with his works.

In conjunction with the metrical rhythms, the general tonal structure of the sentences and the rich semantic constructions of the unusual selection of words, there are also many associations produced by assonance and alliteration. The choice of certain phonemes particularly with regard to the interaction of vowel and consonants in conjunction with the above-discussed rhythmic features adds yet another dimension to the musical aspects of Thomas Mann's poetic prose. As this is a general stylistic feature of Thomas Mann, one example from Seidlin should suffice for illustrative purposes:

> Nehmen wir die ersten Worte der beiden Satzteile, so wird uns die lautmäßige Ähnlichkeit entgehen können. Es sind dunkle Laute, die uns hier wie dort als Akzentträger begegnen: *au, a, o, u, e*in ganz vereinzeltes *ä* und überhaupt kein einziger Laut des oberen Registers, kein *I, ü, e* oder *eu*. Aufklang und Abklang ruhen lautlich auf Vokalen, die eine feierliche und ruhig gesetzte Färbung haben, die Satzsymphonie beginnt und endet majestätisch und schwer - *molto grave* würde die Musiksprache es nennen. (Seidlin 1963: 160)

As with music criticism, it is difficult to prove many critical aspects in a scientific way. Seidlin does try to prove on a probability basis that the metrical patterns in this sentence cannot be a matter of mere chance. Indeed, it would be difficult to prove the contrary. Nevertheless, Seidlin's final court of appeal is simply to read the sentence with sensitivity, "sinngemäßes Lesen", a not unreasonable strategy since poetry, like music, needs in the final analysis to be listened to:

> Wir brauchen uns diesen Aufklang und Abklang nur laut vorlesen, um ihre Parallelität, ihre Gemessenheit und ernste Ruhe, aus dem Klang zu erfühlen: *der Autor der klaren und mächtigen Prosa* und *Gustav Aschenbach also wurde zu L., geboren*. Volltönend beginnt der große Satz, volltönend endet er - ein kurzes Stück deutscher Prosa, aber in seiner stilistischen Vollendung ein Stück Architektur auch, ein Stück musikalischer Komposition. (Seidlin 1963: 160)

Seidlin shows that only a thoroughgoing analysis can penetrate those hidden depths of what is rather loosely termed as 'stylistic features.' The conclusion of Seidlin's excellent, though somewhat effusive analysis, also deserves to be quoted in full:

> Wie wir es in *Joseph der Ernährer* finden, es stehe hier, weil in ihm das Entscheidende gesagt
> scheint, was sich über Stil - sei es nun Lebensstil oder Kunststil - sagen läßt: Die liebste und
> lieblichste Form aber war ihm Anspielung; und wenn es anspielungsreich zuging in seinem
> aufmerksam überwachten Leben und die Umstände sich durchsichtig erwiesen für höhere
> Stimmigkeit, so war er schon glücklich, da durchsichtige Umstände ja nie ganz düster sein
> können. (Seidlin 1963: 160-161)

Even after Seidlin's seemingly exhaustive study of twelve pages devoted to one sentence, there are still several features which have not been covered in his analysis. The whole sentence is pervaded with a deep irony, which, for example, breaks out with the insertion of *also* in line 14, as if mention of the author were almost an afterthought:

14 Gustav Aschenbach *also* war zu L., einer Kreisstadt der

15 Provinz Schlesien, als Sohn eines höheren Justizbeamten

16 geboren. (Seidlin 1963: 149)

There are also other elements of what could be called deliberate 'overwriting' highlighting the aestheticism as well as the exaggerated fastidiousness of Gustav Aschenbach. The stylistic features quoted by Seidlin illustrate this point and in conjunction with a slow, uninterrupted reading of the whole sentence, the poetic and literary density shows signs of deliberate overloading to reflect the exaggerated self-consciousness and aestheticism of the artist as a form of irony. This feature of Mann's style will be analysed in detail in Chapter VI with regard to the opening passage of Chapter IV in *Der Tod in Venedig*. The main point from a translation-theoretic perspective is precisely to show that characteristic features of great style seem almost to tend towards infinity. It is not surprising that this topic has been generally neglected in translation theory as style is difficult enough to define in monolingual studies. Seidlin's study is a bold and generally effective attempt to demonstrate both the range and depth of a great stylist.

(e) Lowe-Porter's and Luke's Versions of the Sentence Analysed by Seidlin

Only a translator with the stylistic gifts of Thomas Mann himself could encode most of the features described by Seidlin. Nevertheless, even an echo of some of these aspects would be a great improvement on the present translations. In the case of Lowe-Porter virtually all the subtle stylistic features are not only lost, but there is also serious distortion of the essential nature of this passage. This can now be established by detailed analysis of her work which will be carried out in note form for the sake of brevity.

Version I: (Lowe-Porter 1978: 12-13)

Gustave[1] Aschenbach was born at L -, *a country town*[2] in the province of Silesia[3]. He was the son of an upper official in the judicature, and his forebears had all been *officers* [4], judges, *departmental functionaries*[5] - men who had lived their strict, decent, sparing lives in the service of king and state. Only once before had *a livelier mentality*[6]- *in the quality of a clergyman*[7] - turned up among them; but swifter, *more perceptive blood*[8] had in the generation before the poet's flowed into the stock from the mother's side, she being the daughter of a Bohemian musical conductor. It was from her he had the foreign traits that betrayed themselves in his appearance. The union of dry, conscientious *officialdom*[9] and *ardent, obscure impulse*[10], produced an artist - and this particular artist: author of the lucid and *vigorous*[11] prose epic on the life of *Frederick the Great*[12]; careful, tireless weaver of the richly patterned tapestry entitled *Maia,*a novel that gathers up the threads of many human destinies in the *warp of a single idea*[13]; creator of that powerful narrative *The Abject* [14], which taught *a whole generation*[15] that a man can still be capable of moral resolution even after he has plumbed the depths of *knowledge*[16]; and lastly - *to complete the tale of works*[17] of his mature period - the writer of that impassioned discourse on the theme of *Mind and Art*[18] whose *ordered force*[19] and *antithetic eloquence*[20] led serious critics to rank it with Schiller's *Simple and Sentimental Poetry.*[21]

1) The Christian name *Gustav* is preferable to *Gustave*. In the English-speaking world reference is always made to Gustav Mahler and all the other versions use the German version.

2) The phrase *a country town* is not equivalent to *Kreisstadt* as the former refers more to 'a town in the country' than to the main town in a particular district. A phrase such as *a small provincial city* or Koelb's (1994) formulation *a district capital in the province of Silesia* could be regarded as roughly equivalent.

3) [This footnote refers to the whole sentence.] As already analysed in Section (d) of this chapter, to begin with this sentence destroys the whole point and effect of the original. The demolition process of the main structural purpose of the sentence is continued by introducing other elements of Aschenbach's life taken from later sentences in the same paragraph, thus nullifying the clearly intended effect.

4) In addition in the above sentence, the noun *officers* is too general because this would refer primarily to civil servants and even policemen in English. Luke's translation *military officers* is preferable.

5) The collocation *departmental functionaries* implies a much lower status for Aschenbach's forebears than is the case by referring to officials working within a department rather than *Verwaltungsfunktionäre* who would be full 'government officials' or 'civil servants'. Koelb (1994) chooses the general term *government*

functionaries whereas Chase (1999) goes one step further in generality with his translation *bureaucratic functionaries*; both translations would seem to be adequate.

6) The phrase *livelier mentality* is a totally wrong translation for *innere Geistigkeit* - a phrase such as *a more inward spirituality* or even *deeper spiritual elements* would convey the meaning and reflect the appropriate connotations. The error is a grave one because the notion of 'inward-looking spirituality' in the source text hints at an intellectual, and thus artistic element entering the family with the emphasis on depth and introspection, ultimately leading to neurosis and decadence. The phrase *livelier mentality*, however, would be a more appropriate characteristic for the 'Bürger' implying a positive, humorous, healthy and cheerful outlook on life. Thus, a basic thematic element has been completely reversed.

7) Lowe-Porter's phrase *in the quality of a clergyman* is an infelicitous expression - phrases such as *in the form of* or *in the person of* are both preferable versions. Luke's version "A more inward spirituality had shown itself in one of them who had been a preacher" is more acceptable.

8) The phrase *more perceptive blood* for "sinnlicheres Blut" is not only a complete mistranslation but is also another confusion of themes at their most elementary level. The 'fiery mother' figure represents the wild, exotic, sensual, passionate artistic elements in Aschenbach's character (as with Tonio Kröger), and thus, the Dionysian passions Aschenbach tries to control by his strictly disciplined life, but which burst out in the end to destroy him. This mistake is an example of a fundamental misreading of the basic themes in the novella at their most elementary and uncontroversial level. The phrase *a more sensual blood* as in Version IV further on in this chapter is adequate.

9) The translation of the noun *Gewissenhaftigkeit* as "officialdom" fails to refer to the human quality of *conscientiousness* (as is correctly translated in the Luke version) and the notion of *officialdom* is closer to the abstract and negative concept of 'bureaucracy', inappropriate in the context of the severe, strict devotion to duty typical of the *Bürger* in Mann's works.

10) The phrase *ardent obscure impulse* fails to capture the Dionysian connotations of "darker, more fiery impulses" (Luke) or even, "darker, more fiery urges" (Version IV).

11) The translation of the adjective *mächtig* as "vigorous" is profoundly misleading. All the other translators interpret *mächtig* to indicate the scope of the work. The

adjective *vigorous* would have the opposite connotations because it is clear from the Appendix III extracts that Aschenbach's prose is described in terms of a classical fastidiousness, even with a hint of anaemic aestheticism i.e. anything but 'vigorous', a quality which clearly belongs to the *Bürger* camp rather than to what is in this case a very rarified artistic camp.

12) The translation of the title *Friedrich von Preußen* as *Frederick the Great* is possible in a communicative translation, but misses some sonic effects, as has already been pointed out by Seidlin in Section (d). There are both sonic and semantic reasons for choosing the title *Friedrich von Preußen* as opposed to *Friedrich, der Große* so that the translation *Frederick of Prussia* would adequately cover both the phonological and connotative aspects of this phrase.

13) The phrase *warp of a single idea* for *im Schatten einer Idee*. At first sight, this seems to be a good solution continuing the imagery of weaving. However, it fails to express the dark Dionysian connotations of the 'shadow' looming over human existence.

14) The book title *The Abject* for *Der Elende* is virtually meaningless. The word *abject* usually works only as a qualifier as in the collocation *abject misery*. On its own, it tends to be meaningless, as in the sentence: *He is abject.** As *der Elende* is personified, it should refer to a particular individual as in Version III *The Vile Wretch*, or should have a vividly clear meaning such as the title *Human Scum* in Version IV. (It is, however, true that the adjective *abject* is used as an adjectival noun by contemporary literary critics such as Julia Kristeva in reference to the horror film genre, but for the general reader, the above point would still apply.)

15) In the phrase *a whole generation* for "einer ganzen dankbaren Jugend", the adjective *dankbar* is ignored without reason, thus losing the connection concerning the salutary effect his work had on a whole generation.

16) The translation of *Erkenntnis* as "knowledge" is appropriate in some contexts, but the term *knowledge* in English has too many scientific or prosaically factual associations as in the German concept of *Wissenschaft*. This is not a case of factual knowledge, but rather of insight or of an awareness penetrating the very depths of existence.

17) The phrase, *To complete the tale of works*, as a translation of "und damit sind die Werke seiner Reifezeit kurz bezeichnet" is an inappropriate collocation - *a tale of woe* is possible, but not "the tale of works."

18) The German noun *Geist* can be a cause of difficulty for the translator, but the translated title *Mind and Art* for *Geist und Kunst* has more psychological connotations whereas the *raisonnement* in question is clearly literary and philosophical so that the translation *Intellect and Art* is far more appropriate here.

19) The phrase *ordered force* for "ordnende Kraft" is inappropriate; in translating the present participle as a past participle, the Apollonian dynamic power of the original collocation is lost.

20) The phrase *antithetic eloquence* is a virtually meaningless. Luke's phrase *antithetical eloquence* makes a little more sense, but Version III, its *eloquent use of antithesis* makes the meaning clear and would seem to be more felicitous. Chase's phrase *dialectic eloquence* is felicitous, but has too many Germanic associations for what Seidlin has cogently argued is supposed to refer to a brilliantly transparent *raisonnement* in a classical French essayist style.

21) The title *Simple and Sentimental Poetry* is a lamentable translation for Schiller's treatise *Über naïve und sentimentale Dichtung*. This commits not only the gross error of being bewitched by 'false friends' but also betrays a complete ignorance of the German philosophical and literary traditions. The connotations in English are ludicrous because 'simple and sentimental' verse could refer to popular verse as in 'greeting card' poetry. The adjective *naiv* can, however, be translated as *naïve* as is the case in collocations such as the *naïve school of painters* referring to Henri Rousseau, for example, with similar import to the *naïve Dichtung* in Schiller's treatise. The German adjective *sentimental* in this context has, of course, little to do with the English 'false friend' *sentimental* in the context of nostalgia or superficial emotion, but it still presents a translation difficulty. Luke's version *reflective* shows an understanding of the German term *sentimental* and no doubt, echoes Wordsworth's idea of verse 'recollected in tranquillity'.

Whilst keeping within the conventions of *academic translation*, Lowe-Porter often tends in the direction of a communicative translation, particularly with the re-arrangement of the sentences and structure. If she had undertaken a free communicative translation, some of the mistakes would have been forgivable, but as this is still a conventional translation, the whole effect of the sentence structure is lost. Worse than this is the confusion of themes, as referred to in the notes and as discussed in detail in Chapter III. This shows a failure to understand Mann's work at a most elementary and obvious level. A reader would miss the basic thematic structure of

Mann's work in the Lowe-Porter version. The certain liveliness and occasional readability of her prose style are, however, sufficient to dupe the unsuspecting reader into having faith in the translator. This could be one of the factors which explain the longevity of the high esteem that Lowe-Porter's translations have enjoyed.

Version II: (Luke 1988: 200)

Luke's version also lies within the conventions of the *academic approach*, but is a closer, more semantic translation than Lowe-Porter's:

> The author of the lucid and massive *prose-epic*[1] on the life of Frederic of Prussia; the patient artist who *with long toil*[2] had woven the great tapestry of the novel called *Maya,* so *rich in characters*[3], gathering so many human destinies together under the shadow of one idea; the creator of that powerful tale entitled *A Study in Abjection*[4], which earned the gratitude of a whole younger generation by pointing to the possibility of moral resolution even for those who have plumbed the depths of *knowledge*[5]; the author *(lastly but not least*[6] in this summary enumeration of his maturer works) of that passionate treatise *Intellect and Art* which in its ordering energy and antithetical eloquence has led serious critics to place it immediately alongside Schiller's disquisition *On Naive and Reflective Literature:* in a word, Gustav Aschenbach, was born in L . . ., an important city in the province of Silesia, as the son of a highly-placed legal official. His ancestors had been military officers, judges, government administrators; men who had spent their disciplined, decently austere life in the service of the king and the state. A more inward spirituality had shown itself in one of them who had been a preacher; a strain of livelier, *more sensuous blood*[7] had entered the family in the previous generation with the writer's mother, the daughter of a director of music from Bohemia. Certain exotic racial characteristics in his external appearance had come to him from her. It was from this marriage between hard-working, sober conscientiousness and darker, more fiery impulses that an artist, and indeed this particular kind of artist, had come into being.

1) The compound noun *prose-epic* misses the connotations (already discussed) of *epopee* in Version IV.

2) The phrase *long toil* for *in langem Fleiß* is an infelicitous formulation in English. *Toil* is rarely, if ever qualified by 'long' or 'short' but, the intensity of the toil is usually subject to qualification, as in 'hard toil' or 'bitter toil.' The phrases *enduring diligence* in Version VI or *long application* in V (as in Appendix II) are adequate, though not ideal translations.

3) The phrase *rich in characters* for *so vielerlei Menschenschicksal* misses the point of Mann's deliberate use of the singular noun after a plural qualifier as has already been discussed in the Seidlin analysis. The singular form could have been used *so rich in character* for a closer, if not equivalent effect.

4) Although the translation of the title *A Study in Abjection* for *der Elende* is an improvement on Lowe-Porter's phrase *The Abject*, the same criticism applies in that *abject* or *abjection* needs immediate context to have any meaning. Versions III and IV express more the tone of moral opprobrium and outrage, which is the main point here, with the respective translations *The Vile Wretch* or even, *Human Scum*.

5) The noun *knowledge* for *Erkenntnis*: see note 16 on Lowe-Porter (above).

6) The phrase *lastly but not least* for *damit sind [...] bezeichnet* is a very unliterary cliché which Mann would, no doubt, have eschewed.

7) The phrase *more sensual blood* would be preferable as in the Chase (1999) translation (Appendix II, Version VI) to the phrase *a more sensuous blood*. The adjective *sensuous* usually has a conscious element, whereas this reference to the typical mother figure in Mann's oeuvre quite clearly refers to her passionate nature deemed as decadent by the *Bürger* camp.

Luke's version is far closer to the original than Lowe-Porter's and the basic argument is sustained, though in a weakened or domesticated form. In Lowe-Porter's version, some of the basic themes are confused whereas Luke's version can, at least, be categorised as an 'adequate' translation despite some inaccuracies and infelicities even though, in Luke as in all the other published versions, virtually all the stylistic subtleties pointed out by Seidlin are either missed or ignored.

After such an exhaustive analysis, the question then arises as to what strategy a translator can choose to encode the information gathered in this way and also as to what methods the translator should adopt to reflect something of the depth and complexity of Mann's style. For the translator, there could be said to be at least four possible strategies:

(f) Alternative Translation Strategies

(i) Strategy I

This would aim at producing a close semantic translation based on a thorough study of the author and would attempt to reflect many of the aspects as illustrated by close textual analysis. Where there are inevitable stylistic losses, these can be compensated by new 'appropriate' stylistic features added by the translator. Some of the poetic rhythms are lost in this version which would be aimed at the serious literary reader and would ideally be placed next to the original as a parallel annotated text. In doing so the reader may glean something of the richness and complexity of Thomas

Mann's style. Unlike Version IV, which I have also offered, this version is not intended for easy reading but more for close textual analysis.

Version III: (Suggested Semantic Version) (Gledhill)

> The author of the lucid and massive prose epopee on the life of Frederick of Prussia, - the long-suffering artist who had patiently and painstakingly woven together so great a variety of human character and destiny into a vast tapestry unified beneath the shadow of one great idea in his novel entitled *Maya* - the creator of that most disturbing story, *A Vile Wretch* which revealed to the new young and grateful generation that it was still possible to have an ethical commitment which transcends even the deepest of philosophical insights - and finally to characterise the works of his later years, the writer whose mature period was exemplified by a passionate treatise on *Intellect and Art*, ranked equally by some serious critics with Schiller's famous raisonnement on naïve and sophisticated poetry because of its creative sense of order and its eloquent use of antithesis - Gustav Aschenbach was born in the town of L., a district capital in the province of Silesia, as the son of a high-ranking official in the judiciary. [End of sentence]
>
> His forebears had been army officers, judges, civil servants, men who had led austere lives of respectable frugality in the service of their king and country. A more inward form of spirituality had once manifested itself amongst his ancestors in the form of a clergyman; the poet's mother, the daughter of a Bohemian music master, introduced more thrilling, more sensual blood into the family. His foreign features came from her. The union of a scrupulous, sober dedication to duty with darker, fiery impulses produced an artist, and indeed, combined to produce this particular artist.

The disadvantage is that the passage can appear stilted and dense in the target language and so, there need to be some 'communicative' aspects to be incorporated for the sake of readability. The advantage, however, is that the reader is receiving something of the flavour, density, musicality, irony and complexity of Thomas Mann's style, even though at second hand. The translation aims at producing equivalents, where possible, such as the noun *epopee* for "Epopöe".

(ii) Strategy II

A close, but communicative literary translation would not even attempt to reflect the myriad complexity of the source text, but would aim at expressing the actual content of the original in a literary but natural style. There would, however, still be an attempt to capture something of the poetic register and, in Mann's case, the intellectual richness of the original. Chase's version (1999) (Appendix II: VII) has something of these qualities. I have written Version IV as an example of a fairly conservative, but natural communicative translation which primarily aims at readability and secondarily, at retaining a close fidelity to the tenor and tone of the original:

Version IV: (Suggested Communicative Version) (Gledhill)

> The author of that colossal prose epic on the life of Frederick of Prussia - the artist who wove a vast tapestry uniting the multifarious strands of human destinies and characters beneath the shadow of one unifying idea in his novel called *Maya* - creator of the powerful story entitled *Human Scum*, which, however, made moral action possible again to a whole generation of grateful readers and take precedence over artistic insights penetrating the nether depths of knowledge - writer of that passionate treatise on *Art and the Intellect* (which characterised his later period) and which was so cogently argued and was so sophisticated in its use of antithesis that some leading critics put it on a level with Schiller's famous treatise defining the difference between naïve, and 'consciously wrought' poetry - Gustav Aschenbach was born in L., a town in Silesia as the son of a highly placed, state lawyer. [End of sentence]
> His ancestors came from the ranks of military officers, judges, civil servants - all men who lead impeccably respectable, though frugal lives in the service of their king and country. There had been one manifestation of a deeper, more spiritual influence in the form of an ancestor who had been a clergyman; the poet's mother, who was the daughter of a Bohemian music director, introduced a more hot-blooded and sensual streak into the family. His foreign-looking appearance came from her. The combination of dry devotion to duty with darker, yet fiery urges was a mixture which could produce an artist and which, in fact, did produce this particular artist.

Version IV interprets and explains the original making it both accessible and easy to assimilate for the English reader. The semantic features of the original such as the progression *Autor→Künstler→Schöpfer→Verfasser* are preserved in this translation as long as they do not detract from the fluency of the SL text (which, however, is not the case with the published versions where virtually all the stylistic features of the SL text listed in this chapter are either omitted or ignored yet without any compensatory stylistic devices.)

Version IV reads well in modern natural English and may be characterised as bold. The opprobrium in *Der Elende* is vividly translated as *Human Scum*. As a communicative translation aims at a wide readership, the reference to Schiller is almost given a metalinguistic explanatory translation as *naïve and consciously wrought poetry* because a wide readership could not be expected to be familiar with Schiller's aesthetic philosophy.

(iii) Strategy III

This takes Strategy II one step further and would be an adaptation (*Bearbeitung*) of the Thomas Mann original. It could be an *English Death in Venice* with an English character and would not attempt to translate sentence by sentence. The seventeenth-century Gotha translators of English Restoration plays as described by Unger (1996) illustrate how imaginative translations of comedies could be produced which, according to Unger, were as successful as theatre in Germany as they had been in England[27]. At the same time, the academic translations extant at the same time were generally ignored.

Another more recent example is Adriana Hunter's translation £9.99 (2003) of Frédéric Beigbeder's novel entitled 99 Francs referred to in a literary article by Bassnett (2203):

> The English title gives a clue as to her special translation strategy. 99 Francs has become £9.99, and just as the money has been transposed from francs to pounds, so Hunter has transposed the entire novel from Paris to London. The novel is a black comedy about a grotesque clique of cocaine-sniffing, violent advertising executives who inhabit an amoral world. The translation is brilliant – the protagonist inhabits a high-octane, high-fashion world, and Hunter has skilfully transposed every reference so that English readers can have a flavour of the corrupt world of advertising and consumerism. This is a very clever example of creative translation, for it is hard to see how a novel that was so rooted in French culture could have succeeded with English readers had Hunter not boldly decided to go far beyond a translator's brief. (Bassnett: 2003: 67)

This is high praise indeed from an eminent translation critic and yet the innate conservatism of contemporary criticism is evident in the phrase "far beyond a translator's brief" in the above extract. What is a 'standard translator's brief'? In this context, it is obviously understood to be what has been defined as the *academic strategy*.

It would, however, in this case seem evident that Strategy III would be inappropriate for one of the greater prose classics of German literature unless the translator had a literary gift similar to that of Thomas Mann. However, particularly for lesser known works, this can be an excellent solution.

(iv) Strategy IV

This would go even further than Strategy III and would be a complete rewriting (*Neudichtung*) of the *Death in Venice* 'legend' or 'myth' as created by Thomas Mann. As in Strategy III, it would also need a literary talent of an appropriate stature to be comparable with Thomas Mann. This is very much in the world of speculation and in the twilight territory between *literarische Bearbeitung*,

---

[27] Unger's (1996) strategy is discussed in detail in Chapter IX of this study.

Neudichtung and original works of literature and so, is not appropriate for detailed discussion on translation theory. In this context, Visconti's film *Death in Venice* can be seen as an example of post-Derridean διαφερειν or transformation as discussed in Chapter V.

(g) Conclusion

It can be confirmed from this analysis that style is an 'umbrella' term for a very complex set of phenomena. These elusive features are still a long way from being open to scientific analysis. It has, however, been seen that mathematical methods such as the bar graph used in this chapter can be a very useful tool to supplement literary analysis. Literary translation theory is still, in my opinion, a literary and philosophical activity. This view is shared by the famous writer and critic Octavio Paz who is an ardent defender of translation as an essentially literary activity:

> In recent years, perhaps because of the increasing primacy of linguistics, there has been a tendency to deemphasise the decidedly literary nature of translation. There is no such thing - nor can there be - as a science of translation, although translation can and should be studied scientifically. Just as literature is a specialized function of language, so translation is a specialized function of literature. And what, we might ask, of the machines that translate? If they ever really translate, they too will perform a literary operation, and they too will produce what translators now do: literature. (Schulte 1992: 157)

Chapter V: Approaches to the Translation of Poetry and Poetic Prose
(a) Introduction: the (Un)translatability of Poetry?

The starting point for the poetics of translation usually begins with the supposition that what is being dealt with is 'the art of the impossible' as in the notorious Robert Frost dictum that what great literature consists of, is what is lost in translation. This entrenched position assumes that the untranslatability of literature is an incontrovertible truth and indeed, there are many eminent proponents for the absolute impossibility of this activity including Jakobson (2000):

> [. . .] - paranomasia reigns over poetic art, and whether its rule is absolute or limited, poetry by definition is untranslatable. *Only creative transposition is possible.* [. . .] (Jakobson 2000: 118. My emphasis.)

Like most linguists, Jakobson's rejection of any form of paranomasia as translatable reflects the lexically bound view of the translation process, even though he does allow for "creative transposition". Interestingly, Hatim and Mason (1988: 13) also use the phrase *creative transposition* to show the impossibility of dialect translation and it is also significant that this most excellent of strategies is qualified by the adverb *only*. Yet, it will be seen that creative transposition is a frequent strategy that must be employed not only with regard to literary texts but also often for commercial translations, particularly in the field of publicity and advertising.

Many contemporary linguists such as House (1997) support Jakobson's belief in the untranslatability of poetry:

> In a poetic-aesthetic work of art, the usual distinctions between form and content (or meaning) no longer hold. In poetry, the form of a linguistic unit cannot be changed without a corresponding change in (semantic, pragmatic and textual) meaning. And since the form cannot be detached from its meaning, this meaning cannot be expressed in any other way, i.e. through paraphrase, explanation or commentary, borrowing of new words etc. In poetry the signifiers have an autonomous value and can therefore not be exchanged for the signifiers of another language, although they may in fact express the same signified concept or referent. Since the physical nature of signifiers in one language can never be duplicated in another language, the relations of signifiers to signified, which are no longer arbitrary in a poetic-aesthetic work, cannot be expressed in another language. (House 1997: 48)

It can be shown that there is a certain circularity (*petitio principii*) in this seemingly watertight argument which is based merely on the self-evident principle of identity as in the well-known Bishop Butler proposition: "A thing is what it is and not another thing." Basically, House's argument states that you can either reproduce form or content, but not both. The fallacy of this argument consists in the covert assumption that translation means *academic translation*.

However, House makes the valid point that the linguistic use of a word, phrase or formulation which is bound to a specific culture is at one level untranslatable. House gives many examples contrasting the exaggerated politeness of English with German directness. She also shows that German signs and requests tend to require 'scientific' justification which is usually omitted in English. One example will suffice to make this point:

> (4) Sign in a hotel bathroom
>
> *Lieber Gast! Weniger Wäsche und weniger Waschmittel schützen unsere Umwelt. Bitte entscheiden Sie sich selbst, ob Ihre Handtücher gewaschen werden sollen. Nochmals benutzen: Handtücher bitte hängen lassen. Neue Handtücher: Handtücher auf den Boden legen.*
>
> Vs
>
> *Dear Guest, will you please decide for yourself, whether your towels shall be washed. Use again: please leave your towels on the towel rack. Clean towels: please put your towels on the floor.*
>
> In the German original, but not in the translation, an explicit justification for the request is offered in the first sentence. Further, the German original seems slightly less polite than the translation, i.e. mentioning "bitte" twice may have seemed too much for the German writer, whereas the English translation inserts a "please" in each of the requests. (House 1997: 87)

Similarly, the concept *bread* is different even in different European languages: let us take a period such as the nineteen fifties as opposed to the present multi-cultural world, the French *pain* may well be a baguette or a bread roll, the German version could vary from *Graubrot* and *Schwarzbrot* to regional varieties whereas the English concept may evoke a traditional brown or white loaf or even white sliced bread depending on the social context[28]. This line of argument, that languages are unique and are therefore fundamentally untranslatable, has many variations from the famous

---

[28] De Man (1986) makes the same point with regard to French culture: "To mean 'bread', when I need to name bread, I have the word *Brot*, so that the way in which I mean this is by using the word *Brot*. The translation will reveal a fundamental discrepancy between the intent to name *Brot* and the name *Brot* itself in its materiality, as a device of meaning. If you hear *Brot* in the context of Hölderlin, who is so often mentioned in this text, I hear *Brot und Wein* necessarily, which is the great Hölderlin text that is very much present in this - which in French becomes *Pain et vin*. 'Pain et vin' is what you get for free in a restaurant, in a cheap restaurant where it is still included, so *pain et vin* has very different connotations from *Brot und Wein*. It brings to mind the *pain français, baguette, ficelle, bâtard,* all those things - I now hear in *Brot* 'bastard'. This upsets the stability of the quotidian." (De Man 1986: 87)

Sapir/Whorf hypothesis to the latest edition of Steiner's *After Babel* including Jakobson (2000: 113-116) and Quine (2000: 98) .

Steiner (1998: 252-253) is also a vociferous proponent of the ultimate untranslatability of poetry. Ironically, to clinch his argument he quotes the Rumanian poet, Marin Sorescu who, in his poem called "Translation", claimed that his translation of a classical poem "utterly failed/At the soul", implying that this is always the case with poetry translations. Incredibly and yet without any reference to the irony of the situation, the poem about the untranslatability of poetry quoted by Steiner is itself an English translation by T. Cribbs. This contradictory attitude is at the heart of the purists' argument against the translation of poetry. Of course, it is better in one sense to read the poem in the original, if possible, but this is often not possible and so translations of poetry abound alongside original works. A cursory glance at the poetry section of any continental bookshop, particularly in Germany, will reveal that about half the titles are translations; the same is true for the many popular compendia with themes such as love and marriage where thoughts and light poems are chosen from a great variety of international sources. The purists themselves, as is obviously the case with Steiner, must often read poetry translations if they are interested in poetry on a world-wide basis unless they are extraordinary polyglots.

The purists whether Benjamin, Heidegger or Steiner seem to base their arguments on Judaeo/Greco philosophy and 'myths', which is well summarised by Barnstone (1993):

> After the expulsion from Eden and the Flood, translation was initiated with the third diaspora, the Babelean linguistic dissemination, as an endeavour to return to that Edenic state when Adam gave names to all cattle, and to the birds of the air, and to every beast of the field. Translation sought to regain the universality of that earthly knowledge that was ours before the fall, when we were a single people with a single tongue. God's dispersal offered an implicit injunction against that knowledge, yet at the same time it hurled mankind into the necessity of translation and the eventual restoration of that single tongue. (Barnstone 1993: 135)

This summary applies particularly to certain aspects of Benjamin's theories concerning the relationship of the translation to its original.

> Die Übersetzung aber sieht sich nicht gleichsam wie die Dichtung im innern Bergwald der Sprache selbst, sondern außerhalb desselben, ihm gegenüber, und ohne ihn zu betreten, ruft sie das Original hinein, an denjenigen einzigen Ort hinein, wo jeweils das Echo in der eigenen den Widerhall eines Werkes der fremden Sprache zu geben vermag. (Benjamin 1961: 63-64)

There are many such statements in Benjamin's work which refer to a sacred hierarchy of meaning. The phrase *im innern Bergwald der Sprache selbst* together with the verb *betreten* implies entering into the holiest of holies (of language) whilst the translation remains "außerhalb", in the outer darkness. The original is sacred text (whether as a work of art or scripture) which echoes something of the "divine" (and which can be understood in a secularised post-Nietzschean world as a reflection of truth via "reine Sprache"). Thus the translation is at best merely an echo of an echo. It is fortunate that there are two words for echo in German (*Widerhall, Echo*) to illustrate his point. Yet, as with Steiner, there is a fundamental contradiction at the heart of this despairing attitude because this whole untranslatability thesis is expounded in the introduction to Benjamin's own translation of Baudelaire's *Tableaux Parisiens*. A similar attitude is reflected in Steiner's main book on translation theory with its title *After Babel*. In interpreting Benjamin, Steiner resorts to mystical and religious (Cabbalistic) terminology as highlighted by the added emphasis:

> A genuine translation evokes the shadowy and yet unmistakable contours of *the coherent design* from which, *after Babel*, the jagged fragments of human speech broke off. (Steiner 1998: 67)

The *Babel* theme is a recurrent motif in Western literature on translation. Derrida (1985) has written in depth on this theme as have many modern critics such as Barnstone as quoted above. Steiner goes on to refer to a pre-Babel *Ursprache* which is to be understood more in mythical than philological terms.

The main fallacy lies in the purists' implied downgrading of the status of the translation as summarised by Nabokov's poem "On Translating *Eugene Onegin*" quoted by Steiner in defence of his purist thesis:

> What is translation? On a platter
> A poet's pale and glaring head,
> A parrot's screech, a monkey's chatter,
> And profanation of the dead. (Steiner 1998: 252)

This fallacy also ignores the fact that a translation can be an *improvement* of the original. This is often the case in technical and commercial translation for the simple reason many translators (of the highest standards) are language experts and writers with a good stylistic sense whereas for some engineers or commercial writers language is of secondary importance.

One of the arguments against untranslatability accepts that the translation does not claim to be the same as the original, but that its validity depends on its function in the target language. This approach is sometimes referred to as "Skopos-theory" as in the exposition of Vermeer (1996) who claims that the main value of the translation is based on its purpose or "skopos" and on its function in the target culture rather than its closeness to the original in the SL. Similarly, Toury (1985) coined the term *polysystem* for his equally target-oriented approach in which the value of a translation depends on its interaction with other genres within the complex system (polysytem) of the target culture. His definition of translation illustrates this point:

> A 'translation' will be taken to be any target-language utterance which is presented or regarded as such within the target culture on whatever grounds. (Toury 1985: 20)

This definition is so broad that it would also include 'pseudo-translations' such as McPherson's *Ossian*, the notorious 'translation' of a non-existent text which fooled writers such as Schiller and Goethe and yet which was influential in its time as an inspiration to poets and literati. Even-Zohar (1990), Holz-Mänttäri (1984) and Kußmaul (1995) have also contributed to target-oriented or "functional" theories of translation. In this approach, there is no more searching after a chimerical ideal translation which finds the set of perfect equivalents in L2 for L1, no more striving after the often mythical yet always elusive *mot juste*. Instead, there are many possible translations so that criteria such as coherence, readability and acceptability assume a new importance. A translation can be assessed as a work in itself, almost or even absolutely independently from its source text. This view is not as radical as it might seem at first sight. Many people in English-speaking countries are only vaguely conscious that the King James Authorised Version of the Bible is only a translation because this text has acquired the status of a 'holy text'. This point has been made very forcefully by Barnstone (1993) with regard to the New Testament:

> So the New Testament, most of which is translated from lost sources, is presented as original gospel, not translation; so the Authorized Version or King James Version of the Bible is popularly perceived to be God's words, delivered by the Creator in English and sacredly original. (Barnstone 1993: 9)

Luther's translation of the Bible has a similar status in Germany. The same principle applies to the Schlegel-Tieck-Baudissin translations of Shakespeare. Whilst not being Shakespeare, they are great literary works in themselves and the German literary tradition would have been very different without them. The point is not controversial. It has been forcefully made by Barnstone (1993) among many others:

> [. . .] so Geoffrey Chaucer's *Troilus* stands alone, without reference to Chaucer's genius in revising versions from Boccaccio and from French epic love poetry; so Richard Crashaw's close translation

of Saint Teresa's famous "Vivo sin vivir in mí" (itself an intralingual *glosa* of a traditional anonymous poem) goes unrecognized in all editions of Crashaw's writings; so even W. B. Yeats's "When You Are Old" (a close version of Pierre de Ronsard's most famous sonnet)[. . .] (Barnstone 1993: 9)

Numerous other examples can be adduced where translations have gained the status of original works. Indeed, the question arises when is a translation a translation. The great medieval German poets Wolfram von Eschenbach, Gottfried von Strassburg and Hartmann von Aue described their activities as translations, insisting even that theirs were more accurate than other versions, even though their works have a much higher status within the literary canon than their source texts. To suggest to a patriotic French scholar that some of the works of Racine could be regarded as adaptations of their classical sources would be greeted with horror, so high is the canonical status of Racine in the French literature and so low is the status of translators and writers of adaptations. Yet many passages in Racine closely parallel their sources. The polysystem school breaks down these barriers and divisions, thus liberating the translator from the tyranny of the source text.

According to Gentzler, deconstructionists go one step further than the polysystem theoreticians by dethroning of the primacy of the source text even to the point of questioning whether the original could not also be regarded as being dependent on the translation rather than vice versa:

> Questions being posed by deconstructionists include the following: What if one theoretically reversed the direction of thought and posited the hypothesis that the original text is dependent on the translation? What if one suggested that, without translation, the original text ceased to exist, that the very survival of the original depends not on any particular quality it contains, but upon those qualities that its translation contains? What if the very definition of a text's meaning was determined not by the original, but by the translation [. . .] What exists *before* the original? An idea? A form? A thing? Nothing? (Gentzler 1993: 144-145).

It could equally be a mistake to imply that the translation is *more* important than the original, but the deconstructionists have the useful function of demythologising translation theory. Whether poetry is translatable or not, there is an enormous literature of translated poems presumably with an even greater readership. At this point, it is relevant to examine the various strategies undertaken by translators of poetry.

(b) Practical Approaches to the Translation Poetry

It can be argued that the whole field of poetry translation is still in its infancy at the theoretical level despite three millennia of practice[29]. The past and present states of the theory regarding the translation of poetry is well summarised in *The Encyclopaedia of Literary Translation* (1998) under the headings *The Poetics of Translation* and *Poetry Translation*. There is no need to repeat these excellent summaries written by Gentzler and Venuti respectively, but instead, it will be of greater relevance to examine the language of discourse in this field. In short, it can almost be said 'anything goes in the theory of poetic discourse translation as there are distinguished theorists, literati and poets who represent more or less every conceivable stance on this most difficult of topics. Based on Lefevere (1975), Bassnett (1991) list of the various possible approaches still applies:

1. *phonemic translation* (imitation of ST sounds);
2. *literal translation* (cf. Nabokov);
3. *metrical translation* (imitation of metre of ST);
4. *prose translation* (rendering as much sense as possible);
5. *rhymed translation* (added constraints of rhyme and metre);
6. *blank verse translation* (no constraint of rhyme but still one of structure);
7. *interpretation* (complete change of form and/or imitation). (Abridged from Bassnett. 1991: 81-82)

More detailed examples of these various stances will be given in the course of this introduction.

There has been much written about poetry translation by poets, translators and literary critics, but there has been little written in a systematic way. The wide range of stances on this issue is also well summarised by Holmes (1978) who also reflects some of the vehemence with which these views are held by the various parties involved:

---

[29] It can be seen from Hatim and Mason (1990) who quote and translate a text taken from Badawi (1968: 33) that the same issues such as literalness versus free and equivalence versus the impossibility of equivalence were current even in the fourteenth century. The procedure quoted below provides a good illustration of the approach of the more 'scientific' wing of the present-day equivalence theoreticians: "The 'literal' versus 'free' controversy has been more or less a constant in translation studies, no matter how far back one goes. The extreme case is that referred to by the fourteenth-century translator Salah al-Din al-Safadi who, writing about earlier generations of Arab translators, complains that they look at each Greek word and what it means. They seek an equivalent term in Arabic and write it down. Then they take the next word and do the same, and so on until the end of what they have to translate. Al-Safadi faults this method of translating on two counts:
> 1. It is erroneous to assume that one-for-one equivalents exist for all lexical items in Greek and Arabic.
> 2. The sentence structure of one language does not match that of another." (Hatim and Mason 1990: 15-16)

> What should the verse form of a metapoem be? There is, surely, no other problem of translation that has generated so much heat, and so little light, among the normative critics. Poetry, says one, should be translated into prose. No, says a second, it should be translated into verse, for in prose its very essence is lost. By all means into verse, and into the form of the original, urges a third. Verse into verse, fair enough, says a fourth, but God save us from Homer in hexameters. (Holmes 1978: 94)

In the history of translation and literature, each school of thought has distinguished representatives. It could also be added that the language of discourse has both a moral and absolutist tone which excludes open debate on these matters. It will be useful to begin with the first category mentioned by Holmes (1970) which refers to those poets and theoreticians who are convinced that *all* poetry in *all* cases (such is the universalist form of their discourse) should be translated into prose.

The literary critic and translator, John Middleton Murry (1923) is a vigorous supporter of the 'poetry-into-prose' school:

> Poetry ought *always* to be rendered into prose. Since the aim of the translator *should be* to present the original as exactly as possible, no fetters of rhyme or metre *should be* imposed to hamper this difficult labour. Indeed they make it impossible. (Murry 1923: 129. My emphasis.)

The argument is based on moral exhortations as illustrated by the emphasis. Similarly, the more recent critic, writer and translator Nabokov, whose essay "Problems of Translation: *Onegin* in English" originally published in 1955, quoted in full in Venuti (2000), takes an equally extreme and absolutist position on this topic. His justification of this stance is based on an uncompromising literalist view of translation:

> The term "free translation" smacks of knavery and tyranny. It is when the translator sets out to render the "spirit" - not the textual sense - that he begins *to traduce* the author. The clumsiest literal translation is a thousand times more useful that the prettiest paraphrase. (Nabokov 2000: 71. My emphasis.)

By his use of the verb *traduce*, Nabokov implies a severe moral condemnation for the 'free' translator, possibly as an echo of the well-known Italian dictum to the effect that *traduttore* (to translate) equals *traditore* (to betray).The same tone of moral indignation concerning 'free' translators pervades the whole essay:

> The person who desires to turn a literary masterpiece into another language has only one duty to perform, and this is to produce with absolute exactitude the whole text and nothing but the text. (Venuti 2000: 77. My emphasis.)

The phrase "the whole text and nothing but the text" is redolent of the oath to be sworn before a jury: "the whole truth and nothing but the truth". This is to imply that free translation is not only betrayal but is also a form of perjury.

It is, however, not very well known that the poet Robert Browning's views on poetry anticipate those of the 'literalist' school[30]. Pound and Benjamin also tend towards this approach to translation where the target language is sometimes violated to preserve the rugged and raw nature of the original.

In between the two extremes of translation into prose versus translation into verse, there are, however, other opinions which include grey areas such as those of Matthew Arnold (1909), whose essay "On Translating Homer" originally appeared in 1861, is a slightly less categorical supporter of the poetry-into-prose school since he restricts his dogmatic ban only to the 'great works' of literature on account of the variety entailed in such literary monuments:

> There are great works composed of parts so disparate that one translator is not likely to have the requisite gifts for poetically rendering all of them. Such are the works of Shakespeare and Goethe's *Faust*; and these it is best to attempt to render in prose only. (Arnold 1909: 274)

Although Arnold's arguments are consistent in theory, they are rather weak in practice as they involve preferring an obscure French prose version of Shakespeare to the universally acclaimed Schlegel-Tieck translations[31]. Similarly, he supports a very weak English prose version of Goethe's *Faust*.[32]

At the other extreme, Alexander Fraser Tytler (1791), who was one of the early theoreticians to discuss the problem of poetry translation into English, takes a

---

[30] Browning's notes are taken from the diary of John Addington Symonds as quoted by Selver (1966). Poets tend towards dogmatic extremes in their theoretical discourse as illustrated by the added emphasis in the following extract: "Browning's theory of translation. *Ought* to be *absolutely* literal, with exact rendering of words, and words placed in the order of the original. *Only* a rendering of this sort gives any real insight into the original. Fitzgerald's 'Omar Khayam' - a fine English poem but no translation [. . .]. Let it be said, then, that the translator of a poem is *not entitled* to *tamper* with the original. He should omit nothing essential. He *should* add nothing extraneous. It is primarily by unsubstantiated additions that the mediocre or slovenly translator *betrays* himself. Frequently he indulges in them merely to engineer a rhyme which would otherwise elude him. The adroit, inspired translator is never reduced to such a *shift* as that. His skill in this respect may be described as a knack, in the same way that juggling billiard balls is a knack."(Selver 1966: 26. My italics.)

[31] He states in main work on translation theory *On Translating Homer*: "People praise Tieck and Schlegel's version of Shakespeare. I for my part would sooner read Shakespeare in the French prose translation, and that is saying a good deal; but in the German poet's hands, Shakespeare so often gets, especially where he is humorous, an air of what the French call *niaiserie* and can anything be more un-Shakespearean than that? Again Mr Hayward's prose translation of the first part of 'Faust' is not likely to be surpassed by any translation in verse." (Arnold 1909: 274)

[32] A brief quotation from his translation of the opening lines of the *Walpurgisnacht* scenes will suffice to show that the quality of this prose translation can hardly be taken to be superior to the verse of Schlegel-Tieck: "Do you not long for a broomstick? For my part, I should be glad of the sturdiest he-goat. By this road we are still far from our destination." (Selver 1966: 14)

diametrically opposite stance to both the translation-into-prose school with an equally confident dogmatism. Tytler asserts:

> To attempt, therefore, a translation of lyric poem into prose, is the *most absurd* of all undertakings; for those very characters of the original which are essential to it, and which constitute its highest beauties, if transferred to a prose translation, become *unpardonable* blemishes. (Tytler 1791: 111. My emphasis.)

Again as with Nabokov, opprobrium is supported by ethical threats with Tytler's use of the adjective *unpardonable*. Tytler also adds the threat of ridicule to possible opponents of stance by his use of the phrase *most absurd*. Sometimes, even national prejudices are invoked to support extreme views on poetry translation as in the case of the poet Coleridge:

> I do not admit the argument for prose translations. I would, in general, rather see verse in so capable a language as ours. The French cannot help themselves, of course, with such a language as theirs. (Quoted in Selver 1966: 13)

Entertaining though it may be to consider the diverse opinions of poets and scholars from the past on the topic of translating poetry, it has already seen to be not very illuminating as there are few arguments other than oracular pronouncements based on the supposed authority of the writer or there are dire moral threats for those who dare to disagree. There have, however, been some dispassionate analyses a classic example of which will be treated in the next Section.

(c) Equivalence Theoreticians

With the advent of machine translation from the 1940s, scientific and mathematical approaches dominated linguistic discourse on translation theory from this period up to the end of the 1980s. The elusive concept of equivalence was the key concept that has almost as many definitions as theorists as noted by Gallagher:

> Übersetzungsäquivalenz ist bekanntlich ein schwer fassbarer und kein einheitlicher Begriff (vgl.. Koller 1979: 176; Stein 1980: 33-34; Reiß/Vermeer 1984: 124; Nord 1986: 30; Snell-Hornby 1988: 13-22; Gallagher 1993c: 150). Deshalb versuchen viele Forscher Missverständnissen vorzubeugen, indem sie verschiedene Äquivalenztypen unterscheiden. So wird in der übersetzungstheoretischen Literatur von denotativer, konnotativer, inhaltlicher dynamischer, formaler, kommunikativer, pragmatischer und wirkungsmäßiger Äquivalenz gesprochen, um nur acht Beispiele wahllos herauszugreifen. (Gallagher 1998: 1)

Similarly, Koller defines five types of equivalence most of which are included in Gallagher's list which, but the impression created by both authors is that the list could well be endless.

Although it has been argued that equivalence theories have limited application in the field of literature, it is clear that in other areas such as science, technology and commerce, they can be useful strategies. To give an obvious example, the German noun *Spannung* can have many different meanings and differing contexts. It could mean *tension, stress, voltage, pressure, strain* and *potential* - to name but a few examples. The simplest and most practical definition of equivalence involves finding the correct meaning of the word in the appropriate context, which can also be a matter of life and death. If a notice such as *Vorsicht Hochspannung* in a context of where *Danger High Voltage* would be an appropriate translation is wrongly translated as 'Be cautious - there is a lot of stress about', this could have fatal consequences for even a wary wanderer on an electrical installation! Obviously such a crass mistake rarely occurs even in the field of technical translation where less dangerous errors abound. Anecdotal evidence alone suffices to make this point. Even here, however, for the experienced translator, stating the necessity for equivalence is merely a case of stating the obvious.

In this Section the 'classical' concept of equivalence is connected with its use in mathematics and formal logic. As there is not space to deal with all the various forms of equivalence, there will only be a formal refutation of Holmes' attempt to formalise the process of literary translation. This is to illustrate the basic theoretical approach of this dissertation which argues that a non-dogmatic and pragmatic use of the notion translation strategies is more fruitful than following the blind alley of scientifically based equivalence.

Van den Broeck (1978) defines translation acts in terms of equivalence with sub-categories such as 'synonymy' or 'semantic equivalence.' He quotes Mates' definition to describe these terms:

> Two expressions are synonymous in a language L if and only if they may be interchanged in each sentence in L without altering the truth value of that sentence.'
> (Mates 1950: 209).

It is surprising that Holmes does not go one step further and give mathematical form to what is already a mathematical definition. A possible formulation of the above could be as follows: where E refers to any translation act which is defined as equivalent for an item (a) in the source language L1 translated into the target language L2 (b) so that, using standard formal logic notation, the Mates' definition could be expressed as follows:

$$E = (L1 \text{ (a)} \Leftrightarrow L2 \text{ (b)})$$

It must also be noted that (a) $\Leftrightarrow$ (b) $\neq$ ((a = b)) or, in other words, equivalence must never be confused with identity even though their truth values may be the same. House rightly expresses a sense of outrage when as distinguished a theoretician as Snell-Hornby fails to make this distinction:

> Given the relative nature of 'equivalence' and the fact that it has nothing to do with 'identity' it is more than surprising that a polemic attack should have been directed against the concept of equivalence, in the course of which an analysis of the English and German dictionary meaning of the term 'Equivalence' was presented. Snell-Hornby singles out one dictionary entry, which supports her claim that equivalence basically equals identity and promptly proceeds to dismiss equivalence as 'an illusion' in translation studies. She writes that equivalence means 'virtually the same thing'. By contrast, I found the following dictionary entries for 'equivalent' and 'equivalence' in my own dictionary searches. 'having the same value, purpose [. . .] etc. as a person or thing of a different kind (Longman Dictionary of Contemporary English 1995), and having the same relative position or function; corresponding [. . .]' (Shorter Oxford English Dictionary 1995), as well as 'equivalence is something that has the same use or function as something else' (Collins Cobuild 1987). And in German, too, 'Äquivalenz' is not only a term in the 'exakte Wissenschaften' as Snell-Hornby claims: in my Brockhaus I read: 'das, was in gewissen Fällen gleiche Wirkung hervorzubringen vermag'.
>
> (House 1997: 26)

This is, however, not a debate which should be solved by an appeal to lexicographers because what needs to be made clear is whether equivalence is defined as in mathematical logic, or, as in ordinary language or again whether a stipulative definition has been made of this term.

In technical translation, there are, however, occasions when formal equivalence and identity are identical such as when dealing with measurements or describing machines, but in literary translation, this is rarely the case. Van den Broeck (1978) also makes this point with his example of the two sentences *I am an orphan* and *I am a child and I have no father and mother* as a case of equivalence of reference, but not of sense as 'orphan' has all kinds of connotations which would be missed by the mere reference to a child without parents. Literary equivalence is completely different from scientific or logical equivalence. To make this point even more clearly, the following example adapted from Frege (1892) should suffice: from a logical point of view the planet *Venus*, the *Morning Star*, the *Evening Star* and *the second nearest planet to the sun within the solar system* refer to the same object and are identical and thus the reference ("Bedeutung") is identical. Particularly from a literary perspective, the various expressions referring to this particular planet are by no means identical with regard to their sense ("Sinn"). In a hypothetical poem referring to a very amorous poet or even philanderer, a line such as:

(a) *My heart leapt for joy when I saw Venus flood the evening sky*

is certainly not equivalent with regard to sense to:

(b) *My heart leapt for joy when I saw the Evening Star flood the evening sky*

as the romantic or in some contexts, erotic connotations are totally lost.

If the Morning Star is substituted, there is a paradoxical effect, but quite different from the original (a) and also, interestingly, from (b):

(c) *My heart leapt for joy when I saw the Morning Star flood the evening sky.*

If we use the scientific equivalent (d), the effect becomes absurd:

(d) *My heart leapt for joy when I saw the second planet nearest to the sun within the solar system flood the evening sky.*

The distinction thus needs to be made whether equivalence refers to the sense (*Sinn*) or whether it is a case of reference (*Bedeutung*). Most European languages have exact equivalents for the various aspects of 'sense' in this case such as in German with the names *Morgenstern, Abendstern* and *Venus*, but the problem arises with cultures in which such equivalents are lacking, particularly those of the southern hemisphere where Venus does not appear either at all or at least in the same way. These problems are dealt with by some theoreticians such as Koller (1979: 187-191, 1979: 100-104) who does distinguish between denotative (*Bedeutung*) and connotative (*Sinn*) meaning, but more as a matter classification than of strategy. Nida's concept of "dynamic" equivalence is relevant for the problem of translating for languages in the southern hemisphere:

> In contrast, a translation which attempts to produce a dynamic rather than a formal equivalence is based upon "the principle of equivalent effect" (Rieu & Phillips 1954). In such a translation one is not concerned with matching the receptor-language message with the source-language message, but with the dynamic relationship, that the relationship between receptor and message should be substantially the same as that which existed between the original receptor and message. (Nida 2000: 129)

As this involves discovering or finding a strategy which would have the same effect in the target language, the notion of equivalence is again strained to its limits.

Although Van den Broeck's recognises the difficulty of always finding a translational equivalent his narrowly scientific approach[33], he does admit to the inherent contradiction in this pursuit with the following reasonable concession:

> Unfortunately, it will be difficult to find any pairs of expressions in natural languages which meet the very stringent requirements this criterion of semantic equivalence seems to impose. (Van den Broeck 1978: 36)

In a similar vein, Van den Broeck refers to the scepticism of both Mates and Leech with regard to the possibility of ever finding true equivalents, particularly with regard to stylistic aspects:

> If we take into account the fact that expressions in context not only have conceptual meanings but also convey connotative, stylistic, affective, reflected, and collocative meanings, it will in fact be difficult to discover any pair of expressions in actual speech which are really equivalent. (Van den Broeck 1978: 36)

Van den Broeck is well aware of the limitations of what has been defined in this dissertation as the *academic approach*:

> In view of the semantic gap between languages and the fact that any text communicates more than mere 'cognitive' (or 'conceptual') meanings, it is impossible to maintain that, for example, the problem of translating a book from German into English simply amounts to 'the problem of producing an English version which faithfully reproduces the sense of the original, that is, of producing a book which contains, for every meaningful expression in the German original, a synonymous expression in English, and conversely' (Mates 1950: 202). (Van den Broeck 1978: 37)

However, his hoped-for solution for an explanatory "elaborate" theory, based presumably on scientific grounds, will be revealed in the next Section to be a chimera:

> It would seem to be quite possible to achieve a very elaborate and quite useful theory about literary translation and yet have to admit that we do not know a single law, in the ordinary sense of the word, which it obeys. (Van den Broeck 1978: 45)

. (d) A Formal Refutation of Holmes' Mathematical Approach

An extreme and extraordinary example of the scientific or mathematical approach can be found in Holmes (1970) who attempts to give scientific definitions in

---

[33] Interestingly, Van den Broeck's more recent publications imply a shift of stance away from 'hard-edged' linguistics to a more literary approach with a tolerant attitude: "Contrary to what I thought some eight years ago, Derrida's philosophical approach may offer a substantial theoretical basis for explaining and describing translational phenomena." (Van den Broeck 1995: 4)
 Even though this is a very valuable and courageous concession on behalf of Van den Broeck, it is interesting that he is still searching for what in my opinion is the chimera that a scientific theory of literary translation is possible. This approach is revealed by his choice of phrases such as *substantial theoretical basis* and *explaining translational phenomena* when the whole thrust of Derrida is to avoid being pinned down by a scientific approach.

mathematical form for the literary translation process. He uses the term *mimetic*[34] to describe the approach of using the same verse form of the original and gives Lattimore's version of Homer's Odyssey (the opening of Book XI) as an example of this form which retains the hexameter form of the original:

> No verse form in any one language can be identical with a verse form in any other, however similar their nomenclatures and however cognate the languages. What in reality happens is that, much as one dancer may perform a pattern of steps closely resembling another's, yet always somehow different, in the same way the translator taking this first approach will imitate the form of the original as best he can. (Holmes 1970: 95)

This is another example of an argument based on Butler's maxim: "A thing is what it is and not another thing." The status of the original is given a transcendental authority like the musical score to the conductor or, to quote Holmes' analogy, like the choreography to the individual dancer. On the contrary, a great dancer might well make even a mediocre choreography seem brilliant simply by the individual and interpretative manifestation of the choreography. Similarly, a good translator may well translate dull conventional mechanical verse into something brilliant and natural as has already been argued in the introduction to this chapter.

Holmes then goes on to give a mathematical definition of 'mimetic' form:

(1)$F_P \, S \,^{35} F_{MP}$

where F_P designates the verse of the original poem, F_{MP} that of the metapoem (i.e. the translation) and S denotes fundamental similarity.

The purpose of putting these ideas into logical form is unclear. The symbol S 'is fundamentally similar to' would seem to be an arbitrary invention of the author on no mathematical basis. It is not clear if logical transitivity rules would apply for the variables x, y and z to produce the following argument: $((x \, S \, y \, \& \, y \, S \, z) \rightarrow x \, S \, z)$. From Van den Broeck's (1978) definition of equivalence in a collection of essays co-edited by Holmes, it would appear that equivalence as defined by the linguists' school does not imply transitivity:

---

[34] Steiner rightly notes: "This word has along and chequered history". (Steiner 1998: 268) On pages 267-268, he discusses Dryden's use of this term, which could be redefined in terms of functional equivalence. See (Nida 2000: 129) for a definition of this term and also the discussion in the previous Section of this chapter.

[35] The diagonal S is used to represent Holmes' horizontal S which has a point or dot placed below the middle of the symbol. This is because Holmes' symbol is an entirely new symbol which does not exist in any symbol index. If S is seen as a metasymbol, then the intended logic of the argument is not impaired.

The properties of a strict equivalence relationship (symmetry, transitivity, reflexivity) do not apply to the translation relationship. (Van den Broeck 1978: 33)

In terms of the formal aspects, the argument would appear to be valid if contrary to Van den Broeck as quoted above, equivalence is understood as a transitive relationship. In metalanguage[36], however, it would appear to be so in some cases, but not in others. A beloved may be compared with a red rose as in the famous line from the Robert Burns' poem, "My love is like a red red rose" with associations of beauty, freshness, symmetry, fragrance, ruddiness of lips or cheeks whereas a martyr's death may also be compared to a rose with different associations such as red blood, the odour of sanctity and the thorns of suffering, but in no way is the similarity logically transitive, because it would imply that the beautiful young woman resembles a martyr undergoing torture and death! Thus, the logical relation 'is fundamentally similar to' is not necessarily transitive and yet the symbol *S* is given the function of a constant.

A secondary point is, however, that *fundamental similarity* cannot be effectively used in mathematical notation without defining more clearly how 'fundamental similarity' differs from 'superficial similarity' or what logical constants are used to determine the continuum between 'identity,' 'similarity' and 'dissimilarity'. With the same casual disregard for the rules of formal logic, Holmes goes on in the next paragraph to invent another new constant: **: :** to express the relation of being "analogical to". Holmes then attempts a mathematical definition of analogy:

The principle underlying this approach, is that of 'analogical form', which might be formulated:

(2) $F_P : PT_{SL} :: F_{MP} : PT_{TL}$

Where PT_{SL} indicates the poetic tradition of the source language and PT_{TL} that of the target language. (Holmes 1970: 95-96)

However, to provide a mathematical constant for analogy would introduce the same objections as have already been applied to similarity[37] except that, in this context, to

[36] This term also used by Holmes is applied here in its strictly logical sense: i.e. the metalanguage of the formal logic in this context is ordinary language.

[37] There is neither an explanation nor a definition of the new, arbitrarily invented constant::: . He then 'derives' a further relationship from (1) and (2) already quoted:

(1 & 2) $(C_P \leftrightarrow F_P) \underset{TR}{\rightarrow} F_{MP} \rightarrow C_{MP}$ (Form-derivative forms)

where C_P indicates the 'content', the non-formal material, of the original poem, C_{MP} that of the meta-poem, and $\underset{TR}{\rightarrow}$ the translingual process. (1970: 96)

Holmes goes on to try to give a precise mathematical form to what he calls the "organic form":

$(F_P \leftrightarrow C_P) \rightarrow C_{MP} \rightarrow F_{MP}$

give precise definition of analogy is an even more arduous a task. Even if there were a precise definition of analogy, how this should work as a logical constant is not only not proven by Holmes, it is not even mentioned by him. His introduction of three hitherto unknown constants is doubly confusing because he uses them in the context of traditional constants within formal logic such as his use of brackets and both the implication → and the equivalence ↔ signs and yet he sometimes uses them in a different way from their usual signification as implication and equivalence. The implication sign is sometimes used to mean 'goes into' or 'translates into' and yet seems to have the force of transitivity by producing derivable arguments. In short, Holmes' symbolism remains unconvincing at the formal level, but the whole enterprise of trying to find a formal symbolic schema to represent poetry translation would seem to be questionable in the light of the difficulty of finding sufficient consensus at the common sense level of ordinary language. It is one of the major goals of this thesis to try to open debate on these issues and to find some clarity amidst the whole confusion of conflicting ideas concerning literary translation, and specifically the translation of poetry. The refutation of the Holmes' approach is important in this context to show that at least at the moment mathematical theories produce more confusion than light on this matter.

Outside the garbled formal aspects, the content of Holmes' article is useful because he makes the following three distinctions: 1) of *mimetic* form to reproduce the same metrical pattern as the original 2) *analogue* form which tries to achieve an equivalent effect in the target language 3) *form determined by content* which implies that the content shapes its own suitable form. Category (3) could be better expressed as appropriacy, i.e. that a form is used which in some ways reflects the content rather than, as according to Holmes, invoking the "mysterious process" of form determining of itself the content. He uses Ezra Pound's adaptation of the *Andreas Divus* 1538 translation of the same passage into Latin as an example of 'content-derivative' form.

TR

In the 'derivations' not only new terms C_P for content but also even more new constants → (TR) for the translingual process are arbitrarily introduced and yet traditional constants such as the use of brackets, → (implication) and ↔ (equivalence) are used with the new nomenclature to reach this final (invalid) conclusion:

(4) $(F_P \leftrightarrow C_P) \xrightarrow{TR} C_{MP} \leftarrow F_{MP}$

The reverse arrow is introduced without explanation. It is obvious that there is no formal logical validity between his various statements nor any clear logical relationship between those propositions which could theoretically stand on their own as descriptive symbolised statements. In such a case, the question arises as to what purpose is served by the use of this hybrid symbolism.

It is a great pity that Holmes does not subject the three passages to detailed analysis and it is perhaps an indictment of the whole 'mathematical' school that, despite all the formulations, the article reaches the rather feeble conclusion that a normative approach will not produce the best results, but that this area is in need of further study:

> As these three quotations emphasise, (*i.e. the three verse translations or adaptations of the Homer passage*) there is an extremely close relationship between the kind of verse form a translator chooses and the kind of total effect his translation achieves. It is, in fact, a relationship so central to the entire problem of verse translation that its study deserves our utmost attention - study, not in order to arrive at normative dicta. So it must be, and not otherwise; but to come to understand the nature of the various kinds of metapoem, each of which can never be more than a single interpretation out of many of the original whose image it darkly mirrors. (Holmes 1970: 101-102)

In his later work of Holmes (1978) sees translation as a decision procedure when he discusses the translation of Baudelaire's poem "La géante" in terms of a hierarchy of correspondences involving 'homologues' (SL-bound form) and anologues (TL-bound form):

> To return to my hypothetical translator Mr X. Should he, in his English translation of 'La géante', 'retain' such features as syllabic verse, the twelve- and thirteen -syllable line, the continental rhyme scheme, all of them homologues, that is to say in the English setting parallel in form to the French, but clearly not in function? Or should he choose analogues: syllabotonic verse, ten-syllable lines, the rhyme scheme of the English sonnet? These are obviously momentous choices, and which ones he is to make and which to reject will be determined by the correspondence rules which the translator has consciously or unconsciously chosen on the basis of his confrontative knowledge of the French and English languages, literatures and cultures. (Holmes 1978: 75-76)

Holmes, however, offers no answers other than suggesting directions for translation theory. He proposes that a 'repertory' of criteria should be set up to assess translations involving several axes with features such as microstructure, mesostructure, macrostructure on one axis, for example and on another axis, form, meaning, function (morphologue, semasiologue, analogue) and on yet another, this time third-dimensional axis, criteria such as contextuality, intertextuality and situationality. The language and methods like many in the equivalence school resemble those of mathematics and the natural sciences. There are formulations, as has already shown with regard to Mates, which could be given a mathematical form; there is a liberal use of block diagrams and charts; rules are formulated using symbolism or the language of mathematics such as 'if and only if'; Cartesian geometrical models are suggested and Linnaeus is explicitly quoted as a model for classification:

> The task of working out such a repertory would be enormous. But if scholars were to arrive at a consensus regarding it, in the way for instance, that botanists since Linnaeus have arrived at a consensus regarding systematic methods for the description of plants, it would then become possible, for the first time, to provide descriptions of original and translated texts, of their respective maps, and of correspondence networks, rules and hierarchies that would be mutually comparable. (Holmes 1978: 80-81)

Despite some successes in the field of machine translation which is still only in its infancy as far as sophisticated translation is concerned, it is not surprising that this school has had a relatively minor effect on literary translation because literature cannot easily be reduced to mathematical models. The project to give a precise scientific description of literary translation is doomed from the start. It is even very difficult sometimes to give an imprecise, *ad hoc* description of a literary text or translation.

Even though Holmes' goal to describe literary translation in terms of mathematics may be rejected, his final appeal for a more precise and rigorous methodology in translation theory would be welcomed by most, if not all translation theoreticians:

> Such goals, of course, the scholars of our generation have tended to reject: they seem to us unattainable, and so outside the range of our less-than vaulting ambition. It is in any case certain that they exceed the grasp of the subjective, largely intuitive and impressionist methods still so often being applied today. And only a more explicit, a more precise, a stricter intersubjective approach holds any promise of greater things to come. (Holmes 1978: 81)

(e) A Semiotic Approach

In this Section, it will be shown that other approaches can be more relevant such as Levý's (1969) semiotic or structural analysis within the Prague school of linguists which reveals how many significant features are hidden even in one line of children's or 'nonsense' poetry. The concept of semiotics is used in a special sense with regard to literary translation which is not so much concerned with semiotics as strictly defined by classical linguists such as De Saussure (1959) in which texts are studied as linguistic entities, but more as *second-order semiotic systems* as defined by Hatim and Mason (1998):

> Roland Barthes, particularly in his work on myth, pioneered investigations into what came to be known as *second-order semiotic systems*. These are systems which, in order to signify, build on other systems. Literature is an ideal example of such systems in that, primarily

through the element of 'creativity', it provides an alternative to the real world. (Hatim and Mason 1998: 112)

Thus a text can be seen as a system of signs with its own internal dynamics rather than as a string of lexical items for which equivalents need to be sought. The semiotic analysis is fruitful because it represents a radical break from the traditional hidebound stances using the outworn *faithful/free* terminology. Fidelity is now seen in terms of fidelity to a certain semiotic process or language game rather than mere semantic fidelity to a string of lexical items. Levý adopts Klemensiewicz's (1955) definition of the semiotic approach, which is used specifically in a translation context:

> Das Original sollte als ein System und nicht als eine Summe von Elementen betrachtet werden, als organische Ganzheit und nicht als eine mechanische Ansammlung von Elementen. Die Aufgabe des Übersetzers besteht weder darin zu reproduzieren, noch darin, die Elemente und Strukturen des Originals umzuformen, sondern darin, *ihre Funktion zu erfassen und solche Elemente der eigenen Sprache anzuwenden*, die, soweit wie möglich, deren Ersatz und Gegenwert mit der gleichen funktionalen Eignung und Wirksamkeit sein könnten. (Levý 1969: 21-22. My emphasis.)

Levý then goes to make the inherent semiotic approach in Klemensiewicz's definition explicit:

> Die strukturelle Linguistik findet ihre logische Fortsetzung in der Semiotik, der allgemeinen Theorie von Zeichensystemen, die die Sprache als Code auffaßt, d. h. als einen Komplex von sprachlichen Elementen (z. B. Wortzeichen) und Regeln für deren Kombination. (Levý 1969: 21-22)

Levý's (1969) attempt at evolving a semiotic theory for poetry translation is particularly interesting because he illustrates the problem of translating poetry in a clear and concrete fashion by taking his examples from Christian Morgenstern whose clever but charming nonsense rhymes may, in fact, seem untranslatable. The Levý proves the opposite is the case both at the theoretical level and by concrete examples taken from Max Knight's translations of Morgenstern. At one level, his examples could be criticised as trivial, but they reveal how a gifted poet such as Morgenstern conceals a multitude of subtleties in a three-line poem. In their very simplicity, they provide a paradigmatic example of the essential problem of literary translation in general and poetry translation in particular. At the same time, they show that even light humorous poetry can conceal a number of subtle language games which are deciphered in Levý's semiotic analysis.

Invidious though the division between form and content may be and even though the greatest poetry is such a subtle blend of both that form and content can hardly be distinguished, the translator needs to make this distinction before work is begun. In narrative verse such as popular ballads, content would seem to be the major factor as long as a basic ballad form is maintained whereas with humorous and nonsense poetry, the content could in certain cases almost be said to be the form itself. This point is illustrated by Levý with regard to Christian Morgenstern's non-sense poem in the following example:

> Ein Wiesel
> saß auf einem Kiesel
> inmitten Bachgeriesel. (Levý 1969: 103)

together with Max Knight's inventive version:

> A weasel
> perched on an easel
> within a patch of teasel. (Levý 1969: 104)

Levý rightly notes that in such verses the form is far more important than the content:

> In Christian Morgensterns Gedicht *Das ästhetische Wiesel* ist das Reimspiel wesentlicher als die zoologische und topographische Genauigkeit, denn Morgenstern selbst fügt hinzu:
>> Das raffinierte Tier
>> Tat's um des Reimes willen. (Levý 1969: 104)

Knight offers several alternatives claiming that they are equally acceptable and is supported by Levý in this opinion as quoted above. Knight's ingenious inventions are as follows:

> A ferret
> nibbling a carrot
> in a garret.

Or

> A mink
> sipping a drink
> in a kitchen sink.

Or

> A hyena
> playing a concertina
> in an arena.

Or

> A lizard
> shaking its gizzard
> in a blizzard.

(Levý 1969: 104)

In an *academic translation* with the stress on semantic equivalence, the 'poem' would be absurdly flat and dull:

A weasel

sat on a pebble

in the midst of a ripple of a brook.* (Translation from Levý 1967)

Levý's semiotic approach attempts to identify the semiotics of the poem and presents these factors diagrammatically. As this approach will be subjected to critical analysis, it is worth quoting Levý in full:

> Die Varianten der Übersetzungen von Morgensterns Wortspielen drängen uns die Frage auf, was alle diese Substitutionen eigentlich bewahren, welche Invariante ihnen allen mit dem Original gemeinsam ist. Wenn wir die allen Lösungen gemeinsamen Zügen abstrahieren, können wir folgendes sagen: allen Übersetzungen bleibt gemeinsam die Konfrontation der Reimübereinstimmung von 1. Dem Namen des Tieres, 2. Dem Objekt, zu dem seine Tätigkeit hinstrebt, 3. Dem Schauplatz. In allen fünf Übersetzungen sind gerade nur diese abstrakten Funktionen der drei einzelnen Verse in der Gesamtheit des Wortspiels erhalten und keineswegs die konkreten Bedeutungen der einzelnen Wörter. Anders ausgedrückt haben einige Wörter in Morgensterns Text zwei semantische Funktionen: 1. Eine denotative eigene Bedeutung, 2. Die Funktion in einer Struktur höherer Ordnung (eben diese blieb in den Übersetzungen gewahrt):

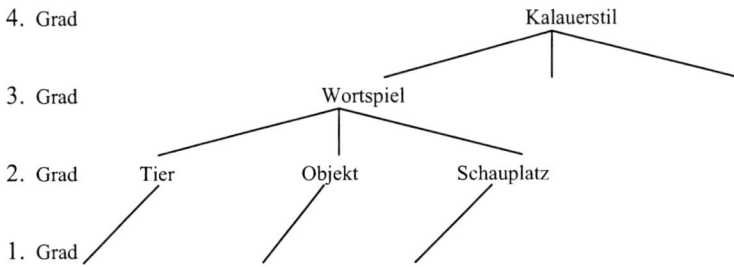

Ein Wiesel saß auf einem Kiesel inmitten Bachgeriesel (Levý 1969: 104)

Levý rightly claims that there is a hierarchy of priorities[38]:

---

[38] Gutt (2000) questions the validity of setting up functional hierarchical criteria: "[. . .] it is not clear on what principles Levý's hierarchy is constructed [. . .]. Thus the overall organization of this hierarchy remains unclear." (Gutt 2000: 383-384). At the formal linguistic level, Gutt has a point, but he goes on to say that this is not of prime importance: "However, it seems more than doubtful anyway that 'such functional hierarchies' play any significant role here at all. What is actually being done here can be both *accounted for* and *evaluated* in terms of interpretive use within the relevance-theoretic framework." (Gutt 2000: 384). As the scientific linguistic approach to these problems has been found to be inadequate, the methodology of this section has been from the outset "within the relevance-theoretic framework." Although a critic from the cognitive approach, Gutt admits in conclusion that the interpretive approach is the more fruitful for this kind of analysis: "Thus it seems that an account of translation as interlingual interpretive use has much to commend it. In fact, it could be said to achieve what translation theory has been attempting to do for a long time - that is to develop a concept of faithfulness that is generally applicable and yet both text- and context-specific." (Gutt 2000: 384).

> Das literarische Werk ist ein System von sprachlichen Zeichen, von denen einige neben ihrer
> konkreten denotativen Bedeutung noch eine allgemeinere Aussagefunktion höherer Ordnung
> haben, d. h. ein Bestandteil von Zeichensystemen höherer Ordnung sind. (Levý 1969: 105)

In this case, the *höhere Ordnung* would refer to the humorous poetry or *Kalauerstil*. It is clear that if a translator were commissioned to translate a book of Morgenstern's lighter verses, possibly to entertain children (and parents!), a prose translation would be absurd as has been shown in the example of literal translation. This also applies to any attempt to stick rigidly to the content in the vain search for equivalents. Versions such as those offered by Knight would be far more acceptable. Even so, objections could be made that they are not really translations, but such objections are easily refuted because they would represent a misunderstanding of the whole translation process. The Morgenstern poem provides the counterargument to the untranslatability school with utmost clarity because Levý's semiotic analysis shows that certain elements of semantic content are either secondary or irrelevant and that other formal features comprise the essence of the poem, and thus, in a certain sense, provide the content. Levý's clear analysis shows that, if the poems are conceived as semiotic systems involving a hierarchical structure, then parallel semiotic systems (semiotically though not semantically equivalent) can be produced with similar material to produce a similar effect, thus, from a semiotic point of view, satisfying adequacy criteria for functional[39] or dynamic[40] equivalence. The concept of 'equivalence' is now being stretched to the limit in comparison with the other precise scientific definitions in the previous chapter so that, at this stage, the use of this term must be questioned. Again, the question arises concerning the scope of the equivalent, which, in this example, refers to the whole of the three-line poem.

Despite his brilliant analysis, Levý fails to differentiate sufficiently with regard to qualitative matters by blithely categorising the five poetic translations as all *equally* valid. He quotes Knight's comments to the same effect:

> [. . .] und fügt im Vorwort *richtig* hinzu, daß anderslautende Übersetzungen *ebenso möglich*
> wären. (Levý 1969: 104. My emphasis.)

To regard each version to be equally good would seem to be a fallacy which will be demonstrated by detailed analysis. It is a pity, however, that, in his analysis, Levý seems to be satisfied with functional equivalence as adequate for literary translation. It is, however, the qualitative differentiation which should be the essential activity of

---

[39] See Osers' clear definition of functional equivalence in the footnote 26.
[40] See also (Nida 2000: 129) together with the discussion at the beginning of part (c) in Chapter VI.

literary translation criticism, but with many linguistic theoreticians, the debate remains merely at the 'adequacy' or, in this case, the functional equivalence level. Just as the translator of poetry has to be something of a poet, the literary translation theoretician has to become involved in literary criticism. Barnstone (1993) goes one step further by claiming that literary criticism and translation are identical in that both are concerned with interpretation or "reading":

> Translation theory and literary theory come together in the act common to them both: reading. Reading is an act of interpretation, which is itself an act of translation (an intralingual translation from graphic sign to mind). [. . .] Hence *reading is translation and translation is reading.* (Barnstone 1993: 7. Author's italics.)

Certainly, from Levý's semiotic analysis all the five poems are formally equivalent in that they fulfil the criteria defined by Levý's analysis, but his analysis is by no means exhaustive. There are other factors such as the naturalness of both the picture painted together with the rhyme, the coherence of the whole picture and the whimsical nature of the humour.

The first version "A weasel/perched on an easel/within a patch of teasel" obviously depends on the very few rhymes for *weasel*, if this subject of the poem is to be retained semantically. However, the idea of a weasel perched on an easel is awkward in comparison with the weasel sitting on a pebble in a brook. In addition, the noun *teasel* is obscure in contrast to *Bachgeriesel* which blends semantically, sonically and even scenically with *Kiesel* together with its echo of both *Geröll* and *Geräusch* (and the idea of *rieseln*).

The second translation, "A ferret/ nibbling a carrot/ in a garret" would seem to be much weaker, partly because of impure feminine rhyme (*fer*ret/*car*rot) in a poem where felicitous use of rhyme is paramount and partly because of the inappropriacy of *garret* which has too poetic and inappropriate literary associations in this context and which result in an incomplete picture so that the last line is something of an anti-climax.

The third version "A mink/sipping a drink/in a kitchen sink" has something of the naturalness and simplicity of the original. The incongruity of the refined activity of *sipping a drink* contrasting with the banality of *kitchen sink* strikes a humorous note which compensates for the lack of unity in the original German version where a full natural picture is conveyed as if in three brush strokes with the three very short lines. If this 'mink' version were to be further 'translated' into a picture, an amusing scene could be provided by the illustrator such as a very refined mink sipping from a cocktail glass in a very sordid kitchen sink. I would go one step further in Levý' hierarchy, which places *Kalauerstil* at the top as the most important element, to maintain that the final 'court of appeal' within the semiotic hierarchy for deciding the success of the poem is the very combination of its humorous and aesthetic impact. Thus, this version would seem to have succeeded the most by producing an almost equally humorous and pleasing effect.

The fourth version "A hyena/ playing a concertina/ in an arena" has now moved entirely away from the rodent world and thus is much semantically 'freer' than the others. A vivid picture is portrayed as in the original although the absurd effect of *playing a concertina* would have been best left to the last line if possible to avoid the slight anti-climax of the conventional context *in an arena*. The last 'poem' would seem to be the weakest, *A lizard/ shaking his gizzard/ in a blizzard* where there seems to be rhyme only for rhyme's sake without any compensating literary effects such as humour.

There are numerous possibilities which would fulfil Levý's semiotic criteria. One more example is offered to illustrate this point:

> A stoat
>
> Almost afloat
>
> In a castle moat.

This version[41] also fulfils Levý's criteria of functional equivalence whilst supplying an element of humour with the qualifier *almost* which could imply that the poor rodent is having trouble keeping its head above water. This version also satisfies more semantic element with the close relative of the rodent world, i.e. the *stoat*, (even though the semantic elements are relatively minor importance, they are not to be wholly ignored). However, there is the loss of the natural surroundings which is only partially compensated by the relatively exotic medieval background.

From this analysis it can be concluded that being 'true' to the original does not necessarily consist in finding a string of semantic equivalents to correspond to each of the original elements but involves the semiotic features included in Levý's analysis and also other factors which lie outside his analysis, i.e. those more elusive though no less real features such as the mood, the spirit, the diction, the humour and the

---

[41] This version was supplied by Andrew Gledhill.

naturalness of the original. Thus a new definition of fidelity is emerging. The analysed examples have made this point clear.

(f) Deconstruction and Implications on Post-Derridean Translation Theory

It will be seen in this analysis that Gentzler is justified when he asserts that the insights of deconstructionists offer many valuable insights to literary translation theory:

> I would like to suggest, however, that the deconstructionists' entire project is intricately relevant to questions of translation theory, and their thinking is seminal to any understanding of the theoretical problems of that translation process. (Gentzler 1993: 146)

Derrida's use of his coined word *différance* as opposed to *différence* to imply a deferring of meaning in a twilight zone of non-existence, an area between the original writer's conception of an idea to the infinity of possible translations is certainly at the opposite end of the spectrum from the formalist and 'scientific' schools of translation which search after 'the' equivalent or, at least, after a restricted number of possible equivalents. It has, however, already been shown that the precision of the scientific schools of translation is illusory. The surface vagueness of Derrida is, by no means, meaningless or too obscure because Derrida has an immediate liberating effect for the translator. It has already been shown that great translations can be great works of art. The translator is now invited to enter into the world of *différance*, "this bottomless chessboard on which Being is put into play" (Derrida 1982: 22), where the original has no automatic priority and where the translator is free to join the eternal game of deferring meaning, of creating his or her own forms and meaning. The difference and status of original and translation, of author and adapter are now blurred.

To illustrate this theory, it would be helpful to look at a theme in European literature such as the 'Faust' legend. The status of the original legend is secondary. The first known compilation of the Faust legend in 1587 was *Die Historie des Dr. Faust* by an unknown author and was no more than a series of entertaining anecdotes. Christopher Marlowe's masterpiece, *The Tragical History of the Life and Death of Dr. Faustus* (1997), first published in 1593, was the first great literary work based on the legend and in a post-Derridean sense could be said to be a 'translation' of the original German set of anecdotes into an English tragedy. Goethe's 'translation' of the legend is yet another step in this direction. These literary transformations which could serve as examples of Derrida's idea of translation as διαφερειν or 'transporting across' can now be taken one step further so that the 'chasm' separating 'original' work from 'translation' is now crossed:

> Différance is never pure, no more so is translation, and for the notion of translation we would have to substitute a notion of transformation: a regulated transformation of one language by another, of one text by another. We will never have, and in fact have never had, to do with some 'transport' of pure signifiers from one language to another, or within one and the same language, that the signifying instrument would leave virgin and untouched. (Derrida 1981: 20)

Now the Derridean paradox of the source being also dependent on the translation is becoming clearer.

Thus, the highest level of literary translation involves a process akin to the highest level of literary creation. This point will be amply illustrated by the two examples in Sections (f) and (g). The medium may change in the process of διαφερειν as is the case with the many musical versions of the Faust legend such as Gounot's *Faust*, Berlioz's *La Damnation de Faust,* Busoni's *Dr. Faust*, Liszt's *A Faust Symphony* and Spohr's *Faust* to name just a few of the more well-known works. In a post-Derridean context, Visconti's (1971) film *Death in Venice* could be said to be a 'translation' of Mann's work, but again into a different medium. These examples of transformation constitute examples of Derrida's notion of survival in the sense of *Fortleben* (continuing to live as a work of art) rather than *Überleben* (merely surviving as manuscript rather than text):

> Just as the manifestations of life are intimately connected with the living, without signifying anything for it, a translation proceeds from the original. Indeed not so much as from its life as from its survival (Überleben). For a translation comes after the original and, for the important works that never find their predestined translator at the time of their birth, it characterises the stage of their survival. ('Fortleben,' this time sur-vival as continuation of life rather than life as post-mortem.) (Derrida 1985: 178)

This discourse has taken translation theory to its extreme limit, but it is a debate which could well be pursued further. An interesting study could be to show, for example, how much hidden translation there can be in an 'original' work and conversely, how much creativity there can be in a successful literary translation. Thomas Mann's *Der Tod in Venedig* is a prime example of this. 'The Phaedo Dialogues', for example, are a translation of a translation:

> Plato may have been the source for both writers. Rilke was a friend of Rudolf Kaßner, whose versions of *Phaedrus* and the *Symposium* Thomas Mann used. (Reed 1994: 118)

Another example is Mann's quotation and translation of the *Liebestod* scenes from *Tristan und Isolde* in his novella *Tristan* – again, the Wagner version itself is a translation as $\delta\iota\alpha\varphi\varepsilon\rho\varepsilon\iota\nu$ of Gottfried von Strassburg's *Tristan* which in turn was a translation (and improvement on) Chrétien de Troyes' *Tristan et Yseut*. To take the post-Derridean discourse one step further, it can be argued that part of Mann's originality is his ability to 'translate' ($\delta\iota\alpha\varphi\varepsilon\rho\varepsilon\iota\nu$) his own everyday experiences into story and myth reflecting the fundamental themes that were a constant part of his life. Translation can thus be understood as one of the most creative intellectual activities, but, like great literary writing, the translation process involves a creativity which combines craftsmanship with a perspicacious interpretation of the source text. It is thus not surprising that, according to Gentzler, translation is 'a', if not 'the' central theme in Derrida's philosophy:

> According to Derrida, *all* of philosophy is centrally concerned with the notion of translation: "the origin of philosophy is translation or the thesis of translatability." (Gentzler 1993: 146)

Inspiring though Derrida's analysis may be, he has little to offer the translator in concrete terms other than advice to the effect that the translator of a great work of literature should simply produce another great work of literature on the same theme in the target language. It is for this reason it will be more useful to illustrate this approach with two case studies: Joyce's own translation of *Finnegans Wake* into Italian and two versions of Hölderlin's translation of twenty lines taken from the chorus of Sophocles' *Antigone*.

(f) A Post-Derridean Case Study: Joyce's Own Italian Version of *Finnegans Wake*

Poetic discourse can have many levels of richness, ambiguity, density and complexity, but perhaps one of the most complex examples of poetic prose in the twentieth century is James Joyce's *Finnegans Wake*. If ever a work has been untranslatable, this must be a prime example. Yet, perhaps precisely for this reason, this text has been tackled by a great number of translators including several German translators such as Ulrich Blumenbach, Reinhard Markner, Dieter Stündel, Friedhelm Rathjen and Arno Schmidt among others whose works appear in Reichert's (1988) collection of *Finnegans Wake* translations into German. Reichert makes this point on the inside sleeve of his translation collection:

> 1998 jährt sich zum 50. Male das Erscheinen von *Finnegans Wake,* des unverständlichsten Werkes der Weltliteratur. Das Werk gilt als unübersetzbar, und dennoch, *oder gerade deshalb,* hat es immer wieder Übersetzer und Schriftsteller, Außenseiter und Fachleute gereizt, Übersetzungen zu probieren. Joyce selbst hat dazu den Anstoß gegeben, als er Beckett und andere Freunde ermunterte, eine längere Passage ins Französische zu übertragen. Inzwischen

gibt es größere Auszüge aus dem Werk auf französisch und italienisch. (Reichert 1988: Frontpiece inside sleeve. My emphasis.)

It is unfortunately beyond the scope of this dissertation to compare any of the various attempts to translate sections of *Finnegans Wake*, other than to mention the fact that some versions of *Finnegans Wake* can, in my opinion, only be described as brilliant. It would be equally interesting to compare Samuel Beckett's and Philippe Soupault's French translation of the "Anna Livia Plurabelle" passage of *Finnegans Wake* with Joyce's own Italian translation, but this would be good material for another dissertation. What is relevant in the context of this dissertation is to disprove the untranslatability school and the best counter-example is Joyce's own translation of a few pages of the "Anna Livia Plurabelle " chapter into Italian, which will act as the case study for this Section. This translation can also be regarded as a classic illustration of what is meant by the post-Derridean approach.

The first article written on Joyce's translation into Italian was by Risset (1985) to which Gentzler (1993) then referred when placing Joyce's translation within a post-Derridean context:

> In circles, much of the discussion of deconstruction, translation and the nature of language centers around writing by James Joyce, and strategies preferred by his translators. Perhaps the best example of the practice of "affirmative productivity" as preferred by deconstructionists is James Joyce's own translation of two passages from *Finnegans Wake*. (Gentzler 1993: 169)

Whether this is the ideal context or not, it is convenient to discuss this work within post-Derridean and deconstructionist discourse. It attempts to describe the process behind what in the cases under discussion can perhaps only be referred to as 'genius-level' translation. The basic meaning of this term is that a great work of art in one language is transformed into a great work art in another language whilst paralleling the original at the deepest level. The second aspect of this definition is that the original does not necessarily have a higher status than the translation, which is fundamentally opposed to the 'canonised' status of the original as in the theorising of Benjamin, for example. Joyce's own Italian translation of *Finnegans Wake* is a transformation ($\delta\iota\alpha\varphi\varepsilon\rho\varepsilon\iota\nu$) of a multilingual text into a monolingual but 'multi-dialectal' text. Risset (1985) maintains that Joyce managed to fuse various Italian dialects with the supporting base of Dante's own rich dialectal usage:

> This out-and-out Italianisation, this liberty in the emendation of the text, is based upon the exact and simultaneous use of different areas and levels of Italian: in particular, dialects (above all Venetian, Triestian, Tuscan), literary archaisms (drawn from Dante, from Florentine comedy or

> from the poetry and drama of D'Annunzio), specialised idiom (that of the opera for instance).
> These layers are not juxtaposed, but mixed and fused. Lofty discourse is assimilated, absorbed in
> the context; one needs a second process of analysis to distinguish under the seemingly
> homogeneous level of the spoken discourse. (Risset 1984: 12)

This is perhaps one of the reasons why Risset does not like the word *translation* in this context even though this is the word used by Joyce and his collaborators in this enterprise as she herself does in the title to this essay "Joyce Translates Joyce":

> But this Italian text from *Finnegans Wake* cannot really be called - in the usual sense of the word -
> a translation at all; for what takes place is a complete rewriting, *a later elaboration of the original*,
> which consequently does not stand opposite the new version as 'original text', but as 'work in
> progress'. (Risset 1984: 3. My emphasis.)

The italicised phrase *a later elaboration of the original* is a concrete example of Derrida's idea of *différance* or, in other words, deferring the final version, deferring meanings in a flux of reworkings. What is generally not understood is that literary translation at the highest level is both 'translation' and rewriting at the same time. As has been argued, the term *translation* includes a wide variety of interpretative activities as listed from Wilss in Chapter I.

At this point, it is appropriate to analyse one sentence of the text in detail to illustrate Joyce's translation technique as a form of post-Derridean translation. The full text of Joyce's Italian translation of the "Anna Livia" chapter is included in the Risset article and the following sentence taken from the "Anna Livia Plurabella" section of *Finnegans Wake* has been selected for analysis because it has been rightly quoted by Gentzler (1993) as an example of post-Derridean translation although Gentzler does not undertake a detailed analysis:

> Annona gebroren aroostokrat Nivia, *dochter* of Sense and Art, with Spark's
> piryphlickathims funkling her fran [. . .]. (Joyce 1993: 199. My emphasis.)

Joyce's Italian translation is also taken from the same page in Gentzler:

> Annona genata arusticrata Nivea, *laureolata* in Senso e Arte, il ventaglio costellata di
> filgettanti [. . .]. (Gentzler 1993: 170. My emphasis.)

As this is such a wonderful example of something that is both translation and rewriting by a great literary and linguistic talent, it might be interesting to begin by dwelling on the translation of one word, the translation of the noun *dochter* by *laureolata*. *Dochter* here is a pun, based on the German nouns *Tochter* (daughter) and *Doktor* implying that Annona is both a specialist (*Doktor*) in "Sense and Art" as well as being formed by them in the most natural way possible (*Tochter*) whereas the Italianate participle *laureolata* is a quite different pun but with similar import whilst being more suited to Italian culture. There is not only the idea of Annona being given the (Roman) 'laurel' crown (*alloro*) by "Sense and Art" because of her accomplishment, but also that art has both beautified and beatified her with its own 'aureole' or 'halo' (*l'aureola*). The translation conveys both ideas, or, in other words, she is both very knowledgeable and gifted or 'blessed' by 'sense and art'. The original involves a heavier more Germanic pun suitable for the Anglo-Saxon world of Northern Europe whereas *laureolata* not only echoes the idea of the *l'aureola* of ancient Italy but also evokes the saints and painters of medieval Italy such as Giotto's famous painting of St. Francis of Assisi with his head surrounded by a very powerful *aureola* or halo. Also *laureata* is the Italian word for some one who has received a doctorate, which is, at the same time, a close translation of the term *doctor* in this context.

In the original version, the rhythmical effects are hard and alliterative with the repetition of fricatives, consonant clusters and plosives so that it has an 'Anglo-Saxon' or 'Germanic' ring. This 'Anglo-Saxon' element is also compounded by a hint of humorous obscenity in the phrase *funkling her fran* taken from the same sentence:

> Annona *gebroren aroostokrat* Nivia, *dochter* of sense and Art, with Spark's *piryphlickathims funkling her fran* . . . (Emphasis added and underling to highlight the alliterative phonic effect.)

In contrast, the Italian version is sonorous and musical depending on the rich play of the endings such as the repetition of the feminine ending *ata* echoing the idea and sound of *Arte* even though this is not a case of perfect rhyme:

> Annona genata arusticrata Nivea, laureolata in Senso e Arte, il ventaglio costellata di filgettanti. (My underlining to emphasise the rhymed endings.)

The process can be described in terms of a multi-dimensional analysis or deconstruction of the source text and a radical reconstruction in the translation so that the two texts closely parallel each other as translations whilst, at the same time, reading as profoundly original works of literature - a multi-lingual but basically European text is transformed into a musical and multi-dialectal Italian creation. It involves semiotics, deconstruction and reconstruction and so is, at a deeper level 'faithful' to the original, i.e. at the semiotic level as defined in Section (e) of this chapter, whilst, at the same time, reading like an original work with a similar richness, density, ambiguity, profundity and musicality to these elements in the original, which, in turn, is seen as *différance* or work in progress. Risset maintains that it is the multi-dialectal language of Dante that holds the work together, but it is not a case of Dante as traditionally understood but more a resurrection and 're-creation'of Dante's language:

> Joyce evokes, in other words, something very different from the traditional Dante: not the corpus of culture, not the Bible, but the living root of the language, beyond sense - yet in a way which takes up the same direction experienced by Dante. What is captured is precisely a movement (generally congealed even in the boldest literary ventures) between 'tongue' (lingua) and sentence (sentenza), a movement along a line of extreme tension between two levels (also between 'langue' and 'parole'), the opposite of the 'normal' movement: not the word which rises from the language and then forgets it, but the word which turns towards the language and 'excavates' it. [. . .] The project of translation, as the analysis illuminates, has finally as its deep aim the *'re-creation' in the Italian language of the experience of Dante*. (Risset 1984: 7. My emphasis.)

However, to describe Joyce's translation as re-creation is not totally accurate as the Italian version is in some ways a very close translation and to describe it as translation in the narrow academic sense of the word is also not totally accurate because the reformulation is, at the surface level, semantically so different that another process is taking place. This is the area where fidelity is more to the density, musicality and diction (in this case, wit) of the text rather a mere search for semantic 'equivalents'. This point is recognised by Risset:

> At the same time this total immersion in the world of idiomatic Italian is far removed from simple mimesis, from a reduction to the spoken level of discourse. On the contrary, analysing the language of the passage one finds the text organized entirely according to the rules of a poetic language within three levels: rhythm, syntactic structure, phonic texture. (Risset 1984: 7.)

The semiotics of the text involves the aspects "rhythm, syntactic structure, phonic texture" as well as semantic richness (paranomasia with multifarious connotations) and cross-cultural language games. The semantic surface is still retained with Joyce so that it is still a translation, which is also a literary work in itself. It is at this interface (translation versus literary creation) that the surface vagueness of many of Derrida's pronouncements over the status of the translation vis-à-vis the original begins to make sense.

Risset concludes her analysis with a clear rejection of the traditional equivalence approach in translation theory even though her article, at times, reflects the language of the linguistic approach with frequent reference to concepts such as *equivalence* itself:

> Every translation which becomes fixed on the problem of semantic and local phonetic
> equivalence is doomed to fail in its purpose, to miss *Finnegans Wake*, the stream of *Finnegans*
> *Wake*. But a translation able to rediscover and extend this stream was perhaps only to be
> achieved in this formula: *Joyce translator of Joyce, under the aegis of Dante*. (Risset 1984: 3.
> Risset's emphasis.)

To translate like Joyce, you have to write like Joyce, or at the very least be a brilliant
imitator of his style. Although Risset does not make any explicit reference to Derrida
or to other deconstructionists, her article uses similar language to describe this
translation process so that there is a tension between the two poles of literary creation
on the one hand and close translation on the other, which explains her reluctance to
regard the work as a translation, at least "in the traditional sense". This is another
reason why Gentzler's coining of the term post-Derridean would seem appropriate in
this context:

> The Italian version affords a special perspective on Joyce's work, permitting us to analyse in
> another language what Joyce termed '*the technique of deformation*', showing how the text is
> worked and *transformed*. Moreover (and it is perhaps what emerges most strikingly and
> fruitfully), in this translation one can catch the complexity and boldness of Joyce's technique
> of linguistic arrangement as it were in the very act, to reveal a very rich process, one perhaps
> unique in this field: namely an exploration of the furthest limits of the Italian language
> conducted by a great writer; a writer who was not Italian, but, according to his collaborators,
> 'italianista unico'. (Risset 1984: 3. My emphasis.)

Risset rightly sees this 'translation' as *transformation*, another Derridean term. This
area of creative twilight beautifully illustrates the Derridean notion of *différance* with
the idea of deferring meaning until the whole text is both deconstructed and
reconstructed in a seemingly endless Heraclitean flux of parallel but constantly
shifting meanings. This is not to imply that Derrida had another hidden agenda of
intending to produce a Joycean translation theory, but rather that his ideas, like those
of the polysystem and *skopos* theories, liberate the translator from the surface-level
semantic 'tyranny' of the original, and, more than this, allow the translator to
participate in the process of creative transformation.

I also agree with Gentzler's coinage *post-Derridean*, which is not the
same as Derridean. Derrida's ideas provoke, stimulate and often infuriate the reader.
Searle (1977), one of the many critics of Derrida as philosopher, has a point with his
assertion:

> Derrida has a distressing penchant for saying things that are obviously false. (Searle
> 1977: 203)

Derrida had no blue-print for a new translation theory or, even more so, could be said to be hostile to such an approach so that there is no embarrassment to the post-Derridean literary translation theorist in being labelled in some respects as anti-Derridean because the post-Derrideans, as defined by Gentzler, try to make sense out of the deliberate Derridean chaos, by finding meaning within the Derridean vacuum.[42] A post-Derridean approach by no means involves abandoning many of the useful insights of the linguists with regard to translation theory, but merely finds the linguists' categories break down when confronted with the highest literature and that many of the paradoxical assertions of Derrida can, in the hands of a post-Derriean theorist, act as a stimulus for a more radical and successful approach to the translation of the highest literature, as will also be seen in the next case study.

(g) A Case Study: Hölderlin's Translation of Sophocles' *Antigone*

According to Schadewaldt (1970) basing his ideas on an earlier study by Beißner, the translations of Hölderlin fall into three phases, which in themselves reflect a progression from *academic translation* to 'foreignising' or 'semantic' translation and finally, to "erneuerndes Nachgestalten" or, in other words, what might be described as post-Derridean 'transformation':

> Wie die eindringlichen Stilbeobachtungen Friedrich Beißners gezeigt haben, lassen sich an dem Übersetzungswerk Hölderlins vor allem drei Stilstufen unterscheiden: eine umsetzende Übersetzungsart, in der nach der herkömmlichen Weise des Übersetzens der im Zusammenhang erfaßte Sinn in freierer Form im ganzen wiedergegeben wird, eine genau hinhörende, nachformende, in der jedes einzelne Wort ernst genommen und vor allem auch die Wortfolge ernst genommen wird, und eine aus einer neu erreichten tiefen 'Innigkeit' des Wort- und Sinnverständnisses geschöpfte frei deutende dichterische Art des 'Übersetzens', das

---

[42] An example of the inherent ambiguity in the various Derridean approaches can be invoked to provide a theory which would seem to be the opposite of Gentzler's, i.e. that words are fundamentally untranslatable as is argued by Delabastita (1997): "Deconstructionists have indeed a clear tendency to conceive translation in function of problematic *words* (especially proper names and polysemic words) rather than texts [. . .] as well as to promote untranslatability to an *absolute* principle or blanket rule. [. . .] These are certainly among the points that would need to be re-examined if deconstructionist critics and more empirically orientated translation scholars should one day attempt to meet halfway." (Delabastita 1997: 226-27; Emphasis as in the original text.) Davies (1997), on the other hand, holds the middle ground between Gentzler and Delabastita: "If a text were *totally* translatable, it would exhibit no difference from some other text (its translation), and it would, therefore, disappear into that with which it would already be identical. Likewise, in order to be *totally un*translatable, a text would bear no relation at all to the language system(s) in which other texts are written: irrevocably self-contained, it would die immediately. Both of these scenarios are unrealistic, of course. Derrida is, in part, pointing out what translation scholars well know: translation is always relative, and relative translation is always possible." (Davies 1997: 33)

Phase one falls within the scope of what has been defined as *academic translation*. Phases two and three are well illustrated by Hölderlin's two translations of the same verses taken from the Greek chorus lines in Sophocles' *Antigone*. Both translations will be analysed in this Section because they are eminently suitable for study being amongst the very best creations and poems of the great poet. They reveal a progression from a foreignised translation to an equally close translation, which becomes poetry at the highest level. The context for these magnificent verses concerns Antigone's tragic decision to bury her brother, Polyneikes against the orders of Creon and the town authorities. Creon has just threatened the death penalty for any one who disobeys his orders. The mood is of extreme tension caused by impending doom and the chorus looks at the situation from the point of view of extreme detachment wondering at the cleverness and power of mortal man who is also capable of great evil and great evil is sure to follow as a result of the conflict:

πολλα τα δεινα κουδεν αν-
θρωπου δεινοτερον πελει
τουτο και τε πολιου περαν
ποντου χειμεριω νοτω
χορει περιβρυχιοισιν
περων υπ οιδμασιν, θεων
τε ταν υπερταταν, Γαν
αφθιτον, ακαματαν αποτρυεται,
ιλλομενων ετοσ εισ ετοσ,
ιππειω γενει πολευων.

κουφονοων τε φυλον ορ-
νιθων αμφιβαλων αγρει
και θηρων αγριων εθνη
ποντου τ' ειναλιαν φυσι
σπειραισι δικτυοκλωστοις,
περιφραδης ανηρ κρατει
δε μαχαναις αγραυλου
θηρος ορεσσιβατα, λασιαυχενα θ'
ιππον υπαξεμεν αμφιλοφον ζυγον

οεριον τ' ακμητα ταυρον. (Sophokles 1985: 215-216: lines: 331-352. Accentuation omitted.)

Constantine (1990), however, appropriately sets the context at a much deeper level, expressing the situation in terms of catastrophe and immanence, using Hölderlin's own vocabulary to interpret the spiritual and philosophical background to the play:

> Antigone is set, according to Hölderlin, like his own Empedokeles, at a time of upheaval and change, and is a document of it. The quarrel between Creon and Antigone is in that sense emblematic. A new order is being brought about, a republican one (v. 272). Creon and Antigone struggle in the meantime, at the turning point, as two principles: law and (in Hölderlin's sense) sobriety versus pure fire, 'lawlessness'. Creon is 'förmlich', she is 'gegenförmlich' (v. 272). Antigone pits herself against Creon with an ecstatic violence; she is as bent on conjuring up catastrophe as Oedipus is. Both figures, in Hölderlin's view, 'force God to appear', they bring about immanence precisely in the moment of their tragedy. This hubristic, coercive tendency is present in Empedokeles too, and in Hölderlin's poetics. The ground of feeling in Hölderlin's work was always the longing for immanence, and his persistent preoccupation with these two holy texts and with the mechanics of tragedy has undertones of an increasing desperation. Steiner detects in Hölderlin's Sophocles 'a solicitation of chaos', rightly, I think. (Constantine 1990: 295)

Using Hölderlin's language, law and order are defined as *das Organische* in contrast with the "ecstatic violence" (*das Aorgische*) with which Antigone embraces her fate. It is tempting to re-interpret these in the post-Nietzschean sense as *das Apollonische* and *das Dionysische*, but something different is meant by Hölderlin's concept of *das Organische* as this repressively structuring principle tends towards rigid order, thus towards tyranny, punishment and death rather than to Apollonian beauty creating form, order and harmony (music). Although *das Aorgische* like Dionysian tendencies is ecstatically destructive, a moral harmony is reached in death through *das Aorgische* whereas the Dionysian destruction destroys all those who have the misfortune to fall within its orgiastic wake. *Das Aorgische* is less a "solicitation of chaos" as Steiner and Constantine maintain, but more a solicitation of God within a 'moral' self-destructive frenzy culminating in a manifestation or 'epiphany' that leads to tragic death and, ultimately to a solemn peace. Hölderlin's translation reflects the 'metaphysical' dimension of these themes.

Hölderlin's first translation written in 1799 fits neatly into Schadewaldt's second category, "eine genau hinhörende, nachformende, in der jedes einzelne Wort ernst genommen und vor allem auch die Wortfolge ernst genommen wird," with the syntax of the very compact Greek compounds being retained:

Vieles gewaltge giebts. Doch nichts

Ist gewaltiger, als der Mensch.

Denn der schweiffet im grauen

Meer' in stürmischer Südluft

Umher in woogenumrauschten

Geflügelten Wohnungen.

Der Götter heiliger Erde, sie, die

Reine, die mühelose,

Arbeitet er um, das Pferdegeschlecht

Am leichtbewegten Pflug von

Jahr zu Jahr umtreibend.

Leichtgeschaffener Vogelart

Legt er Schlingen, verfolget sie,

Und der Thiere wildes Volk,

Und des salzigen Meeres Geschlecht

Mit listiggeschlungenen Seilen,

Der wohlerfahrene Mann.

Beherrscht mit seiner Kunst des Landes

Bergbewandelndes Wild.

Dem Naken des Rosses wirft er das Joch

Um die Mähne und dem wilden

Ungezähmten Stiere.   (v. 42) (Hölderlin 1969: 792)

This version is more what is traditionally understood as translation even though it is at the extreme end of the foreignising spectrum. It is so close to the Greek that German syntax is strained but not broken. Thus, the compound past participial construction *woogenumrauschten* is used partially to translate the equally compact Greek construction: περιβρυχιοισιν. Similarly, very unusual compound constructions such as *listiggeschlungenen* for δικτυοκλωστοις and *Bergbewandelndes* for ορεσσιβατα reflect something of both the density and the feel of the Greek text. Despite the highly convoluted syntax, the poem works. Although the adjectival past participle *listiggeschlungenen* would normally be two words, the compound is extremely effective as it is itself 'cunningly twined together' so that the syntax reflects the sense, reinforcing, perhaps at a subliminal level, the idea of clever, complex nets being spun to trap even 'the birds of the air' *(τε φυλον ορνιθων)*.

In the past participle phrasal construction *woogenumrauschten*, the strangeness of the archaic form of the noun *woogen* contributes both to the tone of alienation running through the whole text - man as controller and destroyer of nature - and to the remoteness of an ancient civilisation with a very different culture. Paradoxically, in Hölderlin's case, it still has the effect of bringing that culture closer to us because it is a strangeness with which we can cope whereas a purely domesticating version arouses the suspicion of trivialisation taking place.

The even more unusual compound present participle *Bergbewandelndes* is also successful for similar reasons. Yet, in the hands of this consummate poet, it still reads like an original, though difficult poem. Despite the translation being so close to the Greek as almost to offend German grammar rules, the poem works as an original of the highest quality owing to the metre, rhythm and tone. The metrical control together with the solemn diction provides a deep coherence below the surface complexity. It is an absurdly close translation yet a work of original genius at the same time.

Hölderlin's later version of the same extract written between 1803 and 1804 fits equally well into Schadewaldt's third category, "eine aus einer neu erreichten tiefen 'Innigkeit' des Wort- und Sinnverständnisses geschöpfte frei deutende dichterische Art des 'Übersetzens', das nun kaum mehr ein Übersetzen, sondern ein erneuerndes Nachgestalten ist" or, in other words, it is more an example of what Schadewaldt calls *Nachdichtung*:

> Ungeheuer ist viel. Doch nichts
> Ungeheuerer, als der Mensch.
> Denn der, über die Nacht
> Des Meers, wenn gegen den Winter wehet
> Der Südwind, fähret er aus
> In geflügelten sausenden Häußern.
> Und der Himmlischen erhabene Erde
> Die unverderbliche, unermüdete
> Reibet er auf; mit dem strebenden Pfluge,
> Von Jahr zu Jahr,
> Treibt sein Verkehr er, mit dem Rossengeschlecht',
> Und leichtträumender Vögel Welt
> Bestrikt er, und jagt sie;
> Und wilder Thiere Zug,
> Und des Pontos salzbelebte Natur
> Mit gesponnenen Nezen,

> Der kundige Mann.
>
> Und fängt mit Künsten das Wild,
>
> Das auf Bergen übernachtet und schweift.
>
> Und dem rauhmähnigen Rosse wirft er um
>
> Den Naken das Joch, und dem Berge
>
> Bewandelnden unbezähmten Stier. (Hölderlin 1969: 748-749)

Even here, the categories break down because this version is pure Hölderlin and yet, whatever that phrase may mean to various generations, it is also pure Sophocles. In its style and diction, it has a similar effect to some of Hölderlin's greatest original poems and in particular, the opening lines resemble his poem *Andenken*:

> Der Nordost wehet
>
> Der liebste unter den Winden
>
> Mir, weil er feurigen Geist
>
> Und gute Fahrt verheißet den Schiffern. *Andenken* (1-4)

The classical rhythms and structure echo those of the chorus as in this extract:

> Denn der, über die Nacht
>
> Des Meers, wenn gegen den Winter wehet
>
> Der Südwind, fähret er aus
>
> In geflügelten sausenden Haüßern. (*Antigone*) (Hölderlin 1969: 194)

As in the first version, the diction of the chorus is one of a high seriousness, a fine balance between tragic passion and philosophical detachment. Yet the language is slightly more fluent and less difficult than in the first version although there are some similar compounds such as *leichtträumend, salzbelebt* and *rauhmähnig* and some difficult constructions which stretch German syntax beyond its normal limits in phrases such as:

> und dem Berge
>
> Bewandelnden unbezähmten Stier. (v. 239-240).

When this high impassioned lyrical fluency is, however, coupled with the alien and fascinating Greek-based compounds, the effect is powerful: the poem works as a poem and it works as an impassioned and 'religious' interpretation of the Greek chorus. Both versions succeed because they display fidelity to the register of the original, to the density of the text and finally because of the mysterious quality of Hölderlin's metre. Archaic usage such as the *et* endings in the third person of verbs as in *wehet*, for example, or the archaic spellings would normally act as an irritant, but with Hölderlin they work. It probably has something to do with the passionate sincerity of the poet, the high diction and the masterly metrical control. Whatever, as

Constantine rightly states, they are both works of "the highest genius": the former being more alien, more Greek more tragic and densely philosophical whereas the second version is more lyrical, more purely Hölderlin writing at his best, more accessible and yet retaining many of the features of the former. If there has ever been a counterexample to the untranslatability school, then these two versions alone would suffice. To assert that one is 'better' than the other is invidious as they both work in different ways as outlined in this analysis. Constantine also rightly refers to the language of these translations as "an ultimate achievement." He also adds:

> But fully to appreciate the interplay of literal and interpretative translation we should have to take a passage word by word from Greek into German. (Constantine 1990: 296)

Even a superficial glance has been sufficient to establish at least that not only creative translation but also great poetry is taking place. Schadewaldt's thirty-page analysis of Hölderlin's translations of Sophocles from the point of view of a classical scholar shows in detail how Hölderlin's translations work not only as translations but as great poetry in their own right.

There is a transition from the former version where Hölderlin chooses the adjective *gewaltig*, which is close to the Greek and expresses the violence of the despot whereas in the second version the horror becomes almost metaphysical with the adjective *ungeheuer*. In Hölderlin's theory of tragedy, the key tragic event involves confrontation with the deity, a kind of negative epiphany which, in death, leads to a new resolution and unity with the absolute. In this 'theology' of tragedy, the concept of the *ungeheuer* is a key theme as illustrated by Schadewaldt:

> Gesammelter, gedrungener und im tiefsten Sinn bestimmter hat Hölderlin dasselbe Verhältnis in den Anmerkungen zum Ödipus und zur Antigone ausgedrückt: "Die Darstellung des Tragischen beruht vorzüglich darauf, daß das Ungeheure (ungehiûre, Unheimliche), wie der Gott und Mensch sich paart und grenzenlos die Naturmacht (das Aorgische) und des Menschen Innerstes (das Individuellste, Organische) im Zorn (Streit) Eins wird, dadurch sich begreift (sich faßt, hält, bestimmt), daß das Grenzenlose-eines durch grenzenloses Scheiden sich reinigt." (Schadewaldt 1970: 782)

The horror expressed by the chorus is not only tragic but is also metaphysical. There is something eerie and alien in the way they express fascinated horror at the human species and the impending confrontation of the finite human being with the Ultimate. The human beings dominate the seas, exhaust the 'holy' earth itself and not only tame the savage beasts, but even subject them to their own purposes.

For Hölderlin, the plays expressed his own view of life at the deepest level so that Hölderlin approaches the translation with a feeling of awe as if he is interpreting and re-creating a holy text, as implied by Schadewaldt who maintains that this comes from Hölderlin's religious attitude to the plays and refers to Hölderlin's translations as "Übersetzungen aus religiösem Geist.":

> [. . .] so mußte ihm auch das Wort des Sophokles als heilges, gottgesprochenes Wort erscheinen und das Geschäft des Übersetzens, wie überhaupt das Geschäft des Dichtens als ein heiliges Geschäft, dazu bestimmt, das ursprünglich Wort des griechischen Dichters neu zu verwirklichen. (Schadewaldt 1970: 805-806)

It is only since the twentieth century that Hölderlin's translations have been recognised to be of an outstanding quality, having a similar impact as the original version, even though, in his time, they were treated with derision. Schadewaldt's article offers at least some explanation as to why this was the case. In the first place, the version of Sophocles used by Hölderlin was faulty and secondly, there were numerous printing errors in the first edition of his translation:

> Um mit dem Äußerlichen zu beginnen, so sei zunächst der Tatsache gedacht, daß der *Text der Erstausgabe von 1804* - die Handschrift des Dichters selbst ist uns bisher verloren - durch Druckfehler auf gröbste entstellt ist. (Schadewaldt 1970: 770)

In addition to the numerous printing errors, there were frequent misinterpretations caused by Hölderlin's relatively limited knowledge of Greek. After confronting the reader with several scholarly and eminent translations set side by side with those of Hölderlin, Schadewaldt rightly comes to this conclusion:

> In all seiner mangelnden Wort- und Regelkenntnis, Kenntnis der üblichen Verstehensroutine, blieb Hölderlin auch vor aller jener übersetzerischen Routine gleichsam fromm bewahrt, die gängigen Übersetzungen seiner und späterer Zeit *so korrekt und zugleich belanglos* machen. Instinktkräftig ergriff er zumal den 'Klang' des Sophokleischen Wortes mit Ernst in seiner Sachlichkeit und Gründlichkeit, aus jener Verantwortung für die Sprache, die alle poetisierenden Unarten nicht erst abzutun braucht. Was ihm so gelang, ist ihm über die Maßen gelungen: Chorlieder wie auch die großen Reden in ihrer Härte, Dichte, Sachlichkeit des Worts. (Schadewaldt 1970: 777. My emphasis.)

Faced with two versions of highest genius, it is not surprising that even an eminent Hölderlin scholar and able translator of Hölderlin's poetry such as Constantine himself, prefers simply to let them stand by themselves for the admiration of the reader. His only comment rightly summarises the situation:

> Wherever that comes from, by whatever means, it is the highest poetry. (Constantine 1990: 298)

Steiner (1998) goes so far as to assert that commentary on Hölderlin's poetry translation is an "impertinence", which is, my opinion, an exaggerated view, but shows the extent of awe and reverence Hölderlin's translation oeuvre inspires:

> We find ourselves here at the far limits of any rational theory or practice of linguistic exchange. Hölderlin's is the most exalted, enigmatic stance in the literature of translation. It merits constant attention and respect by virtue of the psychological risks implied and because it produced an intensity of understanding and 're-saying' such as to make commentary impertinent. (Steiner 1998: 350)

However, we are here at the heart of literary translation theory and practice. Both versions have been compared from translation theoretical point of view, bearing in mind that clear-cut categories break down in the hands of a poet whose language is able to ascend to the very highest levels of genius.

Hölderlin could have chosen to translate many poets such as Homer or Virgil, perhaps, but he wisely kept his range limited to those poets who expressed his own most inner feelings, philosophy and poetry and so, Hölderlin qua Hölderlin can almost perfectly render what is regarded as Sophocles, the great tragedian, afresh to many generations. His translation may be described as re-inspiration. Whatever Sophocles may have felt or tried to express, it is as if Hölderlin felt and expressed the same kind of emotion anew, afresh and this is why his translations stand above all others in the German language. Other translators look at the words and merely render the same words either into felicitous or infelicitous formulations in the target language or "so korrekt und so belanglos" as Schadewaldt refers to the later translations. It is a great tribute to Hölderlin that a Greek scholar of the stature of Schadewaldt pays the poet such homage. If any one were to take exception at the great translations of Hölderlin, it could well be a Greek scholar who is only too aware of the linguistic limitations of the poet with regard to the Greek language and of missed nuances, even of his not too infrequent gross errors. There have been many tributes to Hölderlin as a translator, the most noteworthy being the encomium of Steiner (1998), but it is perhaps more appropriate to leave the final word with the sober scholarship of Schadewaldt:

> Die Einheit indessen, in der die Extreme doch wieder miteinander verbunden sind, ist der Gott und das von Hölderlin mit tiefem Recht als Grund und Inhalt der Tragödie erkannte Gottesgeschehen. *In ihr ist er dem Sophokles so nahe gekommen wie kein anderer Übersetzer.* (Schadewaldt 1970: 805-806. My emphasis.)

(h) Conclusion

Translators such as Hölderlin act as a contradictory to the 'untranslatability' school by showing that great poets can successfully translate great poetry. It may be the case that only great poets can translate great poetry, but even this opinion needs to be proven. The other main conclusion to emerge from this study is that serious literary translation is less a matter of being highly qualified in both languages (reference has already been made to Hölderlin's relatively limited knowledge of Greek), but more a case of sharing the same inspiration, the same muse as the poet one is translating. Sager (1966) cites the Brazilian poet and translator Manuel Bandeira who illustrates this point with regard to his own translation methodology:

> Moreover, I only translate successfully, those poems that I myself should like to have written, that is to say, those poems which express things that were already within me, although my "discoveries" in translations as in my original poems, are always the result of my intuitions.
> (Sager 1966: 198)

Hölderlin was certainly one of the greatest practitioners of poetry translation and so, he acts as a model for poetry translators, even if his example seems impossible to follow. Hölderlin, unlike many literary translators, seemed to know his limitations in that he translated only those works in harmony with his own muse. Similarly, it is important for a translator of Thomas Mann to display some affinity with the great author. It is regrettable that the two translations of Thomas Mann in this study fail even to indicate that poetry is taking place and that the elements of self-caricature, humorous decadence and literary virtuosity are missing and replaced by merely pretentious ungainly prose displaying here and there a slightly poetic moment, but with the general sense, tone, diction, form, rhythm and poetry being completely lost in translation. The example of Hölderlin shows that this need not be the case.

The next chapter will analyse some the classical poetry encoded in *Der Tod in Venedig* and compare not only the versions of the two translators in question but will also look at one French and three Italian versions which do capture something of the poetry of the original.

Chapter VI: The Translation of Poetry and Poetic Prose in *Der Tod in Venedig*

(a) Introduction

It has been seen in Sections (c) of Chapter II that both Lowe-Porter and Thomas Mann belonged to what has already been designated as the untranslatability school. Thomas Mann himself was only too aware of the difficulties involved in translating his own poetic prose. Thirwall, for example, quotes a statement from an interview with Frank Harriot in which Mann is supposed to have said:

> To translate artistic prose into another language is as difficult as to translate poetry.
>
> (Thirlwall 1966: 95)

This chapter will concentrate on the purely poetic aspects of Mann's style.

The analysis of Hölderlin's and Joyce's translations in the previous chapter has shown that 'great' translations of 'great' poetry and prose are possible, but the only hitch in this formula is that perhaps only 'great' poets are capable of this achievement. Lowe-Porter, however, argues that the contrary is the case when she compares W. H. Auden's translation of Goethe's poem commemorating the birthday of Archduke Karl August as quoted on the fly-leaf of *Lotte in Weimar* with her own version:

> It is clear that Auden's version is the work of a poet. It is eight lines of such verse as he might have written had he been the personal friend of, say F. D. R. But it is not, I feel, in spirit or technique, like the simple warm little patriotic Goethe lines. It does not seem eighteenth-century to me. *Auden, I think, cannot be a translator, however hard he tries.* He kept the first rule of a translator, to make, not a translation, which is 'God bless us a thing of naught,' but did not keep the second (which is to keep the words and the spirit). Or am I all wrong? (1966: 199. My emphasis.)

It is debatable whether or not Auden did "keep the words and the spirit" less than Lowe-Porter. It is appropriate at this stage to quote the original alongside Auden's version followed by that of Lowe-Porter:

Goethe	Mit allem Schall und Klang
	Der Transoxanen
	Erkühnt sich unser Sang
	Auf Deine Bahnen.
	Uns ist für gar nichts bang
	In dir lebendig
	Dein Leben dauere lang
	Dein Reich beständig.
Auden	Though conch and tribal gong

Howl in the marches,

Bold be our rebel song,

Thy courts and arches

Stand. We dread no wrong

In thee made able.

O may thy reign be long

Thy kingdom stable.   (Auden's version in Thirlwall 1966: 197)

Lowe-Porter   Through all the bounce and blare

Of border races

Our song makes bold to fare

Upon thy traces.

We fear not any wrong

In thee residing -

Oh, may thy life be long,

Thy realm abiding. (Thirlwall 1966: 197-198)

Auden adheres rigidly to Goethe's repetition of rhyme with the pattern *ababacac* whereas Lowe-Porter varies the scheme slightly with *ababcdcd* thus losing some of the witty tightness of the original. It is true, however, that Auden's version misinterprets an essential point with the phrase "rebel song", which takes the boldness of the subjects in celebrating their ruler so wildly and loudly more than one step too far by implying the wildness has inherent rebellious elements. Otherwise, Auden does seem to capture something of the spirit of the original. The basic idea of stable rule is well conveyed with the *enjambment* of the line "Thy courts and arches/Stand" so that the verb *stand* is highlighted. This theme is clinched in the last line "Thy kingdom stable" with the main emphasis on the final iamb giving this foot almost the force of a spondee, thus ending on a note of solidity and peace. The obscurity of "conch and tribal gong" in the first line reflects something of the 'outlandishness' of Goethe's coinage of the word *Transoxanen* (which could be roughly translated as 'people living beyond the Pale') and adds a slightly humorous pagan or "tribal" touch to the poem. It is quite clear that, for Auden, the semiotics of the poem was more important than the semantics so that his translation of "Auf Deine Bahnen" by "Thy courts and arches" has more to do with finding a suitable rhyme for *marches* than to reflect the sense of the original. It is, however, still within the 'spirit' of the original as the courts and arches emphasise the 'glory' of the enlightened monarch, even though the idea of following the monarch is lost. Despite some semantic loss, Auden in the end has produced a fluent and successful poem from an original which in itself can hardly be regarded as high poetry as it is only an example of Goethe's occasional verse.

Lowe-Porter's version attempts to be semantically closer to Goethe's, but there is still some loss of poetic features. The first collocation in the first line "bounce and blare" for "Schall und Klang" is a not a collocation and thus has a bizarre effect. If some one is 'full of bounce', this means that they are very lively or 'full of beans' as with the very common collocation 'a bouncy baby'. It could also unconsciously be an echo of the felicitous collocation 'full of bounce and flair' to describe an able and energetic person. It also reflects twentieth century colloquial usage so that her claim to have caught the '18th century spirit' of the poem does not hold. When, however, the noun *bounce* is combined with *blare*, the confusion is increased. One may refer to the 'blaring' of trumpets, but, on its own, it has a puzzling effect as if the reference were made to the 'banging of drums', for example, by the word 'bang' and then made into a non-collocation such as *bang and bounce*! Confusion is further compounded when the non-collocation is referred to 'border races', which in turn is a very vague reference. What is a 'border race' and why should they be full of 'bounce and blare'? Goethe's reference, on the other hand, is precise, i.e. *die Transoxanen* and so, makes perfect sense.

Similarly, the next two lines have two non-collocations in the idea that a song 'makes bold' and 'fare upon' which is presumably meant 'to follow'. The idea behind this is very obscure even after allowing for the non-collocations: that a song becomes bold enough to follow the footsteps of the 'great' duke. The second half of the poem is more felicitous, but the iambs in *residing* and *abiding* together with the weak feminine rhymes lack the solidity of Auden's 'able/stable' rhyme. Lowe-Porter would certainly not be justified in her denunciation of Auden as being incapable of translation, "however hard he tries" because the latter understood the semiotics of the poem to a much higher degree, even though there was one serious semantic error, i.e. 'our rebel song'. Secondly, even though Auden's version by no means represents his best poetry, it reads well and fluently besides striking a poetic note whereas the first half of Lowe-Porter's version can only be described as garbled.

A translator of poetry who lacks any poetic gifts is not likely to produce great poetry translations even if the translator may be a great philologist. Lowe-Porter said of herself: 'I am not a literary bird.'She was by no means a gifted poet.[43]

(b) Poetic Elements in Thomas Mann's Prose

As has been demonstrated in the detailed analysis in Chapter IV, Thomas Mann's prose often displays poetic elements not only with regard to associations and connotations, but also with regard to their sonic effects and rhythm. That Mann regarded the rhythmic aspects of his prose an essential feature, there is no doubt as testified by his letter, "An Bruno Walter zum siebzigsten Geburtstag":

> Ich bin überzeugt, daß *die geheimste und stärkste Anziehungskraft einer Prosa in ihrem Rhythmus liegt*, [. . .] dessen Gesetze so viel delikater sind als die offenkundig metrischen.
> (Mann 1961: 738: My emphasis.)

Although most of *Der Tod in Venedig* is written in poetic prose, there are many instances of Mann actually weaving classical rhythms and even full hexameters into his 'prose'. Hayes, recognised two examples: one in the breakfast scene, "Oft

---

[43] It may seem churlish to point out the poetic deficiencies of a translator, but it is necessary in this case to emphasise the point that it takes a poet to translate poetry successfully, particularly in the light of her casual dismissal of Auden's talents as a translator of poetry. The poems, quoted in Thirlwall ostensibly for the readers' admiration, illustrate this point in the following two examples of Lowe-Porter's poetry:
Example 1

> Words are dear,
> And names are dear,
> And words of place fall sweet upon the air.
> But most of all the names of English places,
> Of English settlements and shires,
> Stealing like drowsy music on the ears,
> And specially of all the shires there be
> In Oxford, Bucks and Berks
> The names are dear to me.

Example 2

> **A face is a face is a face:**
>
> A mouth and a nose and an eye
>
> Or two, in the usual place
>
> Make us all look alike, you'll agree,
>
> So how can you tell it is me,
>
> When we're all so alike in the face?
>
>
> I boast no unusual feature,
>
> No arrangement distinctive or odd,
>
> And yet this quite commonplace creature
>
> When modelled by Gina you'll see
>
> Can surely be no one but me. (Thirlwall 1966: viii-ix)

veränderten Schmuck und warme Bäder und Ruhe" and one some 150 words farther on in the text:

> Auf diesem Kragen aber, der nicht einmal sonderlich elegant zum Charakter des Anzugs passen wollte, *ruhte die Blüte des Hauptes in unvergleichlichem Liebreiz, [. . .] (das) Haupt des Eros, vom gelblichem Schmelze parischen Marmors.* (Hayes 1974: 120-121. Italics indicate two hexameters.)

Hayes notes that both Burke and Lowe-Porter missed the hexameters in this extract and claims that there are "some of the dactylic rhythms" in the Lowe-Porter version:

> The lad had [. . .] a simple white standing collar round the neck [. . .] a not very elegant effect [. . .] yet above this collar the head was poised like a flower in incomparable loveliness. It was the head of Eros, with the yellowish bloom of Parian marble. (Lowe-Porter 1978: 34-35)

The few dactylic rhythms could be a matter of chance because any felicitous rhythmic effect is destroyed as Hayes rightly notes arguing, as it were, against himself:

> She does preserve some of the dactylic rhythms: but the phrase "in incomparable loveliness" is so retardant that it interrupts any rhythmic flow. Also, her last sentence has eight accents instead of six. (Hayes 1974: 122)

Luke's version reads quite fluently with a hint here and there of classical rhythms (particularly in the last line), but with nothing to suggest that perfect hexameters are encoded within the text:

> [. . .] the boy was wearing [. . .] a simple white stand-up collar. But on this collar - which did not even match the rest of his suit very elegantly [. . .] there, like a flower in bloom, his head was gracefully resting. It was the head of Eros, with the creamy luster of Parian marble. (Luke 1988: 220)

Hayes demonstrates that it is possible to reproduce the hexameters without too much difficulty by offering his own felicitous rendering:

> The difficulty in producing some sort of passable hexameter does not seem overwhelming: for example, the final translation might be "poised like a flower, his head was crowned with unmatchable charm - - (the) head of an Eros, with yellowing lustre of Parian marble." My own preference, however, would be blank verse: "his head held poised, the flower's crowning charm, was Eros' head, in yellowed Paros marble." (Hayes 1974: 130)

Hayes' preference for the iambic pentameter is clear as he goes on to argue that "the Anglo-Saxon ear is not attuned to the rhythms of the classical hexameter" and he condones Burke's use of the pentameter to translate Homeric hexameters:

> In a passage like this one [i.e. the 'Parian marble passage'] the translator is faced with a choice between preserving the exact form of the original or adjusting the form to transmit another effect by other means, in terms more appropriate to the receptor language. If he decides on the latter course, he will probably render the passage in iambic form, as it was discussed in

> Chapter II, above; and in that case, it seems to me, he should translate the *Odyssey* verse into
> an iambic pentameter, as Burke has done: "A frequent change of dress; warm baths, and rest".
> (Hayes 1974: 121)

In this particular case, I would, however, argue the contrary to Hayes' choice of pentameters over hexameters because the very artificiality of the hexameter reflects Aschenbach's fastidiousness, thus adding to the humour and irony by gently mocking a writer who is a little too self-conscious and over-dexterous. This use of the hexameter also contains an element of Mann's self-mockery. Many of the hexameters are indirect quotations which provide distance from the protagonist so that there is room for that gentle, all-pervading irony that runs through the whole text as recognised to a certain extent by Häfele and Stammel (1992):

> Sicherlich hatte Thomas Mann seine Freude am Zitieren, vielleicht hat sie auch der Leser beim
> Auffinden kryptischer Verbindungslinien. Das Zitat ist vor allem Teil der ironischen
> Erzählstrategie und läßt als Wiedergabe fremder Meinung dem Erzähler die Freiheit, Distanz
> zu den Vorstellungen seines Helden zu wahren. (Häfele und Stammel 1992: 55)

Covert classical references are woven into the text within the Platonic dialogues on the destructiveness of art. There are also 'classical' passages the hexameter predominates with frequent quotations/translations of Homer such as the following example in the same chapter:

> In Anlehnung an einen in Homers *Odyssee* (4. Buch, V 563) beschriebenen idyllischen
> Zustand fühlt er sich dagegen in Venedig und am Lido, wo „der zarten Sinneslust kein Ende"
> (41) ist, „als sei er entrückt ins elysische Land, an die Grenzen der Erde, wo leichtestes Leben
> den Menschen beschert ist, wo nicht Schnee ist und Winter, noch Sturm und strömender
> Regen, sondern immer sanft kühlenden Anhauch Okeanos aufsteigen läßt, und in seliger Muße
> die Tage verrinnen, mühelos, kampflos und ganz nur der Sonne und ihren Festen geweiht.
> (Häfele und Stammel 1992: 54)

Even in the 'less poetic' passages, there are frequent hexameters. Hayes identifies one more passage where the dactylic/spondee rhythms are clearly evident even though the sentences may not be perfect hexameters. The first example is taken from Chapter IV:

> *Er war früh auf, wie sonst bei pochendem Arbeits*drange, *und vor den meisten am Strand,*
> *wenn die Sonne noch milde* war und das Meer weißblendend in Morgenträumen lag. *Er grüßte*
> *menschenfreundlich die Wächter der Sperre, grüßte auch vertraulich den barfüßigen*
> *Weißbart, der ihm die Stätte bereitet,* das braune Schattentuch ausgespannt, *die Möbel der*
> *Hütte hinaus auf die Plattform gerückt hatte, und ließ sich nieder.* (Hayes 1974: 123. Hayes'
> italics)

As Hayes does not offer a detailed scansion analysis, it is difficult to see in the above the justification for the line breaks, but, whatever, there are clear classical rhythms in this extract.

Other critics such as Hofmiller (1966) claim that the nightmare sequence with the Dionysian feast is also rich in hexameters such as in the following extract:

> Aber alles durchdrang und beherrschte der tiefe, lockende Flötenton. Lockte er nicht auf ihn, den widerstrebenden Erlebenden, schamlos beharrlich zum Fest und Unmaß des äußersten Opfers? Groß war sein Abscheu, groß seine Furcht, redlich sein Wille, bis zuletzt das seine zu schützen gegen den Fremden, den Feind des gefaßten und würdigen Geistes. (1977: 393).

Similarly, Dittmann also identified a hexameter in the sixth paragraph of the same chapter:

```
        1        2          3    4        5    6
   -  v  / -    v  v  /- v   v /  - v / -  v v  /- v
```

> Muscheln, / Seepferdchen / Quallen und / seitlich / laufende / Krebse. (Dittmann 1993: 47)

(c) Detailed Analysis of the Opening Lines in Chapter IV of *Der Tod in Venedig*

In Chapter IV, the poetic element is dominant in the passages where the passion and tension increase. This chapter is also full of classical references and displays of metrical virtuosity, so much so, that the author himself referred to it as "das antikisierende Kapitel"[44]. Similarly, Häfele and Stammel (1992) refer to the poetic elements in their study as a case of "der antikisierende Rhythmus" and they also recognise the deliberate exaggeration which is at the root of the self-parody and irony in the passage by describing the poetic elements as "überhöht" (exaggerated):

> Das vierte Kapitel beginnt mit einer ins mythische Bild überhöhte Beschreibung der Sonnenglut am Strand. (Häfele und Stammel 1992: 54)

The opening passage of Chapter IV deserves to be quoted in full because, under analysis, it can be shown that this passage is such an extreme example of poetic prose that it could be regarded as a covert poem. In this passage Mann gives an exalted description in classical style of the 'blissful' days Aschenbach spent in Venice during the latter part of his stay:

> Nun lenkte Tag für Tag der Gott mit den hitzigen Wangen nackend sein gluthauchendes Viergespann durch die Räume des Himmels, und sein gelbes Gelock flatterte im zugleich ausstürmenden Ostwind. Weißlich seidiger Glanz lag auf den Weiten des träge wallendes Pontos. Der Sand glühte. Unter der silbrig flirrenden Bläue des Äthers waren rostfarbene Segeltücher vor den Strandhütten ausgespannt, und auf dem scharf umgrenzten Schattenfleck,

---

[44] This reference is taken from his letter to Heinrich Mann on 2nd April, 1912 (Mann: 1985).

135

den sie boten, verbrachte man die Vormittagsstunden. Aber köstlich war auch der Abend, wenn die Pflanzen des Parks balsamisch dufteten, die Gestirne droben ihren Reigen schritten und das Murmeln des umnachteten Meeres, leise heraufdringend, die Seele besprach. Solch ein Abend trug in sich die freudige Gewähr eines neuen Sonntages von leicht geordneter Muße und geschmückt mit zahllosen, dicht beieinanderliegenden Möglichkeiten lieblichen Zufalls. (Mann 1977: 370)

One aspect which has not been noted and which must, therefore, be argued is that the first four lines all display the distinctive features of Homeric hexameters. The characteristic last two feet consisting of a dactyl followed by a spondee or trochee, thus displaying the typical rhythm - v v \ - - can be recognised in the first four lines which can be set out as almost perfect hexameters. Sometimes, there is one foot too many (which is indicated with a zero) or a word which can be regarded as a link with the next line and thus metrically redundant as a hexameter:

```
       1        2     3    0    4          5       6
   / v  - /  v - / v  - / v /-   v   v  / - v v   / -  v /
   1 Nun lenk/te Tag /für Tag /der/ Gott mit den/ hitzigen /Wangen


       /-   v/
   2. nackend
        1         2          3           4        5          6
    / v   - / -  v    v / -    v  v / -   v   / - v  v  / - -/
   3. sein glut/hauchendes / Viergespann /durch die / Räume des / Himmels,


       /v    -  / - v/
    4. und sein / gelbes
         1      2       3        0     5        6
    / v   - / - v v / v v   -  / - /- v  v    / -  -/
   5. Gelock / flatterte / im zugleich /aus/stürmenden /Ostwind.


    /-      v / - v  v/
   6. Weißlich /seidiger
          1       2      3     4      5      6
    /-    -  / - v / -  v    v / - v / - v  v / - -/
   7. Glanz lag / auf den / Weiten des /träge / wallenden / Pontos.
```

The linking lines are marked with an even number, but despite these 'imperfections' the rhythms of this opening passage do produce a 'classical' effect. Not all the rhythms of the opening paragraph are, however, typically classical. It can also be argued that Thomas Mann's irony and self-parodying are by no means absent in these passages which are a little too purple and a little too precious, though deliberately so, resulting in a brilliant parody of classical aestheticism. The whole paragraph can be set out as a poem in four parts:

I

1. Nun lenkte Tag für Tag der Gott mit den hitzigen Wangen

2. Nackend

3. Sein gluthauchendes Viergespann durch die Räume des Himmels,

4. Und sein gelbes

5. Gelock flatterte im zugleich ausstürmenden Ostwind.

6. Weißlich seidiger

7. Glanz lag auf den Weiten des träge wallenden Pontos.

II

1. Der Sand glühte.

III

1. Unter der silbrig flirrenden Bläue des Äthers

2. Waren rostfarbene Segeltücher aufgespannt

3. Und auf dem scharf umgrenzten Schattenfleck,

4. Den sie boten,

5. Verbrachte man

6. Die Vormittagsstunden

IV

1. Aber köstlich war auch der Abend,

2. Wenn die Pflanzen des Parkes balsamisch dufteten

3. Die Gestirne droben ihre Reigen schritten

4. Und das Murmeln des umnachteten Meeres

5. Leise heraufdringend

6. Die Seele besprach.

This example of line-sequencing is just one of many possibilities. Lines 2, 4 and 6, for example in verse I, are links based on the assumption that their corresponding preceding lines are more or less complete Homeric hexameters as analysed in this Section. The classical rhythms were totally abandoned in verses II-IV as if the poet is returning from the heavens (*Himmel - der Gott*) to earth and so there is a beautiful, but powerful simplicity in this line. Also the division of the first half into three verses makes hermeneutic sense in that the verses are divided according to their role in the structure or semiotics of the 'elements': verse I - the sky and fire; verse II - linking of the element fire with earth; verse III - air to earth via water (the sea) and verse IV - air and sea. A full verse value is given to the one line *Der Sand glühte* because this line acts as a bridge between the land and the sea, and the 'glowing' of the sand is suggestive of the fire theme as in the first verse. The second half of the 'poem' (verses II and IV) returns to the twentieth century so that 'vers libre' form is more appropriate.

(d) Lowe-Porter's and Luke's Translations of the Opening Lines in Chapter IV of *Der Tod in Venedig*

It is then interesting now to examine how many of these rhythmical aspects are encoded in the translations concerned. Hayes claims that Lowe-Porter does use 'iambic combinations' in her translations, (Hayes 1974: 125), but he does not highlight what these 'combinations' are. At best, it could be asserted that there is some attempt at writing rhythmic prose, but this is by no means clear. What is certain is that there is no equivalent poetic effect in her version:

> ***Lowe-Porter:*** Now daily the naked god with cheeks aflame drove his four fire-breathing steeds through heaven's spaces; and with him streamed the strong east wind that fluttered his yellow locks. A sheen, like white satin, lay over all the idly rolling sea's expanse. The sand was burning hot. Awnings of rust-coloured canvas were spanned before the bathing-huts, under the ether's quivering silver blue; one spent the morning hours within the small, sharp square of shadow they purveyed. But the evening too was rarely lovely: balsamic with the breath of flowers and shrubs from the nearby park, while overhead the constellations circled in their spheres, and the murmuring of the night girded sea swelled softly up and whispered to

the soul. Such nights as these contained the joyful promise of a sunlit morrow, brim-full of sweetly ordered idleness, studded thick with countless precious possibilities. (Lowe-Porter 1978: 46-47)

The same criticism could also apply to Luke:

> *Luke:* Now day after day the god with the burning cheeks soared naked, driving his four fire-breathing steeds through the spaces of heaven, and now, too, his yellow-gold locks fluttered wide in the outstorming east wind. Silk-white radiance gleamed on the slow-swelling deep's vast waters. The sand glowed. Under the silvery quivering blue of the ether, rust-covered awnings were spread out in front of the beach cabins, and one spent the morning hours on the sharply defined patch of shade they provided. But exquisite, too, was the evening, when the plants in the park gave off a balmy fragrance, and the stars on high moved through their dance, and the softly audible murmur of the night-surrounded sea worked its magic on the soul. (Luke 1988: 231)

Neither passage attempts to capture the strict classical metre of the original, but both do aim at capturing something of the exalted tone and diction of Mann's poetic prose whilst missing the self-parodying aspects of the extract where the deliberate, even elaborate display of metrical virtuosity can be seen to reflect the affected traits in Aschenbach's character as has also been implied by Häfele and Stammel's use of the adjective *überhöht*. Indeed, the overwriting is so obvious that despite the classical vigour of the hexameters, there is a narcissistic element hinting at Aschenbach's inherent decadence which leads to his final downfall. The Lowe-Porter version does manage, however, to be very slightly poetic with the use of inversion, rhythm and alliteration in the second clause:

> [. . .] and with him streamed the strong east wind that *fluttered* his yellow locks (Lowe-Porter 1978: 46. My emphasis.)

This line reads quite well despite its being marred by the incorrect use of *flutter* as a transitive verb[45]. Compounds such as "night-girded sea" and "brim-full" are generally infelicitous in English. The whole passage has a vigorous and energetic rhythm which contradicts the inherently decadent tone in the original. Luke's version also reads quite well on the first reading, but he too produces some barbaric compounds such as "the out-storming east wind". Although the phrase "night-surrounded sea" may be slightly more preferable to Lowe-Porter's equivalent phrase "night-girded sea", the effect is still clumsy. The embedded hexameters are, however, completely ignored by both translators and the inherent poetic form is lost. The use of the impersonal

---

[45] The wrong use of transitive and intransitive verbs is a typical feature of Lowe-Porter's abuse of English grammar. In Appendix I, the thirteen examples 2. 4111 - 2. 4123 are taken from *Tristan* and *Tonio Kröger* alone, but there are many more examples throughout her oeuvre.

pronoun in both translations also trivialises the high poetic tone by producing an inappropriately 'English' upper-class effect:

> *Lowe-Porter*: *One* spent the morning hours within the small, sharp square of the shadow they purveyed
>
> *Luke:* [. . .] *One* spent the morning hours on the sharply defined patch of shade they provided.
> (My emphasis.)

In short, both versions fail to communicate the sense of excitement, intoxication with language and form of the original; there is no hint that here is a piece of high poetry together with sophisticated self-parodying decadence. Instead, we are presented with two passages of overblown, awkward English prose.

(e) Three Italian Versions of the Opening Lines in Chapter IV of *Der Tod in Venedig*

The three main Italian versions read much better. Both the Maffi (1994) and Rho (1954) versions display poetic qualities with assonance, rhythm and sound repetition for which the Italian language is renowned as does the Castellani (1988) translation to a very high degree.

> *Rho:* Ormai, giorno per giorno, il dio dalle guance ardenti conduceva nudo la quadriga di fuoco attraverso gli spazi del cielo, e la sua chioma d'oro ondeggiava al vento di levante subitamente calmato. Una serica bianchezza posava sulle distese del Ponto torpido e ondoso. La sabbia bruciava. Sotto l'etere azzurro dai barbagli d'argento erano tese davanti alle cabini tende di traliccio color ruggine, e sulla netta macchia d'ombra da esse proiettata si passavan le ore del pomeriggio. Ma non meno deliziosa era la sera, quando gli alberi del parco esalavano profumi balsamici, le stelle compivano lassù la loro danza, e il mormorio del mare notturno saliva dolcemente parlava alle anime. Quelle sere portavano in sé la lieta promessa di una nuova giornata di sole, di facili e ordinati piaceri, abbellita da infinite occasioni di gradevoli casi. (Rho 1954: 53)
>
> *Maffi:* Ormai, giorno per giorno, il dio dalle guance di fuoco guidava nudo negli spazi celesti la rutilante quadriga, e la sua bionda chioma ondeggiava al libeccio improvvisamente calato. Una bianca, serica lucentezza indugiava sulle distese del Ponto pigramente ondoso. La sabbia bruciava. Sotto l'azzurro dell' etere sfavillante d'argento, rudivi teli color ruggine erano stesi davanti ai capanni, e, sulla loro macchia d'ombra nettamente segnata, si transcorrevano le ore pomeridiane. Ma era altrettanto deliziosa la sera, quando nel giardino le piante esalavano balsamici profumi, le stelle eseguivano lassù la loro danza, e il mormorio sommesso del mare avvolto nella notte e parlava all'anima: una sera che portava in sé l'ilare garanzia di una nova giornata di sole e di facile ozio, adorna d'infinite e quasi ininterrotte possibilità di eventi gradevoli. (Maffi 1994: 74-75)

Castellani: Giorno dopo giorno, ormai, il dio dalle guance infocata correva ignudo con la fiammea quadriga attraverso gli spazi celesti e la sua chioma d'oro fluttuava al vento di levante mutatosi in placida brezza. Un lucido biancore di seta posava sulle pigre ondeggianti distese del ponto; la sabbia ardeva, l'etere azzurro sfavillava d'argento. Dinanzi ai cappanni della spiagga erano tese tende color ruggine: alla loro ombrache si proiettava netta, si transcorrevano le ore pomeridiane. Ma deliziosa era pure la sera, quando le piante del parco esalavano effluvi balsamaci e si compiva nel cielo la danza delle stelle, quando il murmure delle acque avvolte nell' oscurità si levava sommesso a parlare all'anima. Ognuna di quelle sere portava con sé la gioiosa certezza di una nuova giornata di sole sotto il segno di un facile ozio, ornato di innumerevoli, ininterrotte probalità di cari incontri. (Castellani 1988: 45)

It is beyond the scope of this analysis to compare all the European versions of the Thomas Mann translations, but, even with a superficial acquaintance of Italian, it is clear that all three versions display a great sense of rhythm and poetry. The Rho version is very close to the original and is the least poetic despite some pleasing effects such as:

Una serica bianchezza posava sulle distese del Ponto torpido e ondoso.

The Maffi version displays greater rhythmical variety with his greater use of dactylic rhythms in phrases such as "subitamente calmato" and in his translation of the line quoted as immediately above:

Una bianca, serica lucentezza indugiava sulle distese del Ponto pigramente ondoso.

The Castellani version, however, attempts to capture the classical rhythms of the original with dactyl/spondee rhythms in phrases such as "correva ignudo", "attraverso gli spazi celesti", "placida brezza","sulle pigre"and "ondeggianti distese del ponto". The choice of vocabulary is also more felicitous with the phrases such as "la gioiosa certezza" as opposed to the more prosaic noun *garanzia* in the Maffi version or in the Rho's use of the noun *promessa* in the relatively dull phrase, "la lieta promessa". All three versions, however, miss the irony and self-parody in that they are merely poetic rather than being over-poetic at the same time. Nevertheless, the reader is aware that poetry as well as prose is embedded in this passage.

(f) A French Translation of the Opening Lines in Chapter IV of *Der Tod in Venedig*

The Bertaux, Nesme and Sigwalt (1997) French version is both a very close translation and highly poetic. The rich mixture of classical metres in phrases such as "conduisait nu son quadrige enflammé" and "au même moment déchaîné" in the first sentence echo one another more in the manner of French alexandrines in the manner of Corneille and Racine. This would seem to be a successful strategy as most literary French readers would perceive high classical metres and rhythms more through the French classics than directly from the Greek whereas the English pentameter has more immediate associations with Shakespeare and the English tradition than with Latin and Greek models:

> Maintenant, tous les jours, le dieu au visage ardent conduisait nu son quadrige enflammé a travers les espaces du ciel, et sa chevelure d'or flottait au vent d'Est au même moment déchaîné. Une blancheur soyeuse et éblouissante s'étendait sur les lointains de la mer et la houle paresseuse. Le sable brûlait. Sous l'éther azuré aux vibrations d'argent, des voiles couleur de rouille étaient tendues devant les cabines, et sur la tâche d'ombre nettement découpée qu'elles projetaient, on passait les heures de la matinée. Mais non moins exquise était la soirée, quand les plantes du parc exhalaient leurs parfums balsamiques, que les constellations accomplissaient là-haut leur ronde et que le murmure de la mer plongée dans la nuit montait doucement vers les âmes pour leur faire ses mystérieuses confidences. (Bertaux, Nesme and Sigwalt 1997: 63-64)

The lines following the opening alexandrines are high prose with poetic effects such as the inversion in the line, "Mais non moins exquise était la soirée" and the rich assonance and alliteration in the final clause, "le murmure de la mer plongée dans la nuit montait doucement vers les âmes pour leur faire ses mystérieuses confidences". Even though the French version almost reads as poetry (a great achievement), the deliberate overwriting and pretentiousness, and thus parody, irony and self-mockery of the original is also lost except perhaps for the phrase, "Mais non moins exquise était la soirée" where the adjective *exquise* is the *le mot juste* being both poetic and pretentious.

(g) Conclusion

It has been seen that the Italian and French versions capture not only many of the poetic aspects, but something of the classical metre. As the passage has an element of self-parody, an exaggerated use of metre, rhythm and poetic effects would be in order as long as the exaggeration can be seen to be deliberate. This is expecting rather a lot from a literary translator, but as has been seen with Joyce's translation into Italian and even the German versions of *Finnegans Wake*, it is remarkable how far translation can go in the hands of skilled writers and poets. Even if one goes half way as do the one French and three Italian versions, something has been achieved, and an echo of Thomas Mann's brilliant and sophisticated language games is preserved, but if no or little attempt is made, as in the English versions in this study, then the result is disastrous: overblown and ungrammatical prose as in the case of Lowe-Porter and dull, pretentious prose as in Luke's case with little evidence of Homeric rhythm or Mann's sophisticated parody of an aesthete. On the other hand, a more parodying version with recondite words and metrical displays of virtuosity is also possible. It is not within the province of the dissertation to give a prescriptive formula for translating Thomas Mann works. The *strategic approach* depends on many other factors (target readership, publishing contract, general strategy domesticating, semantic, communicative, adaptation and rewriting). Lowe-Porter's and Luke's versions reveal the limitations of the *academic approach*. The reader is short-changed. For a brilliant piece of style, in covert poetic form, full of metrical games and self-parody, we receive from both translators two passages of dull, overblown, pedantic prose.

Chapter VII: The Translation of Philosophical, Literary Prose and the Problem of Translating Dialect

(a) General Discussion of the Problem of Translating Philosophy

Venuti (1998) is one of the few recent theorists to tackle directly the problem of philosophy translation to which he devotes a whole chapter in his book *The Scandals of Translation*. His approach is very much from that of a literary stylist rather than from the perspective of a philosopher, but he makes a valuable contribution by highlighting the gross neglect philosophical translation has suffered:

> In philosophical research widespread dependence on translated texts coincides with neglect of their translated status, a general failure to take into account the differences introduced by the fact of translation. The problem is perhaps most glaring in Anglo-American cultures, where native philosophical traditions from empiricism to logical semantics have privileged language as communication and therefore imagined the transparency of the translated text. (Venuti 1998: 106)

This neglect is also particularly marked in the literature concerning the translation of the philosophical passages in Thomas Mann's oeuvre. Both Hellmann's (1992) study of the French translation of *Der Zauberberg* and Hayes' study of *Der Tod in Venedig* make no reference to the difficulties of translating philosophy or philosophical literary prose.[46]

Venuti (1998) sees the main problem as the decision to establish how far a text should be domesticated (or to Newmark's terminology how communicative a translation should be) and how far a text should remain close to the original even at the expense of the idiom of the target language (i.e. a foreignising text). He rightly criticises the philosophers for having a naive view of transparency by simply referring back to the argumentation in the source text. Following more or less directly from the previous quotation, he denounces both the philosophers' neglect of translational problems and their eagerness to domesticate according to their own norms:

> This is never more true than on the rare occasions when a translation is actually noticed in reviews and studies: philosophers assume that transparency is an attainable ideal by evaluating the accuracy of the translation as a correspondence to the foreign text, chastising the translator

---

[46] Despite 47 topics listed for discussion Hellmann's study, *Die französische Version des* Zauberberg *von Thomas Mann* in his otherwise thorough study of Maurice Betz's French translation, there is not a single reference to the philosophising passages. This is surprising because *Der Zauberberg* is a highly philosophical work. Even more surprising is the fact that under linguistic headings such as "ad-hoc Komposita," "Adjektiv und Bindestrich-Doppeladjektiv" and "andere Sondersprachen", there are virtually no examples of philosophical language. This aspect is more or less ignored throughout the whole work, a state of affairs which only reflects the general avoidance of this area by literary scholars and critics.

for missing the foreign philosopher's intention or the full significance of the foreign philosophical terms. (Venuti 1998: 106)

In the context of the *strategic approach*, it is interesting that he devotes a section of this chapter to the theme of *Strategies of Philosophical Translation*, but it is, however, disappointing that he identifies only the two strategies already alluded to, i.e. the choice either to domesticate or not to domesticate:

> The translator's responsibility is not just twofold, both foreign and domestic, but split into two opposing obligations: to establish *a lexicographical equivalence* for a conceptually dense text, while intelligibly maintaining its foreignness to domestic readerships. (Venuti 1998: 115. My emphasis.)

It is also rather disappointing that there is a regression to equivalence strategies as this reverts to the linguists' approach of the sixties and seventies, which he had rejected in his first chapter on the limitation of linguistics (Venuti 1998: 21). The equivalence theories lead to the following unproductive circularity: to assume that to establish "lexicographical equivalence" is all that is needed is to beg the question of difficulty in philosophical translation. Many philosophical concoctions have no "immediately insertible equivalents". There is no better example to illustrate this phenomenon than Thomas Mann's own philosophical concoctions such as the following few typical listed by Hayes from *Der Tod in Venedig*:

> das Tapfer-Sittliche, das Amtlich-Erzieherische, das Mustergültig-Feststehende, das Geschliffen-Herkömmliche, das Göttlich-Nichtsagende, das Nebelhaft-Grenzenlose und Verheißungsvoll-Ungeheuere. (Hayes 1974: 139)

Simply to recommend that equivalents should be substituted for the above examples is, in effect, to offer no strategy at all. Hayes recognises the syntactical difficulties involved in translating these compounds, which are formidable even before the translator has to embark on the even more difficult semantic aspects:

> For the most part these are adjectival nouns: and this circumstance presents an immediate difficulty, because an attempt to reproduce them formally at every occurrence will very probably result in woodenness. The adjectival noun, so common in German, makes rather stiff sounding English [. . .] There is a subtle difference (at least Thomas Mann must have thought so) between "das Verheißungsvoll-Ungeheure" and "das verheißungsvoll[e] Ungeheure"; the second expression lacks the vibrant quality of the first. (Hayes 1974: 140)

This raises the central question as to what comprises a successful philosophical translation. The first point to be made in this context is that philosophy is not a homogeneous activity and different strategies will be needed for different kinds of philosophy. At the extreme ends of the philosophical spectrum, there is the mathematically based philosophy in a work such as Gottlob Frege's *Begriffsschrift* on the one hand, or an abstract, idiosyncratic and creative work such as Jacques Derrida's *De la grammatologie* or Nietzsche's *Also Sprach Zarathustra* on the other. For the practical translator, the approach is clear: i.e. Frege would be translated in a scientific mathematical way so that the translator's grasp of mathematical logic is as important as his or her grasp of German. The translator needs to be familiar with the technical terminology in both languages. This would apply particularly to a work such as Frege's *Über Sinn und Bedeutung* in which the terms *Sinn* and *Bedeutung* would have to be invariantly translated as *sense* and *reference* respectively as these are fixed terms in the English philosophical tradition. At the other extreme, a good literary translator with perhaps only a very limited knowledge of philosophy but with a very wide culture in both the source and target languages may well cope with Nietzsche.

Some philosophers lie between the two extremes such as Ludwig Wittgenstein where both a good literary style and a clear grasp of mathematical logic may well be prerequisites for such an undertaking. Venuti embarks on an interesting, but brief analysis of Anscombe's (1963) translation Wittgenstein's *Philosophical Investigation*s. His examples support his thesis that her translation is overdomesticated.

> Hence, no English translation can ever simply communicate Wittgenstein's German text without simultaneously inscribing it with English-language forms that destabilize and reconstitute his own philosophy.
>
> Consider a typical excerpt from Anscombe's version:
>
> Das Benennen erscheint als eine *seltsame* Verbindung eines Wortes mit einem Gegenstand. - [. .] Denn die philosophischen Probleme entstehen, wenn die Sprache *feiert*.
>
> Naming appears as a *queer* connection of a word with an object. [. . .] For philosophical problems arise when language *goes on holiday.*
>
> The translation is cast mostly in a plain register of the standard dialect of English, but the orthography is British, and Anscombe draws noticeably on British colloquialisms: [. . .] the use of "holiday" and "queer" where American English would substitute "vacation" (or "day off") and "strange". (Venuti 1998: 108-109)

If Venuti's trivial argument concerning the Atlantic divide is ignored, he does make a valid point concerning what he later describes as "unusual" renderings in Anscombe's version. The adjective *queer* can be described as overtranslation (with the force of *wunderlich* in German) and the idea of language going on holiday is far too active an image conjuring up a picture of language packing a trunk and setting off for the seaside. A disappointing aspect of Venuti's contribution on the translation of philosophy is that he treats philosophy as another kind of literary writing without examining the crucial features of philosophical dialogue. For example, much of philosophical discourse involves argument or, more precisely, *argumentation* which, in turn, implies logical form. It is imperative to the philosopher that this form is clearly transposed by the translator. It will be shown in the example to be analysed in this chapter that Thomas Mann has a very clear argumentation even though it is often embedded in a dense literary text. One strategy is to convert the relevant passage into logical form before embarking on a translation, but first it is necessary to return to the translations in question.

That a translator should acquire a clear grasp of the main philosophical ideas and themes of the author s/he is translating before embarking on a translation should be obvious and uncontroversial, but in Lowe-Porter's version, it will be shown that this was not the case.

The following strategy is suggested as one of many possible approaches, but all valid strategies are likely to display similar features: there must be an initial, hermeneutic stage or simply 'decoding' depending on the difficulty of the text in question. The text is analysed in the context of the author's ideas or, in this case, in the context of Mann's various themes and motifs. There should be a clear holistic understanding of the argument, even if this is only a subjective impression, before embarking on the encoding stage. The translator must attempt to interpret the text or else the general sense would remain obscure. (Even a false interpretation is, to a certain extent, preferable to a garbled version. With a clear, but false interpretation, the mistake can easily be remedied after discussion with the good practice of consulting experts in the relevant field.)

(b) Discussion of the Problem of Translating Philosophical Literary Texts with regard to Thomas Mann's Oeuvre

In *Tonio Kröger*, the whole of Chapter IV is devoted to a philosophical dialogue (or more accurately, monologue) on the nature and origin of art as well as the nature and character of the artist. The disquisition involves a setting up of antinomies such as *Bürger* versus *Künstler*, *Natur* versus *Kunst* and *Geist* versus *Leben*. Tonio's argumentation shows how these themes hitherto thought to be complementary are irreconcilable opposites for the contemporary artist of his time. This is felt acutely in his own case because through his background he feels to be as much *Bürger* as *Künstler* and so, he suffers greatly from his conflicting identities. It is just as important for the translator as well as for the teacher of literature that the clear argumentation behind these themes should be explicated.

Der Tod in Venedig has, however, even more 'philosophical' passages than *Tonio Kröger*. In this work, the argumentation is brought forward so that the 'Bürger-Künstler' Gustav von Aschenbach seems to have managed to cope with the antinomies which caused the conflict in Tonio Kröger. However, a new and fatal situation emerges which results in his death. This time key themes are linked together as a chain with an inevitable and fatal concatenation. The - *art→ eros→ decadence→ disease→ death* – argument, to which reference has already been discussed in Section (d) of Chapter III can be summarised as follows: the spiritual appeal of art is beauty, but beauty works through the senses and is thus linked to sensuousness and sensuality. The cultivation of sensuality leads to sexuality which in turn leads to 'sin' and 'sin' leads to disease and death; thus the artist is doomed by his or her love of beauty from the start. Aschenbach had tried to resist the inevitability of this logic by adopting a *Bürger* existence based on hard work, discipline and the defence of morality. However, as is too well known to relate once again here, his brief excursion into a more relaxed *modus vivendi* lets him fall prey to the inevitable logic outlined above. It is important that the translator should keep this argument explicit and clear throughout the novella. Mann's German style which, as has been seen in Chapter IV, can be opaque, spells out the message with transparent clarity. The explicit philosophical dialogues based on Plato's *Gastmahl* and *Phaidros* as translated by Kaßner (1903) are further 'translated' by Thomas Mann into poetic prose which, at the same time, underline his own philosophical argument with utmost clarity as analysed by Häfele and Stammel (1992). One brief extract shows how closely Thomas Mann follows the philosophical dialogue which is 'translated' into poetic prose:

> Sokrates: Nur die Schönheit ist zugleich sichtbar und liebenswürdig, beides. [. . .] Denn der Freund ist göttlicher als der Geliebte. Der Freund trägt den Gott in sich. (Platon 1903: 6)
>
> Thomas Mann: Denn die Schönheit, mein Phaidros, nur sie ist liebenswürdig und sichtbar zugleich. [. . .] dies, daß der Liebende göttlicher sei als der Geliebte, will in jenem der Gott sei, nicht aber im andern. (Mann 1977: 374)

If we look at Mann as a 'translator' of philosophy, he is a very effective interpreter because he does not only rewrite Kaßner's Plato in an even more poetic form but he also explicates the argument to make this theme transparent. The argument is further translated into action by the downfall of his protagonist. The incidents in the novella constantly illustrate these themes in both a vivid and concrete way.

(c) Detailed Analysis of a Philosophical Literary Passage in Chapter II of *Der Tod in Venedig*

It will be seen that Luke generally translates the dialectic of the novella with sufficient clarity despite some philosophically opaque passages, one of which will be subjected to close analysis and translation in the next Section of this chapter. His introduction to his version of Mann's short stories is cogently argued as is to be expected from a German scholar whereas he rightly refers to Lowe-Porter's versions as "garbled". Chapter IV of *Tonio Kröger*, which contains the philosophical monologue, will not be subjected to detailed analysis because it can be seen from Appendix I that there is an enormous density of gross errors in Lowe-Porter's version and that the sense is so grossly distorted at even the most elementary level of surface meaning that a philosophical analysis of this chapter would be rendered superfluous. Instead, a difficult philosophical passage will be taken from *Der Tod in Venedig* where the mistakes are less gross and where the meaning is distorted in a more subtle way. Even in this passage, however, there are some gross mistakes such as her translation of the noun *Wucht* as *fury* because of confusion between *Wucht* and *Wut*. Luke's version, though more accurate, is also not always clear. Suggested translations will be offered as in Chapter IV.

The passage for analysis, however, is taken from Chapter II of *Der Tod in Venedig* and has been chosen because the theme is a 'philosophical' continuation from the literary extract discussed in detail in Chapter V and so, acts as a further commentary on the same themes. It is also a typically condensed text where the meaning is not always immediately apparent and where a confused version can produce disastrous results. These more difficult passages in Mann's oeuvre are often the less popular and thus the less analysed passages on account of their initial difficulty. This is particularly the case in the longer works such as in *Der Zauberberg* where they could, at times, be regarded as too philosophical for what is essentially a literary work. Mann's philosophising passages have a surface obscurity and a surface difficulty, but once this has been penetrated, they do not pose translation difficulties comparable to the stylistic aspects discussed in the previous chapter. However, as the surface difficulties are sufficiently daunting even for an educated German reader, it is all the more important to have a clear translation for the non-native reader. Here, a competent translator can provide a useful service by acting as an interpreter and clarifier. On the other hand, a "garbled" version can only have disastrous results because what was difficult in the original becomes impossible in the confused translation and what was at the limits of comprehensibility becomes totally meaningless. The Luke and Lowe-Porter versions, which will be compared with each other and with other possible strategies, illustrate this point. All seven versions are printed in full at the end of the dissertation in Appendix III for purposes of comparison. Version I is Lowe-Porter's translation, Version II is Luke's, Version III is offered as semantic translation, IV is a suggested communicative translation, V is the first translation of *Der Tod in Venedig* by Kenneth Burke of 1929 and which remains unchanged in the 1971 reprint, VI is the 1993 translation by Koelb and Version VII is the most recent translation of this work (Chase: 1999). It would be tempting to analyse all seven versions, but this would be beyond the scope of the study. They are presented, however, for further comparison to show how varied translations can be, but at the same time, how all the five published versions are well within the parameters of what has been defined as *academic translation*. All fail at the poetic level, but all except for Lowe-Porter's version, succeed at the basic level of transfer of information, and so could be classified as adequate. Version III attempts to capture something of Thomas Mann's style, but still remains a pale reflection. There is, however, very little of Thomas Mann's style in the other five versions. Version IV aims at readability and, to a large extent, succeeds, though at the expense of closeness to the text. However, in this version, the philosophical argument is transparent. The other three versions have a lack-lustre quality in English, no doubt contributing to the reputation of Thomas Mann as being pompous, dull and heavy. Little of the irony is conveyed in all the versions except, possibly, in III, but the irony is so subtle in this paragraph that even a native reader could be forgiven for missing this element. The source text passage will now be quoted in full:

Aber es scheint, daß gegen nichts ein edler und tüchtiger Geist sich rascher, sich gründlicher abstumpft als gegen den scharfen und bitteren Reiz der Erkenntnis; und gewiß ist, daß die schwermütig gewissenhafteste Gründlichkeit des Jünglings Seichtheit bedeutet im Vergleich mit dem tiefen Entschlusse des Meister gewordenen Mannes, das Wissen zu leugnen, es abzulehnen, erhobenen Hauptes darüber hinwegzugehen, sofern es den Willen, die Tat, das Gefühl und selbst die Leidenschaft im geringsten zu lähmen, zu entmutigen, zu entwürdigen geeignet ist. Wie wäre die berühmte Erzählung vom 'Elenden' wohl anders zu deuten denn als

Ausbruch des Ekels gegen den unanständigen Psychologismus der Zeit, verkörpert in der Figur jenes weichen und albernen Halbschurken, der sich ein Schicksal erschleicht, indem er sein Weib, aus Ohnmacht, aus Lasterhaftigkeit, aus ethischer Velleität, in die Arme eines Unbärtigen treibt und aus Tiefe Nichtswürdigkeiten begehen zu dürfen glaubt? Die Wucht des Wortes, mit welcher hier das Verworfene verworfen wurde, verkündete die Abkehr von allem moralischen Zweifelsinn, von jeder Sympathie mit dem Abgrund, die Absage an die Laxheit des Mitleidssatzes, daß alles verstehen alles verzeihen heiße, und was sich hier vorbereitete, ja schon vollzog, war jenes 'Wunder der wiedergeborenen Unbefangenheit,' auf welches ein wenig später in einem der Dialoge des Autors ausdrücklich und nicht ohne geheimnisvolle Betonung die Rede kam. Seltsame Zusammenhänge! War es eine geistige Folge dieser 'Wiedergeburt', dieser neuen Würde und Strenge, daß man um dieselbe Zeit ein fast übermäßiges Erstarken seines Schönheitssinnes beobachtete, jene adelige Reinheit, Einfachheit und Ebenmäßigkeit der Formgebung, welche seinen Produkten fortan ein so sinnfälliges, ja gewolltes Gepräge der Meisterlichkeit und Klassizität verlieh? Aber moralische Entschlossenheit jenseits des Wissens, der auflösenden und hemmenden Erkenntnis - bedeutet sie nicht wiederum eine Vereinfachung, eine sittliche Vereinfältigung der Welt und der Seele und also auch ein Erstarken zum Bösen, Verbotenen, zum sittlich Unmöglichen? Und hat Form nicht zweierlei Gesicht? Ist sie nicht sittlich und unsittlich zugleich - sittlich als Ergebnis und Ausdruck der Zucht, unsittlich aber und selbst widersittlich, sofern sie von Natur eine moralische Gleichgültigkeit in sich schließt, ja wesentlich bestrebt ist, das Moralische unter ihr stolzes und unumschränktes Zepter zu beugen? (Mann 1977: 17-18)

The text could be interpreted as follows: Mann's basic point is that Aschenbach attempted to reintroduce morality into the twentieth century world of high art and literature. His work is a rejection of the 'satanic' view of art as is sometimes portrayed in French Symbolist poets such as Baudelaire or in the Nietzschean view of art as expressed in works such as *Jenseits von Gut und Böse* in which, at least, conventional morality is rejected. Aschenbach (and Mann himself) show that, despite 'Nietzschean insights' beyond good and evil, the artist is still a member of society and that the choice for 'bourgeois' morality is not a step towards mediocrity, but, instead, is the artist's best path to high and sustained creative achievement as evidenced by Achenbach's own artistic career. The moral resolution has neither the effect of stunting nor of stultifying aesthetic sensibility, but on the contrary, leads to progression, to the heights of literary and philosophical achievement, even to a new and fresh classicism as opposed to the 'charms' and 'lures' of creative insight which do, in fact, have the ultimate effect of blunting the intellect.

Having analysed the passage for its main themes, its logical form can now be explicated[47] and it can be further deconstructed for its subtext: its hidden agenda and its implicit assumptions. Aschenbach, however, rejects the argument set out in footnote forty-two, but the rejection is emotional rather than rational. His whole life was based on a rejection of this inevitable concatenation so that his whole life was based on a contradiction or a lie. The lie is borne out by the subsequent events supporting the logical chain; hence, the tremendous tension in this passage and the vehemence with which Aschenbach rejects the enticements of an aesthetically based amorality. Despite the tension between intellect and emotion, there is also an underlying irony of the artist who 'protests too much' and who despite his moral commitment to classicism and truth is dazzled by his own language into grandiloquence and aestheticism, thus already hinting at the truth of the logical outcome together with his own inevitable downfall.

The tone of this passage is intense and impassioned, betraying the inner passion of the artist; yet there is something self-satisfied even to the point of smugness in the exquisitely high literary tone. The phrase "man um dieselbe Zeit ein fast übermäßiges Erstarken seines Schönheitssinnes beobachtete," applies not only to the fictitious author but also to the passage itself. The irony has an element of self-mockery. The tension of the elaborately wrought, long sentences reflects Aschenbach's own tension which will, inevitably, reach breaking point. The vehemence with which he tries to refute the inevitability of the aesthetic logic reflects the tension between reason and Aschenbach's own will. This tension is released in the last sentence in which aesthetic considerations predominate over philosophical content with the result that, yet again, the form not only reflects but also plays with the content both underlining and illustrating the basic point that 'beauty' will rule over 'truth' in the end just as in the story itself *Eros* triumphs over reason. The decay of an exaggerated aestheticism is embodied in a text of magnificently impassioned classical

---

[47] As this demands some knowledge of the propositional calculus within formal logic, it is appropriate in an essentially literary thesis to exhibit this as a footnote:

1. Discipline produces the artist.	$D \Rightarrow A$
2. The artist gains insight into the depths of reality.	$A \Rightarrow I$
3. Insight is not bound by morality (i.e. is amoral).	$I \Rightarrow -M$
4. Amorality leads to immorality and downfall (sin, death)	$-M \Rightarrow S$
therefore,	$A \Rightarrow S$

As is clear from the symbolism, this is a valid but not an obvious argument (as opposed to $D \Rightarrow S$ which has a simple *modus ponens* structure) because this works only by a triple application of the *hypothetical syllogism*.

prose which, however, like the strawberries, that turned out to be the efficient cause of Aschenbach's death, can be described as 'overripe'. The translator should attempt to capture something of the tone of the passage, if the subtext (that the pent-up power in beauty is artificially controlled by morality) is to be conveyed. Although in an abstract and rather difficult way, this passage encapsulates the whole story of the novella.

The second stage is the encoding, reconstruction, rewriting or reconfiguration of the ideas. Before this stage is attempted, a translation decision must be made as to whether the text should be target-language oriented, i.e. a communicative translation written for a specific readership (Version IV) or whether it should be a semantic translation (Version III) remaining as close as possible to the source language as implied by Venuti's argumentation in Section (a) of this chapter.

In philosophical writing, a good communicative translation will express the main ideas clearly and fluently, using meta-text if necessary, but will still strive to capture the spirit and flavour of the original. It will cross cultural and national boundaries. In both Lowe-Porter and Luke's versions, the main argument is lost probably as an effect caused by the *academic approach*, whereas in both Versions III and IV the sense and meaning of the passage is conveyed.

It will also be evident that the explication of the argument in logical form leads to clear and comprehensible texts as in Versions III and IV. The highlighting of structure is also another example of a *translation strategy*. The language game in this and many other philosophical passages is intimately bound with logical form. In the selected passage, it has been shown that several language games are embedded in the text which can be subsumed under the headings *philosophy* and *literature*.

d) Lowe-Porter's and Luke's Translations of the Philosophical Literary Passage in Chapter II of *Der Tod in Venedig*

It is now appropriate to analyse the Lowe-Porter and Luke translations of the extract and to compare them with the suggested free semantic Version III and the suggested free communicative Version IV, as has already been structured in Chapter V.

Version I:

Lowe-Porter: But it seems that a noble and active mind blunts itself against nothing so quickly as the sharp and bitter *irritant of knowledge*[1]. And certain it is that the youth's *constancy of purpose*,[2] no matter how painfully conscientious, was shallow beside the mature resolution of the master of his craft, who made *a right-about-face*[3], turned his back on *the realm of knowledge,*[4] _[5] and passed it by with averted face, lest it lame his will or power of action, paralyse his feelings or his passions, deprive any of these of their conviction or *utility*[6]. How else interpret the oft-cited story of *The Abject,* than as a rebuke to the excesses of a psychology-ridden age, embodied in the delineation of the weak and silly fool who manages *to lead fate by the nose*[7]; driving his wife, out of sheer *innate pusillanimity*[8], into the arms of a beardless youth, and *making this disaster*[9] an excuse for *trifling away*[10] the rest of his life? *With rage*[11] the author here rejects the rejected, casts out the outcast - and the measure of his fury is the measure of his condemnation of *all moral shilly-shallying*[12]. Explicitly he renounces sympathy with the abyss, explicitly he refutes the flabby humanitarianism of the phrase: *'Tout comprendre c'est tout pardonner*[13].' What was here unfolding, or rather was already in full bloom, was 'the miracle of regained detachment,' which a little later became the theme of one of the author's dialogues, dwelt upon not without a *certain oracular emphasis*[14]. *Strange sequence of thought*[15]! Was it perhaps an intellectual consequence of this rebirth, this new austerity, that *from now on*[16] *his style showed an almost exaggerated sense of beauty*[17], a lofty purity, symmetry, and simplicity, which gave his productions a stamp of the classic, of conscious and deliberate mastery? And yet: this moral fibre, surviving the hampering and disintegrating effect of knowledge, does it not result in its turn in a dangerous simplification, *in a tendency to equate the world and the human soul*[18], and thus to strengthen the hold of the evil, the forbidden, and the ethically impossible? And has not form two aspects? Is it not moral and immoral at once; moral in so far as it is the expression and result of discipline, immoral - yes, actually hostile to morality - in that of its very essence it is indifferent to good and evil, and deliberately concerned to make the moral world stoop beneath its proud and undivided sceptre? (Lowe-Porter 1978: 17-18)

1) The phrase *irritant of knowledge* is inappropriate for "Reiz der Erkenntnis" for the following reasons:

(a) The noun *irritant* has the opposite meaning to the one in this context - *charm, lure, enticement* etc., as in the phrase *the lure of artistic insight* or as correctly rendered in the other versions. Thus, the introductory major premise of the passage is given a contrary meaning from the very beginning, thereby undermining the whole structure of the argument.

(b) The noun *knowledge* for "Erkenntnis" needs qualification: as already analysed in Chapter IV, *knowledge* has more associations with *Wissenschaft*; simply the noun *insight* or even *artistic* or *philosophical insight* would be appropriate in this context. This point will be discussed in greater detail at a later stage in this chapter. [48]

---

[48] According to Thirlwall, Lowe-Porter had probably discussed this difficulty with Albert Einstein: "In this interview she pointed out a key difficulty in working with another language: 'It sometimes happens that a foreigner, however fluent his English, will not know *all* the implications of an English word and thus consider its use in an English sentence as incorrect. I once had a discussion on this point with a very great, very modest genius [probably Einstein], who could not believe that the German word

2) The phrase *constancy of purpose* has no German equivalent in the original. This is, perhaps, a relatively harmless interpolation from Lowe-Porter, whose work tends to idealise and romanticise Thomas Mann's themes.

3) The expression *a right-about-face* for "mit dem tiefen Entschluß" is far too colloquial for the high literary tone of the passage as well as being semantically overtranslated because the Lowe-Porter collocation would imply a complete reversal of values or 'U-turn' rather than a *decision*.

4) The phrase *the realm of knowledge* for the gerund *das Wissen*: this is another example of Lowe-Porter's romanticising the darker themes in Mann's work. This *Wissen* separates the artist from the *Bürger* and is more likely to have satanic overtones that later become explicit in Mann's oeuvre as with Leverkühn's insights into music in *Dr Faustus*. The phrase *the realm of knowledge*, on the other hand, is an idealistic term more in tune with Romanticism or even Victorian sentimentality than the sophisticated context of this particular discourse.

5) The phrase *"im geringsten"* is omitted in the Lowe-Porter version, thus lessening the force of the ethical commitment and total rejection of evil. This also misses the *emotional* force behind Aschenbach's decision with a resultant loss of the tension already discussed with regard to this passage.

6) The noun *utility* - another unjustified interpolation which would confuse the issues. It is not clear whether utility is used in the context of a Benthamite hedonistic calculus, i.e. producing the greatest happiness for the greatest number, or merely in its ordinary sense of usefulness. As this concept is not in the original text nor implied in any way, great philosophical confusion results for the reader.

7) The phrase *lead fate by the nose* fails to express the meaning of "der sich ein Schicksal erschleicht" as it implies the protagonist is not only in control of fate in general, but is fooling destiny itself. Luke's version is more accurate "who cheats his way into destiny", or Version IV which is slightly bolder: "who gained a cheap notoriety for himself".

8) The phrase *innate pusillanimity* is a poor translation for "aus Ohnmacht, aus Lasterhaftigkeit, aus ethischer Velleität". Not only is the *Steigerungseffekt* (crescendo) missed which culminates in the ironic *Velleität*, a word itself that hovers on the edge of the German language reflecting its own subtle ambiguity, but Lowe-Porter also

---

Erkenntnis, translated, had in English, as in German, many shades of meaning. The same is true with English renderings of German words, my own included.' " (Thirlwall 1966: 26. Thirlwall's insertion.)

es a completely alien idea into the argument, namely that the weakness was
;, or inherited. The very point of the story is to show that this laxity is
rehensible because there is free consent to moral turpitude, but the idea of innate or
inborn evil would tend to have the opposite effect by exonerating the anti-hero. Thus,
the example aimed to concretise what is otherwise an abstract argument is botched
with yet another loss in the philosophical argumentation.

9) The phrase *making this disaster* has no German source. This again is an unwarranted
addition which distorts the text in the same way as the use of the adjective *innate* in
the previous line. As a disaster generally refers to something external to the speaker
and is often associated with the collocation *natural disaster*, this again has the effect
of lessening the guilt of the anti-hero. Since there is neither explicit nor implicit
reference to a disaster in the text, the interpolation cannot be justified.

10) The phrase *trifling away* for "Nichtswürdigkeiten begehen" is a very weak
translation for the rather strong, but far more appropriate translation in IV *committing
acts of indecency*. The whole shameful and disgusting aspects of the original (no
doubt reminiscent of woeful figures such as *Tobias Mindernickel* in the eponymous
story) are domesticated out of existence in the Lowe-Porter version.

11) The phrase *with rage* for "mit Wucht" is obviously a complete misreading of the
text at the most elementary level, i.e. confusion between *Wucht* and *Wut*.

12) The phrase *moral shilly-shallying* for "ethischer Velleität". This vivid, though very
colloquial phrase is another example of Lowe-Porter's tendency to trivialise the
philosophical passages.

13) The phrase *Tout comprendre, c'est tout pardonner* is perhaps an adequate
translation (by going back to the original), but the high literary tone of the passage is
lowered by the use of this hackneyed saying.

14) The phrase *a certain oracular emphasis* is far too strong a translation for the phrase
"nicht ohne geheimnisvolle Betonung". The adjective *oracular* refers to an
authoritative pronouncement, which again has the effect of heightening the hubris
theme invented by Lowe-Porter (see Chapter III (c)) and is yet another factor
emphasising Lowe-Porter's reduction of the tragedy to a morality play as discussed in
Chapter III. The adjective *geheimnisvoll* with its implication of secret or mysterious
motives, in this context, would seem to refer to private hidden, possibly clandestine
reasons known only to the author himself.

15) In the phrase, *strange sequence of thought*, for "seltsame Zusammenhänge", the German plural form is important here as many different strands within the basic themes of Thomas Mann's philosophy are referred to with the implication that some strands connect in unexpected ways whereas a sequence would imply the opposite such as a chronological or formal logical sequence. Version IV would seem to express the import most clearly, even if with some licence: "How strange the way all these themes connect with each other!"

16) The phrase *from now on* is an embarrassing elementary grammatical mistake for "um dieselbe Zeit". As this reference is to the past, not the present, the translation should be either a close translation such as *at the same time* or at least a phrase such as *from that time onwards* if tense coherence is to be maintained. Any equivalent which keeps the relative future reference within the framework of past time could also be used. This is, of course, not a mistake repeated in the other translations.

17) In the phrase *his style showed an almost exaggerated sense of beauty* for "ein fast übermäßiges Erstarken seines Schönheitssinnes"; it is not his style (an inanimate abstract noun) that has a sense of beauty, but the man himself so that a phrase such as *aesthetic consciousness* or *aesthetic sensibility* would be more appropriate as in versions III and IV, implying that Aschenbach's aestheticism increased to an inordinate degree, an implication which is totally lost in the Lowe-Porter version, but which is important for understanding not only the tone and register of the passage but also its general argumentation.

18) The phrase *in a tendency to equate the world and the human soul* is a philosophically disastrous translation for *eine sittliche Vereinfältigung der Welt und der Seele*. Mann is concerned that a (bourgeois) ethical stance could lead to a simplistic metaphysical position, i.e. a naïve belief in good and evil despite living in a post-Nietzschean world. Lowe-Porter's formulation echoes more idealistic notions such as Schelling's concept of the *Weltseele* or could even be interpreted as a form of solipsism - both possibilities being philosophically totally misleading by distorting the cultural context.

Version II:

Luke: But it seems that there is nothing to which a noble and *active mind*[1] more quickly becomes inured than that pungent and bitter stimulus, the *acquisition of knowledge*[2]; and it is very sure that even the most gloomily conscientious and radical sophistication of youth is shallow by comparison with Aschenbach's profound decision as a mature master to repudiate knowledge as such, to reject it, to step over it with head held high - in the recognition that knowledge can paralyse the will, paralyse and discourage action and emotion and even passion, and rob all these of their dignity. How else is the famous short story *A Study in Abjection* to be understood but as an outbreak of disgust against an age indecently undermined by psychology and represented by the figure *of a spiritless, witless semiscoundrel*[3] who cheats his way into a destiny of sorts, when, *motivated by his own ineptitude*[4] and depravity and ethical *whimsicality,*[5] he drives his wife into the arms of a callow youth - convinced that his intellectual depths entitle him to behave with contemptible baseness? *The forthright words of condemnation which here weighed vileness in the balance and found it wanting*[6] - they proclaimed *their writer's renunciation of all moral scepticism,*[7] of every kind of sympathy with the abyss; they declared his repudiation of the laxity of that compassionate principle which holds that to understand all is to forgive all. And the development that was here being anticipated, indeed already taking place, was that 'miracle of reborn naiveté' to which, in a dialogue written a little later, the author himself had referred with a certain mysterious emphasis. *How strange these associations!* [8] Was it an intellectual consequence of this 'rebirth,' of this new dignity and rigor, that, at about the same time, *his sense of beauty was observed to undergo an almost excessive resurgence,*[9] that his style took on the noble purity, simplicity and symmetry that were *to set upon*[10] all his subsequent works that *so evident and evidently intentional*[11] stamp of the classical master? And yet: moral resoluteness at the far side of knowledge, achieved *in despite of*[12] all corrosive and inhibiting insight - does this not in its turn signify a simplification, a morally simplistic view of the world and of human psychology, and thus also a resurgence of energies that are evil, forbidden, morally impossible? And is form not two-faced? Is it not at one and the same time moral and immoral - moral as the product and expression of discipline, but immoral and even antimoral inasmuch as it houses within itself an innate moral indifference, and indeed essentially strives for nothing less than to bend morality under its proud and absolute scepter? (Luke 1988: 204-205)

1) The phrase *active mind* is a misleading translation for "tüchtiger Geist". As is often the case and despite his explicit reservations concerning Lowe-Porter's competence, Luke often slavishly and disastrously follows Lowe-Porter's version. The moral aspect of diligence, a typical theme for Thomas Mann which is vividly expressed in *Schwere Stunde,* for example, is missed in these two translations. Since the passage is concerned with this aspect of morality and the problem of making ethical choices in general, this is a serious omission.

2) The phrase *the acquisition of knowledge* is very neutral and too scientific for "bitteren Reiz der Erkenntnis" as Luke's phrase implies a mere accumulation of facts, a total misconception, as has already been analysed in note 1(b) referring to the Lowe-Porter version.

3) In the phrase *of a spiritless, witless semiscoundrel* for "jenes weichen und albernen Halbschurken", the adjective *witless* lacks the necessary element of

moral condemnation. (Similarly, the adjective *spiritless* is also too weak by implying a defect rather than the conscious choice for evil. The adjective *weak* would carry the necessary moral connotations.) The noun *semiscroundrel* does not work in English and has, indeed, a ludicrous effect. As scoundrel expresses harsh condemnation, the subject of reference is either a scoundrel or not a scoundrel. We do not, for example, talk of 'semi-thieves' when referring to someone who might be regarded as even the pettiest of thieves. However, the noun *Halbschurke* presents a translation problem because it is also a strange concoction in German so that a literal translation could be just accepted in a close semantic translation.

4) In the phrase *motivated by his own ineptitude* for "aus Ohnmacht", the noun *ineptitude* continues Luke's stress on stupidity and mild condemnation as opposed to moral weakness, which is, in fact, the main theme of the sentence. Again the diminishing of the ethical content reflects the failure to follow the line of argument in the passage.

5) The noun *whimsicality* is also weak for "Velleität" and continues, as in the Lowe-Porter version, the toning down the opprobrium Mann wishes to heap on the protagonist. *Whimsicality* has positive associations in the case of a person merely following what might be eccentric whims, whereas, in this context, the noun *Velleität* has more to do with prevarication, lack of ethical purpose and profound decadence. This is yet another example of domesticating the ethical content out of existence and thus of losing the whole force of the argument.

6) The clause *the forthright words of condemnation which here weighed vileness in the balance and found it wanting* is another domesticated version for "die Wucht des Wortes, mit welcher hier das Verworfene verworfen wurde". In what sense *vileness* can be found wanting is not clear as something is either vile or not and a lacking vileness (in other words, a vileness found wanting would imply the opposite, i.e. that the vileness was not vile enough!) Again this reflects the failure to follow the philosophical thread running throughout the passage.

7) The phrase *the writer's renunciation of all moral scepticism* for "verkündete die Abkehr von allem moralischen Zweifelsinn" continues to domesticate the rejection of immorality. Renunciation is not the same as rejection and usually has connotations of doing without, often connected with asceticism. Repudiation or a more literal phrase such as the *turning away from* would be more suitable in this context. Only in certain formulations such as *renouncing the devil* does the word

renunciation have its full moral force of total rejection, but in the phrase *renunciation of all moral scepticism*, the logical implication becomes confused, because the renunciation of moral scepticism could imply the absurd conclusion that <u>immoral</u> scepticism would be more acceptable. This point is another illustration of the mistake of simply translating a philosophical text sentence by sentence rather than taking a holistic approach to the highly structured argument.

8) The phrase, *how strange these associations*, for "seltsame Zusammenhänge" is again a weak translation. Associations are open-ended echoes of meanings where the term *Zusammenhänge* (*interconnections*) refers to the structure of themes, which seemingly unrelated, prove, in fact, to be connected to each other. The attentive reader can trace the structure of the connections of these themes. *Associations*, on the other hand, are much looser (as in a dream) so that something of the interconnectedness of Mann's universe is lost in Luke's version.

9) The clause *his sense of beauty was observed to undergo an almost excessive resurgence* for "man um dieselbe Zeit ein fast übermäßiges Erstarken seines Schönheitssinnes beobachtete," implies that his aesthetic sense reappeared by the process of *resurgence* whereas the whole point of the sentence is to show that there was a *new* development of aesthetic sensibility, namely an increase in his powers. Thus, the sense of a decadent overripe sensibility, as already discussed in Section (c) of this chapter, is lost.

10) The phrase *to set upon* [. . .] *stamp* is an infelicitous use of English for "Gepräge verleihen". The phrase: *He set his seal upon something* is a possible collocation, but not: **He set upon his works that stamp.*

11) The phrase, *that so evident and evidently intentional stamp*, for "ein so sinnfälliges, ja gewolltes Gepräge" is clever word-play, but fails to work as the collocation *that evident stamp of the classical master* is not semantically transparent unlike an alternative such as *that obvious stamp of the classical master,* and this lack of transparency is blurred even more by adding the adverb *evidently* to qualify yet another adjective, thus producing a confusing effect.

12) The preposition **in despite of* does not, of course, exist. It is to be hoped that this error, more typical in the works of Lowe-Porter, is a printer's oversight.

Luke's condemnation of the Lowe-Porter version as "garbled" would seem to be particularly apt with regard to the translation of 'philosophical' passages. Even though, at times, there is a certain flow, some of the basic ideas have been shown to be either ignored or misunderstood and key-themes played down or omitted. Luke's version is more comprehensible and generally makes sense despite his omission of some vital aspects such as the strong emphasis on moral responsibility as shown in the detailed analysis, but the argument is not clearly highlighted and the passages seem confusing and dull, lacking the intense passion of the original. In short, it lacks a clear structured coherent argument as has been shown in the detailed analysis where some key premises in the argument have been blurred by inaccurate translation. It must be admitted that the source text is difficult, but Luke's translation serves only to increase these surface difficulties partly on account of the various misreadings but mainly because there is no attempt to analyse, clarify, interpret or convey the basic argument. Although Luke is a highly competent German scholar, his translation is a typical product of the *academic approach* of line-by-line, sentence-by-sentence translation.

e) A Source-Text-Based Version

Following Venuti's approach outlined in part (a) of this chapter, two strategies are offered as improvements in the suggested versions. The first (Version III) is a source-text-based translation or to use Newmark's terminology a *semantic* version.

However, different from both Venuti and Newmark, this translation's main point of fidelity is to the argumentation and structure involving some use of meta-language. In this passage as in the more domesticating Version IV, the force of the moral condemnation of amoral aestheticism is highlighted to contrast with the high moral discipline and determination of Aschenbach's career.

Version III: (Source-Text-Based Version) (Gledhill)

> However, it seems that the pungently acrid and bitter allure of knowledge and insight will stupefy the noble and diligent mind more swiftly and more systematically than anything else; and it is also certain that the young artist's absolute thoroughness carried out in glum resignation was sheer superficiality compared with that profound decision of the later mature artist who had become a master of his craft and who had decided to deny insight and knowledge, to reject them and, with his head proudly held high, to walk away as soon as artistic insight showed the slightest tendency to paralyse, discourage or, in any way, debase either the will, action or the emotions including the passions. How else could the story, *A Vile Wretch* be interpreted other than as an outburst of horror against the psychologising tendencies so typical of the age, which were epitomised in the form of that weak and foolish, immature wretch who slimed his way into history by driving his wife into the arms of a beardless youth; and whose motives were determined by lethargy, vice and moral velleity and who fondly believed that his insights entitled him to behave indecently? The force with which the written word rejected the reject in this story heralded a turning away from all forms of moral

ambiguity and from all forms of sympathy with the abyss. It rejected the moral laxity implied by that trite formulation of ultimate compassion that implies to understand is to forgive. What was developing here and, in fact, came to fruition, was 'the miracle of a new-born objectivity' which was explicitly referred to in one of the author's dialogues and was given some special, mysterious emphasis. There were some very strange connections! Could it be as a result of this 'rebirth', of this new dignity and severity, that an almost exaggerated intensity in the author's aesthetic consciousness was simultaneously observed during this period - the aristocratic purity of style, simplicity and formal balance in his structures giving his literary products from that time onwards, their striking classicism and that masterly craftsmanship he had always been aiming for? But does not a moral stance that transcends knowledge and artistic insight (insights which dissolve everything and prevent action) imply a simplification or a simplistically moral attitude to the world and soul? And does not too much knowledge increase the inclination towards evil, the forbidden and what is morally impossible? And does not form have two faces? Is not form both moral and immoral at the same time - moral as a result of and expression of discipline, but also immoral in so far as, by its very nature, it contains a profound moral indifference or even worse, its essential aim is to force morality to bow down to its proud, unbounded sceptre?

(f) A Domesticating Version

Version IV follows from III in that the argumentation is highlighted but this time written in a more reader-friendly form i.e. domesticating, communicative but with all the basic ideas clearly conveyed to the reader. There are some slight explanatory additions and some omissions which do not distort the text as with the mistranslations of Luke and Lowe-Porter, but, on the contrary, which make the text clearer and more digestible for English-speaking readers. It is to a certain extent an interpretation, but hardly a controversial one as the 'message' of the original text is very clearly expressed. The strategic aspect of this translation based on Wittgenstein's language game theory is to demonstrate 'fidelity' to the particular language game being played: here, impassioned philosophical argument. This allows some semantic licence with the text in an explanatory or expanding form whilst at the same time remaining true to the structure and logic of the argument. The text is to seen merely as an illustration that yet another strategy is possible and is certainly an improvement on the academic approach and to be read as offering solutions to the problems that have arisen from the critical notes on Luke's and Lowe-Porter's translations.

Version IV: (Domesticating) (Gledhill)

There is nothing more powerful nor swifter in its effect on this earth for both blunting and stunting the intellects of even the noblest and most conscientious minds than the fascination that yields to pure insight and knowledge. On the other hand, the grim, pedantic diligence of the artist when he was a young man is merely superficial in comparison to the profound resolution made by the mature artist when he completely repudiated this kind of knowledge, proudly walking away from its domain as soon as insight threatened to paralyse the will, to dishonour human passions and emotions, to prevent moral action from taking place or, in any way, to detract from the dignity of the human, ethical areas of life. How else can we interpret the story called *Human Scum* other than as a vilification of the modern tendency to reduce evil to psychology? The outbreak of nausea towards 'psychologism' was symbolised by the protagonist of the story, a spineless and foolish specimen of 'human scum', who gained a cheap notoriety for himself by driving his wife into the arms of a callow youth? His weakness came from an inability to act, from a debauched will and moral equivocation, but he foolishly believed that depth of insight could justify acts of indecency. The eloquence with which the writer denounced this specimen marked a complete rejection of ethical prevarication - no more sympathy with the abyss nor with that decadent cliché: 'Tout comprendre, c'est tout pardonner.' This led to the next stage, 'the miracle of new-born objectivity', a phrase he had coined before in one of his dialogues when he gave it a mysterious, special emphasis. How strange the way all these themes seem to be interrelated! The new classicism and craftsmanship which, from then on, characterised his work could be seen as a consequence of the 'rebirth' which had occurred at the same time. His style had gained a new dignity and austerity; his works had an aristocratic purity, simplicity and balance and his aesthetic sensibility was carried almost to excess. There could, however, be dangers with this step taken in favour of a morality that transcends knowledge and philosophical insight that analyses and dissolves everything, thus atrophying the ability to act. The moral choice could imply a gross oversimplification of the external world and could cause the human soul to tend all the more in the direction of evil, towards forbidden things and towards the ethically impossible. Form itself can be said to have two faces, to be both moral and immoral, at the same time - *moral* as the fruit and expression of discipline, but also *immoral* or even *amoral* as form is, by its very nature, completely indifferent to morality and, what is more, its basic aim is to force morality to bow down to its proud sceptre that knows no limits.

(g) The Problem of Dialect Translation

The language-game theory can also contribute to the still unsolved/unsolvable problem of translating dialectal features in a text. As, however, there is only one passage in the three stories which has strong dialectal features, this aspect of translation theory will be dealt with only briefly. It is, first of all, necessary to distinguish dialect from sociolect, or, more precisely, to assess the proportion of sociolectal to dialectal constituents of any given dialogue. As many languages have a wide range of sociolectal registers, it should not be impossible to encode similar 'language games' in the target languages.

That it is difficult is attested by Raykowski (1979) in his *Nachwort* to his translation of three *Jeeves* stories:

> Manchmal ist es jedoch schwierig, für einen englischen Ausdruck einen sinnentsprechenden deutschen zu finden. Das gilt vor allem für Wörter, die eng mit dem kulturellen und sozialen Hintergrund Englands verbunden sind, also etwas „typisches Englisches" bezeichnen. Hin und wieder kann man so ein Wort um des Lokalkolorits willen stehen lassen, etwa *yard* oder *Colonel*. In anderen Fällen muß durch einen erklärenden Zusatz explizit gemacht werden, was sich für einen englischen Leser von selbst versteht. (Raykowski 1979: 128)

It is a pity that a translator as gifted as Raykowski is so pessimistic about the capturing of dialectal and sociolectal features as his brilliant solution to a pun in *Alice in Wonderland* analysed in Chapter VIII Section (b) shows that he is a highly resourceful translator and so much of the humour in Wodehouse's Jeeves depends on sociolectal colouring. This can be illustrated in the extract below taken from *Jeeves and the Kid Clementina*:

> I was wandering moodily to and fro on the pier, when I observed Jeeves *shimmering* towards me.
>
> 'Good afternoon sir,' he said. 'I had not supposed that you would be returning quite so soon, or I would have remained at the hotel.'
>
> 'I had not supposed that I would be returning quite so soon myself, Jeeves,' I said, sighing somewhat. 'I was *outed* in the first round, I regret to say.'
>
> 'Indeed, sir? I am sorry to hear that.'
>
> 'And to increase the mortification of defeat, Jeeves, by a *blighter* who had not spared himself at the luncheon table and was quite noticeably *sozzled*. I couldn't seem to do anything right.'
>
> 'Possibly you *omitted* to keep your eye on the ball *with sufficient assiduity*, sir?'
>
> 'Something of that nature, no doubt. Anyway, here I am, a *game* and popular loser and . . . ' I paused, and scanned the horizon with some interest.
>
> '*Great Scott,* Jeeves! Look at that girl just coming on to the pier. I never saw anybody so extraordinarily like Miss Wickham. How do account for these resemblances?'
>
> '*In the present instance*, sir, I attribute the similarity to the fact that the young lady is Miss Wickham.'
>
> '*Eh?*'
>
> 'Yes, sir. If you notice she is waving to you now.'
>
> 'But what on earth is she doing down here?'
>
> 'I am unable to say, sir.' (Wodehouse 1989: 131. My emphasis to indicate variation.)

The aristocrat speaks in short, clipped sentences larded with contemporary slang words such as *blighter* and *sozzled* whereas the butler speaks in well-rounded ponderous sentences containing unusual but pedantically correct collocations such as *omitting to keep your eye on the ball with sufficient assiduity* for what in standard

English would be simply *failing to watch the ball*. The translator would need to realise that Bertie Wooster speaks an upper-class nineteen-twenties/thirties slang whereas his butler Jeeves speaks such an erudite and pedantic English that it too has pronounced idiolectal features.

Even Hatim and Mason are reasonably optimistic in this respect in their otherwise pessimistic view with regard to the possibility of relaying idio/sociolectal features in translation:

> The question for the translator is: since idiolects are normally on the margin of situationally relevant variation, is it necessary or possible to translate them? But if variation within any given domain of linguistic activity is systematic (and we believe it is), much more than the actual descriptive label for a given instance of variation is involved. One's idiolectal use of language is not unrelated to one's choice of which standard, geographical, social or temporal dialects to use. It is linked to the purpose of the utterance and will ultimately be found to carry socio-cultural significance. (Hatim and Mason 1998: 44)

That it is possible to relay sociolect is attested by Samuel Beckett's English translation, *Waiting for Godot* of his own French play *En Attendant Godot*. This is an example that has already been chosen but not fully analysed by Hatim and Mason as a model of successful sociolectgal translation:

French version:

> VLADIMIR (*froissé, froidement*). - Peut-on savoir où Monsieur a passé la nuit?
> ESTRAGON . - Dans un fossé.
> VLADIMIR (*épaté*). - Un fossé! Où ça?
> ESTRAGON (*sans geste*).- Par là. (Beckett 1971: 10)

English version:

> VLADIMIR: May one enquire where his Highness spent the night?
> ESTRAGON: In a ditch.
> VLADIMIR: (*admiringly*). A ditch! Where?
> ESTRAGON: (without a gesture). Over there. (Beckett 1965: 9)

In the above example, "Peut-on savoir où Monsieur a passé la nuit?", Beckett uses a formal register (i.e. the use of the third person when addressing his fellow tramp), but a close translation would not quite have the same formal effect in English as in French. To solve this problem, Beckett uses the technique of compensation by raising his companion to royalty. A compensatory humorous effect is achieved in the English version with the bathetic contrast of Estragon's answer.

Beckett uses the same compensation technique throughout the play. One more example should suffice to illustrate this point. In the English version, Vladimir this time raises his tramp companion to the status of a high court judge by using the title *Your Worship*:

> *French version:*
> ESTRAGON. - Quel est notre rôle là-dedans?
> VLADIMIR. - Notre rôle?
> ESTRAGON. - Prends ton temps.
> VLADIMIR. - Notre rôle? Celui du suppliant.
> ESTRAGON. - A ce point-là?
> VLADIMIR. - Monsieur a des exigences à faire valoir?
> ESTRAGON. - On n'a plus de droits? (Beckett 1971: 24-25)
>
> *English version:*
> ESTRAGON. Where do we come in?
> VLADIMIR. Come in?
> ESTRAGON. Take your time.
> VLADIMIR. Come in? On our hands and knees.
> ESTRAGON. As bad as that?
> VLADIMIR. Your Worship wishes to assert his prerogatives?
> ESTRAGON. We have no rights any more? (Beckett 1965: 18-19)

(h) The Problem of Dialect Translation in *Tonio Kröger*

The only passage in the three stories in which dialect or more precisely in this context, regional accent, plays an important role is the scene in Chapter VII of *Tonio Kröger* when Tonio has a conversation with the businessman on board the ship to Denmark. The unnamed businessman speaks in a Hamburg dialect which is further compounded by his own idiolect complicated even further by sinus problems. The scene is a source of humour. Inspired by an excess of food and drink, the businessman waxes both lyrical and philosophical about the immensity of the universe represented by the "glittering" stars on an exceptionally clear night in contrast to the insignificance of mankind:

> Sehen Sie, Herr, bloß die Sderne an. Da sdehen sie und glitzern, es ist, weiß Gott, der ganze Himmel voll. Und nun bitt' ich Sie, wenn man hinaufsieht und bedenkt, daß viele davon hundertmal größer sein sollen als die Erde, wie wird einem da zu Sinn? Wir Menschen haben den Telegraphen erfunden und das Telephon und so viele Errungenschaften der Neuzeit, ja, das haben wir. Aber wenn wir da hinaufsehen, so müssen wir doch erkennen und versdehen, daß wir im Grunde Gewürm sind, elendes Gewürm und nichts weiter, - hab' ich Recht oder Unrecht, Herr? Ja, wir sind Gewürm!" antwortete er sich selbst und nickte demütig und zerknirscht zum Firmament empor. (Mann 1977: 243. Idiolectal variations are indicated by the underlining)

Tonio rather snobbishly says of him: "Der hat keine Literatur im Leib", because he is confronted by another case of a "Bürger" causing embarrassment by straying into the world of poetry and the arts like the lieutenant who recited poetry to the consternation of others as referred to in his conversation with Lisavetta (Chapter IV). Indeed, the next morning after his poetic and philosophical outburst, the businessman is acutely embarrassed. The humorous perspective is obvious as 'the lyrical mood' was also connected with his stomach complaint, after eating too much lobster omelette:

> Beim Frühstück sah er den jungen Mann wieder, der heftig errötete, wahrscheinlich vor Scham, im Dunklen so poetische und blamable Dinge geäußert zu haben [. . .] (Mann 1977: 244)

The approaches of Luke and Lowe-Porter to the problem of translating idiolect/dialect represent the opposite ends of the spectrum. This can be seen by comparing the two versions:

> ***Lowe-Porter:*** Look <u>by</u> dear sir, just look at the stars. There they <u>stahd</u> and glitter; by goodness, the whole sky is full of <u>theb</u>! And I ask you, when you <u>stahd</u> <u>ahd</u> look up at <u>theb</u>!, <u>ahd</u> realize that <u>bany</u> of <u>theb</u> are a <u>huddred tibes</u> larger <u>thad</u> the earth, how does it <u>bake</u> you feel? Yes, we have <u>idvehted</u> the telegraph and the <u>telephode</u> and all the <u>triuphs</u> <u>of</u> our <u>bodern</u> <u>tibes</u>. But <u>whed</u> we look up there, after all we have to <u>recogdize</u> and <u>uhderstad</u> that we are <u>worbs</u>, <u>biserable</u> <u>worbs</u>, <u>ahd</u> <u>dothing</u> else. <u>Ab</u> I right, sir, or <u>ab</u> I <u>wrog</u>? Yes, we are <u>worbs</u>,' he answered himself, and nodded meekly and abjectly in the direction of the firmament. (Lowe-Porter 1978: 174. Idiolectal variations are indicated by the underlining)
>
> ***Luke:*** Look, sir, just look at the <u>sstars</u>! Twinkling away up there; by god, the whole sky's full of them. And when you look up at it all and consider that a lot of them are supposed to be a hundred times the size of the earth, well, I ask you, how does it make one feel! We men have invented the telegraph and the telephone and so many wonders of modern times, yes, so we have. But when we look up there we have to realize nevertheless that when all's said and done we are just worms, just miserable little worms and nothing more - am I right or am I wrong, sir? Yes, "he concluded, answering his own question, "that's what we are: worms!" And he nodded toward the firmament in abject contrition. (Luke 1988: 176. The one idiolectal variation is indicated by the underlining)

In Mann's version there are only four obvious idiolectal variations indicated by non-standard spelling of the words involved whereas Lowe-Porter makes thirty variations in this brief extract. Luke, on the other hand, makes only one alteration, the doubling the letter *s* to form the non-existent noun *sstars* to hint at the North German dialect in which the phoneme *s* replaces the usual German ʃ phoneme as in the noun *Sterne*, for example. However, without a metalinguistic hint, this would not mean anything to the English reader.

It could be argued that at least Lowe-Porter makes an attempt to capture something of the idiolect and to produce a sinus effect, but the result in this extract is laboured causing more a ludicrous rather than a humorous effect. To the unsuspecting reader the passage could seem to be very confusing or even incomprehensible. It might have helped if she had written a metalinguistic comment into her text, i.e. that the businessman's sinus problems had the effect that his *m* sounded like *b* and that the nasal *n* is either omitted or replaced by the phoneme *d*. The non-existent noun *worbs*, for example, is doubly confusing because an English speaker would tend to pronounce this 'word' as *wɔːbz,* rhyming with *orbs*, for example. It is, of course, intended to

represent the noun *worms* (*wɜːmz*), but as two of the phonemes out of four are different, the reader cannot be expected to make the necessary phonetic leap and even if the reader tried, he or she would probably land on *words* rather than *worms* owing to the former's relative phonetic similarity. Other such examples could be given, but, on this occasion, Lowe-Porter's boldness in attempting to encode an idiolect, must be respected even though the encoding was not thoroughly thought out and ultimately fails. In Luke's case, the minimal hint at dialect succeeds to a certain extent, but much of the humour is lost. This could, have been achieved by giving general English dialectal and sociolectal features such as the use of interjections such *ee* and non-standard forms such *them* for *those* so that the opening speech could read something like: "Ee, look at them stars up there, glittering away like that, but it don't half make you think, eh?" and so forth. Thus, the humorous function of using non-standard language to express 'exalted' thoughts is achieved and Tonio's intellectually snobbish reaction ("Der hat keine Literatur im Leib") even if not justified would fit in so that the text would read coherently.

(h) Conclusion

(i) Philosophy Translation

Fidelity in a philosophical context implies fidelity to the argument. In the case of Thomas Mann, the philosophy is deeply embedded in literary language games so that the translator has to be something of a philosopher and poet at the same time. However, a clear semantic or a readable communicative translation have been seen to be an improvement on the academic approach.

(ii) Dialect Translation

This area remains problematic. It has been shown that there are possible strategies and that it is very important to assess both the extent of dialect in any passage and its particular literary function within the text before encoding dialectal features in the target text. It has also been pointed out that more linguistic research is needed in defining the various degrees of dialectal coloration. Similarly, more literary studies such as that of Mace (1987) examining the various functions of dialect within a particular literary work are needed before a thorough or comprehensive treatment of this topic can be successfully undertaken within translation studies. At least, this chapter has opened up once again this fraught area and some possible strategies have been hinted at within the framework of a *strategic approach* to translation theory.

Chapter VIII: The Translation of Humour, Irony and Wordplay with Special Reference to *Tristan*

(a) Theoretical Considerations with regard to the Translation of Humour and Paranomasia

The translation of humour and paranomasia is yet another important neglected field in literary translation theory. Traditionally puns, like poetry, have been deemed untranslatable. Delabastita (1996) goes as far back as Addison (1711) on this subject, who defines puns in terms of their untranslatability. Delabastita's discussion of this topic in the following quotation shows that attitudes have not changed much since the time of Addison in 1711:

> But to return to Punning. Having pursued the History of a Punn, from its Original to its Downfall, I shall here define it to be a Conceit arising from the use of two Words that agree in the Sound, but differ in the Sense. The only way therefore to try a Piece of Wit, is to translate it into a different language: If it bears the Test you may pronounce it true; but if it vanishes in the Experiment you may conclude it to have been a Punn.
>
> (Addison 1965: vol I, 262)

Delabastita rightly sees this area as not only difficult but he also opens up the problem of defining the limits of translation:

> There is indeed a lot more at stake than just the question *is wordplay translatable?* For a start, any answer that this question may prompt is bound to be theoretically biased insofar as it depends on the type of translation one has in mind (in terms of kinds and degrees of equivalence, as well as of genres and communicative situations), but also on the speaker's own position vis-à-vis the actual business of translation (whether one is speaking as a teacher of translation, as a practitioner, a critic, a theorist, a historian, a philosopher of language). Moreover, the discussion is likely to draw us into all sorts of debates about key issues in linguistics, pragmatics, historical poetics and semiotics, down to philosophical questions concerning the nature of language and their ideological implications.
>
> (Delabastita 1996: 127)

Hatim and Mason (1998) also emphasise the difficulty or even the virtual impossibility of translating puns, but, this time, by quoting Jakobson (2000) as an authoritative voice on this topic:

> In recent times, Roman Jakobson (1959: 238) is one of those who, from a linguistic perspective, adopt a pessimistic view [with regard to translatability]. In poetry, 'phonemic similarity is sensed as semantic relationship'; formal aspects of the linguistic code become part of the meaning so that *translation proper is impossible; only creative transposition is possible*. In fact, the point is applicable, well beyond poetry, to all discourse in which properties of the form of the language code are brought to the fore and made to bear particular

This defeatism occurs in many of the usually very brief or cryptic comments made by other translation theorists on this subject. Interestingly, Hatim and Mason unwittingly offer a strategic solution in the above quotation with their coinage *creative transposition* and it is also significant that this most excellent of strategies is qualified by the adverb *only*. This is typical of the narrow, semantically bound definitions of translation which often reflect a lamentably limited experience of professional practice in this field[49]. Any professional translator often has to have recourse to 'creative transposition' because many a commercial, academic and political text contains wordplay as well as many other difficulties or 'impossibilities'. However, the use of the noun phrase *translation proper* in the above extract would implicitly seem to exclude broader definitions with the result that a hidden agenda has been created. (Would Levý's semiotic approach to Max Knight's brilliant translations of Morgenstern's non-sense poetry, for example, be dubbed as 'improper' translation with all the implications of impropriety?) This is often the case among linguists with a 'scientific' approach. Indeed, there seems sometimes to be the assumption that the only form of valid translation is what has been defined as *academic translation*. The above quotations would seem to reflect this prejudice.

Similarly, Peter Newmark refers to the translation of puns as of "marginal importance and of irresistible interest" (Newmark: 1988: 217), but, at least, he does write a couple of pages on this topic even if the tone is also somewhat defeatist:

If the purpose of the pun is merely to raise laughter, it can sometimes be 'compensated' by another pun on a word with a different but associated meaning. This is done in the translation of *Asterix* into many languages, and requires exceptional ingenuity. (Newmark 1988: 217)

---

[49] It is not clear in this quotation whether Leppihalme (1996) is disapproving or not with regard to the strategy of creating puns, but there is the same agonising tone which only seems to take place among professional academic linguists and teachers of translation when they are confronted with brilliantly creative translations. Practitioners tend to rejoice at re-created felicitous puns: "The brilliant examples of creativity in translations of *Asterix* cited by Embleton (1991) and Harvey (1995) notwithstanding, it would seem that some allusive wordplay in translation can hardly be enjoyed by other than bilingual and bicultural readers who are able to back-translate if need be while reading the target text. For the majority of target-text readers who are not in this privileged position, any strategy chosen by the translator is likely to be problematic one way or another, even when the translator identified the frame and its source." (Leppihalme 1996: 213)

The kind of ingenuity required is, unfortunately, not discussed despite the fact that translation practice has many examples to offer as an illustration of the kind of dexterity required. Newmark goes on to mention the difficulty of translating puns in poetry, but only to the effect that it is, in fact, either very difficult or even impossible:

> Puns made by punning poets are most difficult to translate, since they are limited by metre. Often the pun simply has to be sacrificed. (Newmark 1988: 217)

This represents the general attitude in contemporary translation theory, which is reflected in Baker (1998) where there is only the following brief quotation concerning word-play in an encyclopaedia of almost six hundred pages of text. The brief description of this area seems merely to repeat Newmark and Hatim as already quoted:

> Compensation is a technique which involves making up for the loss of a source text effect by recreating a similar effect in the target text through means that are specific to the target language and/or text. Examples cited in the literature often involve the translation of puns. For instance, in a discussion of the translations of the French comic strip *Asterix* (Goscinny and Uderzo 1972), Hatim and Mason conclude that 'Translators abandon the attempt to relay the puns as such and, instead, compensate by inserting English puns of their own which are not part of the source text. But equivalence of intention has been maintained' (1990: 202). Here, the same linguistic device is employed in both source and target texts to achieve a similar humorous effect. (Baker 1998: 37-38)

As with Newmark quoted in the inset, the translation of puns and paranomasia are subsumed under the strategy of compensation. It is quite clear from a work such as *Tristan* that puns are by no means merely of marginal interest[50], but are a major source of humour.

(b) German Translations of Lewis Carroll's *Alice's Adventures in Wonderland*

The world of translation practice has, however, many examples of 'creative transposition' such as Raykowski's translation (1992) of the Mock Turtle's description of his schooldays in Lewis Carroll's *Alice's Adventures in Wonderland*.

---

[50] The Hellman study of the French version of *Der Zauberberg* to which reference has already been made is similarly typical of the narrowly scientific school in that there is very little mention of the problem of translating humour in this great satiric work and that the whole area is designated as a *Grenzphänomen*: "Besonders deutlich treten die Grenzen der Übersetzbarkeit am sprachlichen Grenzphänomen des Wortspiels zutage. Dieses kann insofern als Grenzphänomen bezeichnet werden, als in ihm nicht nur die informationsübermittelnde Funktion der Sprache ganz zugunsten der Autoreferenz zurücktritt, sondern auch die sprachliche Differenz, die nicht vorhandene logische Eindeutigkeit und damit die mangelnde Perfektion der Sprache (mit sprachlichen Mitteln) aufs Korn genommen wird. " (Hellmann 1992: 238)

The English pun depends on the phonetic similarity between tortoise (t ɔːt ə s) and taught us (t ɔːt ə s /z):

> 'When we were little,' the Mock Turtle went on at last, more calmly, though still sobbing a little now and then, 'we went to school in the sea. The master was an old Turtle - we used to call him Tortoise - '
>
> 'Why did you call him Tortoise, if he wasn't one?' Alice asked.
>
> 'We called him Tortoise because he taught us,' said the Mock Turtle angrily. 'Really you are very dull!'
>
> 'You ought to be ashamed of yourself for asking such a simple question,' added the Gryphon; and then they both sat silent and looked at poor Alice, who felt ready to sink into the earth. (Carroll 1986: 125-126).

Again, as in poetry, a straight academic translation would lose all the humour and would be meaningless with the whole point of the passage being totally lost as in the following example of minimal transfer using Raykowski's version as a basis for this purpose:

> *Minimal transfer translation based on Raykowski:*
>
> "Als wir klein waren," fuhr die Ersatzschildkröte[51] schließlich ruhiger, aber immer noch hin und wieder schluchzend fort, "gingen wir im Meer zur Schule. Unser Lehrer war eine alte Landschildkröte - wir nannten ihn Wasserschildkröte. . . "
>
> "Warum denn Wasserschildkröte, wenn er doch keine war? " fragte Alice.
>
> "Wir nannten ihn Wasserschildkröte, weil er uns unterrichtete." sagte die Ersatzschildkröte ungehalten. "Du bist wirklich sehr dumm!"
>
> "Du sollst dich schämen, so dumme Fragen zu stellen" ergänzte der Greif, und dann saßen beide da und musterten stumm die arme Alice, die am liebsten im Erdboden versunken wäre.

In the minimal transfer version, the whole point of the pun is completely lost and thus the whole point of the passage. Alice's perfectly reasonable question is treated with undeserved contempt and the explanatory answer is no explanation so that the resultant indignation of the Mock Turtle and the Gryphon together with Alice's consequent shame are incomprehensible outside the context of the pun. *Alice's Adventures in Wonderland* is a book which is full of word-play and language games whilst, at the same time, presenting highly imaginative tableaux for the delight of both children and adults. The translator has a problem. There is, however, a solution and that is to invent new but appropriate puns with the same semiotic features as the

---

[51] Most of the German translators seem to have missed the point of the 'Mock Turtle' joke with versions such as "Falsche Schildkröte" (1981) and "Pseudoschildkröte" (1992). Mock turtle soup is a substitute soup made from a calf's head and thus an 'ersatz' soup like 'Ersatzkaffee', but the Mock Turtle in *Alice's Adventures Wonderland* is the 'Mock Turtle' (*Ersatzschildkröte)* from which mock turtle soup is made directly!

original (sea creatures, school and, as in Levý's analysis, the higher order of wordplay). This is precisely what the German translator Raykowski attempts to do:

> "Als wir klein waren" fuhr die Suppenschildkröte schließlich ruhiger, aber immer noch hin und wieder schluchzend fort, "gingen wir im Meer zur Schule. Unser Lehrer war eine alte Landschildkröte - wir nannten ihn den Barsch. . . "
>
> "Warum denn Barsch, wenn er doch keiner war? " fragte Alice.
>
> "Wir nannten ihn Barsch, weil er barsch war.", sagte die Suppenschildkröte ungehalten. "Du bist wirklich sehr dumm!"
>
> "Du sollst dich schämen, so dumme Fragen zu stellen" ergänzte der Greif, und dann saßen beide da und musterten stumm die arme Alice, die am liebsten im Erdboden versunken wäre. (Raykowski 1992: 144)

Although the translation may not quite have the naturalness and humour of the original, the solution produces the required effect with the result that the whole passage reads as a coherent text. There are, however, semiotic features which are lacking in Raykowski's translation as his retention of the tortoise theme shows that his translation is too semantically bound. The evolutionary downward leap from the reptilian world of tortoises to fish (*perch* as in "Barsch") is too great to be humorous unlike the very close turtle/tortoise relation of the original. If the translator had kept within the fish range so that the leap from *Kabeljau* or *Schellfisch* to *Barsch* would have been unobtrusive, thus keeping the light humorous tone in tact. The same sort of criticisms applies to other translators. The Von Herwarth translation (1984) seems to have found a less felicitous solution:

> "Warum habt ihr sie Weichtier genannt, wenn sie [die alte Schildkröte] keine war?" fragte Alice.
>
> "Weil vor einem Weichtier ein Schüler niemals weicht hier", antwortete die Falsche Schildkröte. (Von Herwarth 1984: 119. Square brackets added.)

The pun is phonically, semiotically and grammatically awkward so that there is a loss of humour, but at least text coherence is minimally sustained. The same applies to L. Remané & M. Remané's' version (1981) for similar reasons although in this version the pun is slightly more natural despite the fact that the reptilian semiotics of the original are abandoned in favour of elaborating the schoolmaster theme:

> "Unser Lehrer war ein alter Schildkrötenmann, den wir immer ‚Herzog' nannten . . . "
>
> "Warum nanntet ihr ihn, Herzog' wenn er keiner war?" fiel Alice ihr ins Wort.
>
> "Wir nannten ihn ‚Herzog', weil er uns ‚erzog' ", versetzte die Falsche Suppenschildkröte ärgerlich. (Remané, L. & Remané, M. 1981: 118)

Virtually the whole chapter with the Mock Turtle depends on puns to do with elementary education and marine life, but Raykowski produces some ingenious solutions even though they lack the full humour and wit of the original text. Lewis Carroll soon became aware of the translation difficulties of this book so that at first it was deemed as untranslatable:

> He soon became aware of the great problems translation would involve. In a letter he wrote to Macmillan on 24 October 1866, he reported: "Friends here seem to think that the book is *untranslatable* into either French or German, the puns and songs being the chief obstacles". (Weissbrod 1996: 224)

However, when translators did produce inventive and creative translations, far from consigning them to the *belles infidèles*, Carroll expressed his delight:

> Lewis Carroll himself had praised the German translator of *Alice* for replacing the original parodies with new ones based on local German texts. (Weissbrod 1996: 226)

(c) An Analysis of the Humour with regard to Names in *Tristan*

As in *Alice's Adventures in Wonderland*, there are many hidden puns and forms of paranomasia in *Tristan*, particularly with regard to the proper nouns. This feature has been well documented by Dittmann (1993) among many others. Even the name of the sanatorium *Einfried* can be seen as a play on Wagner's residence *Wahnfried* together with the idea of isolation, alienation as in the noun *Einsiedler* with associations of an 'artistic' society far removed from the cares of the prosaic bourgeois world, a highly suitable background for the aesthete Herr Spinell. Dittmann rightly alludes to some of the rich connotations of this pun:

> *Einfried*: Die Namen in den Werken Thomas Manns eröffnen einen weiten Assoziationsraum, der jedoch genau auf die Themen der Erzählung ausgerichtet ist: Mit dem Namen des Sanatoriums verband sich für Thomas Mann - wie auch für das Lesepublikum seiner Zeit - eine Assoziation zu dem Komponisten der Oper, auf die der Titel der Erzählung spielt: Wagners Villa in Bayreuth, in deren Nähe Wagner bestattet wurde, trägt den Namen 'Wahnfried'. - Daneben spielt der Name des Sanatoriums sowohl auf die friedlich abgeschiedene Lage als auch auf die Eingeschlossenheit, das Eingefriedetsein der Patienten an; der Name, der zunächst einen positiven Beiklang besitzt, kann auch einen durchaus negativen Eindruck hervorrufen. (Dittmann 1993: 5)

As names play such an important role in *Tristan* with regard to humour and thematic significance, the problem with proper names is further compounded by the question whether to translate them, leave them alone or simply offer metalinguistic information in the form of footnotes or narration unobtrusively written into the text. However, a wonderfully amusing literary text like *Tristan* can suddenly become a difficult scholarly work, thus destroying the basic tenor of the original. Further, the question arises whether to translate them at all and, if so, when to translate and when not to. Normally, names, particularly surnames are not translated even though first names may be translated into the target language. This point is made by Hayes who quotes the translation theorist Güttinger (1963) on the problem of translating names, which, in fact, only deals with first names:

> Names. In the question of personal and place names, Güttinger advises, in translation from English to German, where there is a German form for an English name, the German form is to be preferred; that is, if the name is *George* in the original, it should be *Georg* in translation. (Hayes 1974: 201)

In contrast, Newmark (1988) suggests the bold solution of translating punning names with new names in the target language with similar or equivalent wordplay:

> A possible method of translating literary proper names that have connotations in the SL (source language) is first to translate the word that underlies the proper name into the TL (target language), and then to naturalize it back into the SL proper name. Thus in translating Wackford Squeers into German, 'wack' becomes *prügeln* becomes *Proogle,* and possibly Sqeers (squint, queer?) could become *schielen* and the name in a German version might be translated as '*Proogle Squeers*' or '*Proogle Sheel*'. (Newmark 1996: 71)

The principle propagated by Newmark may be sound, but his example is rather unfortunate as the non-existent proper name *Proogle* would not mean much in German. Far from being associated with *prügeln*, it would elicit more Dutch connotations as the *oo* combination is relatively rare in German. With reference to this example, Manini (1996) not only takes exception to Newmark's ingenious but unsuccessful example, but also to the very attempt to translate proper names in literature:

> This sounds reasonable enough, but a major objection to Newmark's theory is that Dickens gave the spark of fictional life to neither Proogle Squeers nor Proogle Sheel, but exclusively to Wackford Squeers, with the very specific load of connotations that this name evokes. In other words, the trouble with Newmark's suggestion is that in many cases there will be no single, easily identifiable "word that underlies the proper name", but potentially a whole paradigm of formally and semantically related words. As Newmark's cautious wording suggests, he was not totally unaware of the danger of semantic reductions inherent in his method, which limits its usefulness for a large number of Dickensian names. Who would claim to know the exact associative range of names like Murdstone, Steerforth, Peggoty (in *David Copperfield*) or Miss Havisham, Pip, Abel Magwitch (in *Great Expectations*)? (Manini 1996: 171)

This is a very difficult area where the translator should tread carefully, particularly with regard to 'canonised' literature.

If a readable and enjoyable communicative translation were the aim for *Tristan*, then the answer could well be to translate the names into English or, in other words, find equivalents. This process would involve a semiotic analysis possibly similar to the one carried out by Levý as already discussed in Section (b) of Chapter V. This process is by no means impossible as implied by Manini, but even an imperfectly reconstructed name which captures some of the humour of the original is better than no attempt at all (in the context of translations of popular works as opposed to 'canonised' texts).

(d) A Case Study: Gotter's (1785) Translation of Benjamin Hoadly's (1776) Comedy *The Suspicious Husband*

Unger (1996) provides a successful example of the communicative strategy for the translation of names and humour in general with Gotter's (1785) *Der argwöhnische Ehemann*, a translation of Benjamin Hoadly's (1776) comedy *The Suspicious Husband*. This is a case of radical domestication or (nationalising, to use Unger's term), because not only are all the characters' names changed, the place names and whole 'geography' of the play is shifted to Germany:

> In order to nationalize[52] Hoadly's play, Gotter changes the personal and place names into German names. Thus London becomes Frankfurt am Main, and instead of a trip to Bath we are told about a voyage to Schwalbach. Mr. Strictland's name is Herr Bruno in the Gotter version, his wife's is Klara Bruno. Jacintha, the ward, is named Angelika and her beloved Bellamy becomes Herr Roland. Clarinda is raised to nobility, perhaps because of her happy-go-lucky way of life; Gotter calls her Hedwig von Aue, and Carl Frankly, her lover, is called Karl Reinald. (Unger 1996: 5)

Unger refers to the play as a comedy "success", not only in Gotha where it was first performed, but throughout Germany whereas the earlier *academic* translation by Bode (1776) first published in 1754 was only successful to a limited extent with the reading public:

> Bode sticks to the original, keeping the English personal and place names and avoiding any dramaturgical alterations. Bode's method of translating, which requires the reader to deal with a considerable amount of unfamiliarity and otherness, can be regarded as typical of the early period of comedy translations from the English. In fact, these plays were first received by a reading public. They took a long time to be staged in Germany, but it was felt that the public at least had to be informed about what was being performed at the theatres of the world's greatest power. (Unger 1996: 10)

---

[52] Unger (1996) uses the term *nationalize* (verdeutschen) for what is generally referred to as *domesticate*.

Because of the great success of the domesticating translations, Bode himself later adopted this translation strategy:

> Bode himself, under the influence of Friedrich Ludwig Schröder (1744-1816), wrote the first nationalizing translation of Cumberland's *The West Indian*, which was to be performed at the Gotha Hoftheater. From 1774 on, according to Nover, the adaptations which are sometimes considerably altered and nationalized are predominant and mark the "heyday of English comedy translations and of their popularity on stage in Germany". (Unger 1996: 10)

A brief extract will illustrate the freshness and vitality of Gotter's translations in comparison with Bode's early phase of *academic translation*:

> *Hoadly:* Frank. Buxom and lively as the bounding doe--
>
> Fair as painting can express,
>
> Or youthful poets fancy when they love.
>
> Tol, de rol lol! [Singing and dancing.] (Hoadly 1776: 7)

> *Bode:* Frank. Lustig und fröhlich als springende Ziegen,
>
> Schön, als Maler malen können,
>
> Oder junge Dichter träumen,
>
> Die in Liebesflammen brennen
>
> Tol de rol lol! (Er singet und tanzet.) (Bode 1776: 43)

> *Gotter:* Reinald (im Enthusiasmus hereinhüpfend)
>
> Leicht und fröhlich, wie die Gemse,
>
> Heiter wie der May,
>
> Keine Venus Anadyomene,
>
> Nicht Petrarchs geprießne Schöne
>
> Lotte selbst kömmt ihr nicht bey.
>
> (Singt und tanzt) Tal de ral la. (Gotter 1785: 35.)

The reference in Gotter's poem to Lotte concerns Lotte in Goethe's *Leiden des jungen Werthers* which was popular at that time because Gotter's radical intertextuality goes so far as to reflect references in the original to functionally equivalent references within the German culture of the time:

> It will become clear that Gotter makes use of intertextual allusion as a reservoir for specific German cultural themes. He thus presents the Gotha public a text that is wholly embedded in the context of the target culture, but which still conveys an image of English literature, even though it might be quite different from the original text. (Unger 1996: 2)

Gotter also uses the technique of compensation to keep the humorous tone of the original text such as his play on the invented name *Anadyomene*, (presumably a play on *Anno Domini*, thus meaning *no aged Venus*) and also with regard to the mock

178

build-up of beauties from objects of worship in Petrarch's sonnets to "Lotte selbst" of the then contemporary world. The unpoetic *Gemse* with a hint of dialect associations would also be source of humour in contradistinction to the classical tone of the Anacreontic poets of the period. In comparison, Bode's version is dull and conventional. Unger (1996) avoids any discussion of translation methodologies and it is interesting that he uses the terms *translation* and *adaptation* indiscriminately. Within the framework of translation theory, Gotter's strategy can either be described as radical domestication or as an extreme form of communicative translation. The retention of the word *translation* in this case depends less on semantic fidelity to the original and more on its fidelity to the original as a system of signs and functions. If this strategy of radical domestication is, however, applied to a canonised text, then the translator's preface in such a case is very important. The translator's strategy can and should be made explicit and it is in such a preface that the problem of translating names can be fruitfully discussed.

(e) Communicative Strategies with regard to the Translation of Names in *Tristan*

To offer an illustration of how English equivalents may be found for the German names, the first conversation between Gabriele and Spinell could be taken as an example. In this conversation Spinell asks Gabriele what her maiden name is and expresses his horror and disgust with regard to her married name. Dittmann's (1993) analysis of the name of the ultra-bourgeois philistine Hamburg businessman *Klöterjahn* displays some of the connotations of this name which would, of course, be meaningless or at least incomprehensible to an English reader who did not have a good knowledge of German:

> *Klöterjahn:* Diesen Namen trägt die Figur, die in dem folgenden Geschehen zum Antipoden des Schriftstellers wird, der den Namen irgendeines Minerals oder Edelsteines führt; in gewisser Weise deutet sich die spätere Spannung zwischen den beiden Gestalten schon mit der Umschreibung des einen und der Nennung des anderen - noch häufiger erörterten - Namens an. Mit Klöterjahns Namen, in dem die niederdeutschen Dialektbezeichnung *Klot* Pl.: *Klöte(n)* für Hoden anklingt, verweist der Autor auf den Bereich sinnlich-vitalen Lebens, der mit dem des anorganisch-sterilen Bereichs der Minerale und Edelsteine kontrastiert (zum Gegensatz von Geist und Leben, von Künstlertum und einer unbewußten Menschlichkeit). (Dittmann 1993: 9)

Even German readers who are not familiar with this dialect term may not be aware of all the connotations of *Klöterjahn*, but with this knowledge, the ensuing dialogue not only makes perfect sense but is also extremely humorous:

"Darf ich einmal fragen, gnädige Frau (aber es ist wohl naseweis), wie Sie heißen, wie eigentlich Ihr Name ist?"

"Ich heiße doch Klöterjahn, Herr Spinell!"

"Hm. - Das weiß ich. Oder vielmehr: ich leugne es. Ich meine natürlich Ihren eignen Namen, Ihren Mädchennamen. Sie werden gerecht sein und einräumen, gnädige Frau, daß, wer Sie 'Frau Klöterjahn' nennen wollte, die Peitsche verdient."

Sie lachte so herzlich, daß das Äderchen über ihrer Braue beängstigend deutlich hervortrat und ihrem zarten, süßen Gesicht einen Ausdruck von Anstrengung und Bedrängnis verlieh, der tief beunruhigte.

"Nein! Bewahre, Herr Spinell! Die Peitsche? Ist 'Klöterjahn' Ihnen so fürchterlich?"

"Ja, gnädige Frau, ich hasse diesen Namen aus Herzensgrund, seit ich ihn zum erstenmal vernahm. Er ist komisch und zum Verzweifeln unschön, und es ist Barberei und Niedertracht, wenn man die Sitte so weit treibt, auf Sie den Namen Ihres Herrn Gemahls zu übertragen."

(Mann 1977: 175)

It can be also seen that both Lowe-Porter's and Luke's version (without even adding explanatory footnotes) have produced a more or less meaningless dialogue out of one of the most amusing conversations in the novella. The English reader is not aware of any particular ugliness or humour in the name *Klöterjahn*, only that whatever it is, the aesthete takes great exception to this particular name:

Lowe-Porter: 'May I ask, Madam - though you may very likely think me prying - what your name really is?'

'Why Herr Spinell, you know my name is Klöterjahn!'

'H'm. Yes I know that - or, rather, I deny it, I mean your own name, your maiden name, of course. You will in justice, madam, admit that anybody who calls you Klöterjahn ought to be thrashed.'

She laughed so hard that the little blue vein stood out alarmingly on her brow and gave the pale sweet face a strained expression disquieting to see.

'Oh, no! Not at all, Herr Spinell! Thrashed, indeed! Is the name Klöterjahn so horrible to you? 'Yes, madam. I hate the name from the bottom of my heart. I hated it the first time I heard it. It is the abandonment of ugliness; it is grotesque to make you comply with the custom so far as to fasten your husband's name upon you; it is barbarous and vile. (Lowe-Porter 1978: 100.)

Luke: "I am sure, dear madam, that it is very impertinent of me, but may I ask you what your name is - what it really is?"

"But my name is Klöterjahn, Herr Spinell, as you know!" "H'm. Yes, that I know. Or rather: that I deny. I mean of course your own name, your maiden name. You must in all fairness concede, dear madam, that if anyone were to address you as 'Frau Klöterjahn' he would deserve to be horsewhipped."

She laughed so heartily that the little blue vein over her eyebrow stood out alarmingly clearly and gave her sweet delicate face a strained, anxious expression which was deeply disturbing. "Why, good gracious, Herr Spinell! Horsewhipped? Do you find 'Klöterjahn' so appalling?"

"Yes, dear madam, I have most profoundly detested that name ever since I first heard it. It is grotesque, it is unspeakably ugly; and to insist on social convention to the point of calling you by your husband's name is barbaric and outrageous." (Luke 1988: 107)

If the name, however, were given an English equivalent, there are many possibilities although it is by no means an easy task to invent suitable alternatives. As has been seen from Dittmann's analysis, the equivalent name would have to fulfil at least the following criteria for even the briefest of semiotic analyses:

a) At one level, the equivalent should be a fairly normal prosaic but respectable name, i.e. it must be a plausible everyday name. It must have an ugly sound: the two parts of the name *Klöter* and *jahn* do not harmonise felicitously.

b) There must be a vulgar or obscene association even though at a subliminal level

i.e. to carry over the same connotations as the dialect term *Klöten*

One of many possibilities would be to use a name such as "Shuttlecock". It can be seen that such a name would fulfil the above criteria:

a) The name "Shuttlecock" is a normal respectable English name.

b) The name refers to the commonplace weaving instrument *the shuttle* or a missile in badminton as well as being a curious sounding name. Also, the two halves *Shuttle* and *cock* are similarly infelicitous as a combination.

c) There is a hint of vulgarity with any name ending in *cock* which can mean either a shortened form of the noun *cockerel* or the slang term which is most commonly known for referring to the male sexual organ.

If the same extract is now read with this 'creatively transposed equivalent', it would then make perfect sense to any English reader and the passage now works humorously in this communicative version:

Suggested version: 'I hope you would not find me unduly inquisitive if I were to venture to ask what your real name is?'

'My name really is Shuttlecock, Mr. Spinell.'

'Hm, yes, I know, or rather I repudiate that. What I actually mean is, what is your maiden name? I am sure you will be totally fair in this matter and fully concede that anyone with the audacity to call you *Shuttlecock* deserves to be horse-whipped.'

She laughed so heartily that the vein above her left eyebrow began to be a cause of concern in the way it protruded so prominently causing an anxious strained look to come over her face.

181

'Oh, God forbid, Mr. Spinell. "Deserves to be horse-whipped." Is this name so abominable, Mr Spinell?'

'Oh yes, madam I have loathed this name from the very depths of my heart ever since I had the misfortune to hear it for the first time. It is so ludicrous and so ugly as to drive one to despair or even suicide. It is both a barbarous and despicable custom that forces your husband's gross name onto your own person.'

Some names, if translated literally can, however, carry the same connotations in the target language. For a communicative translation, a literal translation would seem to be the best strategy. For example, the surname *Spinell* can be translated into the English equivalent as *Spinell* with exactly the same associations for those who are familiar with this semiprecious stone which can easily be mistaken for the real thing such as a ruby. Dittmann shows the link between the stone and 'dubious value' of the author:

> *Spinell:* [. . .] der Name bezeichnet ein Mineral, das durch besondere Beimischungen auch farbige Kristalle bilden kann. Diese werden als Edelsteine gehandelt; sie besitzen - je nach Einfärbung - *unterschiedlichen Wert.* (Dittmann, 1993: 13. My emphasis.)

This is obviously an appropriate name for a literary man with high pretensions but with a very low output. Something of the Italianate might, however, become lost with the single letter *l* in the English version, but this could be compensated by awarding the figure a recondite Italian sounding Christian name such as Orlando which would be appropriate for this exotic figure. The name *Orlando* has connotations with both 'artistic' and 'outlandish' associations as well as a hint of effeminacy as with Spinell's first name *Detlev.*

The same principle applies to the minor characters who have amusing names such as *Rätin Spatz* which can be successfully translated literally as *Mrs. Sparrow* if allowance is made for the fact that there is no equivalent in English for including the husband's profession in a name. The noun *sparrow* has associations of a plain, chatty and highly sociable bird and thus by implication a rather gossipy and plain person which very well sums up the character of Rätin Spatz, who is very much a background figure in the novella. It is also significant that she is not even accorded a first name but merely the title of her husband nor is there any description of her character given. All the reader knows about her is that she immediately 'took over' Gabriele, that she participated in the conversations as a background figure and, of course, her name which alone carries sufficient connotations for a character sketch in itself.

The same basic principles apply to Pastorin Höhlenrauch and Fräulein von Osterloh. With Pastorin Höhlenrauch there is a hint of dark, overworn inner passages caused by her giving birth to nineteen children as well as a hint of the 'smoke of hell' (*Höllenrauch*) manifested in her tragic (and comic) madness. Similarly, the name Fräulein von Osterloh carries hidden connotations as in the idea contained in the German verb *lohen*. The noun *Oster(n)* has obvious associations with fertility, but, combined the 'poetic' verb *lohen* would represent more the burning desire for fertility, though overladen the respectable associations of Easter as a religious festival. Even though Dittmann does not analyse this particular name, the name can be linked to his analysis of the following sentence:

> Auf ihren Wangen aber glüht in zwei runden, karmoisinroten Flecken die unauslöschliche Hoffnung, dereinst Frau Doktor Leander zu werden. (Mann 1977: 163)

The glow in her cheeks symbolising her inextinguishable hope of one day marrying Doktor Leander is, of course, reflected in her name. Dittmann shows that this hope is one of her essential characteristics:

> Das Adjektiv *unauslöschlich* intensiviert das herkömmliche Bild vom 'Glühen der Hoffnung'. Indem Thomas Mann den abstrakten Sachverhalt eines starken Hoffnungsgefühls, der durch die bildliche Wendung versinnlicht wird, in unmittelbaren Zusammenhang zu der ganz konkreten Erscheinung der Gesichtsfarbe stellt und *auf* den roten Wangen der eifrigen Hausdame lokalisiert, erscheint das konventionelle metaphorische Sprechen übertrieben und wirkt in dieser Übertreibung komisch. (Dittmann 1993: 7)

In addition, the aristocratic title gives her a special authority and distinction which balance the tragicomic aspect of her character so that a well rounded humorous and convincing portrait ensues. Her name is thus an essential aspect of her portrait.

With these, as with the name *Klöterjahn*, the translator has to play a similarly inventive semiotic game. There are many possible solutions, but the principles remain the same. However, both the translations in question (and this also applies to subsequent translations) simply lose the associations and do not even supply a footnote. This results in chunks of meaningless narrative together with a disastrous loss of humour.

(f) Metalingual Strategies with regard to the Translation of Names in *Tristan*

Even in a communicative translation, the metalingual solution is sometimes the preferable strategy. For example, the explicit reference to Konrad Ekhof (1720-1780), an historical figure, with regard to Gabriele Eckhof's maiden name precludes another equivalent, except in the case of a rewriting or radical adaptation of the work where an equivalent figure may be found or invented:

> "Nun, und 'Eckhof'? Ist Eckhof schöner? Mein Vater heißt Eckhof."
>
> "Oh, sehen Sie! 'Eckhof' ist etwas ganz anderes! Eckhof hieß sogar ein großer Schauspieler. Eckhof passiert." (Mann 1977: 175)

In Luke's and Lowe-Porter's versions, however, the reference to the 'father of the German theatre' would not generally be known to English-speaking readers and so, Spinell's enthusiasm for this German name would not be clear:

Lowe-Porter:

> 'Well, and how about Eckhof? Is that any better? Eckhof is my father's name.'
>
> 'Ah, you see! Eckhof is quite another thing. There was a great actor named Eckhof. Eckhof will do nicely.' (Lowe-Porter 1978: 100)

Luke:

> "Well, what about 'Eckhof'? Is Eckhof any better? My father's name is Eckhof."
>
> "Ah, there now, you see! 'Eckhof' is quite another matter! There was once even a great actor called Eckhof. Eckhof is appropriate." (Luke 1988: 107)

This reference together with the associations of the name could be made more explicit for the non-German readership. In the case of this story in order to preserve the continuity and coherence of the original text by avoiding intrusive footnotes, a metalinguistic solution offers itself in that the narrator often intervenes and interrupts the narrative in this story as will be demonstrated later in this chapter. The translator can join the narrative conspiracy and in a subtle way weave in explanations which should be light and amusing as well as being unobtrusive simply by extending the Spinell reference with a phrase such as the 'Father of the German theatre'. The lightness of touch can be added by a pretentious word such as *venerable, illustrious* or even *immortal* (to add a touch of humour by assigning him to the literary gods) as in the phrase, for example, *that Immortal Creator of the German Theatre* so that the humorous tenor is maintained. This otherwise obscure passage would then make sense to the English reader and the humorous tone would be maintained:

Suggested version:

> "Well, what about 'Eckhof'? Is 'Eckhof' a nicer name? That was my father's name."
>
> "Aha, now you can see that 'Eckhof' is a completely different story. 'Eckhof' was the name of that Immortal Creator of the German theatre. 'Eckhof' is fine."

For a close semantic translation, this latter tactic would be appropriate, but for a modern "racy" communicative translation, transliteration is possible. Although not necessarily the best strategy for an established literary author such as Thomas Mann, this is by far the more interesting strategy. An argument could be made for a lively, humorous, communicative translation of *Tristan* and it is in this context only of a 'Bearbeitung' that possible word-play strategies will be discussed.

(f) Strategies to Capture Irony in *Tristan*

An even more problematic aspect of Thomas Mann's humour for the translator is irony, which is at the heart of Thomas Mann's style as argued by Heller (1975):

> Thomas Mann nannte einmal das Problem der Ironie 'das ohne Vergleich reizendste der Welt' (footnote: *Bemühungen*: 56). Und wahrhaftig, es hat ihn gereizt! Es gab Zeiten, da er darüber mit so erzürnter Leidenschaftlichkeit abhandelte, daß man meinen möchte, Ironie bedeutet den Glaubensfanatismus von Kreuzzüglern. (Heller 1975: 279)

Irony pervades all three stories in this study. In *Tonio Kröger*, the irony is so elusive that it is subordinated to the gentle, lyrical mood of the novella despite some wonderful satirical portraits such as Herr Knaak and the 'philosophical' Hamburg business man with sinus and digestive problems. The irony works at a deeper psychological and philosophical level within Tonio's dilemma of finding himself too bourgeois for the artists and too artistic for the bourgeoisie producing a highly conscious but painful tension mitigated only by the gentle humour and self-parody. In *Der Tod in Venedig*, the irony is also a very subtle, yet predominant feature. Much of Thomas Mann is in Aschenbach, but, unlike the fictional protagonist, the author is prepared to laugh at himself. The precious literary style of Aschenbach together with the deliberately 'overwritten' poetic passages is not only a case of self-parody, but also their decadent features hint at the seeds of inevitable destruction so that the style itself reflects the major themes in the novella. It can easily be missed. Indeed, the two translations in question generally miss the irony as has been illustrated in the various detailed analyses.

However, it is clear that humour and a not so very gentle irony predominate in *Tristan*. Much has already been written about irony in this novella which has been succinctly summarised by Klugkist:

> 'Parodistische Tendenz' (Matter), 'Persiflage' (Hilscher), 'komisch-satirisch'(Diersen), 'feine und zugleich Tragikomödie' (Lukacs), 'der vom Karikieren nicht weit entfernte Humor' (Stresau) oder 'Selbstverhöhnung' (Bauer) lauten einige der sekundärliterarischen Charakterisierungsbegriffe, die mit Bezug auf die von Thomas Mann selbst als 'Burleske' bezeichnete Tristan-Novelle eingesetzt werden. Sie zielen im Grunde alle auf die 'tiefe

ironische Form' (Georg Lukacs), in der hier die Kunst-Leben-Beziehung zur Darstellung gelangt. (Klugkist 1995: 27)

This ironic tone in *Tristan* is evident from the opening paragraph and the same key is maintained throughout the novella:

> Hier ist ‚Einfried', das Sanatorium! Weiß und geradlinig liegt es in seinem langgestreckten Hauptgebäude und seinem Seitenflügel inmitten des weiten Gartens, der mit Grotten, Laubengängen und kleinen Pavillons aus Baumrinde *ergötzlich* ausgestattet ist, und hinter seinen Schieferdecken ragen tannengrün, massig und weich zerklüftet die Berge himmelan. (Mann 1977: 210. My emphasis.)

The perspective of the author's exaggerated enthusiasm has an element of irony as does the rather overblown poetic description of the place in conjunction with the creation of a 'rococo' world consisting of pavilions, arbours and grottoes. That the tone really is ironical is confirmed by the author's deliberately precious use of the adjective *ergötzlich*, thus further highlighting the light-hearted rococo elements. At least two authors have commented on the importance of the narrator's perspective in *Tristan*. Klugkist stresses the significance of time and space within the narrative perspective. The scene is here and now; the author, far from being invisible, acts, as it were, without mediation, as if we were conspirators in the narrative process:

> Hier ist Einfried, das Sanatorium! - Die ersten beiden Wörter bereits sind deiktische Ausdrücke, die zwei der drei Origo-Koordinaten geben: hier und jetzt. Die Frage nach dem Ich ist an diesem Punkt schon zwingend. Der bestimmte Artikel nach der Namensnennung suggeriert Bekanntheit: sichtbar wird nicht irgend etwas und nicht irgendein Sanatorium, sondern das Sanatorium Einfried, von dem jeder zumindest schon einmal gehört hat. (Klugkist 1995: 16)

Dittmann elaborates the same point in greater detail:

> Hier ist "Einfried": Dieser Erzählsatz spiegelt einen im Moment unseres Lesebeginns gegenwärtigen Ort vor; damit fingiert der Autor eine Erzählerfigur, die zunächst wie ein Fremdenführer oder Gast in 'Einfried' uns mit dem Ort des Geschehens vertraut macht, um dann die Geschichte zu berichten. Da diese Erzählerfigur, die in verschiedenen Urteilen und sprachlichen Eigenheiten durch die ganze Erzählung hindurch nachweisbar wird, sich selbst nie als ein 'Ich' nennt, ist zur Abgrenzung 'Tristans' von anderen Ich-Erzählungen nach der Funktion dieser Erzählfigur zu fragen; ihr kommt, da sie nur in ihrem Sprechen - keineswegs aber als aktiver Teilnehmer an dem erzählten Geschehen - greifbar wird, eine andere Bedeutung zu als den Erzählerfiguren, die zugleich Hauptfigur der Geschichte sind. (Dittmann 1993: 3)

It is a pity that Dittmann does not go on to explain what the "andere Bedeutung" could be. It can be argued, however, that the interpolation of the narrator is an invitation to the reader not to take the story too seriously, but simply to sit back and enjoy or even bask in the characters and situations. This point is further illustrated by the portrait of Fräulein von Osterloh in this chapter. It is appropriate at this stage to examine the Lowe-Porter and Luke versions of the opening lines of the novella respectively:

> *Lowe-Porter:* Einfried, the sanatorium. A long, white, rectilinear building with a side wing, set in a spacious garden pleasingly equipped with grottoes, bowers, and little dark pavilions. Behind its slate roofs the mountains tower heavenwards, evergreen, massy, cleft with wooded ravines. (Lowe-Porter 1978: 85)

> *Luke:* Here we are at "Einfried," the well-known sanatorium! It is white and rectilinear, a long low-lying main building with a side wing, standing in a spacious garden delightfully adorned with grottoes, leafy arcades and little bark-pavilions; and behind its slate roofs the massive pine-green mountains rear their softly outlined peaks and clefts into the sky. (Luke 1988: 107)

Luke manages to capture the immediacy of the original whereas Lowe-Porter's opening sentence is merely flat and unidiomatic besides losing the ironic narrative perspective. The irony and humour are lost in both versions. Lowe-Porter domesticates away the deliberate affectation of the phrase *ergötzlich ausgestattet* with her pale translation *pleasingly equipped*. Although Luke's stronger version with his use of the phrase *delightfully adorned* is an improvement, the humour based on exaggeration is still lost on the English reader. An even stronger adverb such as *exquisitely* in the phrase *exquisitely adorned* would be closer to the original as well as having a slightly humorous effect.

This humorous tone is maintained throughout the novella and is at its most delicate in the sketches of the minor characters. Although these humorous descriptions do not present obvious translation difficulties, it is very important for the translator to understand the nuances of each word and thus, the tone of the passage. This, however, refers only to the decoding aspect. It is a naive assumption of non-translators that the nuances and tone of a passage can be encoded by finding *le mot juste* with exactly the same nuances in the target language. Any experienced translator knows that very often a *mot juste* simply does not exist. This does not mean the translator despairs, but that compensatory strategies ensue, which may mean that, to be true to the tone, (in this case light humour), the translator may have to re-write the passage syntactically and use the technique already directly referred to as 'creative transposition', which, in turn, can be subsumed under the heading of 'compensation'. Nevertheless, the translator still acting as translator, can still keep remarkably close to the original and if the tone is true, the minor syntactic and lexical deviations go relatively unnoticed. These points can be illustrated by comparing the Luke, Lowe-Porter and suggested translation with the original description of Fräulein von Osterloh

> *Mann*: Was Fräulein von Osterloh betrifft, so steht sie mit unermüdlicher Hingabe dem Haushalte vor. Mein Gott, wie tätig sie, treppauf und treppab, von einem Ende der Anstalt zum anderen eilt! Sie herrscht in der Küche und Vorratskammer, sie klettert in den Wäscheschränken umher, sie kommandiert die Dienerschaft und bestellt unter den Gesichtspunkten der Sparsamkeit, der Hygiene, des Wohlgeschmacks und der äußeren Anmut den Tisch des Hauses, sie wirtschaftet mit einer rasenden Umsicht, und in ihrer extremen Tüchtigkeit liegt ein beständiger Vorwurf für die gesamte Männerwelt verborgen, von der noch niemand darauf verfallen ist, sie heimzuführen. Auf ihren Wangen aber glüht in zwei runden, karmoisinroten Flecken die unauslöschliche Hoffnung, dereinst Frau Doktor Leander zu werden . . . (Mann 1977: 163)

> *Lowe-Porter:* As for Fraulein von Osterloh, hers it is to preside with unwearying zeal over the housekeeping. Ah, what activity! How she plies, now here now there, now upstairs, now down, from one end of the building to the other! She is queen in the kitchen and storerooms, she mounts the shelves of the linen presses, she marshals the domestic staff; she ordains the bill of fare, to the end that the table shall be economical, hygienic, attractive appetizing. She keeps house diligently, furiously; and her exceeding capacity conceals a constant reproach to the world of men, to no one of whom has it yet occurred to lead her to the altar. But ever on her cheeks there glows two round, carmine spots, the unquenchable hope of one day becoming Frau Dr. Leander. (Lowe-Porter 1978: 85)

> *Luke:* As for Fräulein von Osterloh, she manages all domestic matters here, and does so with tireless devotion. Dear me, what a whirl of activity! She hurries upstairs and downstairs and from one end of the institution to the other. She is mistress of the kitchen and storerooms, she rummages in the linen cupboards, she has the servants at her beck and call, she plans the clients' daily fare on principles of economy, hygiene, taste and elegance. She keeps house with fanatical thoroughness; and in her extreme efficiency there lies concealed a standing reproach to the entire male sex, not one member of which has ever taken it into his head to make her his wife. But in two round crimson spots on her cheeks there burns the inextinguishable hope that one day she will become Frau Dr. Leander. (Luke 1988: 107)

It is very obvious that the tone of the original is one of mild humour. The portrait of Fräulein von Osterloh is, of course, exaggerated yet there is an empathetic delight in her unflagging activity. The author seems so exhausted and astonished at the sight of her relentless zeal that he again disrupts the third person narrative distance and breaks out into an interjection of astonishment: "Mein Gott, wie tätig sie treppauf und treppab, von einem Ende der Anstalt zum anderen eilt!" The breathless nature of her activity is further sustained by the sentence beginning with "Sie herrscht in der Küche und Vorratskammer." This six-clause sentence reflects the tension behind the activities by its very length and yet the structure is simple with four clauses emphasising both her activity and control: *Sie herrscht* [. . .] *sie klettert* [. . .] *sie kommandiert* [. . .] *sie wirtschaftet* [. . .]. There is also a poignant tragi-comical element in her unrequited love for Dr. Leander which takes a brilliantly incarnate form in the scarlet patches in her cheeks. This description also gives her cheeks a doll-like appearance, thus emphasising the burlesque elements in her portrait. In the Lowe-Porter version, however, the humorous tenor is missed. There is almost a whimsical note of regret in her exclamation *Ah, what activity!* Fräulein von Osterloh comes across more as a severe but highly respectable person. This is emphasised by her choice of the Latinate verbs *presides, plies, marshals, ordains* and the phrase *keeps the house* together with the overtranslated adverb *furiously*. Not only is the innocent humour of the original lost but also the resultant picture is distorted: no longer a charming, but outwardly rather domineering lady, but more a severe person who is embittered by self-sacrifice. The lightness of touch is totally missing.

The Luke version is closer to Mann's portrait, but the humour is toned down almost to the point of non-existence. What should be an interjection of exuberant astonishment to which reference has just been made, "Mein Gott, wie tätig sie treppauf und treppab, von einem Ende der Anstalt zum anderen eilt!" is also weakened to an expression of mild, almost supercilious dismay "Dear me, what a whirl of activity". By sticking very closely to the text, Luke's English version is acceptable but still rather dull and domesticated. In contrast, the suggested version which is much freer aims at capturing the humour first and the likeness of the portrait second at the expense of irrelevant liberties with the original syntax and lexis. This is justified as a compensatory strategy:

> ***Suggested version (Gledhill):*** The main thing about Fräulein von Osterloh is that she is utterly dedicated to running the institute, a task in which she succeeds with her unflagging zeal. My goodness, you should just see her! It is an *amazing* sight watching her *rushing* upstairs and downstairs and then *zooming* from one end of the sanatorium to the other. She is queen of both kitchen and store room. You can even see her *clambering around* high up in the linen cupboards. As far as the servants are concerned, she's the real boss. She's also the one who determines exactly what should appear on the table based on her strict interpretation with

> regard to economy, hygiene, taste and, of course, aesthetic appeal. She rules the household with a fanatical eye for detail. Her immoderate industry acts as a constant reproach to the whole world of 'menkind' for failing to recognise her many virtues and not making her into "a 'duly' beloved wife". However, in her cheeks you can *still* distinguish two round glowing crimson patches which are perhaps evidence of her inextinguishable hope one day still to become Frau Dr. Leander.

The italicised words attempt to convey something of the author's amused delight at this formidable person. The tone is one of gentle irony. No doubt the suggested version could be improved with even more use of irony, but this translation serves to illustrate the point that something of the humour of the original can be captured.

The humour and exaggeration in the figure of the aesthete Detlev Spinell is much more obvious and both translators do capture the satirical elements to a certain extent even though many nuances are lost. It is, however, in the minor sketches that this loss is most obviously the case as has been seen in the above example. Thomas Mann produces another highly humorous sketch at the end of the novella, the portrait of the baby Anton Klöterjahn. As this portrait has many interesting semiotic features, it is well worth further examination:

> **Mann**: In diesem Wägelchen aber saß das Kind, saß Anton Klöterjahn der Jüngere, saß Gabriele Eckhofs dicker Sohn! Er saß, bekleidet mit einer Flausjacke und einem großen weißen Hut, pausbackig, prächtig und wohlgeraten in den Kissen, und sein Blick begegnete lustig und unbeirrbar demjenigen Herrn Spinells. Der Romancier war im Begriffe, sich aufzuraffen, er war ein Mann, er hätte die Kraft besessen, an dieser unerwarteten, in Glanz getauchten Erscheinung vorüberzuschreiten und seinen Spaziergang fortzusetzen. Da aber geschah das Gräßliche, daß Anton Klöterjahn zu lachen und jubeln begann, er kreischte vor unerklärlicher Lust, es könnte einem unheimlich zu Sinne werden.
>
> Gott weiß, was ihn anfocht, ob die schwarze Gestalt ihm gegenüber ihn in diese wilde Heiterkeit versetzte oder was für ein Anfall von animalischem Wohlbefinden ihn packte. Er hielt in der einen Hand einen knöchernen Beißring und in der anderen eine blecherne Klapperbüchse. Diese beiden Gegenstände reckte er jauchzend in den Sonnenschein empor, schüttelte sie und schlug sie zusammen, als wollte er jemanden spottend verscheuchen. Seine Augen waren beinahe geschlossen vor Vergnügen, und sein Mund war so klaffend aufgerissen, daß man seinen rosigen Gaumen sah. Er warf sogar seinen Kopf hin und her, indes er jauchzte.
>
> Da machte Herr Spinell kehrt und ging von dannen. (Mann 1977: 197-198)

In this passage, life in the form of the 'bourgeois' baby Klöterjahn triumphs over art as embodied over Spinell who is terrified by the aspect of the baby bursting with health and energy. The perspective is half from that of Spinell's point of view whose highly aesthetic sensibilities are offended by the 'monstrous health' and happiness of the baby and half from that of Thomas Mann who also portrays the baby as monster, but Spinell as utter weakling. It is a tribute to Thomas Mann's skill as a writer that he makes the utterly absurd situation of a grown man being terrified and 'scared off' by a baby in a pram both credible and highly amusing - even more so, that the baby itself is portrayed as an horrific creature with its cavernous mouth and noisy rattle. There is a hint of a 'savage' witch doctor raising the rattle and the teething ring to the sun in order to drive out, or even exorcise the black figure before him. These elements are subtly embedded in Mann's text: firstly the (amusingly absurd) situation that the event of the baby laughing is described in terms of horror: "Da aber geschah das Gräßliche, daß Anton Klöterjahn zu lachen und jubeln begann." The authorial perspective supports the aesthete's horror: "Es könnte einem unheimlich werden". The joy of the baby's triumph is also expressed in terms of horror and savagery in phrases such as "diese wilde Heiterkeit" and "was für ein Anfall von animalischem Wohlbefinden". The baby holds up the objects made of hard materials "blechern" and "knöchern" to the sun emphasise almost as if they possessed totemic power. The portrait culminates in a picture of utter horror (for Spinell): "sein Mund war so klaffend aufgerissen, daß man seinen rosigen Gaumen sah" with the implied violence of the participle *aufgerissen*, emphasising once again the savagery of the baby.

The 'monstrosity' of the baby makes Spinell's fear credible and it is not surprising that he is transfixed by the sight of Anton Klöterjahn. The irony of the assertion concerning Spinell: "Er war ein Mann" is increased by the authorial complicity in wanting to excuse Spinell for not having the courage to walk past the baby by the use of a concessive clause: "Er hätte die Kraft besessen, an dieser unerwarteten, in Glanz getauchten Erscheinung vorüberzuschreiten und seinen Spaziergang fortzusetzen." If the 'creature' had been an apparition ("Erscheinung"), then there might have been some excuse for fear in the aesthete, but the fact that it is a question of actually being terrified of a healthy baby provides both the absurdity and humour of the passage. It can be seen that the Lowe-Porter and Luke versions play down the monstrous aspects so that we are simply left with the absurd, but incomprehensible situation of a grown man being so frightened by a healthy baby that he runs off in fear. At this point, it will be appropriate to compare the three passages.

> **Lowe-Porter:** There he sat among his cushions, in a woolly white jacket and large white hat, plump-cheeked, well cared for, and magnificent; and his blithe unerring gaze encountered

Herr Spinell's. The novelist pulled himself together. Was he not a man, had he not the power to pass this unexpected, sunkindled apparition there in the path and continue on his walk? But Anton Klöterjahn began to laugh and shout - most horrible to see. He squealed, he crowed with inconceivable delight - it was positively uncanny to hear him.

God knows what had taken him; perhaps the sight of Herr Spinell's long, black figure set him off; perhaps an attack of sheer animal spirits gave rise to his wild outburst of merriment. He had a bone teething-ring in one hand and a tin rattle in the other; and these two objects he flung aloft with shoutings, shook them to and fro, and clashed them together in the air, as though purposely to frighten Herr Spinell. His eyes were almost shut. His mouth gaped open till all the rosy gums were displayed; and as he shouted he rolled his head about in excess of mirth.

Herr Spinell turned round and went thence. (Lowe-Porter 1978: 127-128)

Luke: There he sat among his cushions, in a white woolly jacket and a big white hat - chubby, magnificent and robust; and his eyes, unabashed and alive with merriment, looked straight into Herr Spinell's. The novelist was just on the point of pulling himself together; after all, he was a grown man, he would have had the strength to step right past this unexpected sight, this resplendent phenomenon, and continue his walk. But at the very moment the appalling thing happened: Anton Klöterjahn began to laugh - he screamed with laughter, he squealed, he crowed: it was inexplicable. It was positively uncanny.

God knows what had come over him, what had set him off into this wild hilarity; the sight of the black-clad figure in front of him perhaps, or some sudden spasm of sheer animal high spirits. He had a bone teething ring in one hand and a tin rattle in the other, and he held up these two objects triumphantly into the sunshine, brandishing them and banging them together, as if he were mockingly trying to scare someone off. His eyes were almost screwed shut with pleasure, and his mouth gaped open so wide that his entire pink palate was exposed. He even wagged his head to and fro in his exultation.

And Herr Spinell turned on his heel and walked back the way he had come. (Luke 1988: 131-132)

Suggested version (Gledhill): However, in the pram there was a baby, in fact, Anton Klöterjahn Junior himself, the dumpy son of Gabriele Eckhof! The creature wore a coarse woollen jacket and a large white hat; its cheeks were so chubby as to seem bloated, yet the well-cared-for scion looked magnificent amongst its cushions; there was no doubting the way its gaze met that of the aesthete and the way it seemed to be utterly delighted. The littérateur was just about to pull himself together, (after all he was a man!). He would normally have had sufficient strength to stride past this sudden apparition, which was bathed in such splendour, and simply to have continued his walk. But then an horrific event occurred: Anton Klöterjahn started to laugh and become suddenly exuberant. He even screeched with inexplicable delight. It was enough to make your hair stand on end.

God only knows what drove this creature into this frenzy of ecstatic joy and bliss. It could have been the black figure standing opposite him. The little monster of health held a bone teething ring in one hand and a tin rattle in the other. It raised these objects to the sun, rattling and banging them as if wanting to pour scorn on the figure and shoo it away from its presence. Its eyes were half-closed as if intoxicated by some obscure pleasure and its mouth gaped wide open so that the pink inner cavern of its gums could be seen. The creature's head even began to sway backwards and forwards whilst delighting in its triumph.

Herr Spinell turned full circle and walked off.

Thomas Mann maintains this humorous perspective throughout the novella which reaches its climax in Spinell's letter and in the ensuing confrontation with Klöterjahn. As the same principles of translation apply to the Fräulein von Osterloh passage just quoted, it would be unnecessary to labour the point by analysing every character sketch although a full study on the translation of humour is still in need of being written.

(g) Conclusion

Perspective, gentle irony and careful selection of words all set the tone and register of this novella, all of which can easily be lost in translation as is often the case with the translators in question. Mann's humorous semiotics (such as the healthy bourgeois baby as monster and savage) is often deeply embedded in the text so that the translator into English may have to make what is implicit, explicit by highlighting the key themes with a judicious choice of vocabulary. This is very much a case of being faithful to the text. (One could argue that this process involves a much greater fidelity at a much deeper (semiotic) level.) Absolute semantic fidelity is secondary to fidelity to the tone (in this case humour) and to the semiotics. After the first two conditions have been fulfilled, the translator may then add 'semantic' touches to the translation to make the translation even in this area is as close as possible to the original in the conventional sense of academic translation.

Chapter IX: Conclusions

The dissertation has attempted to combine practical criticism with translation theory so that there has been a two-directional deductive/inductive dynamic throughout the work. For this reason, it is helpful to divide the conclusion into four sections. Section (a) gives a quality assessment of the two translations of *Tonio Kröger, Tristan* and *Der Tod in Venedig*. Section (b) summarises the conclusions pertaining to translation criticism. Section (c) defines the *strategic approach* to literary translation and Section (d) describes the implications for the teaching of translation.

(a) The Assessment of the Luke and Lowe-Porter Versions

Both translators work within the narrow confines of what has been defined as the *academic approach*, in other words, the balancing act any teacher of translation goes through in order to produce a key to a set translation text in order to combine close fidelity to the SL text with a fluent TL text. At the level of mere information transfer, Luke essentially succeeds in this task. His versions of the three stories can be said to be competent, reliable and professional. Unlike Lowe-Porter, he rarely makes a lexical translation error or a grammatical mistake. In the appendices and in other quotations his translations are placed alongside Lowe-Porter's for normative reference.

On the other hand, the Error Appendix has proven that Lowe-Porter's translations fail even within the criteria of *academic translation*. The 187 errors in Appendix I (i.e. including those identified by Luke) consist of misreadings of German lexis and grammar at the surface level of meaning and, even worse, basic grammar mistakes in English grammar and usage. These are the kind of errors any teacher of translation is confronted with when teaching students with an inadequate knowledge of German and of the mother tongue. Indeed, some mistakes are even below normal student competence as has been seen in the Error Appendix with howlers such as "bath-hotel" for *Badehotel* (2. 5214) or in Buck's examples such as "with big bones" for *breitbeinig*. The other chapters have shown that these errors are by no means harmless. Not only are poetic and stylistic effects lost in this version but there is a basic misreading and misrepresentation of Thomas Mann's themes at the most elementary level.

(b) Conclusions pertaining to Translation Criticism

The real scandal of the Lowe-Porter translations is not only the fact that translations of such poor quality have continued to be published uncorrected for over half a century (and will, no doubt, continue for some time to be the most widely read versions of Thomas Mann in the world) but also that Lowe-Porter still continues to have defenders. Opinions seem to be almost equally divided concerning the quality of her work. All translators make mistakes, but they are usually rare and relatively harmless as in the case of Luke's versions, but to dismiss Lowe-Porter's grossly inaccurate translations as "recastings" shows that common sense and basic linguistic competence are still criteria which cannot be ignored in the present debate on quality assessment.

The detailed analyses have shown that Thomas Mann's prose has the same richness and density of poetry and that poetic, ironical and philosophical aspects are usually lost in the translations. Even though Luke's translations are semantically reliable, they lack the poetry, humour and irony of the original and are often, in fact, dull. It has been argued that this failure to capture literary nuances is the inevitable result of *academic translation*. It is for this reason other strategies have been source-oriented suggested.

(c) The *Strategic Approach* to Literary Translation

The starting part of the *strategic approach* is the realisation that for high literature and many other areas such as comedy or even marketing, the traditional *academic approach* fails because the semantic demands on the translator means that other aspects such as form, humour and wordplay are lost. It is at this point that a translation decision should be made concerning translating strategy. Present-day theory divides between source-oriented and target-language-oriented translation. The nomenclature varies from *domesticating, communicative* and *Skopos-oriented* to describe target-oriented texts to *foreignising* or *semantic* translations to describe source-oriented translations. These two strategies have been adopted with the suggested versions which by no means and by definition (i.e. in that two separate versions are offered) claim to be ideal translations of Thomas Mann. It is, however, claimed that it is better to produce either a fluent readable and enjoyable text in the target language or a very close text for the literary specialist rather than a compromise between these extremes which usually ends in dull versions following the *academic approach*.

The *strategic approach* has been developed to go further along these lines by suggesting there are many more possible strategies and each strategy is appropriate for differing types of text. The main departure from traditional 'equivalence' theories in translation is the redefinition of fidelity, which has always been assumed to mean semantic fidelity. Thus a faithful translation to any text normally refers to a semantically close translation. However, it has been shown that there are more important factors in certain types of translation. For example, for a translated comedy to be performed on the stage, it might well be more important for the translation to be amusing than to reflect every semantic item of the original with its equivalent. This has seen to be the case with Gotter's highly successful translations for the eighteenth-century Gotha theatre. The techniques of compensation and 'creative transposition' are important in this area.

It has been argued that the proponents who claim that problem areas such as poetry, style, puns and dialect are ultimately untranslatable base their arguments on too narrow definitions of the process of translation. Indeed, they assume translation to be what has been defined as *academic translation*. The second-order semiotic approach of Levý has shown that Christian Morgenstern's poetry can be successfully translated. This has also been implicitly the strategy of the various translators of Lewis Carroll's *Alice* stories. The semiotic approach does not imply limitless, creative freedom. The analysis has shown that the translator should understand the semiotics of the original and then recreate a new text but along the same lines. Finally, as many semantic aspects as possible then need to be re-embedded in the text. Max Knight's translations have been shown to vary considerably with regard to the success of their outcome.

Scientific equivalence-based theories of literary translation have been proven to be woefully inadequate. Not only has the formal refutation of Holmes' use of mathematical models shown that equivalence theories fail even at the theoretical level but also the detailed analyses have revealed how rich in meaning and music great literary style can be and how far away we are from fully understanding these processes. The idea of encoding them in mathematical form is thus at the moment doomed to failure.

The strategic theory of translation derives some of its inspiration from Wittgenstein's (1953) language-game theory. The translator should be playing the same language game as is played in the text. This has already been applied to poetry and to comedy and also applies to philosophy where the main stress of fidelity is to the logical form of the argument. It has been seen that Thomas Mann has many philosophical passages embedded in dense literary prose and that the translation will come across with much greater clarity once the skeleton of the argument has been understood and displayed. The same language-game principles would apply to non-literary translation such as, for example, business letters, advertising and humorous speeches.

It has also been shown that great literary translation is possible. This area has been discussed within the parameters of Gentzler's discussion of post-Derridean translation theory. It is at this level that the distinction between great poetry and great translation becomes blurred. It is no coincidence that the successful translators of literature have also been writers. The examples would seem to corroborate this view: Hölderlin's translation of Sophocles, James Joyce's translation of *Finnegans Wake* and Beckett in French translating Beckett into English. These examples alone refute the school that believes in the essential untranslatability of literature.

The area of dialect translation is another difficult area and relatively little has been written on this topic. Indeed, at the level of practice, most translators ignore dialectal features and most theoreticians claim that dialect is untranslatable. However, it has been shown that the *strategic approach* can be helpful even in this area. First, the translator needs to assess the extent of the dialectal features which may vary from light coloration to a new language. Secondly, the translator needs to find out the function of the particular dialect in the work which may be anything from sociolectal placement, regional coloration, exclusion, inclusion to humour and class dynamics or even any combination of both these and other functions. Thirdly, the encoding will depend on the type of translation which may range from total domestication (as has been seen to be the case with Gotter) to subtle metalanguage in that the translator explains the dialectal effects in an appropriate way in order not to disturb either the coherence or the tenor of the text. This is, however, an area where there is a great need for more research.

(d) Implications for the Teaching and Practice of Translation

Many translation theorists are involved with the teaching of translation. The rejection of semantically bound equivalence-based definitions of translation for the translation of great literature does not imply that these approaches do not have their uses. The exercise of translation both into and from the target language is, in my opinion, one of the most efficient ways of gaining a high level writing and reading competence in both the target language and the mother tongue. For first degree students, the *academic approach* is an excellent discipline particularly for regional studies-based texts, even though this strategy has been shown to be disastrously inadequate for the translator confronted with high literary texts.

The illusion for many is that if a linguist is highly competent in two languages he or she can translate anything in those languages. This is an illusion often held by literary publishers. The drastic effect of this mistake has been demonstrated by this analysis of the Lowe-Porter translations. The analysis is by no means intended as an attack on Lowe-Porter herself but on the whole publishing world and to a certain extent on certain academic and literary people who seem to be so blind with regard to the quality of literary translation.

As a corollary to the above, it can be seen that for the training of translators for an MA in translation studies, for example, other criteria than mere language competence would apply. (This is not to imply, of course, that everyone who studies literary translation will want to be a translator of some kind.) It has been shown that generally one can translate only as well as one can write so that the aspects of a literary translation course relevant for potential translators would not differ drastically from a creative writing course which has the aim of discovering the talents of its participants. One student may have a gift for translating plays and dialogues, another for humour and another may be a highly dextrous poet and so forth.

In conclusion, it is to be hoped that the Lowe-Porter debate will now be over and that a more creative definition of the translator's role will have emerged as a result of this thesis. Literary translation is not the dull dictionary-bound activity suitable for pedants (even though the translator does often have to very precise), but is more akin to creative writing. Finally, it is to be hoped that the gap between creator and translator will be been at least partially narrowed as a result of this dissertation

Appendix I: Selection of Errors in *Tristan, Tonio Kröger* and *Der Tod in Venedig*

A) Errors Identified by David Luke. (All the listed 'Luke' errors in Section A are discussed in detail in Chapter II. The emphasis is added in all the examples unless otherwise stated.)

i) Lexical Confusion

Tristan

1. 111 *Thomas Mann:* Es gibt Zeiten, in denen ich das Empire einfach nicht *entbehren* kann, in denen es mir, um einen bescheidenen Grad des Wohlbefindens zu erreichen, unbedingt nötig ist. (1977: 171-172)

Lowe-Porter: There are times when I cannot *endure* Empire and then times when I simply must have it in order to attain any sense of well-being. (1978: 95)

Luke: Now, there are times when I simply cannot *do without* "Empire", times when it is absolutely necessary to me if I am to achieve even a modest degree of well-being. (1988: 163)

Misunderstanding of *entbehren* probably because of its superficial resemblance to the false friends *entbehren* and *bear*. This could, indeed, be regarded as an example of what Luke condemns as 'undergraduate howlers'. Luke's version is adequate.

1. 112 *Thomas Mann:* [...] ich erzähle lediglich eine Geschichte, eine ganz kurze, unsäglich *empörende* Geschichte [...]. (1977: 124)

Lowe-Porter: I will merely tell a story, a brief, unspeakably *touching* story. (1978: 119)

Luke: I merely wish to tell you about something as it was and now is. It is a quite short and unspeakably *outrageous* story. (1988: 123)

It is clear from the quotation that Lowe-Porter has given the opposite meaning to the adjective *empörend*. As this basic mistranslation refers to Spinell's assessment to Gabriele's whole life story, the error is this time less excusable. Luke's version is adequate.

Tonio Kröger

1. 121 *Thomas Mann:* Und er betrachtete abwechselnd die farbigen Skizzen, die zu beiden Seiten der Staffelei auf Stühlen lehnten, und die große, mit einem *quadratischen Liniennetz* überzogene Leinwand. (1977: 221)

Lowe-Porter: [...] and he looked at the colour-sketches leaning against chairs at both sides of the easel and from them to the large canvas covered with a square *linen mesh*. (1978: 149)

Luke: And he looked by turns at the color sketches propped against the chair backs on either side of the easel, and at the great canvas marked of *in squares* (1988: 153)

Lexical confusion of *Linien* with *Leinen*. Luke's version is correct.

Der Tod in Venedig

1. 131 *Thomas Mann:* Der Vierziger hatte, ermattet von den Strapazen und Wechselfällen der eigentlichen Arbeit, alltäglich eine Post zu bewältigen, die *Wertzeichen* aus allen Herren Ländern trug. (1977: 14)

Lowe-Porter: At forty, worn down by the strains of his actual task, he had to deal with a daily post heavy with *tributes* from his own and foreign countries. (1978: 13)

Luke: By the age of forty he was obliged, weary though he might be by the toils and vicissitudes of his real work, to deal with a daily correspondence that bore *postage stamps* from every part of the globe. (1988: 200-201)

Literal translation of *Wertzeichen* as *tributes* rather than as *postage stamps*.

1. 132 *Thomas Mann:* Aber er hatte die *Würde* gewonnen, nach welcher, wie er behauptete, jedem großem Talente ein natürlicher Drang und Stachel eingeboren ist, ja, man kann sagen, daß seine ganze Entwicklung, ein bewußter und trotziger, alle Hemmungen des Zweifels und der Ironie zurücklassender Aufstieg *zur Würde* gewesen war. (1977: 17)

Lowe-Porter: But he had attained to *honour*, and *honour*, he used to say, is the natural goal towards which every considerable talent presses with whip and spur. Yes, one might put it that his whole career had been one conscious and *overweening* ascent to *honour*, which left in the rear all the misgivings or self-derogation which might have hampered him. (1978: 16)

Luke: But he had achieved *dignity*, that goal toward which, as he declared, every great talent is innately driven and spurred; indeed it can be said that the conscious and defiant purpose of his entire development had been, leaving all the inhibitions of skepticism and irony behind him, an ascent to *dignity*. (1988: 203)

In Lowe-Porter's version, the distinction between *honour* and *dignity* is blurred, which is compounded by the intrusive addition of the adjective *overweening*. *Dignity* together with the loss of dignity is one of the major themes of the novella.
Luke's version is adequate.

ii) Grammatical Errors

Der Tod in Venedig

1. 231 **Thomas Mann:** Fast jedem Künstlernaturell ist ein üppiger und verräterischer Hang eingeboren, *Schönheit schaffende Ungerechtigkeit* anzuerkennen. (1977: 358)

Lowe-Porter: For in almost every artist nature is inborn a wanton and treacherous proneness to side with the *beauty that breaks hearts.* (1978: 31-32)

Luke: Inborn in every artistic nature is a luxuriant, treacherous bias in favor of the *injustice that creates beauty.* (1988: 217)

This syntactical error of failing to distinguish between a subject and an object in a noun phrase in Lowe-Porter's version reveals a fundamental lack of knowledge of elementary German syntax. Luke's version is adequate.

iii) Omissions

Der Tod in Venedig

1. 331 **Thomas Mann:** Unterdessen nähert sich das Dampfboot dem Bahnhof, und Schmerz und Rastlosigkeit steigen bis zu Verwirrung. Die Abreise dünkt den Gequälten unmöglich, die Umkehr nicht minder. So ganz zerrissen betritt er die Station. Es ist sehr spät, er hat keinen Augenblick zu verlieren, wenn er den Zug erreichen will. *Er will es und will es nicht.* Aber die Zeit drängt, sie geißelt ihn vorwärts; er eilt sich sein Billet zu verschaffen. (1977: 368)

Lowe-Porter: Meanwhile the steamer neared the station landing; *his anguish of irresolution* amounted *almost* to panic. *Torn* between two alternatives, he entered the station. To leave seemed impossible to the sufferer, to remain not less so. It was very late, he had not a moment to lose, Time pressed, it scourged him onward. He hastened to buy his ticket [...]. (1978: 44)

Luke: In the meantime the vaporetto was approaching the station, and Aschenbach's distress and helplessness increased to the point of distraction. In his torment he felt it to be impossible to leave and no less impossible to turn back. He entered the station torn by this acute inner conflict. It was very late, he had not a moment to lose if he was to catch his train. *He both wanted to catch it and wanted to miss it.* But time was pressing, lashing him on; he hurried to get his ticket, [...]. (1988: 228)

The italicised sentence in the SL and Luke's texts is omitted in the Lowe-Porter version with the result that both the nature of the conflict and the theme of the *Wille* are played down. Lowe-Porter does, however, make an oblique reference to the dilemma with the italicised phrase *his anguish of irresolution*. For a full discussion of other implications of this omission, see Section (c) of Chapter II.

1. 332 *Thomas Mann:* Ihm war aber, als ob der bleiche und liebliche Psychagog dort draußen ihm lächle, ihm winke; als ob er, die Hand aus der Hüfte lösend, hinausdehnte, voranschwebe ins Verheißungsvoll-Ungeheure. *Und wie so oft, machte er sich auf, ihm zu folgen.* (1977: 398)

Lowe-Porter: It seemed to him the pale and lovely Summoner out there smiled at him and beckoned; as though with the hand he lifted from his hip, he pointed outward as he hovered on before into an immensity of richest expectation. [Omission] (1978: 83)

Luke: But it was as if the pale and lovely soul-summoner out there were smiling to him, beckoning to him: as if he loosed his hand from his hip and pointed outward, hovering ahead and onward, into an immensity rich with unutterable expectation. *And as so often, he set out to follow him.* (1988: 263)

Lowe-Porter's version simply omits the last sentence in the penultimate paragraph of the novella which describes Aschenbach's final action before his death. Luke's version is adequate. (For a full discussion of the enormous implications caused by this omission, see Chapter III Section (e).)

B) A Selection of *Other* Errors in *Tristan* and *Tonio Kröger*

i) Basic Printing and Orthographic Errors from *Tristan* and *Tonio Kröger*
Tristan
2. 111 *Thomas Mann:* Ja, nun zerbrecht *euch die* Köpfe über diese Erscheinung! - Und wir zerbrechen sie uns. (1977: 175)

Lowe-Porter: Look on this, if you like, and break *you* heads over it. And we break them. (1978: 100)

Luke: Well, here's a phenomenon to make you all rack *your* brains! And we rack them we do indeed. (1988: 106)

Correct version: you*r*: misspelling. (Also inadmissible literal translation of the German idiom: *sich den Kopf zerbrechen über etwas*). The misspelling remained uncorrected until the Vintage International edition appeared in March, 1989. Luke's version is adequate.

2. 112 *Thomas Mann:* Wenn *sie nicht das Bett hütete* und Herr Spinell auf den Spitzen seiner großen Füße mit ungeheurer Behutsamkeit zu ihr trat. (1977: 178)

Lowe-Porter: When she *had not to keep her bed*, Herr Spinell would approach her with immense caution. (1978: 104)

Luke: When she was *not confined to her bed* Herr Spinell would approach her, tiptoeing up to her on his great feet with extreme circumspection [...]. (1988: 110)

Correct version: to keep _to_ her bed: omission of the preposition. The mistake still remains uncorrected in the Vintage International edition which appeared in March, 1989. Luke's version is adequate.

2. 113 **_Thomas Mann:_** 'Wahrhaftig, ja, alles _liegt in Schatten_', antwortete Herrn Klöterjahns Gattin. (1977: 181)

Lowe-Porter: 'Yes, it is all _overcase_,' replied Herr Klöterjahn's wife. (1978: 108)

Luke: 'Yes indeed, there are _shadows everywhere_', replied Herr Klöterjahn's wife. (1988: 113)

Correct version: overcas_t_: misspelling. This misspelling remained uncorrected until the Vintage International edition appeared in March, 1989.

2. 114 **_Thomas Mann:_** Eigentlich von plumper Konstitution [...] sind Sie [...]. (1977: 191)

Lowe-Porter: [...] _you_ own constitution is coarse-fibred [...] (1978: 120)

Luke: Although in fact _your_ natural constitution is _coarse_ [...]. (1988: 124)

Correct version: you_r_ misspelling: omission of the letter 'r'. This misspelling remained uncorrected until the Vintage International edition appeared in March, 1989.

2. 115 **_Thomas Mann:_** [...] und wenn sie [...] stolz und selig unter dem tödlichen Kusse der Schönheit vergeht, so ist das _meine_ Sorge gewesen. (1977: 192)

Lowe-Porter: [...] and if she [...] _passes_ in an ecstasy, with the deathly kiss of beauty on her brow - well, it is I, sir, who have seen to that! (1978: 120)

Luke: [...] and if she _perishes_ [...] proudly and joyfully under the deadly kiss of beauty, then it is _I_ who have made it my business to bring that about. (1988: 125)

Correct version: passes _away_: word omission. The mistake still remains uncorrected in the Vintage International edition (March, 1989).

Tonio Kröger

2. 121 **_Thomas Mann:_** Und _für_ diesen kalten und eitlen Scharlatan wollen Sie ernstlich eintreten? (1977: 228)

Lowe-Porter: And will you seriously enter the lists *in* behalf of this vain and frigid charlatan? (1978: 158)

Luke: Can we seriously defend this vain coldhearted charlatan? (1988: 161)

Correct version: misspelling of the preposition: <u>o</u>n behalf of.

2. 123 *Thomas Mann:* Übrigens wissen Sie *sehr wohl*, daß Sie die Dinge ansehen, wie sie nicht notwendig gesehen brauchen. (1977: 226)

Now, you *perfectly* know that you are looking at things as they do not necessarily have to be looked at [...] (1978: 156)

Luke: And in any case you know *very well* that it is not necessary to take such a view of things as you are taking [...]. (1988: 159)

Correct version: perfectly <u>well</u>: word omission.

2. 124 *Thomas Mann:* Er war ein wenig niedergeschlagen gewesen, daß man ihn als Hochstapler hatte verhaften wollen, ja - *obgleich* er es gewissermaßen in Ordnung gefunden hatte. (1977: 241)

Lowe-Porter: The episode at the hotel, their wanting to arrest him for a swindler, had cast him down a little, *even although* he found it quite in order - in a certain way. (1978: 173)

Luke: [...] The experience of being nearly arrested in his native town as a criminal adventurer had somewhat damped his spirits, to be sure - *even although* in a certain sense he had felt that this was just as it should be. (1988: 175)

The conjunction **even although* does not exist in English unlike *even though*. Incredibly, Luke repeats Lowe-Porter's mistake.

ii) Lexical Errors
Tristan
2. 211 *Thomas Mann:* Eine fünfzigjährige Dame, die Pastorin Höhlenrauch, die *neunzehn* Kinder zur Welt gebracht hat und absolut keines Gedankens mehr fähig ist, *gelangt <u>dennoch</u> nicht zum Frieden*, [...] (1977: 163-164)

Lowe-Porter: There is an elderly lady, a Frau Pastor Höhlenrauch, who has brought nineteen children into the world and is now incapable of a single thought, *yet has <u>thereby</u> attained to any peace of mind.* (1978: 86)

Luke: There is a lady of fifty, Pastorin Höhlenrauch, who has had nineteen children and is now totally incapable of thought *despite which her mind is still not at peace*: (1988: 94)

The italicised phrase in Lowe-Porter's version barely makes any sense; if the phrase is reformulated into grammatical English as *and has, because of this, attained peace of mind*, it would seem to imply the opposite of the original and the Luke version.

2. 212 *Thomas Mann:* [...] alle diese Individuen, die, *zu schwach sich selbst Gesetze zu geben und sie zu halten,* ihm ihr Vermögen auszuliefern, um sich von seiner Strenge stützen lassen zu dürfen. (1977: 163)

Lowe-Porter: [...] holds those sufferers who, *too weak to be laws unto themselves,* put themselves into his hands that his severity may be a shield unto them. (1978: 85)

Luke: [...] all these individuals who, *too weak to set up a regime for themselves and keep to it,* pay a fortune to him so that they can let themselves be carried along by his strict methods. (1988: 93)

The phrase *to be a law unto oneself* has an entirely different meaning from setting oneself laws or goals; the former would refer to a 'loner' or some one who ignores conventions whereas Luke's version clearly expresses the meaning of the source text.

2. 213 *Thomas Mann:* [...] die Herren mit den entfleischten Gesichtern lächelten und versuchten angestrengt ihre Beine *zu beherrschen,* wenn sie in ihre [Gabrieles] Nähe kamen [...]. (1977: 166)

Lowe-Porter: [...] the gentlemen with the fleshless faces smiled and did their best to keep their legs *in order.* (1978: 89)

Luke: [...] the gentlemen with the shriveled faces, when they came anywhere near her, smiled and made a great effort to keep their legs *under control.* (1988: 97)

In the context of a sanatorium, the Lowe-Porter version would imply that the gentlemen were trying to keep their legs in an acceptable condition rather than keeping them under control after experiencing the presence of the beautiful Gabriele. It is significant that Lowe-Porter omits the translation of the phrase *in ihre Nähe* with the result that the erotic effect of Gabriele is lost together with the humour. Luke's version is adequate.

2. 214 *Thomas Mann:* Sie zeigte *einen nervösen Sinn* für differenzierte Klangfarbe [...]. (1977: 183)

Lowe-Porter: She displayed a *nervous feeling* for modulations of timbre [...]. (1978: 110)

Luke: She showed a *fastidious ear* for differences of timbre [...]. (1988: 115)

Error type: false friend, i.e. misunderstanding of the meaning of the adjective, *nervös*, which, in this context, would almost have the opposite meaning. Luke's version is adequate.

2. 215 ***Thomas Mann:*** Ich *gebe zu*, daß es vielleicht aus der Lunge kommt [...]. (1977: 196)

Lowe-Porter: Yes, *I give in*, it may be from the lung [...]. (1978: 125)

Luke: Maybe it does come from the lungs. *I admit* that it may be [...]. (1988: 130)

Error type: possible confusion of the German verbs *aufgeben* and *zugeben*. Luke's version is correct.

2. 216 ***Thomas Mann:*** [...] es war jene Kranke, die *neunzehn* Kinder zur Welt gebracht hatte und keines Gedankens mehr fähig war. (1977: 186)

Lowe-Porter: [...] It was that patient who had borne *fourteen* children and was no longer capable of a single thought. (1978: 114)

Luke: [...] it was the lady who had had *nineteen* children and was no longer capable of thought [...]. (1988: 119)

Error type: elementary lexical confusion. Although trivial, there are many errors of this kind in Lowe-Porter's work. In this context, as in reality, a difference of five children is a significant distinction. (There is an implication that Pastorin Höhlenrauch's insanity was the result of having 'too many' children.)

2. 217 ***Thomas Mann:*** [...] sondern mit der liebenswürdigen Freude und Teilnahme gutgearteter Kranker an den zuversichtlichen Lebensäußerungen von Leuten, die *in ihrer Haut sich wohlfühlten.* (1977: 168)

Lowe-Porter: [...] but the sympathetic participation of a well-disposed invalid in the manifestations of people *who rejoice in the blessing of abounding health.* (1978: 91)

Luke: [...] taking genuine pleasure in *the hearty self-assurance of persons blessed with good health.* (1988: 99)

Luke, as is often the case, rather slavishly follows the Lowe-Porter version. The more likely version could be along the following lines: *but displaying that charming delight and interest well-disposed sick* *people show towards the confident comments of <u>people who feel at home in the world</u>.* This is an important aspect of the outsider theme in Thomas Mann's works. The particular reference is to the smugness of the healthy 'Bürger' types.

2. 218 **Thomas Mann:** Der Überschwang einer ungeheuren *Lösung und Erfüllung* brach herein, wiederholte sich, ein betäubendes Brausen maßloser Befriedigung, unersättlich wieder und wieder [...]. (1977: 186-187)

Lowe-Porter: [...] it was repeated, swelled into deafening, unquenchable tumult of immense *appeasement* that wove and welled [...]. (1978: 114)

Luke: The triumph of a vast release, *a tremendous fulfillment,* a roaring tumult of immense delight, was heard and heard again [...]. (1988: 119)

The noun *appeasement* is a totally misleading translation so that the English sentence hardly makes any sense (particularly in conjunction with *wove* ('a weaving appeasement'?)). Luke's version makes better sense in this respect although the idea of infinite satisfaction/fulfilment (with both spiritual and sexual connotations) is trivialised in his translation by his phrase *immense delight.*

Tonio Kröger

2. 221 **Thomas Mann:** Bist du noch *Primus*? (1977: 208)

Lowe-Porter: Still *head of the school*? (1978: 133)

Luke: Still *top of the class?* (1988: 139)

Error type: cultural misunderstanding: in a British context, Lowe-Porter's version would refer to the headmaster of a school whereas in an American context, it would be virtually meaningless. Luke's version would be acceptable on both sides of the Atlantic.

2. 222 **Thomas Mann:** Sagen Sie nicht 'Natur', Lisaweta, 'Natur' ist nicht *erschöpfend.* (1977: 222)

Lowe-Porter: Don't say nature, Lisabeta, 'nature' isn't *exhausting.* (1978: 150)

Luke: Don't call it 'nature,' Lisaveta, 'nature' isn't an *adequate* term. (1988: 153)

Error type: failure to distinguish between the two meanings of the adjective *erschöpfend,* which can mean either *exhausting* or *exhaustive.* The former interpretation is obviously meaningless in this context. Luke's translation is acceptable.

2. 223 *Thomas Mann:* Aber hie und da riß alles mit frommen Augen die Mützen herunter vor dem Wotanshut und dem *Jupiterbart* eines gemessen hinschreitenden Oberlehrers. (1977: 205)

Lowe-Porter: But one and all pulled off their caps and cast down their eyes in awe before the Olympian hat and *ambrosial beard* of a master moving homewards with a measured stride. (129: 1978)

Luke: [...] and then they would one and all snatch off their caps with an air of pious awe as some senior master with *the beard of Jove* and the hat of Wotan strode solemnly by [...]. (1988: 135)

The adjective *ambrosial* can only refer to the food of the gods; it is unclear, in this context, as to how *ambrosial* can refer to a beard. Lowe-Porter blandly omits the mythological references and thus the comical admixture of a Zeus-like beard and a 'Wotan' hat. Luke's version is acceptable, but there seems to be no good reason to use the lesser known name *Jove* for *Jupiter*. The Greek name *Zeus* might be even more appropriate to emphasise the ironical high classical tone.

2. 224 *Thomas Mann:* Kleines Volk setzte sich lustig in Trab, daß der Eisbrei umherspritzte und die Siebensachen der Wissenschaft in den *Seehundsränzeln* klapperten. (1977: 205)

Lowe-Porter: Small people trotted gaily off, splashing the slush with their feet, the tools of their learning rattling amain in their *walrus-skin* satchels. (1978: 129)

Luke: [...] the little ones trotted merrily off with their feet splashing in the icy slush and the paraphernalia of learning in their *sealskin* satchels. (1988: 135)

Even though this might be a minor error, there seems to be no justification in changing *sealskin,* a standard type of leather, into the obscure *walrus-skin* variety. Luke's version is correct.

2. 225 *Thomas Mann:* [...] und er war *so geartet*, daß er solche Erfahrungen wohl vermerkte [...]. (1977: 207)

Lowe-Porter: [...] and he was *so organized* that he received such experiences consciously [...]. (1978: 131)

Luke: [...] and *his nature* was *such* that when he learned something in this way he took careful note of it. (1988: 136)

The Lowe-Porter version is misleading: the normal surface meaning would imply that Tonio was such an organised person that he was able to make notes concerning his feelings, thus implying that Tonio belongs the 'Bürger' camp, which, in this case, is the complete contrary of Mann's argumentation. The Luke version has obviously the correct interpretation.

2. 226 **Thomas Mann:** Aber kam ein dritter, so schämte er sich dessen und *opferte ihn auf.* (1977: 211)

Lowe-Porter: But let a third person come, he was ashamed *and offered up his friend.* (1978: 137)

Luke: [...] but when anyone else was there he would feel ashamed and *throw him over* [...]. (1988: 142)

Lexical confusion between *offer* and *sacrifice.* (Lowe-Porter was possibly misled by the similarity of *offer* with its German cognate form *Opfer*). Luke's version is adequate.

2. 227 **Thomas Mann:** [...] und niemand schritt wie er, elastisch, wogend, wiegend, *königlich* - auf die Herrin des Hauses zu [...]. (1977: 214)

Lowe-Porter: [...] and nobody tripped like him, so elastically, so weavingly, *rockingly,* - up to the mistress of the house [...]. (1978: 140)

Luke: [...] - and no one but he could walk with so rhythmic, so supple, so resilient, *so royal* a tread - up to the lady of the house [...]. (1988: 145)

The adjective *rockingly* could describe the absurd aspect of Herr Knaak's movements, but it has completely different connotations from Mann's ironic use of *königlich*. Luke's solution is adequate.

2. 228 **Thomas Mann:** [...] der Macht des Geistes und des Wortes, die lächelnd *über* dem unbewußten und stummen Leben *thront.* (1977: 219)

Lowe-Porter: [...] the power of the intellect, the power of the Word, that *lords* it with a smile *over* the unconscious and the inarticulate. (1978: 147)

Luke: [...] the power of intellect and words, a power that *sits* smilingly *enthroned* above mere inarticulate, unconscious life. (1988: 151)

The verb *lord over* has an obtrusive connotation of a deliberate form of dominance, implying even a bullying attitude, totally inappropriate for this abstract use of the nouns in the phrase, "der Macht des Geistes und des Wortes". Luke's version is adequate.

2. 229 **Thomas Mann:** [...] und ich erröte bei dem Gedanken, wie sehr dieser redliche Mensch *ernüchtert* sein müßte, wenn er einen Blick hinter die Kulissen täte [...]. (1977: 224)

Lowe-Porter: [...] I positively blush at the thought of how these good people would *freeze up* if they were to get a look behind the scenes [...]. (1978: 153)

Luke: [...] I blush to think what a *sobering effect* it would have on the honest man who wrote such a letter if he could ever take a look behind the scenes [...]. (1988: 156)

Overtranslation: the phrasal verb *freeze up, i.e. go rigid with fear or horror* is far too strong a translation for *ernüchtert*. Luke's version is perfectly accurate.

2. 2210 *Thomas Mann:* [...] daß ein *rechtschaffener*, gesunder und anständiger Mensch nicht schreibt. (1977: 224)

Lowe-Porter: [...] a *properly constituted* decent man never writes. (1978: 152)

Luke: [...] any *proper,* healthy *decent* human being ever does is to write or act or compose. (1988: 156)

Inappropriate collocation for a human being: the phrase *properly constituted* could refer to a meeting or to an organisation, but hardly expresses the idea of a *rechtschaffener Mensch*. Luke's version is adequate.

2. 2211 *Thomas Mann:* [...] eine Versammlung von ersten Christen gleichsam: Leute mit *ungeschickten* Körpern und feinen Seelen [...]. (1977: 229)

Lowe-Porter: [...] the same old gathering of early Christians, so to speak: people with fine souls in *uncouth* bodies [...]. (1978: 159)

Luke: [...] a sort of gathering of early Christians: people with *clumsy* bodies and refined souls, [...]. (1988: 162)

The adjective *uncouth* generally refers to behaviour and fails to translate *ungeschickt* in this context, which is adequately translated by Luke. The theme of *clumsiness* refers back to Tonio's unfortunate experiences at the dancing class where he discovers that artists are usually 'clumsy' with matters to do with life whereas the 'Bürger' excels in this area. This theme is lost in the Lowe-Porter version.

2. 2212 *Thomas Mann:* [...] wie es denn Tatsache ist, daß es nirgends in der Welt *stummer* und hoffnungsloser zugeht als in einem Kreise von geistreichen Leuten [...]. (1977: 227)

Lowe-Porter: It is a fact that there is no society in the world so *dumb* and hopeless as a circle of literary people who are hounded to death as it is. (1978: 157)

Luke: It's well known that you'll never find such *mute* hopelessness as among a gathering of intellectuals, all of them thoroughly hagridden already. (1988: 160)

The adjective *dumb* compounded with *hopeless* would immediately imply *dumb* in the sense of *stupid.* In this context, a collocation involving a phrase such as *awkward silences* would also be a possible alternative to Luke's version.

2. 2213 *Thomas Mann:* [...] und in dem es dem Menschen genügt, eine Sache zu durchschauen, um sich bereits zum Sterben angewidert (durchaus nicht *versöhnlich gestimmt* zu fühlen, - der Fall Hamlets) [...]. (1977: 227)

Lowe-Porter: [...] when it is enough for you to see through a thing in order to be sick to death by it and not in the least *in a forgiving mood.* Such was the case of Hamlet [...]. (1978: 157)

Luke: [...] a man has no sooner seen through a thing than so far from *feeling reconciled* to it, he is immediately sickened to death by it. This was how Hamlet felt, [...]. (1988: 160)

Too literal translation: in the context of that insight which leads to nausea, the literary figure still refuses to compromise with regard to this kind of knowledge. Again, the Lowe-Porter trivialises this delicate argument by reducing the insights to a level of mere moodiness. (For a similar form of trivialisation, see discussion in Section (c) of Chapter III concerning the errors in *Tristan.*)

2. 2214 *Thomas Mann:* Ich bin es nicht, sage ich Ihnen, in bezug auf das *lebendige Gefühl* [...]. (1977: 228)

Lowe-Porter: I am not a nihilist, with respect, that is, to *lively feeling.* (1978: 158)

Luke: I tell you I am not a nihilist inasmuch as I affirm the value of *living emotion.* (1988: 161)

As in the previous example, the argument is trivialised by relegating the dialectics of *Geist* and *Kenntnis* against *Leben, Natur* and *Gefühl* to the level of changing moods. Many such examples may seem to be relatively harmless, but their cumulative effect is disastrous.

2. 2215 *Thomas Mann:* Er ist mir nichts, dieser Cesare Borgia, ich halte nicht *das geringste auf ihn* [...]. (1977: 229)

Lowe-Porter: He is nothing to me, your Caesar Borgia. I have *no opinion of him* [...]. (1978: 158)

Luke: This Cesare Borgia is nothing to me, I feel not *a particle of respect* for him [...]. (1988: 161)

Mistranslation: The infelicitous collocation *having no opinion* is not the same as *having a poor opinion of someone.* The Luke version is accurate.

2. 2216 **Thomas Mann:** [...] „Man macht, was die Herkunft, die Miterscheinungen und Bedingungen des Künstlertums betrifft, immer wieder die merkwürdigsten *Erfahrungen* [...]. "
„*An anderen* - verzeihen Sie - oder nicht nur *an anderen?*" (1977: 226)

Lowe-Porter: [...] "The origin, the accompanying phenomena, and the conditions of the artist life - good God, what I haven't observed about them over and over!"
"*Observed,* Tonio Kröger? If I may ask, only *observed?*"(1978: 155-156)

Luke: [...] "The sources and side-effects and preconditions of artist talent are something about which one constantly makes the most curious *discoveries* [...]."
"*Discoveries*, Tonio Kröger - forgive my asking - *about other artists? Or not only about others?*" (1988: 159)

This is a slightly obscure passage in the original. Luke's interpretation is possible whereas Lowe-Porter's version barely makes sense. If the phrase *or experienced* were added to the end of the Lowe-Porter version, then something of the original's sense would be preserved.

2. 2217 **Thomas Mann:** So kam es nur dahin, daß er, haltlos zwischen krassen Extremen, zwischen eisiger Geistigkeit und *verzehrender Sinnenglut* hin und her geworfen [...]. (1977: 220)

Lowe-Porter: So for all result he was flung to and fro forever between two crass extremes: between icy intellect and *scorching sense* [...]. (1978: 148)

Luke: [...] and so he could do no more than let himself be cast helplessly to and fro between gross extremes, between icy intellectuality on the one hand and *devouring feverish lust* on the other. (1988: 152)

Luke's more explicit, interpretative translation would seem to be justified. Lowe-Porter's contrast of the concepts of *sense* and *intellect* is unclear. The noun *sensuality* would be an obvious and adequate translation, but the noun *sense* by no means implies sensuality so that this confusion is further compounded by her choice of the adjective *scorching*, which implies that the heat has an immediate burning or scalding effect as opposed to a perpetual consuming flame implied by Mann's use of *verzehrend.* (Lowe-Porter's opening phrase "So for all result" is a totally non-English collocation which is presumably supposed to mean *as a result of all this.*)

2. 2218 **Thomas Mann:** [...] *daß ich mich schäme, mich schäme* vor seiner reinen Natürlichkeit und seiner siegenden Jugend. (1977: 223)

Lowe-Porter: I quail before its sheer naturalness and triumphant youth. (1978: 152)

Luke: I am put to shame by its pure naturalness, its triumphant youthfulness. (1988: 155)

The unusual verb *quail* would imply fear (as in *quiver* and *quail*) rather than shame, which is the clear meaning of the original. Luke's version is correct.

2. 2219 *Thomas Mann:* Denn *man* muß wissen, *was* man *will*, nicht wahr? (1977: 223)

Lowe-Porter: A *man* has to know what *he* needs, eh? (1978: 151/152)

Luke: One must know what one *wants*, mustn't one? (1988: 155)

Confusion of the German pronoun *man* and the English noun *man*. Luke's version is perfectly adequate. (In the context of this mistranslation, Lowe-Porter's use of the interjection *eh* produces an inappropriately gross and salacious effect, which is not implied in the slightest in the German version.)

2. 2220 *Thomas Mann:* Ach *reden* Sie mir nicht *darein*, Lisaweta! (1977: 224)

Lowe-Porter: Oh, don't *talk* to me, Lisabeta! (1978: 153)

Luke: Oh, don't start *contradicting* me [...]. (1988: 156)

Omission of the import of the particle *darein*. Luke's version is correct.

2. 2221 *Thomas Mann:* [...] so ließe sich ein Mensch denken, der, von Hause aus gutgläubig, sanftmütig, wohlmeinend und ein wenig sentimental, durch die psychologische *Hellsicht* ganz einfach aufgerieben und zugrunde gerichtet wurde. (1977: 227)

Lowe-Porter: Can't you imagine a man, born orthodox, mild mannered, well-meaning, a bit sentimental, just simply overstimulated by his psychological *clairvoyance*, and going to the dogs? (1978: 156/157)

Luke: [...] can you not imagine someone with an innately skeptical disposition being quite literally worn out and destroyed by psychological *enlightenment*? (1988: 159)

The noun *clairvoyance* is theoretically possible for *Hellsicht*, but, in the context of the artist's intellectual insight, this translation trivialises the argument by introducing an untoward occult element.

2. 2222 *Thomas Mann:* Sich von der Traurigkeit der Welt nicht *übermannen* lassen. (1977: 227)

Lowe-Porter: Not to let the sadness of the world *unman* you [...]. (1978: 157)

Luke: Not to let oneself be *overwhelmed* by the sadness of everything [...]. (1988: 159)

The verb *unman* in the Lowe-Porter version introduces an unwarranted 'castration' theme, which is certainly not justified by *übermannen*. The meaning of the sentence is adequately translated by Luke.

2. 2223 *Thomas Mann:* [...] und jedermann wird wissen, daß Sie kein Mensch sind, sondern irgend etwas Fremdes, *Befremdendes* anderes [...]. (1977: 225)

Lowe-Porter: [...] before everyone knows you are not a human being but something else: something queer, different, *inimical*. (1978: 154)

Luke: [...] before everyone will know that you are not a human being but something strange, something *alien*, something different. (1988: 157)

Overtranslation. The adjective *inimical* is usually used only with the preposition *to* so that *hostile* would be a grammatically, though not semantically acceptable variant. Luke's translation is accurate.

2. 2224 *Thomas Mann:* [...] als der Zug in die schmale *verräucherte*, so wunderlich vertraute Halle einfuhr [...]. (1977: 232)

Lowe-Porter: [...] the train pulled into the narrow, *reeking* shed [...]. (1978: 163)

Luke: [...] when the train steamed into the little *smoke-stained* terminus [...]. (1988: 165)

Mistranslation: possible confusion of the verbs *riechen* and *rauchen*. The Luke version is accurate.

2. 2225 *Thomas Mann:* Er schlief lange, unter verworrenen und *seltsam sehnsüchtigen* Träumen. (1977: 234)

Lowe-Porter: He slept for a long time and had curiously confused and *ardent* dreams. (1978: 165)

Luke: He slept long and had confused, *strangely nostalgic* dreams. (1988: 167)

There is no justification for Lowe-Porter's failure to translate the adjective *sehnsüchtig* as the dreams in this context refer to Tonio's childhood and adolescence. Luke's version is adequate.

2. 2226 *Thomas Mann:* Der Portier und ein sehr *feiner* und schwarzgekleideter Herr, welcher die Honneurs machte [...]. (1977: 233)

Lowe-Porter: There was a porter, and a *lordly* gentleman dressed in black, to do the honours [...]. (1978: 164)

Luke: He encountered the inquiring gaze of the porter and of a *very smartly dressed* gentleman in black who was doing the honors [...]. (1988: 167)

Overtranslation in Lowe-Porter's version whereas Luke tries to include the connotation of the adjective *fein* by emphasising the smartness of the dress.

2. 2227 *Thomas Mann:* Er wäre gern lange so *dahingegangen*, im Wind durch die dämmerigen, traumhaft vertrauten Gassen. (1977: 233)

Lowe-Porter: He would have liked *to go on so*, for a long time, in the wind, through the dusky dreamily familiar streets. (1978: 164)

Luke: He would have liked to *stroll on* indefinitely, in the wind and the dusk, along these familiar streets of his dreams. (1988: 167)

Literal translation of the verb *gehen*: here *gehen* is used in the sense of *to walk*. Luke's version is adequate. (The phrasal verb *to go on* with the adverb *so* usually means to *harp on* a theme, but, in the above context, this translation would simply cause some puzzlement.)

2. 2228 *Thomas Mann:* [...] die blonden und lässig-*plumpen* Menschen mit ihrer breiten und dennoch rapiden Redeweise rings um ihn umher [...]. (1977: 232)

Lowe-Porter: [...] the *plump,* fair easy-going populace, with their broad but rapid speech. (1978: 163)

Luke: [...] the fair-haired, easygoing, *unsophisticated* people with their broad yet rapid way of talking. (1988: 166)

False friend: the adjective *plump* in German does not have the same meaning in English. Luke's version is correct.

2. 2229 *Thomas Mann:* Und er führte Tonio Kröger unter einladendem Gestenspiel in den *Hintergrund* des Vestibüls. (1977: 238)

Lowe-Porter: And he ushered Tonio Kröger into the *background* of the vestibule. (1978: 170)

Luke: And with polite gestures he ushered Tonio Kröger to the *back* of the hall. (1988: 172)

Sense complicated by overliteral translation. Luke's version is adequate. In the source text, there is a hint that the vestibule is kept in the background for 'less respectable' activities such as the dealings with the police in this instance, but this connotation would have to be woven into the text, perhaps with a phrase such as *discreetly whisked away into a hidden back room which was the hotel vestibule*.

2. 2230 *Thomas Mann:* Herr Seehase hob den Kopf und *sah* neugierig in sein Gesicht *empor*. (1977: 239)

Lowe-Porter: Herr Seehase lifted his head and *looked him* curiously *in the face*. (1978: 171)

Luke: Herr Seehase raised his head and *looked up at him* with curiosity. (1988: 173)

Mistranslation: the idiom *looking someone in the face* implies a more challenging posture than is implied here. Luke's translation is adequate.

2. 2231 *Thomas Mann:* Auch Herr Seehase legte sich *beschwichtigend* ins Mittel. (1977: 239)

Lowe-Porter: Herr Seehaase *threw himself into the breach*. (1978: 171)

Luke: Herr Seehase *attempted a conciliatory intervention*. (1988: 173)

The idea of conciliation (*beschwichtigend*) is lost in the Lowe-Porter version with the result that Herr Seehase's behaviour is portrayed as aggressive whereas the opposite is the case. Luke's version is correct.

2. 2232 *Thomas Mann:* Der *strenge* Wind und sein herbes Arom hatten ihn *seltsam erregt*, und sein Herz war unruhig wie in ängstlicher Erwartung von etwas Süßem. (1977: 243)

Lowe-Porter: The *strong* wind with its sharp tang had *power to rouse him*; he was strangely restless with sweet anticipations. (1978: 175)

Luke: The *strong* gale with its sharp tang had *strangely excited him*, and his heart beat anxiously, as if troubled by the expectation of some sweet experience. (1988: 177)

Confusion with the English verbs *to rouse* and *to arouse*: the very intimate relationship many of Mann's characters have with the sea is lost in this Lowe-Porter version. The verb *rouse* merely means to wake up. Luke's version is correct. Similarly, both translators misunderstand the German adjective *streng* by translating it as *strong* rather than *severe*, thus with the consequent loss of the moral opprobrium Tonio constantly feels when he returns to his roots.

2. 2233 ***Thomas Mann:*** [...] ging breitbeinig und *mühsam* balancierend auf dem Verdecke hin und her. (1977: 243)

Lowe-Porter: [...] went straddling *painfully* up and down the deck. (1978: 176)

Luke: [...] was pacing the deck with straddled legs, keeping his balance *with difficulty*. (1988: 177)

Overtranslation: the collocation *painful straddling* is also both obscure and awkward. Luke's translation is adequate.

2. 2234 ***Thomas Mann:*** [...] der Fischhändler und die Wirtin zuweilen konversierten, wechselte hie und da mit dem ersteren eine schlichte Bemerkung *über den Barometerstand* [...]. (1977: 245)

Lowe-Porter: [...] the fish dealer and the landlady desultorily conversed; modestly exchanged views with the fish-dealer on *the state of the barometer* [...]. (1978: 178)

Luke: [...] in the speeches the fish-dealer and the proprietress now and then addressed to each other; with the former he would exchange an occasional simple remark about *the state of the weather* [...]. (1988: 180)

Literal translation: in German, the noun *Barometer* is understood as a case of synecdoche referring to the weather, but in English, this can only refer to a concrete object in Lowe-Porter's collocation; hence Luke's solution. Both versions, however, lose something of the deliberately affected tone in the original.

2. 2235 ***Thomas Mann:*** Er sah sie an, sah, wie Hans Hansen *so keck und wohlgestaltet* wie nur jemals, breit in den Schultern und schmal in den Hüften, in seinem Matrosenanzug dastand [...]. (1977: 251)

Lowe-Porter: Hans Hansen was standing there in his sailor suit, *lively and well built* as ever, broad in the shoulders and narrow in the hips [...]. (1978: 185)

Luke: [...] Hans Hansen standing there in his sailor suit, *bold and handsome* as ever, broad in the shoulders and narrow in the hips [...]. (1988: 185)

Lowe-Porter's choice of the adjective *well built* would imply that a very solid physique is being described, when, in fact, the reverse is the case. Luke's translation *handsome* is weak because this does not refer specifically to Hans' figure. A simple solution such as the adjective *well-proportioned* or the

217

use of the phrase *athletic figure* would suffice. (Thus, the homoerotic undertone is lost in both translations.)

2. 2236 **Thomas Mann:** [...] meine Mutter von unbestimmt exotischem Blut, schön, sinnlich, naiv, zugleich *fahrlässig* und leidenschaftlich und von einer impulsiven Liederlichkeit. (1977: 255)

Lowe-Porter: [...] My mother, of indeterminate foreign blood, was beautiful, sensuous, naïve, passionate and *careless* at once [...]. (1978: 190)

Luke: [...] My mother was of a vaguely exotic extraction, beautiful, sensuous, naïve, both *reckless* and passionate, and given to impulsive, rather disreputable behaviour. (1988: 191)

Mistranslation of the adjective *fahrlässig* as *careless*: Luke's version is adequate.

2. 2237 **Thomas Mann:** Denn wenn etwas imstande ist, aus einem Literaten einen Dichter zu machen, so ist diese meine Bürgerliebe zum Menschlichen, Lebendigen und *Gewöhnlichen.* (1977: 255)

Lowe-Porter: For if anything is capable of making a poet of a literary man, it is my bourgeois love of the human, the living and *usual.* (1978: 190)

Luke: For if there is anything that can turn a *littérateur* into a true writer, then it is this bourgeois love of mine for the human and the living and the *ordinary.* (1988: 191)

The translation *usual* is an inappropriate collocation: e. g. *He is* an <u>*ordinary*</u> *person* is acceptable, but *He is a* <u>*usual*</u> *person* would only fit in special circumstances.

2. 2238 **Thomas Mann:** [...] - frei vom Fluch der Erkenntnis der schöpferischen Qual leben, lieben und loben in *seliger* Gewöhnlichkeit [...]. (1977: 250)

Lowe-Porter: [...] – to live free from the curse of knowledge and the torment of creation, live and praise God in *blessed mediocrity*! (1978: 185)

Luke: If only I could be freed from the curse of insight and the creative torment and live and love and be thankful and *blissfully* commonplace! (1988: 186)

Lowe-Porter introduces a conventional religious element with inserting the idea of praising God coupled with the possible translation of the adjective *selig* as *blessed.* In doing so, however, all irony is lost and her version could give the false impression that Tonio has an unqualified love of the mediocre, which is, of course, both a profound and obvious distortion of his ambiguous attitude to ordinary people and to life in general.

iii) Omissions

Tonio Kröger

2. 321 ***Thomas Mann:*** Was war das alles, was unter der Asche seiner Müdigkeit, ohne zur klaren Flamme zu werden, so dunkel *und schmerzlich* glomm. (1977: 233)

Lowe-Porter: What was it burning darkly beneath the ashes of his fatigue, refusing to burst out into a clear blaze? (1978: 164)

Luke: Under the ashes of his weariness something was glowing, obscurely and *painfully*, not flickering up into a clear flame: what was it? (1988: 166/7)

Omission of the phrase *und schmerzlich*: the reference to pain is important to highlight the extremity of his feelings of both longing and guilt with regard to his home town and childhood. Luke's version is adequate.

iv) Grammatical Errors
a) Confusion of Transitive and Intransitive Verbs

Tristan

2. 4111 ***Thomas Mann:*** [...] während das Kind [...] seinen Platz im Leben [...] behauptete, schien die junge Mutter in einer sanften und stillen Glut *dahinzuschwinden* [...]. (1977: 167)

Lowe-Porter: [...] while the child [...] seized on his place in life [...], low, unobservable fever seemed *to waste the young mother daily* [...]. (1978: 90)

Luke: [...] whereas the child [...] held his place in life [...], his young mother seemed to be *gently fading away, quietly burning herself out* [...]. (1988: 98)

A sentence such as *The young mother seemed to be wasting away daily with a low, unobservable fever* would be acceptable. *The fever is wasting me away* could also be grammatically acceptable but the phrase:*The fever wastes me* is totally ungrammatical. Luke's version is adequate.

2. 4112 ***Thomas Mann:*** "Zweifelsohne", sagte Doktor Leander und *funkelte* sie *mit seinen Brillengläsern an.* (1977: 166)

Lowe-Porter: 'Surely not,' said Dr Leander, and *glittered at* her with his *eye-glasses.* (1978: 89)

Luke: 'Indubitably not,' said Dr Leander, *flashing* his *spectacles* at them. (1988: 96)

The construction *to glitter at* with an object does not exist. The phrasal verb *glared at* is, of course, possible, but Luke's version is adequate. (Also, Lowe-Porter's lexical choice of "eye-glasses" for *spectacles* is archaic.)

2. 4113 **Thomas Mann:** Er trug einen englischen Backenbart, war ganz englisch gekleidet und *zeigte sich entzückt,* eine englische Familie, [...] in 'Einfried' anzutreffen [...]. (1977: 167)

Lowe-Porter: He wore English side-whiskers and English clothes, and *it enchanted him* to discover at Einfried an entire English family [...]. (1978: 91)

Luke: He wore English side-whiskers and a complete outfit of English clothes, he *was delighted to* encounter an English family at Einfried [...]. (1988: 98)

The construction *it enchanted him to* is ungrammatical: *he was enchanted to find* is possible, but Luke's solution is more natural.

Tonio Kröger

2. 4121 **Thomas Mann:** [...] sondern in bleichem und flackerndem Licht, war die See zerrissen, zerpeitscht, *zerwühlt,* leckte und sprang in spitzen, flammenartigen, Riesenzungen empor [...]. (1977: 243)

Lowe-Porter: [...] but far out in the pale and flickering light the water was lashed, torn, and *tumbled;* leaped up like great licking flames [...]. (1978: 175)

Luke: [...] [the waves] were being lashed and torn and *churned* into frenzy as far as the eye could reach. In the pallid, flickering light they licked and leaped upward like gigantic pointed tongues of flame [...]. (1988: 177)

The water was tumbled would be non-sensical as in the sentence: *The wind tumbled the water.* Luke's solution is acceptable.

2. 4122 **Thomas Mann:** Ein langbeiniger Mensch [...] wie die fleischgewordene komische Figur *aus* einem dänischen Roman, schien Festordner und Kommandeur des Balles zu sein. (1977: 250)

Lowe-Porter: [...] a long-legged man [...] was like a comic figure *stepped* bodily out of a Danish novel; and he seemed to be the leader and manager of the ball. (1978: 184)

Luke: The master of ceremonies appeared to be a long-legged man [...] . - a comic character *straight out* of a Danish novel. (1988: 185)

The sentence *He was like a comic figure who had stepped bodily out of a Danish novel* is grammatically possible as is, alternatively, the sentence *He was like a comic figure cut bodily out of a Danish novel*, but this past participle construction normally only allows transitive verbs. A non-grammatical formulation such as **He was like a prince wandered out of a fairytale* clearly illustrates this point. Luke's rearrangement of the sentence is felicitous.

2. 4123 ***Thomas Mann:*** "Nun, *das genügt!*" sagte Herr Seehase mit Entschluß [. .]. (1977: 240)

Lowe-Porter: 'All right, that *will answer,*' said Herr Seehaase with decision [...]. (1978: 172)

Luke: 'Well *that's good enough!*' said Herr Seehaase decisively. (1988: 174)

The verb *answer* normally requires an object – e. g. in this context, *That will answer the problem* would be acceptable, but Luke's solution is better.

b) Tense
Tristan

2. 4211 ***Thomas Mann:*** *Beständig lag* auf seinem Tische, für jeden sichtbar, der sein Zimmer betrat, das Buch, das er geschrieben hatte. (1977: 168)

Lowe-Porter: On his table, for anybody to see who entered his room, *there always lay* the book he had written. (1978: 92)

Luke: On his desk, *permanently on view* to anyone who entered his room, *lay* the book he had written. (1988: 100)

In order to translate the ironic implication of *beständig* emphasising an uninterrupted permanence, a compound, i.e. a progressive tense is necessary as in *The book was always lying on the table*. Lowe-Porter's version is not only ungrammatical but also infelicitous. Luke's solution is also acceptable.

2. 4212 ***Thomas Mann:*** So saß sie [...] *eine Handarbeit im Schoße, an der sie nicht arbeitete* [...]. (1977: 175)

Lowe-Porter: So she sat [...] holding *some sort of sewing which she did not sew* [...]. (1978: 99)

Luke: [...] she would sit with Rätin Spatz [...] *holding her needlework idly in her lap.* (1988: 106)

Lowe-Porter's version would be very inelegant even in the correct tense, i.e. *holding some sort of sewing which she was not sewing at the time*. Luke's solution is acceptable.

Tonio Kröger

2. 4221 *Thomas Mann:* Er ging den Weg, den er gehen *mußte* [...]. (1977: 218)

Lowe-Porter: He went the way that go he *must* [...]. (1978: 146)

Luke: He went the way he *had to go.* (1988: 150)

Tense sequence: Luke's version is correct.

c) Confusion of adverbs and adjectives

Tristan

2. 4311 *Thomas Mann:* Das gute Wetter hielt an. Weiß, hart und sauber, in Windstille und lichtem Frost, *in blendender Helle* und bläulichem Schatten lag die Gegend [...]. (1977: 173)

Lowe-Porter: The fine weather continued. Rigid and spotless white the region lay, the mountains, the house and garden, in a windless air that *was blinding clear* and cast bluish shadows [...]. (1978: 97)

Luke: The fine weather continued. Everything was bright, hard and clean, windless and frosty; the house and garden, the surrounding countryside and the mountains, lay mantled *in dazzling whiteness* and pale blue shadows. (1988: 104)

Besides the obvious confusion of an adjective with an adverb *blinding/blindingly* in the Lowe-Porter version, the singular form of the verb *was* would imply that the air was also casting blue shadows. The important element of frost is also omitted in the Lowe-Porter version.

2. 4312 *Thomas Mann:* Überhaupt liebte er es, *viel und gut zu speisen und zu trinken*, [...]. (1977: 167)

Lowe-Porter: He set great store by *good* eating and drinking. (1978: 91)

Luke: He had a great predilection for eating and drinking *plentifully and well.* (1988: 98)

Failure to recognise the verbal dominance of the gerund; e. g. the sentence *I like eating well* is possible, but not **I like good eating* (although this construction is sometimes used in American slang.). Luke's version is acceptable.

Tonio Kröger

2. 4321 *Thomas Mann:* [...] und voller Verachtung für jene Kleinen, denen das Talent ein geselliger Schmuck war, die, ob sie nun arm oder reich waren, *wild und abgerissen* einhergingen. (1977: 220)

Lowe-Porter: He worked withdrawn out of sight and sound for the small fry, for whom he felt nothing but contempt, because to them a talent was a social asset like another; who whether they were poor or not, went about ostentatiously *shabby*. (1978: 149)

Luke: [...] for he utterly despised those minor hacks who treated their talent as a social ornament - who whether they were poor or rich, whether they affected an unkempt and *shabby appearance* [...]. (1988: 152)

Although the phrase *ostentatiously shabbily* is infelicitous, it would be grammatically correct unlike Lowe-Porter's phrase. A simple solution would be *in an ostentatiously shabby fashion*, but Luke's version is preferable.

2. 4322 *Thomas Mann:*[...] ein bejahrtes Mädchen, [...] das immer seine roten Hände auf dem Tafeltuche *ein wenig vorteilhaft zu gruppieren* trachtete. (1977: 245)

Lowe-Porter: She was forever arranging her red hands *to look well upon* the table-cloth. (1978: 178)

Luke: [...] an elderly spinster [...] who always tried to arrange her reddened hands on the tablecloth in a manner that *would display them to their best advantage.* (1988: 179)

With the five senses, normally the adjective is used instead of the adverb *to look good* would be grammatically possible, but Luke's version is stylistically preferable.

2. 4323 *Thomas Mann: Hellsehen* noch durch den Tränenschleier des Gefühls hindurch [...]. (1977: 227)

Lowe-Porter: To see things *clear*, if even through your tears [...]. (178: 157)

Luke: To be *clear-sighted* even through the mist of tears [...]. (1988: 160)

Although certain idioms such as *to make things clear* can have an adjectival qualifier for the verb, this certainly does not apply to the verb *to see*.

2. 4324 *Thomas Mann:* Und über eine Weile, *unmerklich*, ohne Aufsehen und Geräusch, war sie [die Flamme seiner Liebe] dennoch erloschen. (1977: 218)

Lowe-Porter: [...] and in a little while, *unobservably,* without sensation or stir, it went out after all. (1978: 145)

Luke: [...] he found that after a time, *imperceptibly,* silently and without fuss, the flame had nevertheless gone out. (1988: 149)

This is another example where Lowe-Porter confuses adjectives with adverbs. Luke's version *imperceptibly* refers to *how* the flame went out whereas *unobservably* refers to the fact that the flame remained unobserved and so, *unobserved* should remain an adjective.

2. 4325 *Thomas Mann:* [...] und [Tonio] im übrigen grau und *unauffällig* umhergeht, wie ein abgeschminkter Schauspieler, der nichts ist, solange er nichts darzustellen hat. (1977: 220)

Lowe-Porter: [...] [Tonio] moving about grey and *unobtrusive* among his fellows like an actor without his make-up [...]. (1978: 148)

Luke: [...] [Tonio] spends the rest of his time in *a grey incognito*, like an actor with his makeup off [...]. (1988: 152)

This mistake is the reverse of the previous example, i.e. Lowe-Porter uses an adjective where an adverb is necessary: *moving about* is quite clearly a verb of motion which demands the adverb *unobtrusively* even though *grey* can remain an adjective as it is clearly a predicate of the subject. This solution, though grammatical, would be infelicitous. Luke's solution is also not wholly acceptable as the use of the indefinite article seems stylistically unjustifiable because it makes *a grey incognito* sound like a physical object.

d) Confusion with Other Parts of Speech
Tonio Kröger
2. 4421 *Thomas Mann:* Ich bin so *gramvoll ehrlich* veranlagt, [...]. (1977: 173)

Lowe-Porter: I have a hideously *downright* nature [...]. (1978: 97)

Luke: I have a *melancholically honest disposition,* [...]. (1988: 104)

Confusion of adjectives with qualifiers: although the word *downright* can be used as an adjective, in this context, only an adverbial use could be acceptable. (Even Luke's translation would seem to be infelicitous because of translating too literally.) *I am sickeningly honest* would seem to be more natural or for a closer semantic version. *I have a grievously honest temperament* would reflect something of Spinell's rather elaborate use of language without offending English usage.

2. 4422 *Thomas Mann:* [...] dieser aus Süd und Nord *zusammengesetzte* Klang, dieser exotisch angehauchte Bürgersname zu einer Formel, die Vortreffliches bezeichnete [...]. (1977: 220)

Lowe-Porter [...] those syllables *compact* of the north and the south, that good middle-class name with the exotic twist to it – became a synonym for excellence [...]. (1978: 148)

Luke [...] this *mixture* of southern and northern sounds, this respectable middle-class name with an exotic flavor-became a formula betokening excellence. (1988: 152)

Confusion of an adjective with a past participial construction. Even the grammatically correct formulation, *those syllables compacted of the north and the south,* would be odd when *combined, compounded* or even *composed* would be more acceptable. Lowe-Porter's use of an noun for a verb could also be a printing error. Luke's version is adequate.

2. 4423 *Thomas Mann:* Man ist als Künstler immer Abenteurer genug. Äußerlich soll man sich gut anziehen, *zum Teufel* [...]. (1977: 223)

Lowe-Porter: Every artist is as bohemian *as the deuce inside!* Let him at least wear proper clothes [...]. (1978: 151)

Luke: As an artist I'm already enough of an adventurer in my inner life. So far as outward appearances are concerned one should dress decently, *damn it.* (1988: 155)

Failure to recognise the interjection *zum Teufel*: the word *deuce* is normally used only as an interjection and not as an alternative name for the devil (except in a few phrases that are now archaic (See OED)). Lowe-Porter also omits any reference to the artist as adventurer. Lowe-Porter's version only reflects half the original. (For example, there is no implication in the original that the devil is a bohemian.) Luke's translation is accurate.

2. 4424 *Thomas Mann:* Ein Sang an das Meer, *begeistert von Liebe* tönte in ihm. (1977: 243)

Lowe-Porter: [...] within himself he chanted a song to the sea, *instinct with* love for her [...]. (1978: 176)

Luke: Inwardly he began to sing a song *of love,* a paean of praise to the sea. (1988: 1978)

Confusion of the noun *instinct* with a past participial construction such as *inspired* would fit into this context, but the phrase as it stands makes no sense at all. This is such a basic mistake that one can only hope that it is a printing error although it is not clear what such an error could be in this context. (Luke's translation also misses the use of *von* as agent. The content of the song is about the sea not *about* love, but is inspired *by* love. A translation such as *An ode to the sea inspired by pure love seemed as if it were being chanted within him* would seem to be more within the spirit of the original although it must be admitted that this is a difficult sentence to translate satisfactorily.)

2. 4425 *Thomas Mann:* [...] noch in Augenblicken, wo Hände *sich umschlingen*, Lippen sich finden, wo des Menschen Blick, erblindet von Empfindung sich bricht [...]. (1977: 227)

Lowe-Porter: [...] at the very moment when hands *are clinging*, and lips meeting, and the human gaze is blinded with feeling [...]. (178: 157)

Luke: [...] even at moments when hands *clasp* and lips touch and eyes fail, blinded by emotion [...]. (1988: 160)

Confusion of the verbal aspect with a predicate. (For example, there is a big grammatical difference in the following two sentences: *She is caring for her mother* and *She is caring, but he is selfish.)* The verb *cling* is also wrong here as the German verb *sich umschlingen* clearly refers to hands holding each other whereas *cling* implies clinging to an object such as the edge of a cliff or building. Luke's version is grammatically correct.

2. 4426 *Thomas Mann:* So schön und *heiter* wie du kann man nur sein, wenn man nicht *Immensee* liest [...]. (1977: 217)

Lowe-Porter: So lovely and *laughing* as you are one can only be if one does not read *Immensee* [...]. (1978: 143/144)

Luke: Only people who do not read *Immensee* and never try to write anything like it can be as beautiful and *light hearted* as you; that is the tragedy! (1988: 148)

Confusion of an adjective and a verb: the phrase, *you are laughing*, can only have a verbal sense in the present continuous tense and cannot be used as a predicate participle, e. g. *running* is used differently in a phrase such as the *running* water from the water is *running*, i.e. the water is running *now*, but as she uses laughing with the predicative adjective *lovely*, this would be like the (non-sensical) sentence: *The water is cold and running*! (This could, however, be understood as an elliptical construction for the sentence *The water is cold and (is now) running*!, but the basic argument holds.) See also previous example.

e) Illicit negatives
Tristan
2. 4511 *Thomas Mann: Weil es nicht selten geschieht,* daß ein Geschlecht mit praktischen, bürgerlichen und trockenen Traditionen sich gegen das Ende seiner Tage noch einmal durch die Kunst verklärt. (1977: 176)

Lowe-Porter: *Because it not infrequently happens* that a race with sober practical bourgeois traditions will towards the end of its days flare up in some form of art. (1978: 101)

Luke: *Because it often happens that* an old family, with traditions that are entirely practical, sober and bourgeois, undergoes in its declining days a kind of artistic transfiguration. (1988: 108)

The formulation *it does not infrequently happen* is grammatically possible, but Luke's solution is simpler and more felicitous.

2. 4512 ***Thomas Mann:*** [...] (denn er hatte bislang *mit keiner Seele Gemeinschaft* gehalten). (1977: 170)

Lowe-Porter: [...] (for he had up to now *held communion with not a single soul*). (1978: 95)

Luke: [...] (for hitherto he had *kept company* with no one). (1988: 102)

Ungrammatical negative and overtranslation: again with an overlay of religious language with words such as *communion* and *soul*. Luke's simpler version is adequate.

Tonio Kröger

2. 4521 ***Thomas Mann:*** [...] und er *tat nichts, als sich hierauf freuen,* mit einer so ängstlichen und süßen Freude, wie er sie durch lange, tote Jahre hindurch nicht mehr erprobt hatte. (1977: 248)

Lowe-Porter: [...] and he *did nothing but be glad of this*, with a sweet and timorous gladness such as he had never felt through all these long dead years. (1978: 182)

Luke: [...] and he *did nothing all day but look forward to this* with a sweet and apprehensive excitement such as he had not felt throughout all these long, dead years. (1988: 183)

The formulations **did be* or **did nothing but be* are profoundly ungrammatical. In this example, there is the further lexical confusion of *sich freuen über (to be glad about)* with *sich freuen auf (to look forward to)*. Luke's version is correct. For other aspects with regard to this extract, see example 2. 5243.

2. 4522 ***Thomas Mann:*** Aber sie kam *keines Weges*. (1977: 254)

Lowe-Porter: But she *came not at all*. (1978: 188)

Luke: But she *did not come*. (1988: 189)

Lowe-Porter frequently avoids using the auxiliary verb *to do* in negative constructions, possibly for poetic effect, but even in the English of her time this would not be an acceptable archaism. *She came not* could be minimally acceptable as a poetic effect, but is then rendered absurd in the sentence **She came not at all* by the intensifier phrase *not at all*.

2. 4523 ***Thomas Mann:*** [...] *ohne* doch zu einem beruhigenden Ergebnis *gelangen zu können,* weshalb sie sich für eine gemäßigte Höflichkeit entschieden. (1977: 234)

Lowe-Porter: He *seemed not to come* to any clear decision and compromised on a moderate display of politeness. (1977: 164)

Luke: [...] they *were unable, however, to reach* a satisfying conclusion on this point, and therefore decided on a on a moderate show of politeness. (1988: 167)

More a matter of usage rather than a grave error. Luke's version is adequate.

2. 4524 ***Thomas Mann:*** [...] denn der Treppenkopf war durch eine Glastür verschlossen, die *ehemals nicht dagewesen war* [...]. (1977: 238)

Lowe-Porter: [...] the top of the stairs was shut off by a glass door which *used not to be there* [...]. (1978: 169)

Luke: [...] or the staircase ended in a glass door which *had not previously been there,* [...]. (1988: 171)

Even if Lowe-Porter's negative is corrected to *did not used to be there,* the effect is still confusing because of the wrong tense sequence. Luke's solution is acceptable.

f) Word Order
Tonio Kröger

2. 4621 ***Thomas Mann:*** Wenn er *nur* nicht mit uns geht und den ganzen Weg nur von der Reitstunde spricht. (1977: 210)

Lowe-Porter: [...] if he *only* doesn't go with us all the way and talk about the riding-lessons! (1978: 135)

Luke: If *only* he doesn't join us and spend the whole walk talking about their riding lessons! (1988: 141)

Lowe-Porter slavishly follows the German word order in this instance and thereby produces an ungrammatical construction. Luke's version is adequate.

2. 4622 **Thomas Mann:** *Einen Künstler,* einen wirklichen, nicht einen, dessen bürgerlicher Beruf die Kunst ist, *sondern einen vorbestimmten und verdammten,* ersehen Sie mit geringem Scharfblick aus der Menschenmasse. (1977: 225)

Lowe-Porter: A genuine artist - not one who has taken up art as his profession like any other, but *artist foreordained and damned* - you can pick out, without *boasting very sharp perceptions,* out of a group of men. (1978: 154)

Luke: A real artist is not one who has taken up art as his profession, *but a man predestined and foredoomed to it:* and such an artist can be picked out from a crowd by anyone with the slightest perspicacity. (1988: 157)

The ungrammatical word order compounded with the unwarranted omissions of the indefinite article in Lowe-Porter's version together with illicit syntactical gaps for the clause, *You can pick out an artist from a group of men,* causes confusion rather than an intended literary effect whereas Luke's version is perfectly adequate.

2. 4623 **Thomas Mann:** [...] *die Matrosenmütze mit den kurzen Bändern hielt er* in der hinabhängenden Hand [...]. (1977: 248)

Lowe-Porter: [...] *the sailor cap with its short ribbons* he was dangling carelessly in his hand. (1978: 181)

Luke: [...] in his free hand he held *his sailor's cap with its short ribbons.* (1988: 183)

This is just one of many examples where Lowe-Porter follows German word order with out any apparent justification. Luke's version is acceptable.

g) Other grammatical mistakes

Tristan

2. 4711 **Thomas Mann:** [...] und Gott wußte, aus was für eitlen Gründen Herr Spinell *es behauptete.* (1977: 189)

Lowe-Porter: And God knows what sort of vanity it *was made* Herr Spinell put it down. (1978: 117)

Luke: God knows what foolish vanity *induced* Herr Spinell *to make* such an assertion. (1988: 122)

And God knows what sort of vanity <u>it</u> *was* <u>that</u> *made Herr Spinell put it down* would be grammatically acceptable. It is to be hoped that Lowe-Porter's profoundly ungrammatical formulation is more a case of an oversight on the part of her proof readers or printers than a misreading of English grammar at its most basic level. (This mistake still remains uncorrected in the 1989Vintage International edition. Luke's version is correct.

2. 4712 *Thomas Mann:* Es war eine *rührende* und friedvolle Apotheose, *getaucht in die abendliche Verklärung des Verfalles,* der Auflösung und des Verlöschens. (1977: 190)

Lowe-Porter: It was a peaceful apotheosis and *a moving, bathed in a sunset beauty of decadence,* decay and death. (1978: 119)

Luke: It had been a *moving,* tranquil apotheosis *immersed in the transfiguring sunset glow of decline* and decay and extinction. (1988: 124)

Lowe-Porter's eccentric word order leaves the adjective *moving* dangling with no reference point, but even if it had a reference, the sentence would still be profoundly ungrammatical on account of her placing an adjective in front of a preceding past participle. Thus a phrase such as *a moving, bathed in pathos play* would similarly be totally ungrammatical. Luke's version is adequate.

2. 4713 *Thomas Mann:* "Sie *stirbt,* mein Herr!" (1977: 191/2)

Lowe-Porter: 'She *dies,* sir!' (1978: 120)

Luke: 'She *is dying,* sir!' (1988: 125)

Even poetic licence cannot justify the wrong use of aspect here. This mistake is repeated in the other two references to Klöterjahn's wife who is dying from a lung disease. The simple present is just possible in a context such as the end of a duel when the victor might say to the vanquished opponent *You die, sir,* but it is obviously inappropriate in this context. The same applies to the example below. Luke's version is correct.

2.4714 *Thomas Mann:* "[...] und Sie mit Ihrem, 'sie *stirbt,* mein Herr!' Sie sind ein Esel!" (1977: 195)

Lowe-Porter: ' [...] no matter what you say with your "She *dies,* sir," you silly ass!' (1978: 124)

Luke: ' [...] and as for you and your "she *is dying,* sir" - why, you crazy ninny, you [...].' (1988: 128)

See example 2. 4713 as above.

2. 4715 *Thomas Mann:* Andererseits muß man zugeben, *daß das, was* schließlich zustande kam, den Eindruck der Glätte und Lebhaftigkeit erweckte, wenn es auch inhaltlich einen wunderlichen, fragwürdigen und oft sogar unverständlichen Charakter trug. (1977: 189)

Lowe-Porter: Yet so much was true: *that what* had managed to get written sounded fluent and vigorous, though the matter was odd enough, even almost equivocal, and at times impossible to follow. (1978: 117)

Luke: On the other hand it must be admitted *that what* he finally produced did give the impression of smooth spontaneity and vigor, notwithstanding its odd and dubious and often scarcely intelligible content. (1988: 122/123)

Luke's formulation *that what* may be inelegant, but it is at least grammatical as *what* functions as a direct object whereas the Lowe-Porter version is profoundly ungrammatical with *what* as a subject, as in a phrase such as **That what has been achieved is very good*. The ungainly phrase, *what had managed to get written*, would at least be grammatical.

2. 4716 *Thomas Mann:* Und nun, da das Meer sich öffnete, sah er von fern den Strand, an dem er als Knabe die sommerlichen Träume des Meeres *hatte belauschen dürfen* [...]. (1977: 241)

Lowe-Porter: The sea opened out and he saw in the distance the beach where he as a lad *had been let listen to* the ocean's summer dreams [...]. (1978: 173)

Luke: And now as they passed out of the estuary, he saw in the distance the shore where as a boy he *had listened to* the sea's summer reveries. (1988: 175)

This example is a case of grammatical breakdown. It would seem that Lowe-Porter had slavishly followed German syntax and had not allowed for alternative translations of the modal verb 'dürfen'. Her formulation *had been let listen to* can only be regarded as a gross error offending against the basic rules of English syntax. Even the semantically inaccurate formulation *had been allowed to listen to* would at least have been grammatically correct, but the expression *he [...] had been let listen to* is ungrammatical as the verb *let* in English cannot have a passive form, as is clear in the ungrammatical sentence **The boy was let play out*. Luke's simplification is adequate, but the idea of the sea 'allowing' Tonio to eavesdrop on its 'secret' summer dreams is lost in Luke's version. (The verb *belauschen* is treated as if it had the same meaning as *zuhören*. A formulation such as *The ocean's summer dreams shared their secrets with the youth who listened into their mysterious murmuring* might be regarded as long-winded, but perhaps justified in a communicative translation.

2. 4717 *Thomas Mann:* [...] dieser lichten, stahlblauäugigen und blondhaarigen Art, die eine Vorstellung von Reinheit, Ungetrübtheit, Heiterkeit und einer zugleich stolzen und schlichten, unberührbaren Sprödigkeit *hervorrief* [...]. (1977: 251)

Lowe-Porter: This was the blond, fair-haired breed of the steel-blue eyes, which *stood to him for* the pure, the blithe, the untroubled in life [...]. (1978: 184/5)

Luke: [...] they too had that radiant blondness, those steely blue eyes, *that air of* untroubled purity and lightness of heart, of proud simplicity and unapproachable reserve. (1988: 186)

Lowe-Porter's use of the phrasal verb *to stand for* something in the sense of representing something is split in an ungrammatical way with the resultant loss of meaning. Luke's solution is acceptable.

Tonio Kröger
2. 4721 *Thomas Mann:* [...] und seine Augen *trübten sich.* (1977: 205)

Lowe-Porter: [...] and his eyes *were clouded.* (1978: 129)

Luke: [...] and his eyes *clouded over* with sadness. (1988: 135)

Failure to distinguish between a state and a change of state. Luke's version is correct.

2. 4722 *Thomas Mann:* [...] er versuchte leise, die Betonung nachzuahmen, mit der sie das gleichgültige Wort ausgesprochen hatte, und erschauerte *dabei.* (1977: 213)

Lowe-Porter: [...] he tried in a whisper to imitate the tone in which she had uttered the commonplace phrase, and felt a shiver run *through and through* him. (1978: 139)

Luke: [...] he tried to imitate the particular way she had pronounced that insignificant word and a tremor ran *through* him as he did so. (1978: 144)

The phrase *through and through* cannot be used as a preposition, but only adverbially as in a phrase such as *He was soaked through and through. *He threw the stone through and through the window* is obviously ungrammatical. Luke's version is correct.

2. 4723 *Thomas Mann:* [...] und man *muß fürchten,* daß das lange dauert. (1977: 247)

Lowe-Porter: [...] and I *fear me* it will keep up till late. (1978: 180)

Luke: [...] and you *can depend upon it,* they'll go on till all hours. (1988: 182)

Possibly, there was a confusion with *ich fürchte mich* in order to produce the non-existent English reflexive conjugated as **I fear me*, but even this explanation would seem to be inadequate in view of the fact that Thomas Mann does not use a reflexive verb in this case. Luke's solution is adequate although there is no reason not to use the idiomatic English equivalent *I fear*.

2. 4724 **Mann:** [...] während die blonde Inge, saß er auch neben ihr, ihm fern und fremd und befremdet erschien [...]. (1977: 217)

Lowe-Porter: [...] while Inge the fair, *let him sit never* so near her, seemed remote and estranged [...]. (1978: 145)

Luke: [...] whereas fair-haired Inge, *even when he was sitting beside her*, seemed distant and alien and embarrassed by him [...]. (1988: 149)

Word order. The phrase *never let him sit so near her* would be grammatically possible as would the grammatically acceptable formulation, though with an entirely different meaning, *let him sit ever so near her*. This possibility might have caused the confusion. The phrase is also semantically incorrect whereas Luke's version adequately expresses the sense.

2. 4725 **Thomas Mann:** [...] alle diese wundervoll beherrschte Körperlichkeit ihm im Grunde etwas wie *Bewunderung abgewann*. (1977: 215)

Lowe-Porter: [...] roused in him something like *admiration of* all this wonderfully controlled corporeality. (1978: 141)

Luke: [...] he could not help feeling a certain grudging *admiration for* the dancing master's impressively controlled physique. (1988: 146)

Preposition: the phrase *admiration of* is possible only in the sense of passive agent e. g. he won the admiration *of* his parents, but when referring to the object of admiration, the preposition *for* is necessary as in the sentence: *He felt nothing but admiration for his parents*. Luke's version is correct with regard to this phrase, but the German noun *Körperlichkeit* is not the same as *physique* as translated by Luke so that the important element of Knaak's grossness is lost in this version. In this case, Lowe-Porter's choice is more accurate

2. 4726 **Thomas Mann:** Und schnell ward sein Name, derselbe, *mit* dem ihn einst seine Lehrer scheltend gerufen hatten [...]. (1977: 220)

Lowe-Porter: In no long time his name - the same *by* which his masters had reproached him [...]. (1978: 148)

Luke: [...] the same name that had once been *shouted at him by* angry schoolmasters [...]. (1988: 152)

Preposition: as the verb *reproach* takes the preposition *for*, the passive cannot be used in this instance: *The name by which he used to be summoned by the masters when they were angry with him* is grammatically possible if a similar construction were to be used, but this would be a slightly clumsy solution. Luke's solution would seem to be better although the interpretation of *einst* as *once* is at least ambiguous because this was probably a repeated action in the past so that some construction with *used to* would be preferable.

2. 4727 *Thomas Mann:* [...] ein seltener zäh ausharrender und ehrsüchtiger Fleiß, der im Kampf mit der wählerischen Reizbarkeit seines Geschmacks unter heftigen Qualen ungewöhnliche Werke *entstehen ließ*. (1977: 220)

Lowe-Porter: [...] a tenacious ambition and a persistent industry, joined battle with the irritable fastidiousness of his taste and under grinding torments *issued in* work of a quality quite uncommon. (1978: 148)

Luke: [...] and of this perseverance, joined in anguished combat with his fastidiously sensitive taste, works of quite unusual quality *were born*. (1988: 152)

The phrasal verb *to issue in* does not exist in English. Luke's translation of *entstehen ließ* is adequate.

2. 4728 *Thomas Mann:* "Nach Dänemark?"
"Und ich *verspreche mir Gutes* davon." (1977: 231)

Lowe-Porter: 'To Denmark?'
'Yes. I'm quite sanguine *of* the results.' (1978: 162)

Luke: 'Denmark?'
'Yes. And I think I shall *benefit from it*.' (1988: 164)

Preposition: *sanguine about* would be possible, but is still very awkward. Luke's version is still much more natural.

2. 4729 *Thomas Mann:* [...] denn er fand, daß hier weder das Volk noch die Literatur etwas zu suchen *hatte*. (1977: 236)

Lowe-Porter: [...] What *were* either literature or the public doing here? (1978: 167)

Luke: [...] for in his opinion *this was* no place either for the public or for literature. (1988: 170)

Verb agreement: Lowe-Porter's formulation implies an inclusive correlative with the plural verb, thus causing semantic confusion. Luke's solution is adequate.

2. 47210 *Thomas Mann:* Anderseits gewährte eine Glastür den Ausblick *auf die* breite Terrasse und den Garten. (1977: 172)

Lowe-Porter: On the opposite side of the room a glass door gave *on* the broad veranda and garden. (1978: 96)

Luke: On the other side was a glass door giving *on to* the wide terrace and the garden. (1988: 103)

There are numerous similar examples where Lowe-Porter fails to express motion with prepositions.

2. 47211 *Thomas Mann:* "Unsere Ausflügler werden doch noch Schnee bekommen, wie es scheint." (1977: 181)

Lowe-Porter: 'It looks as though our sleighing party *would* have some snow after all [...].' (1978: 108)

Luke: 'I should think it *may well be* snowing before our sleighing party gets back [...].' (1988: 113)

Tense sequence: the reference is to a sleigh ride which was about to take place at the time of the speaker's reference to the weather. Luke's tense usage is correct.

v) Stylistic Errors and Errors of English usage

Tristan
2. 511 *Thomas Mann:* [...] sowie mit ihrem schönen, breiten Munde, der blaß war und dennoch *zu leuchten* schien [...]. (1977: 165)

Lowe-Porter: [...] whose lips were so pale and yet seemed to *flash* [...]. (1978: 88d)

Luke: [...] her mouth which [...] seemed *to shine* despite its pallor. (1988: 96)

In the context of this very ill patient, the verb *to flash* to describe Gabriele's lips would seem to be particularly inappropriate. Luke's choice of a neutral verb is acceptable, but a more 'eerie' connotation such as *gleam* might well reflect Mann's macabre humour.

2. 512 *Thomas Mann:* [...] das dunkle Geäst der Bäume stand scharf und *zart gegliedert* gegen den hellen Himmel. (1977: 197)

Lowe-Porter: [...] and the dark network of branches stood out sharp and *articulate* against the bright sky. (1978: 127)

Luke: [...] twigs stood sharply and finely *silhouetted* against the bright sky. (1988: 131)

Lowe-Porter uses a very unusual image by applying a vocal image to a visual one; however, more context would be needed as the image in isolation produces the merely eccentric picture of **articulate branches*. Luke's version is adequate.

2. 513 *Thomas Mann:* Ja, es geht lebhaft zu hierselbst. *Das Institut steht in Flor.* (1977: 164)

Lowe-Porter: Yes, a deal happens hereabouts - *the institution is in a flourishing way.* (1978: 86)

Luke: Ah yes, this is a lively place. *The establishment is flourishing.* (1988: 94)

Lowe-Porter's formulation is almost ungrammatical. This construction tends only to be used negatively - as in the phrase: *He is in a bad way.* The first part of the sentence is also awkwardly formulated in the Lowe-Porter version, but it has also to be admitted that the original German is probably deliberately affected in order to satirise Dr. Leander.

2. 514 *Thomas Mann:* [...] ich habe Besseres zu bedenken, als ihre *unaussprechlichen* Visionen. (1977: 193)

Lowe-Porter: [...] I have other things to do than think about your *unspeakable* visions. (1978: 123)

Luke: [...] I have more important things to think about than your *indistinguishable* visions [...]. (1988: 127)

Lowe-Porter often uses the pejorative adjective *unspeakable* when the more exalted translation such as *ineffable* or *inexpressible* would be more appropriate. Luke's version is also acceptable as he had indulged in an ironic wordplay on this theme.

2. 515 *Thomas Mann:* "*Wirklichkeitsbegierig.* Das ist ein sehr sonderbares Wort! Ein richtiges Schriftstellerwort, Herr Spinell!" (1977: 103)

Lowe-Porter: '*Avid of actuality* - what a strange phrase, a regular literary phrase, Herr Spinell!' (1978: 98)

Luke: '*Appetite for reality* - what a strange phrase! That really is a phrase only a writer could have used, Herr Spinell!' (1988: 105)

Although this phrase might be regarded as a translation difficulty, the collocation *avid of actuality* is not only ungrammatical (avid *for* something), but also makes little sense as the noun *actuality* is normally contrasted with concepts such as *potentiality*. Luke's version is preferable. A freer translation such a *having a raging thirst for grim reality* could be possible in communicative version or *irredeemably addicted to reality* could be a solution in a semantic version.

2. 516 *Thomas Mann:* Es *spielte* in mondänen Salons, in üppigen Frauengemächern, die voller erlesener Gegenstände waren, voll von Gobelins, uralten Meubles, köstlichen Porzellan, *unbezahlbaren Stoffen,* und künstlerischen Kleinodien aller Art. (1988: 169)

Lowe-Porter: Its scenes were *laid* in fashionable salons, in luxurious boudoirs full of choice, old furniture, gobelins, rare porcelains, priceless *stuffs*, and art treasures of all sorts and kinds. (1977: 92-93)

Luke: Its scenes *were set* in fashionable drawing rooms and luxurious boudoirs full of 'objets d'art', full of Gobelin tapestries, very old furniture, priceless porcelain, *rare materials* and artistic treasures of every sort. (1988: 100)

The verb *laid* is unsuitable for this collocation (cf. the Luke version) and the translation of *Stoffe* as *stuffs* is a typical translation howler based on 'false friends'. Luke's version is adequate.

2. 517 *Thomas Mann:* Ja, gnädige Frau, ich hasse diesen Namen aus Herzensgrund, seit ich ihn zum erstenmal vernahm. Er ist komisch und *zum Verzweifeln unschön*, und es ist Barbarei und Niedertracht, wenn man die Sitte so weit treibt, auf Sie den Namen Ihres Herrn Gemahls zu übertragen. (1977: 175)

Lowe-Porter: Yes, madam. I hate the name from the bottom of my heart. I hated it the first time I heard it. It is *the abandonment of ugliness*; it is grotesque to make you comply with the custom so far as to fasten your husband's name upon you; it is barbarous and vile. (1978: 100)

Luke: Yes, dear madam, I have most profoundly detested that name ever since I first heard it. It is grotesque, *it is unspeakably ugly;* and to insist on social convention to the point of calling you by your husband's name is barbaric and outrageous. (1988: 107)

If Lowe-Porter's collocation *the abandonment of ugliness* means anything in this context, it would seem to imply the opposite of the German version, i.e. that the name abandons all ugliness. Luke's version is adequate.

2. 518 **Thomas Mann:** "Kur? [...] Ich *werde ein bißchen elektrisiert.*" (1977: 171)

Lowe-Porter: 'Cure? Oh, *I'm having myself electrified a bit.*' (1978: 95)

Luke: 'Oh. I am having *a little electrical treatment.*' (1988: 102)

Lowe-Porter's version makes no sense. A system such as a railway can be literally electrified, but not a person unless *electrified* is used figuratively. Her usage in an American context would have unfortunate associations with being electrocuted! Luke's translation, however, makes perfect sense.

2. 519 **Thomas Mann:** Hierauf verlangte Herr Klöterjahn Kaffee, - Kaffee und Buttersemmeln [...]. *Er bekam, was er wünschte.* (1977: 166)

Lowe-Porter: Whereupon Herr Klöterjahn asked for coffee, - coffee and buttered rolls [...]. *His order was filled* [...]. (1978: 89)

Luke: Whereupon Herr Klöterjahn ordered coffee, - coffee and rolls. [...] *He was served with the desired refreshments* [...]. (1988: 96)

The expression *filling an order has a completely different meaning from *receiving what has been ordered*. Luke's version is acceptable.

2. 5110 **Thomas Mann:** [...] und sie lächelten mit ihren Augen, die *ein wenig mühsam* blickten, ja hie und da eine kleine Neigung zum Verschießen zeigten [...]. (1977: 165)

Lowe-Porter: [...] [she] spoke [frankly and pleasantly in her rather husky voice,] with a smile in her eyes - though they *were* again sometimes a little *difficult* [...]. (1978: 95)

Luke: She spoke [with candour and charm in her slightly husky voice], and she smiled with her eyes, although she seemed to find it a little *difficult to focus them.* (1988: 96)

Without qualification, the notion *difficult eyes* makes little sense. Luke's version is slightly too specific, but at least it is comprehensible. Another solution could give a different emphasis such as: *There was just a hint of weariness in the way her eyes stared.* Lowe-Porter also omits the reference to focussing.

2. 5111 **Thomas Mann:** "Er soll sich *eines gewissen Rufes* erfreuen [...]."(1977: 170)

Lowe-Porter: 'I understand he has a certain *amount* of reputation [...].' (1978: 94)

Luke: 'I am told he has *a certain* reputation.' (1988: 101)

Confusion of an abstract noun with a mass noun: you can have a certain *amount* of sugar, but not a certain *amount* of fame, glory etc. Luke's version is correct.

2.5112 *Thomas Mann:* "Sie stirbt, mein Herr! Und wenn sie nicht *in Gemeinheit* dahinfährt, wenn sie dennoch sich aus den Tiefen ihrer Erniedrigung erhob [...]." (1977: 192)

Lowe-Porter: 'She dies, sir! And if she does not *go hence with your vulgarity upon her head;* if at the end she has lifted herself out of the depths of degradation [...].' (1978: 120)

Luke: 'She is dying, sir! And if nevertheless her departure is not *vulgar and trivial*, if at the very end she has risen from her degradation.' (1988: 125)

Lowe-Porter's version *go hence* would seem to imply that she did not realise that death was being referred to. This is compounded with the inappropriate usage of the idiom *Be it upon your head.* Luke's version is adequate although the adjective *trivial* is not justified by the source text.

2. 5113 *Thomas Mann:* [...] da sie [...] weich und ermüdet in *den weißlackierten, gradlinigen Armsessel* zurückgelehnt [...]. (1977: 165)

Lowe-Porter: [...] as she leant back pale and weary in her *chaste* white-enamelled arm-chair [...]. (1978: 96)

Luke: [...] leaning softly and wearily back in her *straight, white-lacquered* armchair [...]. (1988: 95)

Intrusive insertion: the personification of the arm-chair as *chaste* does not seem appropriate in the context of a married woman who may indulge in 'spiritual' flirtation.

2. 5114 *Thomas Mann:* [...] und noch drei Tage später *hielt* er um meine Hand an. (1977: 177)

Lowe-Porter: [...] and three days later he *proposed for* my hand. (1978: 127)

Luke: [...] and only three days later he *asked for* my hand. (1988: 109)

A non-English collocation: either a phrase such as *he proposed to me* or Luke's translation would be acceptable. See also example 2. 5244.

2. 5115 **Thomas Mann:** "*Wollen wir nicht* ins Konversationszimmer hinuntergehen, Frau Rätin?"(1977: 180)

Lowe-Porter: '*Shan't we go* down to the salon, Frau Spatz?' (1978: 107)

Luke: '*Shall we* go down into the drawing room, Frau Rätin?' (1988: 113)

Lowe-Porter's follows too closely the German formulation which results in unnatural English for a positive suggestion. Luke's version is acceptable.

2. 5116 **Thomas Mann:** 'Störe ich?' fragte er noch an der Schwelle mit sanfter Stimme, während er ausschließlich Herrn Klöterjahns Gattin anblickte [...]. (1977: 181)

Lowe-Porter: '*Shall I be* disturbing you?' he asked mildly from the threshold, looking only at Herr Klöterjahn's wife [...]. (1978: 107)

Luke: '*Do I* disturb you?' he asked softly, pausing on the threshold, addressing Herr Klöterjahn's wife and her alone [...]. (1988: 113)

This phrase occurs both in *Tristan* and *Tonio Kröger* in circumstances in which the protagonist is obviously apologising for an unannounced interruption. A phrase such as *I hope I am not disturbing you* would seem preferable to Luke's translation whereas the Lowe-Porter use of the modal verb *shall* has the force of a suggestion rather than an apology for an interruption, but when compounded with an unidiomatic use of the progressive aspect (be disturbing), the whole construction borders on the absurd whereas the German phrase is perfectly idiomatic.

2. 5117 **Thomas Mann:** [...] der mich zwingt, in unvergeßlich und *flammend richtig an ihrem Platze stehenden Worten* meine Erlebnisse zu denen der Welt zu machen. (1977: 189)

Lowe-Porter: [...] which urges me to put my own experiences into *flamingly right* and unforgettable words. (1978: 118)

Luke: [...] to communicate them in unforgettable words each chosen and placed with *burning accuracy* [...]. (1988: 123)

The intensifier *flamingly* in the collocation *flamingly right* is very inappropriate as this intensifier is usually used in the context of vulgar language e. g. *flaming(ly) obvious*. Luke's collocation *burning accuracy* is also obscure. Suggested solution: *which induces me to communicate my experiences to the world in words that are <u>emblazoned</u> in their correct place for all eternity* [...].

240

2. 5118 **Thomas Mann:** "Dies Bild *war ein Ende,* mein Herr [...]."(1977: 190)

Lowe-Porter: 'That scene, sir, was an end and *culmination.*' (1978: 119)

Luke: 'That scene, sir, was the *end of a tale.*' (1988: 124)

This is another case of intrusive insertion: the noun *culmination* is particularly inappropriate here as the case in hand is the opposite of a culmination. If Gabriele had met someone who in Spinell's eyes had been worthy of her love, then this would have culminated her development, but her marriage to Klöterjahn is seen by Spinell to be the very reverse such a situation. Luke's version is adequate, but the point behind the assertion could be highlighted by a translation such as *That was the end of the fairy tale.*

2. 5119 **Thomas Mann:** Sie erniedrigen die müde, scheue und in erhabener Unbrauchbarkeit blühende *Schönheit des Todes* in den Dienst des gemeinen Alltags [...]. (1977: 191)

Lowe-Porter: You take *that deathly beauty* - spent, aloof, flowering in lofty unconcern of the uses of this world - and debase it to the service of common things [...]. (1978: 120)

Luke: You degraded that weary diffident *beauty, which belonged to death* and was blossoming in sublime uselessness, by harnessing it to the service of everyday triviality [...]. (1988: 125)

The phrase *deathly beauty* when applied to a person would normally imply a 'death-bringing' rather than a dying beauty whereas if *deathly* is applied as a qualifier to another adjective as in *deathly pale*, then the adjective *deathly* would have the effect intended by Lowe-Porter in this context. Luke's translation of this phrase gives the true meaning of the original, but by adhering too closely to the text the clear meaning of the whole sentence becomes obscured.

2. 5120 **Thomas Mann:** Rosig und weiß, sauber und frisch gekleidet, dick und duftig lastete er auf dem nackten roten Arm seiner *betreßten Dienerin* [...]. (1977: 188)

Lowe-Porter: Pink and white and plump and fragrant, in fresh and immaculate attire, he rested heavily upon the bare red arm of his *bebraided body-servant* [...]. (1978: 116)

Luke: Pink and white, cleanly and freshly clothed, fat and fragrant, he reposed heavily upon the bare red arm of *his gold-braided nurse* [...]. (1988: 121)

The phrase *bebraided body-servant* has a ludicrous effect. The inappropriate and obscure noun *body-servant* for *nurse* is made even more confusing when compounded with the non-existent participle *bebraided.* Luke's version is also not entirely satisfactory because a person cannot be *braided.* A possible solution could be: *he rested heavily on the bare red arm of the nurse who wore a blouse/uniform which was covered in gold braid.* (Luke's idea of giving the braid a golden colour is in keeping with the colour themes within the passage.)

Tonio Kröger

2. 521 **Thomas Mann:** *Große Schüler* hielten mit Würde ihre Bücherpäckchen hoch *gegen die linke Schulter* gedrückt [...]. (1977: 205)

Lowe-Porter: *Elder pupils* held their books in a strap high *on the left shoulder* [...]. (1978: 128)

Luke: *The older ones* held their bundles of books in a dignified manner, high up *against their left shoulders* [...]. (1988: 135)

Wrong use of the adjective *elder.* This form is normally used attributively only with family members or specific comparisons (Quirk: 459). The phrase *the elder pupils* is just possible, but Luke's formulation is correct. Lowe-Porter's use of the definite article in the phrase *the left shoulder* is a typical elementary stylistic error: see also number 2. 5220 for similar mistakes.

2. 522 **Thomas Mann:** [...] auch *hatte er Mühe*, sein Kinn in der Gewalt zu halten, das beständig ins Zittern geriet [...] (1977: 211)

Lowe-Porter: [...] he *had hard work* to control the trembling of his lips. (1978: 136)

Luke: [...] and his chin kept trembling so that he *could hardly control it.* (1988: 142)

Stylistically ungainly: The sentence *It was hard work for Tonio to control the trembling of his lips* would be possible, but Luke's version is also acceptable.

2. 523 Thomas **Mann:** [...] und darauf sprang er auf eine Bank, die *am Wege* stand, [...]. (1977: 212)

Lowe-Porter: [...] he jumped on a bench that stood *by the way* [...]. (1978: 137)

Luke: Whereupon he jumped onto a wooden seat *at the side of the avenue* [...]. (1988: 142)

Literal translation of *Weg* as *way* leads to the confusing ambiguity with the adverb *incidentally* so that the sentence would have to have the absurd meaning: **He jumped on a bench that <u>incidentally</u> stood.* Luke's version is adequate.

2. 524 *Thomas Mann:* "Das nächste Mal *begleite* ich dich nach Hause, sei sicher."
(1977: 212)

Lowe-Porter: 'Next time I'll *take* you home, see if I don't.' (1978: 138)

Luke: 'Next time I'll *walk you* home, I promise.' (1988: 142)

Overtranslation: the phrase *taking someone home* when not applied to using a vehicle usually has some proprietary overtones such as in the case of a boyfriend taking his partner home. Despite some hint of the sexual in Tonio's relationship with Hans, Lowe-Porter's translation of the verb *begleiten* does not warrant this bold interpretation. (Usually, Lowe-Porter's versions tone down any hint of the sexual aspects cf. Section (c) of Chapter III.) Luke's version is acceptable.

2. 525 *Thomas Mann:* Was für *ein unbegreiflicher Affe*, dachte Tonio Kröger in seinem Sinn. (1977: 215)
Lowe-Porter: '*What an unmentionable monkey!*' thought Tonio Kröger to himself. (1978: 141)

Luke: '*What a preposterous monkey!*' thought Tonio Kröger to himself. (1988: 146)

The noun *Affe* in German often has the connotation *pretentious and preposterous* which is clearly appropriate in the context of describing the highly affected dancing master whereas 'monkey' in English has different connotations as when describing a child as *a cheeky monkey*. Luke's collocation would make sense even though, in the context, a collocation such as 'pretentious clown' would seem to be nearer to the connotations of *Affe*, but Lowe-Porter's use of the adjective *unmentionable* together with *monkey* produces an absurd translation as *unmentionable* has moral associations as in an 'unmentionable' crime or as in the Victorian reference to the private parts as the 'unmentionables'. (OED) Even though the use of *unmentionable* may exist in a rare context as inexpressible, its immediate meaning even in the twenties was always associated with moral opprobrium.

2. 526 *Thomas Mann:* [...] und keine Worte schildern, wie wunderbar der Mann den *Nasallaut* hervorbrachte. (1977: 215)

Luke: [...] no words can tell how marvellously he pronounced the *nasal* [...]. (1978: 142)

Luke: [...] and no words can do justice to his elegant muting of the *e* in "*de*". (1988: 147)

Omission of the noun *sound*. The adjective *nasal* normally requires a noun or can be a plural noun Luke, however, finds an ingenious equivalent which, however, misses something of the effeminate affectation that can only be achieved by the overpronunciation of French nasal sounds. A possible freer version could be along the lines: *no words can describe how exquisitely he managed to produce French nasal sounds.*

2. 527 **Thomas Mann:** [...] denn er war abgehärtet gegen Herr Knaaks *Wirkungen.* (1977: 216)

Lowe-Porter: [...] he was hardened against Herr Knaak's *effects.* (1978: 143)

Luke: [...] he was inured against Herr Knaak's *devices.* (1988: 147)

The next example is of a similar nature to the previous one in which a totally inappropriate word is used with ludicrous effect. Although the usual translation of the noun *Wirkung* as *effect* may be correct in many contexts, it is obviously out of place in this context because, when combined with a possessive, the meaning changes to refer to his belongings.
 Luke's translation is acceptable as would be other possible translations such as *displays*, *eccentricities* or a collocation with *effect* such as *attempts to create an effect.*

2. 528 **Thomas Mann:** Ein Ekel und Haß gegen die Sinne erfaßte ihn und *ein Lechzen nach Reinheit* und wohlanständigem Frieden, während er doch die Luft der Kunst atmete, die laue und süße, duftgeschwängerte Luft eines beständigen Frühlings, in der es treibt und braut und keimt in heimlicher Zeugungswonne. (1977: 220)

Lowe-Porter: Then he would be seized with disgust and hatred of the senses; *pant after purity* and seemly peace, while still he breathed the air of art, the tepid sweet air of permanent spring, heavy with fragrance where it breeds and brews and burgeons in the mysterious bliss of creation. (1978: 148)

Luke: Then he was seized by revulsion, by a hatred of the senses, by *a craving after purity and decency* and peace of mind; and yet he was breathing the atmosphere of art, the mild, sweet, heavily fragrant air of a continual spring, in which everything sprouts and burgeons and germinates in mysterious procreative delight. (1988: 151)
Lowe-Porter's use of the phrase to describe the artist's yearning for purity as <u>*pant*</u> *after purity* would seem extraordinarily infelicitous even though the verb *lechzen* does have associations of physical yearning. In various biblical translations, such as the King James' Bible, the phrase *to pant after* in the simile, "As the hart panteth after the water brooks, so panteth my soul after thee, O God". (King James Authorised Version, Psalm 42, verse (i)), is used to express the soul's yearning for God, but if the expression *to pant after* something with its associations of physical desire is placed next to an abstract noun such as justice, the effect is ludicrous, the absurdity of which is increased when coupled with the noun *purity*. The whole passage is included because it can be seen that the Lowe-Porter version lacks coherence whereas Luke's more prosaic passage at least makes some sense.

2. 529 ***Thomas Mann:*** Aber obgleich er einsam, ausgeschlossen und ohne Hoffnung vor einer geschlossenen Jalousie stand und in seinem Kummer *tat, als könne* er hindurchblicken [...]. (1977: 217)

Lowe-Porter: He stood there aloof and alone, staring hopelessly at a drawn blind and *making,* in his distraction, *as though* he could look out. (1978: 144)

Luke: [...] it was therefore absurd to stand in front of this window *pretending* to be looking out of it. (1988: 148)

Literal translation of the German idiomatic construction *tun, als ob.* Luke's version or a phrase such as *he acted as if* are well-known standard translations of this construction whereas the Lowe-Porter version is totally unidiomatic. This is yet another example of what Luke rightly refers to as a "schoolboy howler".

2. 5230 ***Thomas Mann:*** Es ist nötig, daß man irgend etwas Außermenschliches und *Unmenschliches* sei, daß man zum Menschlichen in einem seltsam fernen und unbeteiligten Verhältnis stehe [...]. (1977: 223)

Lowe-Porter: The artist must be *unhuman,* extra-human; he must stand in a queer aloof relationship to our humanity [...]. (1978: 152)

Luke: [...] one simply has to be something *inhuman,* something standing outside humanity, strangely remote and detached from its concerns [...]. (1988: 156)

Even poetic license cannot justify the non-existent word *unhuman,* when the adjective *inhuman* or even *non-human* would seem to be perfectly adequate, as in Luke's translation. This mistake could also be a printing error.

2. 5231 ***Thomas Mann:*** Sehen Sie Lisaweta, ich hege auf dem Grunde meiner Seele - ins Geistige übertragen - *gegen den Typus des Künstlers* den ganzen Verdacht, den jeder meiner ehrenfesten Vorfahren droben in der engen Stadt irgendeinem Gaukler und abenteuerenden Artisten entgegengebracht hätte, der in sein Haus gekommen wäre. (1977: 225)

Lowe-Porter: Now you see, Lisabeta, I cherish at the bottom of my soul all the scorn and suspicion of *the artist gentry* - translated into terms of the intellectual - that my upright old forbears there on the Baltic would have felt for any juggler or mountebank that entered their houses. (1978: 155)

Luke: You see, Lisaveta, I harbor in my very soul a rooted suspicion of *the artist as a type* - I suspect him no less deeply, though in a more intellectual way, than every one of my honorable ancestors up there in that city of narrow streets would have suspected any sort of mountebank or performing adventurer who had strolled into his house. (1988: 158)

Lowe-Porter's use of the word *gentry* in conjunction with the artist is very confusing. As the noun *gentry* generally refers to the lesser aristocracy, the meaning is unclear. It would be possible to refer to artists metaphorically as 'aristocrats of the intellect' but never as 'gentry' except in a very unusual context. However, as there is nothing in the original sentence that remotely connects with *gentry*, this insertion can only be seen as obtrusive. The total result for the reader who may have no access to the original is one of total confusion whereas the Luke version makes the sense perfectly clear to the English reader.

2. 5232 *Thomas Mann:* „Trotz - ich sage 'trotz' - dieser sublimen Veranlagung ist *dieser Mann nicht völlig unbescholten* [...]". (1977: 226)

Lowe-Porter: 'But despite - I say despite - this excellent gift *his withers are by no means unwrung.*' (1978: 155)

Luke: "Despite - I call it despite - this admirable gift he is a *man of not entirely blameless reputation.*" (1988: 157)

Lowe-Porter's use of the obscure colloquial expression *his withers are by no means unwrung* misses the implied criminality of the artist. The withers refers to the area of a horse's back between the shoulder and the neck and the recondite expression of *wringing* a horse's withers implies bad horsemanship as the horse's withers suffer pressure and become strained. If referred to a person, it can only mean that the person has experienced and suffered a lot as opposed to having a criminal past. Luke's version is adequate.

2. 5233 *Thomas Mann:* Der gute Dilettant! In uns Künstlern sieht es gründlich anders aus, als er mit seinem "warmen Herzen" und "ehrlichen Enthusiasmus" sich träumen mag. (1977: 226)

Lowe-Porter: Poor young dilettante! In us artists it looks fundamentally different from what he *wots of*, with his 'warm heart' and 'honest enthusiasm'. (1978: 155)

Luke: Poor decent dilettante! We artists have an inner life very different from what our 'warmhearted' admirers in their 'genuine enthusiasm' *imagine*. (1988: 158)

As in the previous example, Lowe-Porter often uses obscure and archaic word without any apparent justification other than perhaps to produce some sort of literary effect. The obsolete verb 'woten' (to know) which, in this context, has the opposite effect to the original (i.e. *wissen* as opposed to *sich träumen*), was current in the fifteenth and sixteenth centuries, but was used only as occasional archaism in the nineteenth century by writers such as Sir Walter Scott and Mrs. Browning (OED). Luke's version makes the meaning perfectly clear.

2. 5233 *Thomas Mann:* [...] daß dies bei Leuten mit gutem Gewissen und *solid gegründetem* Selbstgefühl nicht zuzutreffen pflegt. (1977: 225)

Lowe-Porter: [...] just as everybody knows that ordinary people with a *normal bump of self-confidence* are not. (1978: 155)

Luke: [...] this is not usually the case with people who have a good conscience *and solidly grounded* self confidence [...]. (1988: 158)

The racy phrase *bump of self-confidence* is very obscure and certainly reflects an inappropriate register for a literary context. Luke's more literal version is preferable as this version underlines the solid respectable *Bürger* theme.

2. 5234 *Mann:* [...] bis er an seinem letzten und eigentlichen Ziele hielt, dem kleinen weißen *Badehotel* mit den Fensterläden [...]. (1977: 244)

Lowe-Porter: [...] reaching at length his ultimate goal, the little white *bath-hotel* with green blinds. (1978: 177)

Luke: [...] until he reached his final and true destination. It was a little white *seaside hotel* with green shutters [...]. (1988: 179)

This is a fairly typical example of what Luke refers to as "schoolboy howlers". (Similarly, Lowe-Porter translates *Kurgast* on page 92 as *guest of the cure* and on page 170, *ein dänisches Seebad* as *a Danish seashore* resort and on page 95, *eine strenge Tagesordnung* as *the stern service of the cure*. It is not necessary to display such examples in full.)

2. 5235 *Thomas Mann:* [...] ein Fischhändler aus der Hauptstadt, der *des Deutschen mächtig* war. (1977: 245)

Lowe-Porter: [...] a fish-dealer he was, from the capital, and *strong at the German*. (1978: 178)

Luke: [...] he was a fish dealer from the capital and *could speak German*. (1988: 179)

The comments on the previous example also apply to this one. The idiomatic use of *mächtig* has obviously been misunderstood and taken literally. Luke's version is correct

2. 5236 *Thomas Mann:* Diese Haltung und Miene war ihm *eigentümlich.* (1977: 206)

Lowe-Porter: Posture and manner were *habitual.* (1978: 130)

Luke: [...] This attitude and facial expression were *characteristic* of him. (1988: 136)

The adjective *habitual* would normally need qualification as in a collocation such as *an habitual smoker*. This omission compounded with the lack of articles makes Lowe-Porter's version virtually meaningless. Luke's version is adequate.

2. 5237 *Thomas Mann:* Er vermied sie, *wie* er konnte [...]. (1977: 215)

Lowe-Porter: He avoided her *where* he could [...]. (1978: 142)

Luke: He avoided her *as best* he could [...]. (1988: 146)

The verb *avoid* implies motion whereas *where* implies rest: *He avoided her <u>wherever</u> he could*, is possible. A translation such as *He avoided her <u>whenever</u> he could*, would be grammatically preferable, but Luke's solution is more felicitous.

2. 5238 *Thomas Mann:* [Tonio] [...] blickte hie und da in den *abendlichen* Garten hinaus, wo der alte Walnußbaum schwerfällig knarrte. (1977: 216)

Lowe-Porter: [...] lifting his eyes to the *twilight* garden outside, where the old walnut tree moaned. (1978: 143)

Luke: [...] and occasionally glancing out into the garden *where it lay in the evening light* [...]. (1988: 148)

Overliteral translation on the part of Lowe-Porter: only rarely can parts of the day be used successfully as descriptive adjectives; a phrase such as the *night air* is possible whereas phrases such as the *night garden* or the *night park* do not work as English collocations. Luke's version overcomes the difficulty, but is still slightly stilted. The phrase *where it lay* is redundant and, if omitted, the sentence reads more naturally.

2. 5239 *Thomas Mann:* Mochten die anderen tanzen und *frisch und geschickt bei der Sache* sein! (1988: 216)

Lowe-Porter: Others might dance, others *bend* their fresh and lively minds *upon* the pleasure in hand! (1978: 143)

Luke: Let the others dance and *enjoy themselves and be good at it* [...]. (1988: 148)

The formulation *bend upon the pleasure* is both unusual and ungainly, i.e. the notion of straining the mind to enjoy pleasures is obscure. Luke's version is adequate.

2. 5220 *Thomas Mann:* [...] sein Vater könnte aus einer der Türen zu ebener Erde, an denen er vorüberschritt, hervortreten und im Kontor-Rock und *die Feder* hinterm Ohr [...]. (1977: 236)

Lowe-Porter: [...] his father might come out of one of the doors on the ground floor, in his office coat, *with the pen* behind his ear [...]. (1978: 167)

Luke: [...] his father had thrown open one of the doors on the ground floor, emerging in his office coat and *with his pen* behind his ear [...]. (1988: 169)

This is yet another example of a typical second language-interference mistake. Most traditional course grammars in elementary German advise the use of the possessive adjective to translate everyday phrases in the context of articles of clothing and parts of the body. See also example 2. 221.

2. 5241 *Thomas Mann:* [...] verließ auch das Meer, das er so sehr liebte, und *empfand keinen Schmerz dabei.* (1977: 219)

Lowe-Porter: [...] left the sea too, that he loved so much, and *felt no pain to go.* (1978: 146)

Luke: [...] he left the sea too, his beloved sea, and *left it all without a pang.* (1988: 150)

The phrase *felt no pain in going* or better *felt no pain in having to leave it all behind* would be possible instead of Lowe-Porter's ungrammatical version. Luke's version is also acceptable.

2. 5242 *Thomas Mann:* Man vergegenwärtige sich einen Brünetten *am Anfang der Dreißiger* und von stattlicher Statur [...]. (1977: 168)

Lowe-Porter: Imagine a dark man *at the beginning of the thirties*, impressively tall [...]. (1978: 92)

Luke: Let us imagine a tall well-built man *in his early thirties* [...]. (1988: 99)

Lowe-Porter's use of the definite article would tend to refer to the decade rather than to the age of a particular person. Luke's version is correct.

2. 5243 **Thomas Mann:** Denn das, was man sagt, darf niemals die Hauptsache sein, sondern nur das *an und für sich* gleichgültige Material, aus dem das ästhetische Gebilde in *spielender und gelassener Überlegenheit* zusammenzusetzen ist. (1977: 223)

Lowe-Porter: For what an artist talks about is never the main point: it is the raw material, *in and for itself* indifferent, out of which, with *bland and serene* mastery, he creates the work of art. (1978: 151)

Luke: Because, of course, *what* one says must never be one's main concern. It must merely be the raw material, *quite indifferent in itself*, out of which the work of art is made; and the act of making must be a game, aloof and detached, performed in tranquillity. (1988: 155)

In Lowe-Porter's version, the phrase *an und für sich* is literally translated to produce a meaningless collocation in English. (Adjectives such as *extrinsic* and *intrinsic* are the usual solution in philosophical translations). The adjective *bland* is a poor translation for *spielend* when, in this case, a more literal translation such as *playful* would be preferable. On the contrary, *bland* works of art belong to the world of the *Bürger* and not to the artist. Again, Lowe-Porter's version confuses one of the basic themes running throughout the novella. Luke's version which, in this extract, is untypically communicative is, however, adequate.

2. 5244 **Thomas Mann:** Kein Problem, keines in der Welt, ist quälender *als das* vom Künstlertum und seiner menschlichen Wirkung. (1977: 226)

Lowe-Porter: No problem, none in the world, is more tormenting *than this of* the artist and his human aspect. (1978: 155)

Luke: There's no problem on earth so tantalizing *as the* problem of what an artist is and what art does to human beings (1988: 158)

Lowe-Porter's version is ungrammatical; correct usage would be in this case *than that of* the artist. Luke's version is also correct.

26. 5245 **Thomas Mann:** Italien ist mir bis *zur Verachtung gleichgültig!* (1977: 231)

Lowe-Porter: I'm fed up with Italy, I *spew it out of my mouth.* (1978: 161)

Luke: [...] I am bored with Italy *to the point of despising it!* (1988: 164)

Overtranslation resulting in an absurd effect, i.e. the image of 'spewing up' a whole country. This notion could be a misapplication of the biblical phrase referring to the Deity: "So then because thou art lukewarm, and neither cold nor hot, I will spue thee out of my mouth." (King James Authorised Version, Revelations III, Verse (xvi)). Luke's version is adequate.

2. 5246 ***Thomas Mann:*** [...] denn das sehe ich genau, daß Sie heute *geladen sind.* (1977: 223)

Lowe-Porter: [...] for I can perfectly well see that you are *too full for utterance.* (1978: 151)

Luke: [...] for I can see well enough that you have *got a lot on your mind.* (1988: 155)

The phrase *too full for utterance* is ungainly and implies the opposite because Tonio needs to speak to unburden himself, but Luke's solution is perfectly natural and adequate.

2. 5247 ***Thomas Mann:*** Aber nehmen Sie die Bücher, die dort oben geschrieben werden, diese *tiefen,* reinen und humoristischen Bücher, Lisaweta [...]. (1977: 231)

Lowe-Porter: [...] books that are written up there, that clean, *meaty,* whimsical Scandinavian literature, Lisabeta [...]. (1978: 162)

Luke: But think of the books they write up there in the north, Lisaveta, books of *such depth,* purity and humor [...]. (1988: 164)

Wrong register: the adjective *meaty* is far too colloquial. The other adjectives Lowe-Porter uses (*clean* and *whimsical*) continue the trivialisation process whereas Luke's accurate version is felicitous and acts as a just description of Scandinavian literature. Lowe-Porter's list of adjectives, however, produces a ludicrous effect.

2. 5248 ***Thomas Mann:*** Ein Kellner, ein milder Mensch mit *brotblonden* Backenbartstreifen [...]. (1977: 234)

Lowe-Porter: A mild-mannered waiter with *yellow-white* side whiskers [...]. (1978: 164)

Luke: A mild-mannered waiter with *sandy* side whiskers [...]. (1988: 167)

Infelicitous: yellowish white would be acceptable, but Luke's version is better.

2. 5249 ***Thomas Mann:*** [...] wo Fleischer *mit blutigen Händen* ihre Waren wogen [...]. (1977: 235)

Lowe-Porter: [...] where the butchers were weighing out their wares *red-handed* [...]. (1978: 166)

Luke: [...] here were the butchers weighing their wares with *bloodstained* hands [...]. (1988: 168)

Lowe-Porter's version is confusing because the adverb *red-handed* is usually used idiomatically as in the sentence, *He was caught red-handed* and can only exceptionally be used as an adjective. This ambiguity causes minor irritation, but the Luke version is adequate.

2. 5250 ***Thomas Mann:*** Tonio Kröger malte mit seitwärts geneigtem Kopf etwas darauf, das aussah wie Name, *Stand* und Herkunft. (1977: 234)

Lowe-Porter: Tonio Kröger, his head on one side, scrawled something on it that might be taken for a time, *a station*, and a place of origin. (1978: 165)

Luke: Tonio Kröger, with his head tilted to one side, scrawled something on it that had *his name and status* and place of origin. (1988: 167)

Lowe-Porter's wrong use of the indefinite article here has the curious effect of changing the abstract noun *station* into a concrete noun as in *a railway station* or *stage* on a journey! Luke's version is correct.

2. 5251 ***Thomas Mann:*** Wie war ihm doch? [...] *Still, still und kein Wort! Keine Worte!* (1977: 233)

Lowe-Porter: What was at the bottom of this? [...] Only *don't make words!* (1978: 164)

Luke: [...] what was it? Hush, he must not say it! He must *not put it* into words. (1988: 167)

Lowe-Porter's version is very unidiomatic in comparison to Luke's translation because words can be either *expressed* i.e. written or spoken or *made up*, i.e. invented, but not simply *made*.

2. 5252 ***Thomas Mann:*** [...] dann setzte er sich mit gekreuzten Armen auf das weitschweifige Sofa, *zog seine Brauen zusammen* und pfiff vor sich hin. (1977: 234)

Lowe-Porter: [...] then he sat down on the wide sofa, crossed his arms, *drew down his brows* and whistled to himself. (1978: 165)

Luke: [...] then he sat with folded arms on the commodious sofa, *frowning* and whistling to himself. (1988: 167)

Unidiomatic: curtains may possibly be *drawn down*, but not eyebrows. Luke has found the simplest and most elegant solution.

2. 5253 *Thomas Mann:* Er schwieg. Er zog seine *schrägen* Brauen zusammen und pfiff vor sich hin. (1977: 234)

Lowe-Porter: He was silent, knitting his *oblique* brown brows and whistling softly to himself. (1978: 156)

Luke: [...] He contracted his *slanting* brows in a frown and whistled to himself. (1988: 158)

The adjective *oblique* is too abstract to describe eyebrows. Luke's version is adequate.

2. 5254 *Thomas Mann:* Sein geschorener *Backenbart war* weiß geworden [...]. (1977: 238)

Lowe-Porter: His *shaven side-whisker was* white [...]. (1978: 170)

Luke: His *clipped side-whiskers were* white [...]. (1988: 172)

By using the singular, Lowe-Porter's version would imply that Herr Seehase had only half a beard, but, even more confusing still, her choice of the adjectival past participle *shaven* leads to a further contradiction because *a shaven beard* is a beard that no longer exists and so would in turn imply that Herr Seehase had no beard at all! Luke's version is correct.

2. 5255 *Thomas Mann:* [...] und mit einem *schwimmenden Silberglanz* stieg schon der Mond empor [...]. (1977: 239)

Lowe-Porter: The moon *swam up with a silver gleam* as Tonio Kröger's boat reached the open sea. (1978: 173)

Luke: The moon *was rising, its silver radiance floating up* the sky [...]. (1988: 174)

The Lowe-Porter version could imply that the moon was 'swimming' in the sea rather than rising in the sky. Lowe-Porter ignored the fact that the German verb *schwimmen* can also mean *to float* as well as *to swim*. Luke's version translates the meaning adequately.

2. 5256 *Thomas Mann:* Ja, ich bin auf der Reise in ein dänisches *Seebad.* (1977: 238)

Lowe-Porter: I am on the way to a Danish *seashore* resort. (1978: 170)

Luke: [...] I am on my way to a Danish *seaside* resort. (1988: 172)

Wrong collocation. See Luke's version, cf. examples cited in 2. 5214

2. 5257 *Thomas Mann:* Als er völlig wach wurde, war es schon *Tag* [...]. (1977: 244)

Lowe-Porter: When he really roused, it was *broad day* [...]. (1978: 176)

Luke: By the time he was fully awake it was already *broad daylight* [...]. (1988: 1978)

Wrong collocation. See Luke's version.

2. 5258 *Thomas Mann:* [...] und die grüne See *ging ruhiger.* (1977: 244)

Lowe-Porter: [...] and the sea *had gone down.* (1978: 176)

Luke: [...] the green sea *was calmer.* (1988: 178)

Poor style: the idiom *go down* could apply to waves or tides, but not to the whole sea. Luke's version is acceptable, but as there had been a storm on the previous evening, a translation with a clause such as *the sea had calmed down* would be more appropriate.

2. 5259 *Thomas Mann:* [...] hielt ihre *schmal geschnittenen Augen* abgewandt [...]. (1977: 248)

Lowe-Porter: [...] Ingeborg's *narrow eyes* were turned away [...]. (1978: 181)

Luke: [...] Ingeborg kept her *narrow-cut eyes* averted [...]. (1988: 183)

Lowe-Porter's version would refer to the eyes themselves rather than their position in the face. Luke's version makes the meaning clear.

2. 5260 *Thomas Mann:* "Sie *kommen* von München?" fragte endlich der Polizist [...]. (1977: 238)

Lowe-Porter: 'You *came* from Munich?' the policeman asked at length [...]. (1978: 170)

Luke: '*Have* you *come* here from Munich?' asked the policeman eventually [...]. (1988: 172)

The original could be questioning whether Tonio is a resident at Munich or whether he has just travelled from Munich, the former being the more likely variant whereas the Lowe-Porter use of the preterite tense could imply a previous journey or residence, outside the immediate context of the interviewee, and is thus in the wrong tense.

2. 5261 *Thomas Mann:* Er *verkehrte nicht gern* mit Beamten [...]. (1977: 239)

Lowe-Porter: He *hated relations with officials* [...]. (1978: 170)

Luke: He *did not like dealing with* officials [...]. (1988: 173)

Unidiomatic: the sentence *He hated having any relations with officials* would be more grammatical, but Luke's version is more natural.

2. 5262 ***Thomas Mann:*** Gleich dieses Tages *Anfang* gestaltete sich festlich und entzückend. (1977: 246)

Lowe-Porter: The very *opening* of the day had been rare and festal. (1978: 179)

Luke: There was something festive and delightful about that day from *its very beginning*. (1988: 181)

Lowe-Porter's version is confusing: an *opening* of a festival is possible, but not the phrase *the opening of the day* except in as a metaphor. Luke's version is acceptable.

2. 5263 ***Thomas Mann:*** [...] er tat nichts, als sich hierauf freuen, mit einer so *ängstlichen* und süßen Freude [...]. (1977: 248)

Lowe-Porter: [...] and he did nothing but be glad of this, with a sweet and *timorous* gladness. (1978: 182)

Luke: [...] and he did nothing all day but look forward to this with a sweet and *apprehensive* excitement [...]. (1988: 83)

Timorous is awkward as a qualifier to an abstract noun. Luke's version is acceptable, but a communicative translation highlighting the contraries such as *a delight which was exquisite and yet laden with anxiety* would convey the full import of the sentence more clearly. (The other grosser mistakes in this quotation are dealt with in example 2. 4521)

2. 5264 ***Thomas Mann:*** [...] dich *zum Weibe nehmen,* Ingeborg Holm [...]. (1977: 251)

Lowe-Porter: To *take you,* Ingeborg Holm *to wife* [...]. (1978: 185)

Luke: [...] and *marry you,* Ingeborg Holm [...]. (1988: 185)

The collocation *to take to wife* is unidiomatic cf. example 2. 5114. Luke's version is correct.

2. 5265 *Thomas Mann:* [...] um die Schultern trug sie einen breiten, weißen Tüllbesatz mit spitzem Ausschnitt, der *ihren weichen, geschmeidigen* Hals freiließ. (1977: 248)

Lowe-Porter: [...] and it had a tulle fichu draped with a pointed opening that left her *soft throat* free. (1978: 181)

Luke: [...] round her shoulders was a broad white tulle collar cut well down in front and exposing her *soft supple neck.* (1988: 183)

The meaning of the collocation *soft throat* is very obscure because the noun *throat* normally refers to the inner aspect of the neck such as the collocation *a sore throat*, despite exceptions such as the sentence: *He seized his enemy by the throat*, whereas Luke's version is perfectly adequate.

2. 5266 *Thomas Mann:* Der Adjunkt *entfaltete eine umfassende Tätigkeit.* (1977: 252)

Lowe-Porter: The leader *developed a comprehensive activity.* (1978: 187)

Luke: The assistant postmaster *burst into ubiquitous activity.* (1988: 188)

When the noun *activity* is used with an article, it has a different meaning, but when compounded with an inappropriate literal translation of the adjective *umfassend* i.e. as *comprehensive*, the sentence loses its sense. Luke's solution is also not totally satisfactory. A sentence such as *The leader seemed to be busy everywhere at once*, would make more sense in a communicative translation despite some literary loss whereas an alternative formulation such as *The leader blossomed out to take over the floor with bustling omnipresence* would capture something of the literary overtones of the original, though not as succinctly. The Lowe-Porter version is, however, meaningless.

2. 5267 *Thomas Mann:* [...] ihr Blonden, *Lebendigen,* Glücklichen [...]. (1977: 254)

Lowe-Porter: [...] you blond, you *living*, you happy ones! (1978: 188)

Luke: [...] you the fair-haired, the happy, *the truly alive* [...]. (1988: 189)

Although the Lowe-Porter version is comprehensible, it is stylistically weak in comparison with Luke's version because the adjective *living* merely contrasts in this context with the *dead*.

2. 5268 *Thomas Mann:* [...] und bei all dem flogen die Bänder der großen, bunten Schleife, die als Zeichen seiner Würde auf seiner Schulter befestigt war und nach der er manchmal liebevoll den Kopf drehte, flatternd liebevoll *hinter ihm drein.* (1977: 250)

Lowe-Porter: [...] here, there and everywhere, and glancing over his shoulder in pride at his great bow of office, the streamers of which fluttered grandly *in his rear.* (1978: 184)

Luke: [...] as he moved, the ribbons of the gaily coloured bow which had been pinned to his shoulder in token of his office fluttered *behind him.* (1988: 185)

The phrase *in his rear* would normally have merely anatomical reference, thus with absurd effect in this case. The phrase *at his rear* is possible, but Luke's solution is acceptable.

2. 5269 *Thomas Mann:* [...] und er war allein und *ausgeschlossen* von den Ordentlichen und Gewöhnlichen [...]. (1977: 211)

Lowe-Porter: [...] and he was alone, the regular and usual *would none of him* [...]. (1978: 137)

Luke: [...] he was *isolated,* he did not belong among decent *normal* people [...]. (1988: 142)

The italicised phrase in the Lowe-Porter version is presumably intended to mean: *wanted nothing to do with him,* but even this phrase is stilted because the past form *would* cannot mean *wanted* in modern English so that, once again, her version is totally meaningless. Luke's version is adequate, but his translation of *Gewöhnlichen* as "normal" in contrast with *ordinary,* for example, loses the ambiguity of the original because *das Gewöhnliche* can also be pejorative with the implications not only of dullness but also of crassness or even vulgarity.

2. 5270 *Thomas Mann:* [...] Sehnsucht war darin und ein schwermütiger Neid und ein wenig Verachtung und *eine ganz* keusche Seligkeit. (1977: 213)

Lowe-Porter: [...] longing was awake in it, and a gentle envy; a faint contempt and *no little* innocent bliss. (1978: 138)

Luke: [...] in it there was longing, and sad envy, and just a touch of contempt, and *a whole world of innocent delight* (1988: 143)

Although this example could be classified under *illicit negatives,* it could be argued that the artificial construction: **There is <u>no little</u> milk in the fridge* is impossible. Luke's version is adequate.

2. 5271 *Thomas Mann:* [...] Namen, die ihm aus alten Tagen bekannt waren, die ihm etwas Zartes und Köstliches zu bezeichnen schienen und bei alledem etwas wie Vorwurf, Klage und Sehnsucht *nach Verlorenem* in sich schlossen. (1977: 244)

Lowe-Porter: [...] names that had a tender and precious quality and withal in their syllables an accent of plaintive reproach, of repining after *the lost and gone*. (1978: 177)

Luke: [...] names symbolizing for him something tender and precious, and containing at the same time a kind of reproach, the sorrowful nostalgic reminder of *something lost*. (1988: 178)

The use of the definite article in Lowe-Porter's infelicitous version could imply <u>everything</u> that is lost *and gone* whereas Luke's version is correct.

2. 5272 *Thomas Mann: Da geschah dies auf einmal*: Hans Hansen und Ingeborg Holm gingen durch den Saal. (1977: 247)

Lowe-Porter: Then all at once *a thing came to pass*: Hans Hansen and Ingeborg Holm walked through the room. (1978: 181)

Luke: [...] then suddenly *it happened*: Hans Hansen and Ingeborg Holm walked through the dining room. (1988: 182)

Lowe-Porter's use of the 'unliterary' noun *thing* in conjunction with the rather biblical phrase *came to pass* creates a curiously contradictory effect. Luke's simpler version is more acceptable.

2. 5273 *Thomas Mann:* Er betrachtete des Königs Neumarkt und das "Pferd" in seiner Mitte, blickte achtungsvoll an der Säulen der *Frauenkirche* empor [...]. (1977: 244)

Lowe-Porter: He looked at the king's New Market and the 'Horse' in the middle of it, gazed respectfully up the columns of the *Frauenkirch* [...]. (1978: 177)

Luke: [...] He inspected Kongens Nytorv and the 'Horse' in its midst, glanced up respectfully at the columns of the *Fruekirk* [...]. (1988: 178)

Luke's solution for translating *Frauenkirche* as *Fruekirk* in this context would seem to the best strategy whereas Lowe-Porter's version *Frauenkirch* would mean little to English readers particularly with regard to the missing final *e*, which one hopes is merely another printing error. (Lowe-Porter's failure to capitalise the letter *k* in *King's* could also cause semantic confusion).

2. 5274 *Thomas Mann:* Erstarrung; Öde; Eis; und Geist! Und Kunst! (1977: 254)

Lowe-Porter: Icy desolation, solitude: mind and art, forsooth! (1978: 189)

Luke: Paralysis, barrenness; ice and intellect and art! (1988: 189)

It can be seen that whilst Luke's list is accurate, though rather literal, Lowe-Porter's linkage of 'ice' with 'desolation' misses the whole point of the very important semicolons which separate the great themes of the artist's life, thus distorting the central themes of the work. Her use of the noun *solitude* to translate *Öde* is inappropriate because solitude has positive associations, as in Wordsworth's phrase "the bliss of solitude" and by no means conveys the barrenness of the lonely desert. The archaic interjection *forsooth* merely trivialises the whole tone to create an absurd effect.

Appendix II: Translations of One Key Sentence in Thomas Mann's *Der Tod in Venedig* as Analysed in Chapter IV

(The sentence is set out as in the Seidlin analysis together with the rest of the paragraph):

Thomas Mann:

1 Der Autor der klaren und mächtigen Prosa-Epopöe vom Leben

2 Friedrichs von Preußen; der geduldige Künstler, der in langem

3 Fleiß den figurenreichen, so vielerlei Menschenschicksal

4 im Schatten einer Idee versammelnden Romanteppich, 'Maja'

5 mit Namen, wob; der Schöpfer jener starken Erzählung, die

6 'Ein Elender' überschrieben ist und einer ganzen dankbaren

7 Jugend die Möglichkeit sittlicher Entschlossenheit jenseits

8 der tiefsten Erkenntnis zeigte; der Verfasser endlich (und

9 damit sind die Werke seiner Reifezeit kurz bezeichnet) der

10 leidenschaftlichen Abhandlung über 'Geist und Kunst,' deren

11 ordnende Kraft und antithetische Beredsamkeit ernste Beur-

12 teiler vermochte, sie unmittelbar neben Schillers Raisonne-

13 ment über naïve und sentimentalische Dichtung zu stellen:

14 Gustav Aschenbach also war zu L., einer Kreisstadt der

15 Provinz Schlesien, als Sohn eines höheren Justizbeamten

16 geboren. (Seidlin 1963: 149)

Seine Vorfahren waren Offiziere, Richter, Verwaltungsfunktionäre gewesen, Männer, die im Dienst des Königs, des Staates, ihr straffes, anständig karges Leben geführt hatten. Innere Geistigkeit hatte sich einmal, in der Person eines Predigers, unter ihnen verkörpert; rascheres, sinnlicheres Blut war der Familie in der vorigen Generation durch die Mutter des Dichters, Tochter eines böhmischen Kapellmeisters, zugekommen. Von ihr stammten die Merkmale fremder Rasse in seinem Äußern. Die Vermählung dienstlich nüchterner Gewissenhaftigkeit mit dunkleren, feurigeren Impulsen ließ einen Künstler und diesen besonderen Künstler erstehen. (Mann 1977: 14)

Version I: Lowe-Porter

Gustave Aschenbach was born at L -, a country town in the province of Silesia. He was the son of an upper official in the judicature, and his forebears had all been officers, judges, departmental functionaries - men who had lived their strict, decent, sparing lives in the service of king and state. Only once before had a livelier mentality - in the quality of a clergyman - turned up among them; but swifter, more perceptive blood had in the generation before the poet's flowed into the stock from the mother's side, she being the daughter of a Bohemian musical conductor. It was from her he had the foreign traits that betrayed themselves in his appearance. The union of dry, conscientious officialdom and ardent, obscure impulse, produced an artist - and this particular artist: author of the lucid and vigorous prose epic on the life of Frederick the Great; careful, tireless weaver of the richly patterned tapestry entitled *Maia,* a novel that gathers up the threads of many human destinies in the warp of a single idea; creator of that powerful narrative *The Abject,* which taught a whole generation that a man can still be capable of moral resolution even after he has plumbed the depths of knowledge; and lastly - to complete the tale of works of his mature period - the writer of that impassioned discourse on the theme of Mind and Art whose ordered force and antithetic eloquence led serious critics to rank it with Schiller's *Simple and Sentimental Poetry.* (Lowe-Porter 1978:12-13)

Version II: Luke

The author of the lucid and massive prose-epic on the life of Frederic of Prussia; the patient artist who with long toil had woven the great tapestry of the novel called *Maya,* so rich in characters, gathering so many human destinies together under the shadow of one idea; the creator of that powerful tale entitled *A Study in Abjection,* which earned the gratitude of a whole younger generation by pointing to the possibility of moral resolution even for those who have plumbed the depths of knowledge; the author (lastly but not least in this summary enumeration of his maturer works) of that passionate treatise *Intellect and Art* which in its ordering energy and antithetical eloquence has led serious critics to place it immediately alongside Schiller's disquisition *On Naive and Reflective Literature:* in a word, Gustav Aschenbach, was born in L., an important city in the province of Silesia, as the son of a highly-placed legal official. His ancestors had been military officers, judges, government administrators; men who had spent their disciplined, decently austere life in the service of the king and the state. A more inward spirituality had shown itself in one of them who had been a preacher; a strain of livelier, more sensuous blood had entered the family in the previous generation with the writer's mother, the daughter of a director of music from Bohemia. Certain exotic racial characteristics in his external appearance had come to him from her. It was from this marriage between hard-working, sober conscientiousness and darker, more fiery impulses that an artist, and indeed this particular kind of artist, had come into being. (Luke 1988: 200)

Version III: Suggested Semantic Version: Gledhill

The author of the lucid and massive prose epopee on the life of Frederick of Prussia, - the long-suffering artist who had patiently and painstakingly woven together so great a variety of human character and destiny into a vast tapestry unified beneath the shadow of one great idea in his novel entitled Maya - the creator of that most disturbing story, *A Vile Wretch* which told the new young and grateful generation that it was still possible to have an ethical commitment which transcends even the deepest of philosophical insights - and finally to characterise the works of his later years, the writer whose mature period was exemplified by a passionate treatise on *Intellect and Art,* ranked equally by some serious critics with Schiller's famous *raisonnement* on naïve and sophisticated poetry because of its creative sense of order and its eloquent use of antithesis - Gustav Aschenbach was born in the town of L., a district capital in the province of Silesia, as the son of a high-ranking official in the judiciary. [End of sentence]

261

His forebears had been army officers, judges, civil servants, men who had led austere lives of respectable frugality in the service of their king and country. A more inward form of spirituality had once manifested itself amongst his ancestors in the form of a clergyman; the poet's mother, the daughter of a Bohemian music master, introduced more thrilling, more sensual blood into the family. His foreign racial features came from her. The union of a scrupulous, sober dedication to duty with darker, fiery impulses produced an artist, and, did indeed produce, this particular artist.

Version IV: Suggested Communicative Version: Gledhill

The author of that colossal prose epic on the life of Frederick of Prussia - the artist who wove a vast tapestry uniting the multifarious strands of human destinies and characters beneath the shadow of one unifying idea in his novel called *Maya* - creator of the powerful story entitled *Human Scum*, which, however, made moral action possible again to a whole generation of grateful readers and take precedence over artistic insights penetrating the nether depths of knowledge - writer of that passionate treatise on *Art and the Intellect* (which characterised his later period) and which was so cogently argued and was so sophisticated in its use of antithesis that some leading critics put it on a level with Schiller's famous treatise defining the difference between naïve, and 'consciously wrought' poetry - Gustav Aschenbach was born in L., a town in Silesia as the son of a highly placed, state lawyer. [End of sentence]

His ancestors came from the ranks of military officers, judges, civil servants - all men who lead impeccably respectable, though frugal lives in the service of their king and country. There had been one manifestation of a deeper, more spiritual influence in the form of an ancestor who had been a clergyman; the poet's mother who was the daughter of a Bohemian music director introduced a more hot-blooded and sensual streak into the family. His foreign-looking appearance came from her. The combination of dry devotion to duty with darker, yet fiery urges was a mixture to produce an artist and, in fact, made this particular artist.

Version V: Burke

The author of that lucid and powerful prose epic built around the life of Frederick of Prussia; the tenacious artist who, after long application, wove rich, varied strands of human destiny together under one single predominating theme in the fictional tapestry known as *Maya*; the creator of that stark tale which is called *The Wretch* and which pointed out for an entire oncoming generation the possibility of some moral certainty beyond pure knowledge; finally, the writer (and this sums up briefly the works of his mature period) of the impassioned treatise on *Art and the Spirit*, whose capacity for mustering facts, and, further, whose fluency in their presentation, led cautious judges to place this treatise alongside Schiller's conclusion on naïve and sentimental poetry - Gustav Aschenbach, then, was the son of a higher law official, and was born in L_____, a leading city in the province of Silesia. His forbears had been officers, magistrates, government functionaries, men who had led severe, steady lives serving their king, their state. A deeper strain of spirituality had been manifest in them once, in the person of a preacher; the proceeding generation had brought a brisker, more sensuous blood into the family through the author's mother, daughter of a Bohemian bandmaster. The traces of foreignness in his features came from her. A marriage of sober painstaking conscientiousness with impulses of a darker, more fiery nature had had an artist as its result, and this particular artist. (Burke 1971: 11)

Version VI: Koelb

Gustav Aschenbach, the author of the clear and vigorous prose epic on the life of Frederick the Great; the patient artist who wove together with enduring diligence the novelistic tapestry *Maia*, a work rich in characters and eminently successful in gathering together many human destinies under the shadow of a single idea; the creator of that powerful story bearing the title *A Man of Misery*, which had earned the gratitude of an entire young generation by showing it the possibility of a moral resolution that passed through and beyond the deepest knowledge; the author, finally (and this completes the short list of his mature works), of the passionate treatment of the topic *Art and Intellect*, an essay whose power of organization and antithetical eloquence had prompted serious observers to rank it alongside Schiller's *On Naïve and Sentimental Poetry*; Gustav Aschenbach, then, was born the son of a career civil servant in the justice ministry in L., a district capital in the province of Silesia. His ancestors had been officers, judges, and government functionaries, men who had led upright lives of austere decency devoted to the service of king and country. A more ardent spirituality had expressed itself once among them in the person of a preacher; more impetuous and sensuous blood had entered the family line in the previous generation through the writer's mother, the daughter of a Bohemian music director. It was from her that he had in his features the traits of a foreign race. The marriage of sober conscientiousness devoted to service with darker, more fiery impulses engendered an artist and indeed this very special artist. (Koelb 1994: 7)

Version VII: Chase

The author of that lucid and majestic prose epic based on the life of Frederick the Great, the patient artist and painstaking weaver of that densely populated novelistic tapestry known as *Maya*, which manages to subordinate so many individual human destinies to a single basic pattern, the creator of that powerful narrative which bears the title "The True Wretch" and which showed an entire grateful generation of youth the possibility for moral resolution more profound than any intellectual knowledge, and finally (to complete the short catalogue of his mature works) the author of that passionately argued treatise "Mind and Art", whose analytic force and dialectic eloquence had led serious critics to place it on a par with Schiller's great meditation "On Naive and Sentimental Poetry" - Gustav Aschenbach was born the son of a ranking district court official in L., a country seat in provincial Silesia. His ancestors had been military officers, judges and bureaucratic functionaries, men who had dedicated their strict, respectably austere lives to the service of crown and state. More inwardly directed spirituality had manifested itself within the family but once, in the person of a preacher; more sensual passionate blood had been introduced during the previous generation, by the writer's mother, the daughter of a Bohemian *Kapellmeister*. The foreign traits in his appearance came from her.

It was the marriage of the servant's sober devotion to duty with darker, more fiery impulses that had allowed an artist - this *particular* artist - to develop. (Chase 1999: 145)

Appendix III: The Translation of a Philosophical Text

The extract is taken from *Der Tod in Venedig* as discussed in detail Section (c) of Chapter IX.

Mann: Aber es scheint, daß gegen nichts ein edler und tüchtiger Geist sich rascher, sich gründlicher abstumpft als gegen den scharfen und bitteren Reiz der Erkenntnis; und gewiß ist, daß die schwermütig gewissenhafteste Gründlichkeit des Jünglings Seichtheit bedeutet im Vergleich mit dem tiefen Entschlusse des Meister gewordenen Mannes, das Wissen zu leugnen, es abzulehnen, erhobenen Hauptes darüber hinwegzugehen, sofern es den Willen, die Tat, das Gefühl und selbst die Leidenschaft im geringsten zu lähmen, zu entmutigen, zu entwürdigen geeignet ist. Wie wäre die berühmte Erzählung vom "Elenden" wohl anders zu deuten denn als Ausbruch des Ekels gegen den unanständigen Psychologismus der Zeit, verkörpert in der Figur jenes weichen und albernen Halbschurken, der sich ein Schicksal erschleicht, indem er sein Weib, aus Ohnmacht, aus Lasterhaftigkeit, aus ethischer Velleität, in die Arme eines Unbärtigen treibt und aus Tiefe Nichtswürdigkeiten begehen zu dürfen glaubt? Die Wucht des Wortes, mit welcher hier das Verworfene verworfen wurde, verkündete die Abkehr von allem moralischen Zweifelsinn, von jeder Sympathie mit dem Abgrund, die Absage an die Laxheit des Mitleidssatzes, daß alles verstehen alles verzeihen heiße, und was sich hier vorbereitete, ja schon vollzog, war jenes "Wunder der wiedergeborenen Unbefangenheit", auf welches ein wenig später in einem der Dialoge des Autors ausdrücklich und nicht ohne geheimnisvolle Betonung die Rede kam. Seltsame Zusammenhänge! War es eine geistige Folge dieser "Wiedergeburt", dieser neuen Würde und Strenge, daß man um dieselbe Zeit ein fast übermäßiges Erstarken seines Schönheitssinnes beobachtete, jene adelige Reinheit, Einfachheit und Ebenmäßigkeit der Formgebung, welche seinen Produkten fortan ein so sinnfälliges, ja gewolltes Gepräge der Meisterlichkeit und Klassizität verlieh? Aber moralische Entschlossenheit jenseits des Wissens, der auflösenden und hemmenden Erkenntnis,- bedeutet sie nicht wiederum eine Vereinfachung, eine sittliche Vereinfältigung der Welt und der Seele und also auch ein Erstarken zum Bösen, Verbotenen, zum sittlich Unmöglichen? Und hat Form nicht zweierlei Gesicht? Ist sie nicht sittlich und unsittlich zugleich - sittlich als Ergebnis und Ausdruck der Zucht, unsittlich aber und selbst widersittlich, sofern sie von Natur eine moralische Gleichgültigkeit in sich schließt, ja wesentlich bestrebt ist, das Moralische unter ihr stolzes und unumschränktes Szepter zu beugen? (Mann 1977: 17-18)

Version I: Lowe-Porter

But it seems that a noble and active mind blunts itself against nothing so quickly as the sharp and bitter irritant of knowledge. And certain it is that the youth's constancy of purpose, no matter how painfully conscientious, was shallow beside the mature resolution of the master of his craft, who made a right-about-face, turned his back on the realm of knowledge, and passed it by with averted face, lest it lame his will or power of action, paralyse his feelings or his passions, deprive any of these of their conviction or utility. How else interpret the oft cited story of *The Abject*, than as a rebuke to the excesses of a psychology-ridden age, embodied in the delineation of the weak and silly fool who manages to lead fate by the nose; driving his wife, out of sheer innate pusillanimity into the arms of a beardless youth, and making this disaster an excuse for trifling away the rest of his life?

With rage the author here rejects the rejected, casts out the outcast - and the measure of his fury is the measure of his condemnation of all moral shilly-shallying. Explicitly he renounces sympathy with the abyss, explicitly he refutes the flabby humanitarianism of the phrase: 'Tout comprendre c'est tout pardonner.' What was here unfolding, or rather was already in full bloom, was the 'miracle of regained detachment,' which a little later became the theme of one of the author's dialogues, dwelt upon not without a certain oracular emphasis. Strange sequence of thought! Was it perhaps an intellectual consequence of this rebirth, this new austerity, that from now on his style showed an almost exaggerated sense of beauty, a lofty purity, symmetry, and simplicity, which gave his productions a stamp of the classic, of conscious and deliberate mastery? And yet: this moral fibre, surviving the hampering and disintegrating effect of knowledge, does it not result in its turn in a dangerous simplification, in a tendency to equate the world and the human soul, and thus to strengthen the hold of the evil, the forbidden, and the ethically impossible? And has not form two aspects? Is it not moral and immoral at once; moral in so far as it is the expression and result of discipline, immoral - yes, actually hostile to morality - in that of its very essence it is indifferent to good and evil, and deliberately concerned to make the moral world stoop beneath its proud and undivided sceptre? (Lowe-Porter 1977: 17-18)

Version II: Luke

But it seems that there is nothing to which a noble and active mind more quickly becomes inured than that pungent and bitter stimulus, the acquisition of knowledge; and it is very sure that even the most gloomily conscientious and radical sophistication of youth is shallow by comparison with Aschenbach's profound decision as a mature master to repudiate knowledge as such, to reject it, to step over it with head held high - in the recognition that knowledge can paralyse the will, paralyse and discourage action and emotion and even passion, and rob all these of their dignity. How else is the famous short story *A Study in Abjection* to be understood but as an outbreak of disgust against an age indecently undermined by psychology and represented by the figure of a spiritless, witless semiscoundrel who cheats his way into a destiny of sorts, when, motivated by his own ineptitude and depravity and ethical whimsicality, he drives his wife into the arms of a callow youth - convinced that his intellectual depths entitle him to behave with contemptible baseness? The forthright words of condemnation which here weighed vileness in the balance and found it wanting - they proclaimed their writer's renunciation of all moral scepticism, of every kind of sympathy with the abyss; they declared his repudiation of the laxity of that compassionate principle which holds that to understand all is to forgive all. And the development that was here being anticipated, indeed already taking place, was that "miracle of reborn naiveté" to which, in a dialogue written a little later, the author himself had referred with a certain mysterious emphasis. How strange these associations! Was it an intellectual consequence of this 'rebirth,' of this new dignity and rigor, that, at about the same time, his sense of beauty was observed to undergo an almost excessive resurgence, that his style took on the noble purity, simplicity and symmetry that were to set upon all his subsequent works that so evident and evidently intentional stamp of the classical master? And yet: moral resoluteness at the far side of knowledge, achieved in despite of all corrosive and inhibiting insight - does this not in its turn signify a simplification, a morally simplistic view of the world and of human psychology, and thus also a resurgence of energies that are evil, forbidden, morally impossible? And is form not two-faced? Is it not at one and the same time moral and immoral - moral as the product and expression of discipline, but immoral and even antimoral inasmuch as it houses within itself an innate moral indifference, and indeed essentially strives for nothing less than to bend morality under its proud and absolute scepter? (Luke 1988: 204-205)

Version III: A Source-Text-Based Version: Gledhill

However, it seems that the acrid and bitter charms of insight stupefy the noble and diligent mind more swiftly and more systematically than anything else; and it is also certain that the young artist's resigned and absolutely scrupulous thoroughness in all things was shallowness compared with that profound decision of the mature artist and master of his craft who decided to deny insight, to reject it and, with his head proudly held high, to walk away from it as soon as artistic insight showed the slightest tendency to paralyse, discourage or debase either the will, action, the emotions or even human passions themselves. How else could the story, *A Vile Wretch* be interpreted other than as an outburst of horror against the psychologising tendencies so typical of the age, which were epitomised in the form of that weak and foolish, immature wretch who slimed his way into history by driving his wife into the arms of a beardless youth; and who was motivated by hopelessness, vice and moral velleity, fondly believing his insights entitled him to behave indecently? The force with which the written word rejected the reject in this story heralded a turning away from all forms of moral ambiguity and from all forms of sympathy with the abyss. It rejected the moral laxity implied by that formulation of ultimate compassion, *Tout comprendre, c'est tout pardonner*. What was developing here and, in fact, came to fruition, was 'the miracle of a new-born objectivity', which was explicitly referred to in one of the author's dialogues and was given some special, mysterious emphasis. There were some very strange connections! Could it be as a result of this 'rebirth', of this new dignity and severity, that an almost exaggerated intensity in the author's aesthetic consciousness was simultaneously observed during this period - the aristocratic purity of style, simplicity and formal balance in his structures giving his literary products from that time onwards, their striking classicism and the masterly craftsmanship he was aiming for? But does not moral resolution transcending knowledge and artistic insight (insights which dissolve everything and prevent action) imply a simplification or a simplistic moral attitude to the world and soul? And does not too much knowledge increase the inclination towards evil, the forbidden and what is morally impossible? And does not form have two faces? Is not form both moral and immoral at the same time - moral as a result of and expression of discipline, but also immoral in so far as, by its very nature, it contains a profound moral indifference or even worse, its essential aim is to force morality to bow down to its proud, unbounded sceptre?

Version IV: Suggested Domesticating Version: Gledhill

There is nothing more powerful nor swifter in its effect on this earth for both blunting and stunting the intellects of even the noblest and most conscientious minds than those bitter yet so exquisite charms of insight into the abysses of human knowledge. On the other hand, the grim, pedantic diligence of the artist when he was a young man is merely superficial in comparison to this profound decision made by the mature artist when he completely repudiated knowledge, proudly walking away from this domain as soon as insight threatened to paralyse the will, to dishonour human passions and emotions, prevent

267

moral action from taking place or, in any way, to detract from the dignity of the human, ethical areas of life. How else can we interpret the story called *Human Scum* other than as a vilification of the modern tendency to reduce evil to psychology? The outbreak of nausea towards 'psychologism' was symbolised by the protagonist of the story, a spineless and foolish specimen of 'human scum', who gained a cheap notoriety for himself by driving his wife into the arms of a callow youth? His weakness came from an inability to act, from a debauched will and moral equivocation, but he foolishly believed that depth of insight could justify acts of indecency. The eloquence with which the writer denounced this specimen marked a complete rejection of ethical prevarication - no more sympathy with the abyss nor with that decadent cliché: 'Tout comprendre, c'est tout pardonner.' This led to the next stage, 'the miracle of new-born objectivity', a phrase he had coined before in one of his dialogues when he gave it a mysterious, special emphasis. How strange the way all these themes seem to be interrelated! The new classicism and craftsmanship which, from then on, characterised his work could be seen as a consequence of the 'rebirth' which had occurred at the same time. His style had gained a new dignity and austerity; his works had an aristocratic purity, simplicity and balance and his aesthetic sensibility was almost carried to excess. There could, however, be dangers in with the choice in favour of a morality that transcends knowledge and philosophical insight that analyses and dissolves everything, thus atrophying the ability to act. The moral choice could imply a gross oversimplification of the external world and the human soul, tending all the more in the direction of evil, towards forbidden things and towards the ethically impossible. Form itself can be said to have two faces, to be both moral and immoral, at the same time - *moral* as the fruit and expression of discipline, but also *immoral* or even *amoral* as form is, by its very nature, completely indifferent to morality and, what is more, its basic aim is to force morality to bow down to its proud sceptre that knows no limits.

Version V: Burke

But it seems that nothing blunts the edge of a noble, robust mind more quickly and more thoroughly than the sharp and bitter corrosion of knowledge; and certainly the moody radicalism of the youth, no matter how conscientious, was shallow in comparison with his firm determination as an old man and a master to deny knowledge, to reject it, to pass it with raised head, insofar as it is capable of crippling, discouraging, or degrading to the slightest degree, our will, acts, feelings, or even passions. How else would the famous story *The Wretch* be understood than as an outburst of repugnance against the disreputable psychologism of the times: embodied in the figure of that soft and stupid half-clown who pilfers a destiny for himself by guiding his wife (from powerlessness, from lasciviousness, from ethical frailty) into the arms of an adolescent, and believes that he may through profundity commit vileness? The verbal pressure with which he here cast out the outcast announced the return from every moral skepticism, from all fellow-feeling with the engulfed: it was the counter-move laxity of the sympathetic principle that to understand all is to forgive all - and the thing that was here well begun, even nearly completed, was that 'miracle of reborn ingenuousness' which was taken up a little later in one of the author's dialogues expressly and not without a certain discrete emphasis. Strange coincidences! Was it as a result of this rebirth, this new dignity and sternness, that his feeling for beauty - a discriminating purity, simplicity, and evenness of attack which henceforth gave his productions such an obvious, even such a deliberate stamp of mastery and classicism - showed an almost excessive strengthening about this time? But ethical resoluteness in the exclusion of science, of emancipatory and restrictive knowledge - does this not in turn signify a simplification, a reduction morally of the world to too limited terms, and thus also a strengthened capacity for the forbidden, the evil, the morally impossible? And does not form have two aspects? Is it not moral and unmoral at once - moral in that it is the result and expression of discipline, but unmoral, and even immoral in that by nature it contains an indifference to morality, is calculated, in fact, to make morality bend beneath its proud and unencumbered scepter? (Burke 1971: 18-19)

Version VI: Koelb

But it seems that nothing so quickly or so thoroughly blunts a high-minded and capable spirit as the sharp and bitter charm of knowledge; and it is certain that the melancholy, scrupulous thoroughness characteristic of the young seems shallow in comparison with the solemn decision of masterful maturity to disavow knowledge, to reject it, to move beyond it with head held high, to forestall the least possibility that it could cripple, dishearten, or dishonour his will, his capacity for action and feeling, or even his passion. How else could one interpret the famous story *A Man of Misery* save as an outbreak of disgust at the indecent psychologism then current? This disgust was embodied in the figure of that soft and foolish semi-villain who, out of weakness, viciousness, and moral impotence, buys a black-market destiny for himself by driving his wife into the arms of a beardless boy, who imagines profundity can justify committing the basest acts. The weight of the words with which the writer of that work reviled the vile announced a decisive turn away from all moral skepticism, from all sympathy with the abyss, a rejection of the laxity inherent in the supposedly compassionate maxim that to understand everything is to forgive everything. What was coming into play here - or rather, what was already in full swing - was that 'miracle of ingenuousness reborn" about which there was explicit discussion, not without a certain mysterious emphasis, in one of the author's dialogues published only slightly later. Strange relationships! Was it an intellectual consequence of this 'rebirth," of this new dignity an rigour, that just then readers began to notice an almost excessive increase in his sense of beauty, and noble purity, simplicity, and a sense of proportion that henceforth gave his works such a palpable, one might say deliberately classical and masterful quality? But moral determination that goes beyond knowledge, beyond analytic and inhibiting perception - would that not also be a reduction, a moral simplification of the world and of the human soul and therefore also a growing potential for what is evil, and morally unacceptable? And does form not have two faces? Is it not moral and amoral at the same time - moral insofar as form is the product and expression of discipline, but amoral and indeed immoral insofar as it harbours within itself by nature a certain indifference and indeed is essentially bent on forcing the moral realm to stoop under its proud and absolute scepter? (Koelb 1994: 10-11)

Version VII: Chase

There seems to be nothing, however, to which unalloyed imagination, conscious of its duty, becomes more quickly inured than to the stinging, bitter lure of the intellect. There can be no doubt that the apprentice's most dourly conscientious labor proves shallow against the experienced master's profound resolve to reject intellectual knowledge, to dismiss it, to step over it with head held high, insofar as it serves in the least to lame, discourage or derogate his own will, his capacity for action, his feelings or even his passion. How else would the famous short story *A True Wretch* be understood except as an outburst of contempt for the vulgar pseudopsychology of his age, embodied in that ridiculous weakling, that half-pint scoundrel, who inspired by moral velleity, weakness and turpitude, attempts to glorify his own pathetic existence by driving his wife into the arms of a fresh-faced boy, telling himself that plumbed depth justifies despicable deeds? The brunt of whose words, in which dissipation was disdained, signalled Aschenbach's own repudiation of moral relativism, of all sympathetic attraction to the abyss. It announced his rejection of that all-forbearing maxim which says that to know is to forgive: what was being prepared, indeed realized here was that "miraculous rebirth of unfettered innocence," to which the talk returned, explicitly and not without a portentous emphasis, in one of his interviews shortly thereafter. Strange coincidences! Was it not a creative consequence of this "rebirth," this new dignity and rigor, that readers then began to notice in him an almost hypertrophic increase in aestheticism, that aristocratic purity, simplicity and formal symmetry which would henceforth give his entire output an unmistakable, surely intended stamp of classical mastery of technique? And yet moral conviction beyond the realm of knowledge of all-unravelling and all-inhibiting intellect- did this not amount to a simplification in its own right, a moralistic reduction of the world and the human soul? And did it not also entail an encouragement of what was evil, forbidden, ethically indefensible? Does not form have two faces? Is it not simultaneously moral and amoral - moral, insofar as it is the ultimate expression of discipline; amoral, even immoral, insofar as it automatically entails ethical indifference, aspiring to make all that is ethical bow down before its own proud, unchecked scepter? (Chase 1999: 149-150)

Bibliography

Works by Thomas Mann

Mann, T. (1985) *Thomas Mann - Heinrich Mann: Briefwechsel 1900-1949*, herausgegeben von Wysling, H., Frankfurt/M: Fischer Verlag.

Mann, T. (1977) *Die Erzählungen*, Vol. I, Hamburg: Fischer Taschenbuch Verlag.

Mann, T. (1965) *Briefe 1948-1955 und Nachlese*, Vol. III, herausgegeben von Mann, E., Frankfurt/M: Fischer Verlag.

Mann, T. (1961) "An Bruno Walter zum siebzigsten Geburtstag", *Altes und Neues,* Frankfurt/M: Fischer Verlag.

Translations of Thomas Mann

Bertaux, F. & Sigwalt, C. & Nesme, A. (1997) *Thomas Mann: La Mort à Venise, Tristan,* Paris: Fayard.

Burke, K. (1971) *Death in Venice*, New York: Bantam Books.

Castellani, E. (1988) *Thomas Mann: La Morte a Venezia, Tristano - Tonio Kröger,* Milan: Arnoldo Mondadori.

Chase, J. (1999) *Death in Venice and Other Stories,* Harmondsworth: Penguin.

Koelb, C. (1994) *Death in Venice,* New York: W. W. Norton.

Lowe-Porter, H. (1977) *Thomas Mann: Death in Venice, Tristan, Tonio Kröger,* Harmondsworth: Penguin.

Lowe-Porter, H. (1952) *Buddenbrooks,* New York: Vintage Books.

Luke, D. (1988) *Death in Venice and Other Stories by Thomas Mann,* New York: Bantam Books.

Maffi, B. (1994) *Thomas Mann: La Morte a Venezia,* Milan: Biblioteco Universale Rizzoli.

Rho, A. (1954) Thomas Mann: La Morte a Venezia, Turin: Einaudi.

Literature on Thomas Mann

Dittmann, U. (1993) *Erläuterungen und Dokumente: Thomas Mann: Tristan,* Stuttgart: Reclam.

Häfele, J. & Stammel, H. (1992) *Thomas Mann: Der Tod in Venedig,* Frankfurt/M: Diesterweg.

Hayman, R. (1995) *Thomas Mann,* London: Bloomsbury.

Heller, E. (1975) *Thomas Mann: Der Ironische Deutsche,* Frankfurt/M: Suhrkamp Verlag.

Heller, E. (1965) *Thomas Mann: The Ironic German*, New York: The World Publishing Company.

Hofmiller, J. (1966) "Thomas Manns Tod in Venedig". *Interpretationen: Deutsche Erzählungen von Wieland bis Kafka,* herausgegeben von Schillmeit, J. Frankfurt/M: Fischer Bücherei KG.

Klugkist, T. (1995) *Glühende Konstruktion: Thomas Manns Tristan und das "Dreigestirn" Schopenhauer, Nietzsche und Wagner*, Würzburg: Königshausen & Neumann.

Koch-Emmery, E. (1953) "Thomas Mann in English Translation", *German Life and Letters*, July, 1952-1953, New Series VI, 275-284.

Reed, T. (1994) *Death in Venice: Making and Unmaking a Master,* New York: Twayne Publishers.

Seidlin, O. (1963) "Stiluntersuchung an einem Thomas Mann-Satz", *Von Goethe bis Thomas Mann: Zwölf Versuche,* Göttingen: Vandenhoeck & Ruprecht, 148-161.

Literature on Lowe-Porter

Adelbert, J. (1936) "Review of *Stories of Three Decades*", *Boston Transcript*, June 6.

Berlin, J. (1992a) "On the Making of *The Magic Mountain*: The Unpublished Correspondence of Thomas Mann, Alfred A. Knopf and H. T. Lowe-Porter", *Seminar, A Journal of Germanic Studies*, Vol. XXVII, Number 4. Toronto: University of Toronto Press.

Berlin, J. (1992b) "Approaches to Teaching Mann's *Death in Venice* and Other Short Fiction", in: *Approaches to Teaching World Literature*, Vol. IVXIII, New York: Modern Language Association of America.

Connolly, C. (1936) "Review of *Stories of Three Decades*", *New Statesman and Nation*, November 7.

Follett, W. (1936) "Review of *Stories of Three Decades*", *Saturday Review of Literature,* June 6.

Hayes, J. (1974) *A Method of Determining the Reliability of Literary Translations: Two Versions of Thomas Mann's Der Tod in Venedig,* Massachusetts: University Microfilms.

Mandel, S. (1982) "Helen Tracy Lowe-Porter: Once A Translator, Always A Translator", Volume XVII, *Denver Quarterly*.

Thirlwall, J. (1966) *In Another Language: A Record of the Thirty-Year Relationship between Thomas Mann and his English Translator*, New York: Alfred A Knopf.

West, P. (1969) "Thomas Mann and English Taste", *The Southern Review*, Vol. V, Louisiana: Louisiana State University.

Ziolkowski, T. (1961) "German". in: Arrowsmith, W. & Shattuck, R. (eds.) *The Craft and Context of Translation*, Austin: University of Texas Press.

Source Texts and Translations

Banner, A. (1855) *Schwere Zeiten*, Stuttgart: Hoffmann.

Beckett, S. (1971) *En Attendant Godot*, Paris: Les Éditions de Minuit.

Beckett, S. (1965) *Waiting for Godot*, London: Faber and Faber.

Beheim-Schwarzbach, M. (1955) *Oliver Twist*, München: Droemer.

Bode, J. (1766) "Der argwöhnische Ehemann: ein Lustspiel von D. Benjamin Hoadly aus dem Englischen übersetzt", *Neueste Proben der englischen Schaubühne*, Hamburg: Christian Herolds Wittwe.

Frege, G. (1892) "Über Sinn und Bedeutung", *Zeitschrift für Philosophie und philosophische Kritik* 100, 25-50.

Gotter, F. (1785) *Der argwöhnische Ehemann: ein Lustspiel in fünf Aufzügen*, Hamburg: Heroldsche Buchhandlung.

Heichen, P. (1893) *David Copperfield Junior, Was Er Erlebt und Erfahren, von Ihm Selbst Erzählt,* Naumburg: Schirmer.

Heichen, P. (1892) *Leben und Abenteuer des Oliver Twist*, Naumburg: Schirmer.

Heinrich, K. (1968) *David Copperfield: Charles Dickens*, Berlin: Neues Leben.

Hoadly, B. (1776) *The Suspicious Husband: A Comedy*, London: Bell.

Hölderlin, F. (1969) *Hölderlins Werke und Briefe,* herausgegeben von Beißner F. & Schmidt J., Frankfurt/M: Insel Verlag.

Hoeppener, C. (1968) *Oliver Twist,* Berlin: Rütten & Loening.

Joyce, J. (1992) *Finnegans Wake*, Harmondsworth: Penguin.

Kolb, C. (1842) *David Copperfield: Roman von Charles Dickens,* herausgegeben von Wessely, J., Stuttgart: Franckhaus.

Kolb, C. (1841) *Die Pickwickier*, Stuttgart: Krabbe.

Lawrence, D. (1960) *Lady Chatterley's Lover,* London: Heinemann.

Lawrence, D. (1960) *Lady Chatterley: Roman,* Übersetzung von Rebhuhn W., Reinbek bei Hamburg: Rowohlt.

Lawrence, D. (1928) *Lady Chatterley's Lover,* New York: Bantam Books.

Meyrink, G. (1910) *Die Pickwickier*, München: Langen.

Marlowe, C. (1997) *The Tragical History of the Life and Death of Doctor Faustus* herausgegeben von Landes, W., Studio City: Players Press.

Morgenstern, C., (1990) *Galgenlieder und andere Gedichte*, (transl.) Knight, M., *Gallows Songs and Other Poems*, München: Piper.

Raykowski, H. (1992) *Alice im Wunderland*, München: Deutscher Taschenbuch Verlag.

Raykowski, H. (1979) *Jeeves Takes Charge: Three Stories. Jeeves übernimmt den Ruder: Drei Erzählungen,* München: Deutscher Taschenbuch Verlag.

Reichert, K. (1988) *James Joyce Finnegans Wake*, Frankfurt/M: Suhrkamp.

Reichhardt, D. (1992) *David Copperfield: Charles Dickens*, Hamburg: Xenos.

Remané, L. & Remané, M. (1981) *Alice im Wunderland*, Leipzig: Reclam.

Roberts, H. (1838) *Oliver Twist*, Leipzig: J. J.Weber.

Roberts, H. (1837) *Die Pickwickier oder des Herrn Pickwick's und der correspondirenden Mitglieder des Pickwick-Clubs Kreuz- und Querzüge, Abentheuer und Thaten,* Leipzig: J. J. Weber.

Plato (1970) *The Laws*, herausgegeben & übersetzt von Saunders, T., Harmondsworth: Penguin.

Seybt, J. (1849) *Lebensgeschichte und Erfahrungen David Copperfield's des Jüngern*, Leipzig: Lorck.

Sophokles (1985) *Dramen,* herausgegeben & übersetzt von Bayer K., München: Artemis Verlag.

Thanner, J. (1955) *David Copperfield: Roman*, München: Winkler.

Von Bauernfeld, E. (1844) *Die Hinterlassenen Papiere des Pickwick-Clubs*, Wien: Mausberger.

Von Herwarth, C. (1984) *Alice im Wunderland*, Bayreuth: Loewe.

Wilding, K. (1906) *David Copperfield jun. aus Blunderstone Krähenhorst. Seine Lebensgeschichte, Abenteuer, Erfahrungen und Beobachtungen,* Berlin: Weichert.

Wittgenstein, L. (1998) *Philosophische Untersuchungen*, herausgegeben von Savigny, E., Berlin: Akademie-Verlag.

Wittgenstein, L. (1953) *Philosophical Investigations*, herausgegeben & übersetzt von Anscombe, G., Rhees, R. & Von Wright, G., Oxford: Blackwell.

Wodehouse, P. (1989) *Very Good Jeeves*, London: Arrow Books.

Translation Theory and Stylistics

Addison, J. (1965) *The Specator*, (ed.) Bond, D. F.,Vol. I, Oxford: Oxford UP.

Albrecht, J (1998) *Literarische Übersetzung: Geschichte, Theorie, kulturelle Wrikung:*, Darmstadt: Wissentschaftliche Buchgesellschaft.

Arnold, M. (1909) "On Translating Homer", in: *Essays Literary and Critical*, London: Dent.

Baker, M. (1998) (ed.) *Encyclopaedia of Translation Studies*, London: Routledge.

Barnstone, W. (1993) *The Poetics of Translation: History, Theory, Practice,* New Haven: Yale UP.

Bassnett, S. (2003) "Literary Translation is alive and well", in: *The Linguist: Journal of the Institute of Linguists*, Vol. XLII, Issue: III, London: Institute of Linguists, 66-67.

Bassnett, S. (1991) *Translation Studies: Revised Edition*, London: Routledge.

Benjamin, Walter (1972) "Die Aufgabe des Übersetzers", *Walter Benjamin: Gesammelte Schriften*, Vol. IV, Frankfurt/M: Suhrkamp.

Brower, R. (1966) (ed.) *On Translation*, Cambridge, MA: Harvard University Press.

Buck, T. (1996) "Loyalty and Licence. Thomas Mann's Fiction in English Translation", *The Modern Language Review* 91.

Constantine, D. (1990) *Hölderlin,* Oxford: Clarendon.

Davis, L. (1997) "Signature in Translation" in: *Essays on Punning and Translation*, Delabastita, D., (ed.) *Traductio*, Naumur: St Jerome Publishing.

Delabastita, D. (1996) "Introduction", in: Delabastita, D. (ed.) *Wordplay and Translation*. Special issue of *The Translator. Studies in Intercultural Communication.*(2.2), Manchester: St Jerome Publishing, 127-135.

De Man, P. (1986) *The Resistance to Theory,* Minneapolis: University of Minnesota Press.

Derrida, J. (1985) "Des Tours de Babel", Übersetzung von Graham, J., Ithaca: Cornell UP.

Derrida, J. (1982) *Margins of Philosophy*, Übersetzung von Bass A., Chicago: University of Chicago Press.

Derrida, J. (1981) *Positions*, Übersetzung von Bass A., Chicago: University of Chicago Press.

De Saussure, F. (1959) *Course in General Linguistics*, Übersetzung von Baskin, W., New York: Philosophical Library.

Even-Zohar, I. (1990) "Polysystem Studies", *Poetics Today,* XI (1), Tel Aviv: Duke UP.

Even-Zohar, I. (1978) "The Position of Translated Literature within the Literary Polysystem", in: Holmes, J., Lambert, J. & Van den Broeck, R., (eds.) *Literature and Translation: New perspectives in Literary Translation*, Leuven: acco.

Gallagher, J. "Möglichkeiten und Grenzen der Übersetzungsäquivalenz", in: Börner, W.& Vogel, K. (eds.) *Kontrast und Äquivalenz*, Tübingen: Gunter Narr Verlag.

Gentzler, E. (1993) *Contemporary Translation Theories*, New York: Routledge.

Gutt, E. (2000) "Translation as Interlingual Interpretative Use" in: Venuti, L. (ed.) *The Translation Studies Reader,* London: Routledge.

Güttinger, F. (1963) *Zielsprache: Theorie und Praxis des Übersetzens*, Zürich: Manessa Verlag.

Hatim, B. & Mason, I. (1998) *Discourse and the Translator,* New York: Longman.

Hellmann, J. (1992) *Die französische Version des* Zauberberg *von Thomas Mann,* Hamburg: Verlag Dr. R. Krämer.

Holmes, J. (1978) "Describing Literary Translations: Models and Methods", in: Holmes, J., Lambert, J. & Van den Broeck, R. (eds.) *Literature and Translation: New perspectives in Literary Translation*, Leuven: acco.

Holmes, J. (1970) "Forms of Verse Translation and the Translation of Verse Form", in: Holmes, J. (ed.), *The Nature of Translation: Essays on the Theory and Practice of Literary Translation*, The Hague: Mouton.

Holz-Mänttäri, J. (1984) "Translatorisches Handeln: Theorie und Methode", *Annales Academiae Scientarum Fennicae B 226*, Helsinki: Finnish Academy of Science.

House, J. (1997) *Translation Quality Assessment: A Model Revisited*, Tübingen: Gunter Narr Verlag.

Jakobson, R. (2000) "On Linguistic Aspects of Translation," in: Venuti, L. (ed.) *The Translation Studies Reader,* London: Routledge.

Joyce, J. (1997) "The Concept of Error Analysis Applied to Third Level Translation Courses": in:*Translationsdidaktik: Grundfragen der Übersetzungswissenschaft*

Klemensievicz, K. (1958) "Przeklad jako Zagadnienie Jezykoznawstwa" (*Die Übersetzung als sprachwissenschaftliches Problem*) in: *Jezyk Polski*, 38.

Klinkel, Elke (2001) "Thomas Mann in Amerika: Interkultureller Dialog im Wandel? Eine rezeptions- und übersetzungskritische Analyse am Beispiel des *Doktor*

Faustus", in: Baumann, U. and Friedl, H. (eds.) *Beiträge aus Anglistik und Amerikanistik*, Peter Lang Verlag: Frankfurt am Main.

Koller, W. (1979) *Einführung in die Übersetzungswissenschaft*, Heidelberg: Quelle & Meyer.

Koller, W. (1972) *Grundprobleme der Übersetzungstheorie: Unter besonderer Berücksichtigung schwedisch-deutscher Übersetzungsfälle*, Bern: Francke.

Kraszewski, C. (1998) *Four Translation Strategies Determined by the Particular Needs of the Receptor*, New York: Edwin Mellen Press.

Kußmaul, P. (1995) *Training the Translator*, Amsterdam: John Benjamins.

Leech, G. & Short, M. (1981) *Style in Fiction. A Linguistic Introduction to English Fictional Prose*, London: Longman.

Lefevere, A. (1992) *Translation, Rewriting, and the Manipulation of Literary Fame*, London: Routledge.

Lefevere, A. (1975) *Translating Poetry: Seven Strategies and a Blueprint*, Assen: Van Gorcum.

Leppihalme, R. (1996) "Caught in the Frame. A Target-Culture Viewpoint on Allusive Wordplay", in: *Wordplay and Translation*. Special issue of *The Translator. Studies in Intercultural Communication*.(2.2), Manchester: St Jerome Publishing, 199-218.

Levý, J. (1969) *Die literarische Übersetzung: Theorie einer Kunstgattung*, Übersetzung von Schamschula, W., Frankfurt/M: Athenäum Verlag.

Levý, J. (1967) "Translation as a Decision Process" in: *To honour Roman Jakobson II,* The Hague: Mouton, 1171-1182.

Manini, L. (1996) "Meaningful Literary Names. Their Forms and Functions and Their Translation", in: *Wordplay and Translation*. Special issue of *The Translator. Studies in Intercultural Communication*.(2.2), Manchester: St Jerome Publishing, 161-178.

Mates, B. (1950) "Synonymity" in: Mates, B. (ed.) *Meaning and Interpretation*, Berkeöey: University of California Press.

Murry, J. (1923) "Classical Translations" in: *Pencillings: Little Essays on Literature",* London: Books for Libraries Pr.

Nabokov, V. (2000) "The Art of Translation" in: Venuti, L. (ed.) *The Translation Studies Reader,* London: Routledge.

Newmark, P. (1988) *A Textbook of Translation*, New York: Prentice Hall.

Newmark, P. (1981) *Approaches to Translation*, Oxford: Pergamon Press.

Nida, E. (2000) "Principles of Correspondence" in: Venuti, L. (ed.) *The Translation Studies Reader,* London: Routledge.

Nida, E. & Taber, C. (1964) *The Theory and Practice of Translation* Leiden: E. J. Brill.

Nida, E. (1964) *Towards a Science of Translating*, Leiden: E. J. Brill.

Osers, E. (1998) "Translation Norms: Do They Really Exist?", in: Beylard-Ozeroff, A., Králova J. & Moser-Mercer B. (eds.) *Translators' Strategies and Creativity: Selected Papers from the 9th International Conference on Translation and Interpreting, Prague, September 1995 in Honor of Jirí Levý and Anton Popovic,* Amsterdam: Benjamins.

Quine, W. (2000) "Meaning and Translation" in: Venuti, L. (ed.) *The Translation Studies Reader,* London: Routledge.

Rieu, E. & Phillips, J. (1954) " Translating the Gospels," Bible Translator 6, 150-159.

Risset, J. (1984) "Joyce Translates Joyce", Übersetzung von Pick, D., in: Shaffer, E. (ed.) *Comparative Criticism,* Vol. VI, Cambridge: Cambridge UP.

Sager, Juan C. (1966) "A Brazilian Poet's Approach to the Translation of German Poetry", *Babel: International Journal of Translation,* Vol. XII, Budapest: 198-204.

Schadewaldt, W. (1970) "Hölderlins Übersetzungen des Sophokles", *Hellas und Hesperien,* Vol. II, Zürich: 275-332.

Schulte, R. (1992) *Theories of Translation: An Anthology of Essays from Dryden to Derrida*, Chicago: University of Chicago Press.

Selver, P. (1966) *The Art of Translating Poetry*, Boston: The Writer.

Snell-Hornby, M. (1988) *Translation Studies an Integrated Approach,* Amsterdam: John Benjamins Publishing co.

Steiner, G. (1998) *After Babel,* Oxford: Oxford UP.

Stolze, R. (1994) *Übersetzungstheorien*, Tübingen: Gunter Narr Verlag.

Toury, G. (1985) "A Rationale for Descriptive Translation Studies", in: Hermans, T. (ed.) *The Manipulation of Literature: Studies in Literary Translation*, London: Croom Helm.

Unger, T. (1996) "English Plays on the Gotha Stage: Friedrich Wilhelm Gotter's Translation of Benjamin Hoadly's Comedy: *The Suspicious Husband*", *Erfurt Electronic Studies in English 1996*, Erfurt: University of Erfurt EESE.

Van den Broeck, R. (1995) "Translational Interpretation as a Prerequisite for Creativity" in: Beylard-Ozeroff, A., Králova, J. & Moser-Mercer, B. (eds.) *Translators' Strategies and Creativity: Selected Papers from the 9th International Conference on Translation and Interpreting, Prague, September 1995 in Honor of Jirí Levý and Anton Popovic*, Amsterdam: Benjamins.

Van den Broeck, R. (1978) "The Concept of Equivalence in Translation Theory: Some Critical Reflections", in: Holmes, J., Lambert, J. & Van den Broeck, R. (eds.) *Literature and Translation: New Perspectives in Literary Translation*, Leuven: acco.

Venuti, L. (2000) *The Translation Studies Reader,* London: Routledge.

Venuti, L. (1998) *The Scandals of Translation,* London: Routledge.

Venuti, L. (1995) *The Translator's Invisibility,* London: Routledge.

Vermeer, H. (1996) *Skopos Theory of Translation: Some Arguments For and Against,* Heidelberg: Textcontext Verlag.

Weissbrod, R. (1960) "'Curiouser and Curiouser': Hebrew Translation of Wordplay in 'Alice's Adventures in Wonderland'", in: *Wordplay and Translation*. Special issue of *The Translator. Studies in Intercultural Communication*.(2.2), Manchester: St Jerome Publishing, 219-235.

Wilss, W. (1988) *Kognition und Übersetzen*, Tübingen: Niemeyer.

Wilss, W. (1977) *Übersetzungswissenschaft: Probleme und Methoden*, Stuttgart: Ernst Klett Verlag.

Dialect

Chambers, J. & Trudgill, P. (1998) *Dialectology*, Cambridge: Cambridge UP.

Czennia, B. (1992a) "Der fremde Dia/Soziolekt: 'Cockney', 'Cant' und andere Sondersprachen in Übersetzungen zu Charles Dickens Van den Broeck, R. (1978), *Göttinger Beiträge zur internationalen Übersetzungsforschung, Die literarische Übersetzung als Medium der Fremderfahrung*, Vol. VI, herausgegeben von Lönker, F., Berlin: Schmidt.

Czennia, B. (1992b) *Figurenrede als Übersetzungsproblem: untersucht am Romanwerk von Charles Dickens und ausgewählten deutschen Übersetzungen*, Frankfurt/M: Lang.

Diller, H. & Kornelius, J. (1978) *Linguistische Probleme der Übersetzung,* Tübingen: Niemeyer.

Hoeppener, C. (1953) "Bemerkungen zur Übersetzung belletristischer Werke", *Zur Frage der Übersetzung von schöner und wissenschaftlicher Literatur*, herausgegeben von Matthias, C., Berlin: Verlag Kultur und Fortschritt.

Mace, R. (1987) *Funktion des Dialekts im regionalen Roman von Gaskell bis Lawrence*, Tübingen: Gunter Narr.

Werlen, I. (1988) "Swiss German Dialects and Swiss Standard High German", in: Auer, P. & Di Luzio, A. (eds.). *Variation and Convergence*: *Studies in Social Dialectology*, New York: Walter de Gruyter.

VDM

Verlag
Dr. Müller

Wissenschaftlicher Buchverlag bietet

kostenfreie

Publikation

von aktuellen

wissenschaftlichen Arbeiten

Diplomarbeiten, Magisterarbeiten, Master und Bachelor Theses
sowie Dissertationen und wissenschaftliche Monographien

innerhalb von Fachbuchprojekten (Monographien und Sammelwerke)

**in den Fachgebieten Wirtschafts- und Sozialwissenschaften
sowie Wirtschaftsinformatik.**

Sie verfügen über eine Arbeit zu aktuellen Fragestellungen aus den genannten
Fachgebieten, die hohen inhaltlichen und formalen Ansprüchen genügt,
und haben **Interesse an einer honorarvergüteten Publikation**?

Dann senden Sie bitte erste Informationen über sich und Ihre Arbeit per Email
an info@vdm-verlag.de. Unser Außenlektorat meldet sich umgehend bei Ihnen.

VDM Verlag Dr. Mueller e.K. · Dudweiler Landstraße 125a
D - 66123 Saarbrücken · www.vdm-buchverlag.de